MAKING GLOBAL ECONOMIC GOVERNANCE EFFECTIVE

Global Finance Series

Edited by
John Kirton, University of Toronto
Michele Fratianni, Indiana University, USA
Paolo Savona, LUISS University, Italy

The intensifying globalisation of the twenty-first century has brought a myriad of new managerial and political challenges for governing international finance. The return of synchronous global slowdown, mounting developed country debt, and new economy volatility have overturned established economic certainties. Proliferating financial crises, transnational terrorism, currency consolidation, and increasing demands that international finance should better serve public goods such as social and environmental security have all arisen to compound the problem.

The new public and private international institutions that are emerging to govern global finance have only just begun to comprehend and respond to this new world. Embracing international financial flows and foreign direct investment, in both the private and public sector dimensions, this series focuses on the challenges and opportunities faced by firms, national governments, and international institutions, and their roles in creating a new system of global finance.

Forthcoming titles in the series

Debt Relief Initiatives
Policy Design and Outcomes
Marco Arnone and Andrea Presbitero
ISBN 978 0 7546 7742 0

Global Financial Crises
National Economic Solutions and Geopolitical Impacts
Edited by John Kirton and Chiara Oldani
ISBN 978 1 4094 0271 8

Safeguarding the World Bank
Politics of Institutional Reform and Retrenchment
Eva T. Thorne
ISBN 978 0 7546 7763 5

Full listing of previous titles at the back of the book

Making Global Economic Governance Effective

Hard and Soft Law Institutions in a Crowded World

JOHN KIRTON
University of Toronto, Canada

MARINA LARIONOVA
State University-Higher School of Economics, Russia

PAOLO SAVONA
LUISS University, Italy

Routledge
Taylor & Francis Group
LONDON AND NEW YORK

First published 2010 by Ashgate Publishing

Published 2016 by Routledge
2 Park Square, Milton Park, Abingdon, Oxon OX14 4RN
711 Third Avenue, New York, NY 10017, USA

Routledge is an imprint of the Taylor & Francis Group, an informa business

British Library Cataloguing in Publication Data
Making global economic governance effective : hard and soft
law institutions in a crowded world. -- (Global finance
series)
1. International economic relations. 2. Globalization--
Economic aspects. 3. Group of Eight (Organization)
I. Series II. Kirton, John. III. Larionova, Marina.
IV. Savona, Paolo, 1936-
337.1-dc22

Library of Congress Cataloging-in-Publication Data
Kirton, John J.
Making global economic governance effective : hard and soft law institutions in a crowded world / by John Kirton, Marina Larionova and Paolo Savona.
p. cm. -- (Global finance)
Includes bibliographical references and index.
ISBN 978-0-7546-7671-3 (hardback) -- ISBN 978-0-7546-7672-0 (e-book)
1. Group of Eight (Organization) 2. Economic policy--International cooperation. 3. Economic development--Finance. 4. Economic assistance. 5. International law. I. Larionova, Marina. II. Savona, Paolo, 1936- III. Title.
HF1359.K574 2009
337.1--dc22

2009030159

ISBN 13: 978-0-7546-7671-3 (hbk)

Contents

List of Figures

List of Contributors

Ade Adefuye is the Advisor on Democracy and Good Governance for the Economic Community of West African States (ECOWAS).

Andrew F. Cooper is the Associate Director of the Centre for International Governance Innovation and a professor in the Department of Political Science at the University of Waterloo.

Robert Fauver served as US President Bill Clinton's sherpa for the G7 economic summits in 1993 and 1994, and Deputy Under Secretary of State for Economic Affairs from 1991 to 1992.

Jenilee Guebert is Research Coordinator of the G8 Research Group.

John Kirton is Director of the G8 Research Group and Professor of Political Science at the Munk Centre for International Studies at Trinity College in the University of Toronto.

Catherine Kunz holds a Master of Arts in Economics from McGill University and is a member of the G8 Research Group.

Marina Larionova is Head of the International Organizations Research Institute at the State University – Higher School of Economics and the Head of International Programs at the National Training Foundation in Moscow.

Roy MacLaren served as Canada's Minister of International Trade from 1993 to 1996.

Sylvia Ostry is the Distinguished Research Fellow at the Centre for International Studies at the University of Toronto, and served as Canadian Prime Minister Brian Mulroney's sherpa for the 1988 Toronto G7 Summit.

Victoria V. Panova is Director of the G8 Research Group Moscow Office and teaches in the Department of International Relations and Foreign Policy of Russia at Moscow State University of International Relations (MGIMO).

Nikolai Roudev is a PhD candidate at Stanford University in California.

Ivan Savić is a PhD candidate at Columbia University and a doctoral fellow at the Munk Centre for International Studies at Trinity College in the University of Toronto.

Paolo Savona is a Professor of Political Economy at LUISS University in Rome.

Nodari A. Simonia served as African Personal Representative for the Russian Federation until 2007.

Gina Stephens works for the Ministry of Finance of the Government of Ontario in Toronto.

Laura Sunderland works at the Canadian International Council and is a member of the G8 Research Group.

List of Abbreviations and Acronyms

AfDB	African Development Bank
AMF	Asian Monetary Fund
APF	African Partnership Forum
APR	African personal representative
APRM	African Peer Review Mechanism
APEC	Asia-Pacific Economic Cooperation
AU	African Union
BCBS	Basel Committee on Banking Supervision
BIS	Bank for International Settlements
BTC	Baku–Tbilisi–Ceikhan oil pipline
CGFS	Committee on the Global Financial System
CIS	Commonwealth of Independent States
COMESA	Common Market for Eastern and Southern Africa
CPSS	Committee on Payment and Settlement Systems
CTD	World Trade Organization Committee on Trade and Development
CTE	World Trade Organization Committee on Trade and the Environment
DAC	Development Assistance Committee
DOT Force	Digital Opportunities Task Force
ECOSOC	United Nations Economic and Social Council
EFA	Education for All
EITI	Extractive Industries Transparency Initiative
EMIT	GATT Group on Environmental Measures and International Trade
ENGO	environmental non-governmental organization
FAO	Food and Agriculture Organization
FASS	Foreign Affairs Sous-Sherpa
FATF	Financial Action Task Force
FDI	Foreign Direct Investment
FSB	Financial Stability Board
FSF	Financial Stability Forum
FTI	Fast Track Initiative
G5	Group of Five (Brazil, China, India, and Mexico, South Africa; also known as Outreach Five or Plus Five)

G7	Group of Seven (France, United States, United Kingdom, Germany, Japan, Italy, and Canada, with representatives from the European Union)
G8	Group of Eight (Group of Seven plus Russia)
G10	Group of Ten
G20	Group of 20
G22	Group of 22 (also known as the Willard Group)
G33	Group of 33
GAID	Global Alliance for ICT and Development
GATT	General Agreement on Tariffs and Trade
GDP	gross domestic product
GEF	Global Environment Facility
GIS	Global Information Society
GMO	genetically modified organism
HDP	Heiligendamm Dialogue Process
HIPC	heavily indebted poor country
IAEA	International Atomic Energy Agency
IAIS	International Association of Insurance Supervisors
IASB	International Accounting Standards Board
IBRD	International Bank for Reconstruction and Development
ICT	information and communications technology
IDA	International Development Association
IEA	International Energy Agency
IEF	International Energy Forum
IETG	International Energy Technology Group
IFI	international financial institution
IGO	intergovernmental organization
ILOLR	international lender of last resort
IMF	International Monetary Fund
IOSCO	International Organization of Securities Commissions
IPCC	Intergovernmental Panel on Climate Change
IPEEC	International Partnership for Energy Efficiency Cooperation
IPR	Intellectual Property Rights
ISEDC	International Sustainable Energy Development Centre
IT	information technology
ITU	International Telecommunications Union
JODI	Joint Oil Date Initiative
L20	Leaders Level G20
LDC	least developed country
LNG	liquefied natural gas
LOLR	lender of last resort
M^3	cubic meters
MAI	Multilateral Agreement on Investment
MDB	multilateral development bank

MDG	Millennium Development Goal
MEA	multilateral environmental agreement
MO	multilateral organization
NAFTA	North American Free Trade Agreement
NAM	Non-Aligned Movement
NATO	North Atlantic Treaty Organization
NEPAD	New Partnership for Africa's Development
NGO	non-governmental organization
NPT	Non-Proliferation Treaty
O5	Outreach Five (Brazil, China, India, and Mexico, South Africa; also known as Group of Five or Plus Five)
OAU	Organisation for African Unity
ODA	official development assistance
OECD	Organisation for Economic Co-operation and Development
OPEC	Organization of Petroleum Exporting Countries
P5	Permanent Five members of the United Nations Security Council
R&D	research and development
SARS	severe acute respiratory syndrome
SADC	Southern African Development Community
SBN	Sustainable Buildings Network
SPR	Strategic Petroleum Reserve
SPS Agreement	Agreement on the Application of Sanitary and Phytosanitary Measures
TARP	Troubled Asset Relief Program
TB	tuberculosis
TBT Agreement	Technical Barriers to Trade Agreement
TRIPS	Trade-Related Aspects of Intellectual Property
UNAIDS	Joint United Nations Programme on HIV/AIDS
UNAMIS	United Nations Mission to Sudan
UNCTAD	United Nations Conference on Trade and Development
UNDP	United Nations Development Programme
UNECA	United Nations Economic Council for Africa
UNEP	United Nations Environment Programme
UNESCO	United Nations Educational, Scientific and Cultural Organization
UNFCCC	United Nations Framework Convention on Climate Change
UNICEF	United Nations Children's Fund
UN ICT	United Nations Information and Communications Techonologies Task Force
UNSC	United Nations Security Council
WHO	World Heath Organization
WIPO	World Intellectual Property Organization
WTO	World Trade Organization

Preface

This book is the 13th in Ashgate Publishing's Global Finance series. It continues a tradition, begun in 1998, of using the annual G7/8 summit as a catalyst for edited volumes that report the results of international research programs exploring the central themes in the emerging dynamic of global governance with a particular relevance to the field of finance. This volume continues the series' central concern with core finance issues, but includes the broader economic issues of macroeconomics, trade, development, energy, education, information and communication, and health. The book takes a close look at the way the Bretton Woods–United Nations and G8 systems are working together, apart and against each other to meet the challenges faced by the global community in these fields in a globalizing crisis-scared world.

This volume reports the results of research conducted by the Research Group on Global Financial Governance, a joint venture between the Associazione Guido Carli and the G8 Research Group, by the Centre for International Governance Innovation (CIGI) as a partner and by the State University – Higher School of Economics (HSE) in Moscow. These strands of research were brought together at authors' workshops in Moscow in the summer of 2006, in 2007, in the Spring of 2008 and in the summer of 2009. The chapters reviewed there have been subsequently revised, updated, supplemented by other contributions and integrated into a common framework for their presentation here.

This book draws its contributors from North America, Europe and Africa. It involves established and emerging scholars and practitioners who bring first-hand professional experience with the G8, Organisation for Economic Co-operation and Development, and several other multilateral economic organizations. These contributors come largely from the disciplines of economics and the international political economy and international organization fields of political science. Many of the authors have experience at senior levels in core governmental and intergovernmental institutions involved in managing and governing the global economy or have served in senior advisory capacities. With this wide variety of perspectives, analytical approaches and judgments, the collection combines the insights of scholars and practitioners who draw on a rich assortment of regional experiences, theoretical traditions, interpretative frameworks and concluding convictions, on a G8-wide and broader global scale.

Acknowledgments

In producing this volume, we have enjoyed the exceptional support of those who have contributed in many different ways. Our first debt is to the Associazione Guido Carli, which provided part of the funding that made our research possible. Our second debt is to the Centre for International Governance Innovation (CIGI) in Waterloo, Canada, Canada's Department of Foreign Affairs and International Trade, and the Jackman Foundation for their essential financial contribution. We are also grateful to David Dodge, former Governor of the Bank of Canada, his senior advisor, John Murray, and Canada's former Associate Deputy Minister of Finance, Jonathan Fried, for their support of the Research Group on Global Financial Governance. We indeed owe much to Foreign Affairs Canada and International Trade Canada, where Peter Harder, David Mulroney, Leonard Edwards, Drew Fagan, Patricia Malikail and their colleagues provided consistent support. We further thank the State University – Higher School of Economics (HSE), the Moscow Institute of International Relations (MGIMO) and their outstanding leaders and scholars who saw the exceptional opportunity that such a project offered, provided essential support, rich collegiality and warm hospitality, and mobilized the superb intellectual resources to make this project a success.

We very much appreciate the efficient help from the many talented staff that made our venture possible, at HSE and MGIMO in Moscow, at LUISS University in Rome and Milan, and at CIGI in Waterloo, Canada. In Toronto, we owe a special word of thanks to Madeline Koch, the Managing Director of the G8 Research Group, whose managerial and editorial skills were essential in helping organize the contributions and ensuring that initial thoughts and rough drafts were transformed into a polished, integrated book. We are also grateful to Helen Walsh, President of Think Content, for her vital role in ensuring that a global audience could participate in our authors' workshops, and to Zaria Shaw, Nadia Buccarelli and Kathryn Kotris for their editorial assistance in the final stages. More broadly, we note with deep appreciation the indispensable contributions of Ella Kokotsis, Director of Analytical Studies of the G8 Research Group, of Sandra Larmour, the Director of Development of the G8 Research Group, and of Shinichiro Uda, Director of the G8 Research Group's office in Japan.

At the University of Toronto, we are grateful to former President Robert Birgineau, Carolyn Tuohy and their colleagues for their support. We also acknowledge the continuing support of our colleagues at the Centre for International Studies: its director, Professor Louis Pauly, who oversees our research activities, and Professor Peter Hajnal, who assisted with the vital task, led by Michele Fratianni of Indiana University, of securing the anonymous referees who reviewed our draft manuscript and who collectively approved it for publication. We owe much to the comments of our referees, whose often trenchant but generally supportive comments have been taken fully into account. At Trinity College, we acknowledge the critical support of former provost Margaret MacMillan, bursar Geoffrey Seaborn, who manages the G8 Research Group's accounts, Head Librarian Linda Corman, who oversees the development of the G8 Research Library Collection, and Robert Bothwell, Director of the International Relations Programme. At the Department of Political Science, Robert Vipond and David Cameron, as chairs, provided encouragement and support. At the University of Toronto Library, Chief Librarian Carole Moore and Project Managers Marc Lalonde and Richard Hydal have been consistently supportive.

As always, we reserve a special word of thanks for Kirstin Howgate and her colleagues at Ashgate, for recognizing the virtue of producing this volume and for working so effectively and patiently to ensure the smooth adoption and publication of the manuscript. Finally, we acknowledge the understanding, patience and support of our families as we labored to convert raw drafts into published text. We are also indebted to the alumni of the G8 Research Group and our students at universities throughout the G8. They provide a constant source of inspiration and constructive criticism as we pursue our work.

John Kirton, Marina Larionova and Paolo Savona
2009

PART I
Introduction

Chapter 1
Introduction, Arguments and Conclusions

John Kirton, Marina Larionova and Paolo Savona

The Challenge

Today's world is crowded with international institutions governing the global economy. They come in a vast number and diversity of forms. At the center stand the 1944 Bretton Woods bodies – the International Monetary Fund (IMF) for finance, and the International Bank for Reconstruction and Development (IBRD) and World Bank for development. They are closely followed by the 1947 General Agreement on Tariffs and Trade (GATT) that became the World Trade Organization (WTO) in 1995, a host of United Nations (UN) bodies – notably the United Nations Conference on Trade and Development (UNCTAD) of 1964, the United Nations Development Programme (UNDP) of 1965 and a galaxy of functional organizations such as the United Nations Education, Science and Cultural Organization (UNESCO) of 1945 and the World Health Organization (WHO) of 1948.

Since the creation of this Bretton Woods–UN system in the 1940s, its formal, hard law, broadly multilateral, heavily organized bodies have been joined by a cornucopia of softer, informal institutions with smaller membership, lighter legal obligations, less bureaucracy and a greater reliance on open, flexible, voluntary approaches (Kirton and Trebilcock 2004). Among such bodies engaged in global as opposed to geographically regional governance, the pioneer is the Organisation for Economic Co-operation and Development (OECD), formed in 1961 to deal with a wide range of macroeconomic, microeconomic, social and development concerns. It was joined by the International Energy Agency (IEA) in 1974. These Atlantic-centered global bodies are accompanied by a host of even more informal institutions, such as the Bank for International Settlements (BIS) and the Group of Ten (G10).

At the center of this emerging alternative system of global economic governance stands the G8 club of major market democracies. First formed in 1975 and anchored in an annual summit of the leaders of its major power members, this G8-plus system is now replete with G7 and G20 finance ministers' and central bankers' forums, ministerial institutions for trade, development, environment and energy, and a galaxy of often invisible official-level bodies below. Since 2008, the leaders of the G20 have also begun holding summits.

This post-World War II accumulation of hard multilateral and soft plurilateral bodies has now created an institutionally crowded world. But as the 2008 US-turned-global financial and economic crisis dramatically revealed, it by no means constitutes a comprehensive, coherent or credible system of global economic governance. Indeed, there are no genuinely global intergovernmental multilateral organizations of consequence dedicated to such critical domains as energy, investment competition policy or critical components of the complex world of finance. In some areas several bodies claim control of a single policy space, such as food and agriculture with the Food and Agriculture Organization (FAO), the World Food Programme and the International Fund for Agricultural Development. And in the middle, existing bodies such as the FAO reach out to assert authority over ungoverned realms such as forestry and fisheries to deal with them in their own skewed way.

As intensifying globalization thrusts many long-domestic issues onto the international stage, there is a growing need to create at the global level the more comprehensive, coherent, effective governance system that citizens of most countries have long taken for granted at home. Yet the traditional means of producing such an integrated, updated, appropriate architecture for global economic governance have not been at hand. The great Cold War victory of 1989 did not lead to a major peace conference where the victor powers could erase the old order and re-design the international institutional world anew (Ikenberry 2001). Nor did it produce a unipolar movement where a single imperial power could reshape the institutionalized international system in its own image. Even less did the 1989 victory that brought intensifying openness, connectedness and democratization merely extend into an indefinite future the essentially unchanged Bretton Woods and UN institutions and ideals to govern as the dominant center the much changed twenty-first-century world.

The 1989 victory brought instead both a new world of globalization and a new system of global governance to guide it. That system, grounded in the institutions of the G8 with Russia now a full member, was genuinely global in the comprehensive range of issues and geographic space it encompassed and in the increasing inclusion of all the consequential powers in its emerging post-2003 "G8 plus five" core (Hajnal 2007, Payne 2008). It provided genuine governance, in responsively, legitimately and effectively shaping on key issues the otherwise autonomous behavior of countries and other actors, to have them seek and reach collectively desired ends. But for the first time since the modern world of exclusive, territorial, Westphalian sovereign states began in 1648, this new system of global governance was born into a crowded world – one where its predecessor, the Bretton Woods–UN system, had not been blown away by a destructive great power war. The institutions and ideals of a new and an old order thus had to compete, converge and cooperate with each other as they sought to govern this ever more demanding and globalizing crowded world.

Their challenge in doing so was compounded by several factors. First, neither system was created from a single omniscient vision or act of conscious creation to produce a coherent whole. Rather, each was the product of continuing experimentation in response to the defining global challenges arising at any time.

Each was thus more a loosely connected global governance galaxy rather than a tightly knit system. Second, both shared the same set of great powers at their core, especially as Russia and then China became increasingly involved with the G8. Third, the two systems were born with antithetical purposes – to preserve the system of sovereign states in the case of the Bretton Woods–UN bodies, and to transform these states into open democracies in the case of the G8. And fourth, they had a very different approach to governance, with the Bretton Woods–UN system relying on universal multilateralism, hard international law and international bureaucracy, and the G8 on plurilateralism, informality and great power leaders and governments instead.

The Scholarly Debate

How and why have these two great galaxies come to cooperate and converge, rather than compete and conflict, to govern the twenty-first-century world? Only recently have scholars taken up this central question of contemporary international relations (Kirton and Trebilcock 2004, Bayne 2004, Fratianni et al. 2005, Kirton 2009a, 2009b). Thus far their work has focused on the clear choice between the two grand alternatives. Here international relations scholars in the liberal institutionalist tradition and its legalization variant have emphasized the many advantages that heavily organized hard law allegedly brings (Abbott et al. 2000). Others operating from realist premises that privilege great power capabilities and choices, or from constructivist insights that emphasize the importance of direct communication, belonging and socialization, have argued for the importance of informal, exclusive, summit-level great power clubs (Kirton 1989, Bayne 2005). More recently, attention has turned to forum shopping, in which states turn to those international institutions and forums that best meet their needs (Drezner 2007). Interest has also arisen in which formal multilateral organizations are acquiring soft law features, such as the summits which the UN system has increasingly mounted for critical concerns such as development and climate change. And many conclude that the G8 could provide better global governance if it became more multilateral by expanding its membership, and more bureaucratic by adding a secretariat of its own (Cooper and Antkiewicz 2008, Ikenberry 1993).

The Contribution of this Book

Yet amidst this upsurge of interest, there have been few theoretically guided, systematic, empirical analyses of how these two great galaxies of global governance actually relate to each other and the results that their various forms of association bring. This book offers the first comprehensive look at this critical question of international relations. It examines how and how well the multilateral organizations and the G8 are dealing with the central challenges facing the contemporary international community, how they have worked well and poorly together, and how they can work together more effectively to provide badly needed global public goods.

Two points focus the detailed examination that such a subject requires. The first, substantive, one is an emphasis on global economic governance, broadly interpreted to embrace the classic components of finance, macroeconomics, microeconomics, and trade and development, but extending to the newer concerns with energy, information and communication, education and human health. It is in this field that the old multilateral order created its first and still most powerful organizations, the IMF and IBRD. It is where the first plurilateral supplements to this order arose, with the Organisation for European Economic Co-operation, the OECD and the IEA. And it is here where the full-scale alternative of the G8 first appeared in 1975, to deal with the crises of finance, energy, trade and East–West economic relations arising from 1970 to 1975. Economics is also the leading edge of the process of post-Cold War globalization, where the institutional playing field is most crowded, and where recurrent global financial crises now demand new forms of action, association and architecture on the part of all. The great global financial and economic crisis that erupted in 2008, and the emergence of G20 summitry in response, confirm how central this area is (Kirton and Koch 2008, 2009).

The second, institutional, focus is on the G8, especially as it operated at and since the first summit hosted by its newest member, Russia, at St. Petersburg in 2006. The G8's role as the selective, soft law alternative to the old multilateral order was reinforced when Russia, long both a core member and challenger of the UN system, became a full member of the G8 by hosting a summit of its own. Russia chose as the priority themes for its summit three economic issues where the relationships of the G8 with the old multilateral order were very diverse. In the first field of energy, the G8 had long been central, the plurilateral IEA helpful, and the UN system devoid of a dedicated organization of its own. In health, the G8 has assumed a growing role, while the WHO had long commanded center stage. In education and information, the G8 was a recent entrant, while UNESCO and the International Telecommunications Union stood as pillars of the 1945 UN system and the OECD was active in a broad range of issues in the field. These different configurations of the old, middle-aged and new institutions allow analysts and actors to see how the dynamics of cooperation and competition unfold in each case.

Together this allows for an examination of the G8's relationship with a large number of multilateral organizations of great diversity in date of birth, number and composition of members, geographic and functional focus, and degree of hard law form. While the G8 provides a constant focal point in the cross-case and chapter comparisons, a few chapters explore the relationship from the vantage point of the hard law multilateral organizations themselves.

The Contributors

To explore this subject, this book combines the talents of established and emerging scholars and practitioners from several scholarly disciplines and geographic regions. It includes political scientists, economists and legal scholars. It combines scholars with those who have been or are practitioners or participants in many of the institutions under scrutiny, notably the G8, OECD, WTO and Commonwealth. It thus enables scholarly analysis to be tested against and refined by a detailed knowledge of how things work in practice on the inside. And it embraces contributors from North America, Europe and Africa, thus permitting a more global perspective on how the international institutions under scrutiny do and should work.

The Contributions

These contributors offer in turn an analytic framework and academic application for exploring the multilateral organization–G8 relationship, the core economic issues of finance, macroeconomics, trade and development, practitioners' perspectives on this relationship, and the relationship in the extended economic issue areas of energy, information and communication, education and health, highlighted as priorities at the 2006 G8 St. Petersburg Summit, and their convergence at that summit and since.

Part II, "Multilateral Organizations and the G8: Academic Analyses," provides an analytical framework for exploring the multifaceted relationships between formal, hard law, multilateral organizations such as those of the Bretton Woods–UN system and informal plurilateral soft law institutions such as the G8. It does so at three levels. The first is a general categorization of the full range of possible relationships between the two. The second is a more specific set of propositions about how multilateral organizations (MOs) affect G8 performance. The third is the way the first global economic hybrid hard law but plurilateral organization – the OECD – seeks to enhance global economic governance in relationship with both the G8 and the broader multilateral world.

In Chapter 2, "Multilateral Organizations and G8 Governance: A Framework for Analysis," John Kirton focuses on the analytic foundations for examining and improving the relationship between multilateral organizations and the G8. In doing so, the chapter takes up five essential tasks. First, it looks at the existing debate and evidence about the relationship between the G8 and MOs, focusing largely on the impact of this relationship on G8 commitment and compliance. These are placed into six schools of thought, which explore the six possibilities of G8–MO cooperation. Second, the author offers an analytic framework which identifies how MOs can improve G8 compliance, using the dimensions of the level, timing and intentionality of the connection. Based on this framework, Kirton identifies 15 contributions that MOs can and do make to G8 governance, at the latter's preparatory, summit and implementation stages. Third, the chapter identifies ten hypotheses about how MOs' contributions to G8 governance will arise. Fourth, Kirton tests the first two of these hypotheses against new evidence and analysis from the recent record of G8 compliance, finding varying support for both. Finally, the chapter concludes by presenting policy options about how MOs could assist the G8 more effectively in the process of implementation.

In Chapter 3, "The New Partnership between Multilateral Organizations and the G8," Marina Larionova explores the debate between competing schools of thought on the nature of engagement between the G8 and other international institutions: G8 governance through the multilateral organizations, G8 governance against multilateral organizations and G8 governance without multilateral organizations. To develop and arbitrate this debate, she puts forward a fourth model based on two assumptions. The positivist assumption is that the G8 and international organizations seek to serve a common cause, and thus should be natural allies. The second, constructivist, assumption is that given the challenges of global governance, the G8 members' choice of the mode of interaction with the international institutions will rationally tilt toward a "G8 governance in alliance with the multilateral organizations" based on the democratic institutionalism and network of networks models.

Her study of the summits' documents over the period 1998–2007 reveals that there has been a steady increase in the G8 members' cooperative actions with the multilateral institutions from 1998 to 2007. Governance through international institutions remains the preferred choice of engagement. But the trend is gradually pushing toward G8 governance in alliance with multilateral organizations. The trend is especially pronounced in the spheres of development, security and health. However, in the more sensitive spheres – security and energy – governance through the international institutions remains predominant. These trends are likely to persist in the current and next summit sequence. They should be considered in forging decisions, building consensus and defining international mechanisms for the summit commitments' implementation. As the international multilateral institutions' role, influence and involvement in G8 governance increase, the imperative for their reform and efficiency becomes even more pronounced. G8 members should invest more effort in reforming the international institutions to ensure that the latter have sufficient capacity to act as partners in the global governance process.

In Chapter 4, "Financial Crises, the International Monetary Fund and the G8," Ivan Savić argues that G7 commitments are a crucial component of international efforts to combat financial crises. The members of the G7 are the source of much of the world's capital. Through individual action, regular coordination and their large voting shares in the IMF, they effectively regulate and structure the international financial architecture. Moreover, the G7 regularly supports and often supplements the efforts of the IMF to contain and reverse financial crises. Savić examines the relationship between the G7 and the IMF to show how it affects the ability of both organizations to deal with financial crises. Specifically, he examines the influence of the G7 in the IMF and how the G7 coordinates and works with the IMF in crisis response. In doing so, he develops a model of coordination between the G7 and the IMF, discusses the G7–IMF role in global financial bail-outs, including those created in response to the Asian crisis of 1997/98 and the 2007–09 global financial and economic crises.

In Chapter 5, "Finance and Development Compliance in the G8: The IMF and World Bank Role," John Kirton, Nikolai Roudev and Laura Sunderland ask whether the world's major powers keep the international commitments they make. To provide an answer, they develop a recently created multilevel model of G8 member country compliance with the finance commitments the leaders make at their annual summit, and test it with an expanded data set of 54 cases from 1996 to 2006. They first examine how G8 leaders as agents deliberatively craft the commitments in ways that embed 12 "compliance catalysts" designed to improve the chances that their commitments will be complied with during the following year. They then explore how the spontaneous work of the G8's ministerial institution for finance improves compliance. Finally, they assess the distribution of vulnerability and capability in the international system to determine whether agency and institutions act autonomously or are predetermined or overwhelmed by system structure in their compliance effects.

The findings suggest that the agency of G8 leaders matters, but G8 institutionalization does not. The compliance catalyst of a "timetable" and the "total number" of catalysts embedded in a commitment improve compliance. Moreover, the multilateral organizations most relevant to the field of finance – the IMF and World Bank – have a strong compliance-catalytic effect. But the IMF strongly increases while the World Bank strongly decreases the finance compliance that comes about. The G7 finance ministers do not matter, either as a catalyst or as an autonomous institution. On development commitments, compliance is strongly increased by the total number of catalysts and those of priority placement, target, specified agent and the IMF, but lowered by the World Bank. On non-development commitments, compliance is increased, more weakly, by priority placement, timetable and G8 bodies beyond the G7 finance ministers' forum. This suggests the need to go beyond the debate about G8 governance through, against or without the multilateral organization, beyond crude distinctions between hard and soft law bodies and among multilateral, plurilateral and regional ones, to refine and test more specific hypotheses about how multilateral organizations relate to the G8, especially in the latter's compliance task. In the mean time, the advice to G8 leaders is "trust yourself and the Fund, but not the Bank" to deliver the decisions you make.

Part III, "Multilateral Organizations and the G8: Practitioners' Perspectives," takes the academic frameworks offered in Part I for the classic core economic issues of finance, macroeconomics, trade and development and explores how they appear to practitioners from the inside.

In Chapter 6, "Finance, Macroeconomics and the Multilateral Organization–G8 Connection," Robert Fauver focuses on the relationship between the G8 and the IMF, World Bank and international financial institutions (IFIs) in general, the delegation of implementation tasks by the G8 to the IFIs, and whether or not the G8 should act as a directoire for these institutions. He begins with early G8–IMF cooperation during the late 1970s. He then discusses the influence the G8 has within the World Bank and IMF, using the cases of the 1994 Naples and 1986 Tokyo summits as evidence. He also explores a growing resentment on the part of emerging market economies within IFIs against the delegation of implementation tasks by major industrial nations. He ends with recommendations for how the G8 can see more effective implementation when delegating tasks to the hard law IFIs.

In Chapter 7, "Development, the Commonwealth and the G8," Ade Adefuye studies the relationship between the G8 and many multilateral institutions, focusing on the Commonwealth. He feels the Commonwealth can create pressure within the G8 to deal with African issues, help the G8 put its plans into action through its extensive contacts in the continent, and hold the G8 accountable because the latter lacks a secretariat to do so on its own. He points to four issue areas of extreme importance in Africa. On the first, peace and security, Adefuye argues that through support of the African Union (AU) and the UN, conflict on the continent has decreased, and that through cooperation with the Commonwealth, the G8 can be come more effective in further reducing conflicts. On the second, strengthening institutions and governance, he asserts that thanks to G8 support, the AU and the New Partnership for Africa's Development (NEPAD) have made impressive changes. Again he recommends cooperation with the Commonwealth as a way to strengthen G8 governance. Third, Adefuye addresses debt relief, noting some of the problems the G8 has in this area. On the final issue, economic growth and sustainable development, Adefuye argues that the G8 has been successful, by working with the OECD, NEPAD and the WTO. Adefuye concludes with recommendations on how G8–MO cooperation can benefit Africa even further through cooperation with the UN, IFIs, the OECD and the African Development Bank (AfDB).

In Chapter 8, "Trade, the World Trade Organization and the Doha Development Agenda," Roy MacLaren studies the role of the G8 within the WTO and, more specifically, the Doha round of trade negotiations. MacLaren argues that the G8 pursues contradictory policies on the international level – in the IMF, WTO and World Bank – and on the national level with respect to conflicting official development assistance (ODA) and trade policies. He finds it imperative that national priorities of G8 countries are aligned, and recommends a more global, rather than domestic protectionist, trade focus. He then discusses the failure of the Doha round and the influence of the G8 countries over its outcome. MacLaren argues that although the G8 produces communiqués calling for an end to the round and pushes the blame on the WTO or unnamed WTO member states, the blame ultimately lies with the influential G8 countries. Next, MacLaren discusses possible futures for the Doha round and the trend in international trade away from the multilateral hard law WTO toward a series of bilateral free trade deals. He suggests a way in which the WTO can embrace this new trade climate. Finally, MacLaren recommends that the G8 turn its calls for a more effective WTO onto itself, thus beginning collaboration with the WTO, which would turn it into the ideal negotiating forum for the many regional and bilateral free trade agreements. The failure of Doha, allowed by the G8, would cause a serious blow to the international economy and call into question the value and credibility of the G8 itself.

Part IV, "The St. Petersburg Priorities: Energy, Education, Information and Health," applies the general framework to the newer, increasingly relevant, economic issues that globalization has lifted up from national governance onto the global stage.

In Chapter 9, "Energy Security and Sustainable Development: The WTO and the Energy Charter Treaty," Sylvia Ostry begins with a history of the concept of sustainable development within the GATT and the WTO and its increasing importance within international trade negotiations. She next discusses the possibility of the failure of the Doha round and the fragmentation of international trade into bilateral trade deals. She offers suggestions for how the WTO can reform in order to strengthen environmental values. Ostry then turns to the importance of cooperation between international institutions on issues such as the environment, using the case of the EU's energy charter treaty. She outlines the problems with the treaty and suggests a course of action for the G8 in order to create an effective energy security regime by collaborating with the WTO and the OECD on energy investment.

In Chapter 10, "Energy Security: Russia, the European Union and the G8," Nodari A. Simonia reviews from the perspective of late 2006 the tensions over the energy issues at the St. Petersburg Summit. He looks into the most persistent arguments in the preparation of the G8 summit's final documents, which centered on the concept of "energy security." Whereas the majority of Western representatives insisted on understanding this term as a supply guarantee – security for consumers – Russia insisted that guarantees for supply ought to be supplemented with demand guarantees, and that consumer countries' governments and business must share responsibility and risks with producing countries.

Experts managed to find compromise formulas, which allowed the St. Petersburg Summit to adapt the joint declaration and plan of action for the provision of global energy security. They affirmed producers' and consumers' mutual responsibility for sustainable and stable development of world energy. However, unsettled problems remained. The dispute flared up with new force soon after the summit, especially on the threshold of the Russia–EU Summit in November 2006, where negotiations were to start on a new partnership and cooperation agreement. The positions of the three major players, the EU, US and Russia, show that there was a marked contrast between the real cooperation of Russian and European business and the loud, sometimes panicky reaction of European Commission officials to any Russian step toward integration into the European economic space on equal and mutually beneficial terms, even though this was stipulated by the St. Petersburg G8 Summit.

In Chapter 11, "Energy Security, the International Energy Agency and the G8," Victoria V. Panova begins with a review of the four phases of G8 energy governance. The first was the 1975–82 phase of governance in cooperation with the OECD, the World Bank and the IEA based on the reaction to the oil crises of 1973 and 1979. The second phase, the 1980s, saw a more politically driven G8 with little cooperation on energy security with international institutions. The third phase in the late 1980s to early 1990s saw a shift to nuclear safety and environmental concerns, with delegation of tasks to the World Bank and the IEA. The fourth phase, the beginning of the twenty-first century, saw a renewed G8 interest in energy security with resurgent oil prices and cooperation with the International Energy Forum (IEF), the IEA and World Bank. Panova argues that the G8, along with the IEA and other international institutions, has been successful in governing global energy both environmentally and economically. Their cooperation has countered energy shocks from military, political and economic risks and led to stability. She outlines how the G8, both on its own and with the cooperation of institutions such as the IEA, can govern global energy more effectively.

In Chapter 12, "Education, the G8 and UNESCO," John Kirton, Laura Sunderland and Jenilee Guebert examine the G8's performance since 1977, paying particular attention to the "great leap forward" in G8 global education governance at the Okinawa Summit in 2000 and the demands of the rapidly developing twenty-first-century world for education governance. They argue that the G8 has both a supportive and directive relationship with the relevant MOs. The G8 has stepped in to govern education when the hard law MOs have failed to do so, and supported the MOs when they have created worthwhile initiatives. After laying out the schools of thought on G8 education governance, the authors discuss the most important G8 summits for education. This includes a close look at the 2000 Okinawa Summit and the Digital Opportunity Task Force (DOT Force) that filled a gap in global education governance, leading the international institutions to cooperate on education when they had failed to do so themselves. The authors find that the G8 governance on education in the twenty-first century has been very effective, due to the lack of governance on the part of the MOs, the influence of the Dakar Framework for Education under UNESCO and the cooperation of MOs at summits in driving commitments and compliance.

In Chapter 13, "Information and Communication: G8 Institutionalization and Compliance in the DOT Force," Gina Stephens examines the role of G8 institutional expansion, notably the growth of expert working groups, in enhancing cooperation and compliance. Using insights from constructivism and social identity theory, she analyzes the case of the DOT Force working group. She observes that an increase in institutionalization and specialization in "top-down" created working groups effects a change in their participants' interests and identities, thereby increasing cooperation, and eventually compliance. These tightly focused groups, especially those tasked with policy areas that are relatively novel and where there is little pre-existing national policy among G8 members such as information technology, provide a forum that favors the evolution of a group-centric identity that mitigates a competitive concentration on national conceptions of relative capability and gain.

In Chapter 14, "Health Compliance in the G8 and APEC: the World Health Organization's Role," John Kirton, Nikolai Roudev, Laura Sunderland, Catherine Kunz and Jenilee Guebert argue that the annual G8 summits and the Asia-Pacific Economic Cooperation (APEC) leaders' meetings are promising forums for integrating health with foreign policy in ways that reflect the priorities of the WHO and the global community as a whole. Such summits are directly delivered by the most powerful leaders of many of the most influential countries in the world. These leaders are ultimately responsible abroad and at home for both health and foreign policy, including its peace and security core. They use their summits simultaneously to make many commitments in both fields and in the closely related ones of human rights, climate change and development, including the Millennium Development Goals. Moreover, commitments made at G8 summits in these fields are quickly complied with by the member governments to a substantial degree. Such compliance is caused, and can thus be improved, by the leaders themselves, through crafting their commitments to catalyze compliance, and by using their international institutions and own governments to help implement them. But the prevailing processes of implementing G8 and APEC leaders' commitments through international institutions, national governments or non-governmental networks are not well designed to foster compliance, monitoring and reporting in ways that integrate health and foreign policy in a mutually supportive fashion. There are many ways to improve compliance in support of this objective, including through a multi-stakeholder global health diplomacy network of civil society, national governments and international organizations, including the WHO.

Part V, "The G8's St. Petersburg Summit and Beyond," offers a focused conclusion by explaining in detail the intersection of the G8 and MOs at and after the G8's 2006 summit. It pays particular reference to that summit's priority issues of energy, education and health, as well as the G8's "built-in" economic agenda of finance, macroeconomics, trade and development.

In Chapter 15, "The G8 at St. Petersburg and Beyond," John Kirton discusses the process and outcome of the St. Petersburg Summit. He argues that its agenda, focused on energy security, infectious disease and education, went well beyond the current hard law institutions in effective governance. The St. Petersburg Summit marked a new relationship between the G8 and MOs, one where relevant MOs were invited to take part in the summit process and provide support to fill the "commitment–compliance gap." By moving away from the rigid regimes of the MOs, the G8 was able to create strong commitments on a broad variety of issues. However, the cooperation with the MOs did not close the commitment–compliance gap. One very successful aspect of the summit was the democratization of the G8 summit process, contrary to the non-democratic UN system. Inviting the "Plus Five" emerging economies sometimes referred to as the Outreach Five (O5) or the Group of Five (G5), four of which are democratic nations, and setting a course for permanent cooperation showed an ability to reform where the UN had failed with the United Nations Security Council (UNSC). The inclusion of the newly formed Civil 8 gave civil society a voice in G8 commitments. This civil society pressure led to real results, winning the environment an important place on the energy security agenda at the summit.

Kirton suggests that the OECD, IEA and WTO should all make Russia a member, since Russia invited these institutions to take part in the preparations for the G8 summit which it hosted. He also calls for the creation of a "G8 compliance consortium" to coordinate the several systems of G8 compliance monitoring "so that G8 governors can join with their own legislators, judiciaries, auditors general and civil society to know how well their promises at the summit are subsequently being transformed into practice on the ground."

In Chapter 16, "The 2006 St. Petersburg G8 Summit: Conclusions and Critiques," Andrew F. Cooper maintains that at the 2006 G8 summit in St. Petersburg, Russia exhibited unparalleled global governance from state and non-state actors. Including for the first time the Civil 8, Russia hosted a summit that connected "the informal nature of the G8 with 'hard law.'" This effort to foster increased transparency and continued commitment from G8 members and the international community highlighted Russia's governance goals for the summit.

Now, Cooper argues, there is a need to more clearly define MOs' mandates and how they can most benefit the work of the G8. Cooper refers to John Kirton's 2009 G8/MOs framework analysis to assess how this could best be accomplished. From his research, Cooper insists that although there is no direct correlation between the number of times MOs are referenced at G8 summits and actual compliance scores of commitments made therein, it can be argued that governance in alliance with MOs is more pronounced in certain areas (such as health and development) than governance through MOs (energy and security).

During the recent financial crisis, through an effective division of resources, the G8 and the IMF are an example of a cooperative relationship that has mixed components of soft and hard law to produce results. Cooper concludes that this G8 outreach is instrumental for its accountability, effectiveness and global governance.

Conclusions

From these analyses, several conclusions emerge. They cover the descriptive patterns of how the MO–G8 relationship has changed over time and across policy space, the causes of these changes, their consequences for particular actors and global governance for the global public good, policy recommendations for improvements based on the current state of knowledge, and suggestions for further research.

The Changing MO–G8 Relationship

There is considerable consensus among the authors regarding what the G8–MO relationship is and how it has changed and is changing now. A few authors see the G8 as a directoire to the MOs. The G8 deliberates on a given issue, makes commitments, and then delegates the implementation of these tasks to relevant MOs. Fauver sees growing resentment on the part of MOs and their non-G8 members within international financial institutions. Kirton notes that the OECD acts in certain areas of policy as a *de facto* secretariat to the G8.

Another consensus concerns the growing G8–MO cooperation, specifically a rise in cooperation with MOs on the part of the G8 since the late 1990s. Larionova shows that since 1998, the G8 has increasingly chosen to work in alliance with MOs rather than through, with or without them. Others see a re-emergence of cooperation. Panova notes high periods of cooperation with the IEA in the late 1970s, and a subsequent lull in cooperation until its renewal in the new millennium.

Another school, led by MacLaren, sees the G8 taking contradictory policies within MOs, while continuing to urge the MOs in their G8 communiqués to solve problems whose solution ultimately lies with the G8 countries themselves. In contrast, Savić sees the G8 working in harmony with IFIs, especially the IMF. He sees since the 1970s a three-part institutional division of labor between the G8 and the IMF to deal with the global financial system and international financial crises. The G8 works independently to keep the core of international trade and finance strong, while the IMF works to keep the middle- and low-income countries afloat. In times of severe crisis, they come together to solve the problem.

A final school sees the G8 as filling gaps in the international system, which arise due to neglect or failure by MOs. Kirton, Sunderland and Guebert assert that since the 1980s, the G8 has stepped in to provide global governance in education where the MOs such as UNESCO and the United Nations Children's Fund (UNICEF) have failed to do so.

The Causes of Change and Continuity in the MO–G8 Relationship

There are also differing views about why these G8–MO relationships are created, continued and changed. A first school asserts that G8 membership within MOs matters. If an MO's inner management core contains all or nearly all the members of the G8, most notably IFIs (such as the IMF) and the OECD, or G8 members as a bloc possess a major voting share in the institution, G8 initiatives are likely to become those of the MO. Fauver believes that G8 member-based leadership in the hard law IFIs drives the delegation of G8 implementation tasks to the MOs and the growing resentment from their non-G8 member states. MacLaren blames G8 domination of the WTO for the deadlock in the Doha round.

Another school sees the G8 as cooperating with MOs at points in the past, and increasingly so in the future, due to the fact that both the G8 and the MOs seek the same ends. Larionova gives such an explanation for why the G8 has increasingly worked with MOs as an ally since the late 1990s. This stands in sharp contrast to the political security sphere where the core missions of the UN and G8 are antithetical in fundamental ways (Kirton 2002).

Yet another school of authors sees changing G8 priorities as the driver behind which MOs the G8 cooperates with and how much it does. By explaining the changing G8 priorities in global energy governance from concerns about oil prices in the early 1970s to the environmental concerns of the 1990s and the re-emergent high oil prices in the new millennium, Panova outlines the phases of G8 cooperation with the IEA. Adefuye argues that cooperation with MOs on Africa came about only when the G8 had made Africa one of its highest priorities in the late 1990s.

Consequences

In their analysis of the G8–MO relationship, the authors also come to some consensus about the overall effect of these relationships in providing adequate global governance. Several authors see a positive outcome. Within this school there are two variants. The first argues that the collaboration of the G8 and MOs has led to greater global governance and stability in a given area. Panova praises the work of the IEA and the G8 in creating stability in the face of energy shocks generated by military, political and economic risks. The second variant argues that cooperation has led to greater compliance with G8 commitments. Kirton, Sunderland and Guebert note that the cooperation of MOs at summits has led to higher compliance in education. Stephens argues that bringing MOs into the top-down institutionalization process of the G8 creates more impetus for compliance.

Another school offers a mixed conclusion. In some ways, global governance has benefited from the G8–MO relationship, and in others it has not. There are two variants of this school as well. The first sees success in the case of some MOs, and failure in others. Kirton, Roudev and Sunderland found that "the IMF and World Bank have a strong compliance catalytic effect, but the IMF strongly increases, while the World Bank strongly decreases compliance." The second variant sees the G8–MO relationship as a success, but asserts that the G8 and other institutions are still not doing enough. Kirton et al. see successful cooperation among the G8, APEC and the WHO in the area of global health governance, but argue that the relationship is not living up to its potential.

A third conclusion comes from MacLaren. He sees clear failure for global trade liberalization as a result of the G8–MO relationship. He feels that the Doha round and the future of the WTO are being jeopardized by the contradictory policies of the G8 within the IFIs and the unwillingness on the part of G8 members to change their domestic policies in order to conclude the round.

Policy Recommendations

Several authors offer policy recommendations based on their analyses. The first is a call for greater cooperation with MOs on the part of the G8. In some cases this means exerting G8 influence on the MOs so they fit more harmoniously within the G8 system. Larionova suggests reforming MOs so that they can create better alliances with the G8. Fauver recommends creating consensus within the IFIs before delegating tasks so that the IFI will work more efficiently toward achieving G8 aims. In other cases, new areas are suggested where the G8 can branch out in collaboration with MOs. Ostry suggests that a new joint effort be implemented on the part of the G8, the WTO and the OECD in energy security and investment.

A second recommendation is for more cooperation with the G8 on the part of the MOs. Kirton suggests that the OECD, IEA and the WTO make Russia a member, effectively making all G8 member states members of these MOs, with a view toward more effective cooperation, especially in years where Russia is the G8 summit host.

A third recommendation is a call for a new forum for collaboration and discussion among the G8 and MOs. Ostry suggests a new forum be created to discuss energy security through investment. Adefuye recommends a new G8–Africa forum as a permanent part of the G8. Members would include African leaders, the UN Secretary-General, IFIs and the AfDB. Other new forums are suggested to raise G8 compliance. Kirton et al. propose a "a multi-stakeholder global health diplomacy network of civil society, national governments and international organizations, including the WHO." Kirton recommends a "G8 compliance consortium [that] would coordinate the several systems of G8 compliance monitoring so that G8 governors can join with their own legislators, judiciaries, auditors general and civil society to know how well their promises at the summit are subsequently being transformed into practice on the ground."

Suggestions for Scholarly Research

Some authors also identify areas for further research. Some important questions posed in common concern the MOs as secretariats for the G8. Kirton calls for further research on whether the OECD should assume a larger role with the G8 as a type of secretariat, whether other MOs could assist in implementation and compliance monitoring, and whether or not this would increase compliance with G8 commitments. Kirton et al. also feel that research on the implementation process of G8 commitments is lacking.

Other authors see a need to study the G8–MO relationship in more depth, with an emphasis on how the MOs can increase compliance. Kirton, Roudev and Sunderland suggest the need to go beyond the debate about G8 governance through, against or without the multilateral organization's help, and beyond crude distinctions between hard and soft law bodies and among multilateral, plurilateral and regional ones, to refine and test more specific hypotheses about how MOs relate to the G8, especially in the latter's compliance task.

Bibliography

Abbott, Kenneth et al. (2000), "The Concept of Legalization," *International Organization* 54 (Summer).

Bayne, Nicholas (2004), "Hard and Soft Law in International Institutions: Complements, Not Alternatives," in John Kirton and Michael Trebilcock, eds (2004), *Hard Choices, Soft Law: Voluntary Standards in Global Trade, Environment and Social Governance* (Aldershot: Ashgate), pp. 347–51.

Bayne, Nicholas (2005), *Staying Together: The G8 Summit Confronts the Twenty-First Century* (Aldershot: Ashgate).

Cooper, Andrew and Agata Antkiewicz, eds (2008), *Emerging Powers in Global Governance: Lessons from the Heiligendamm Process* (Waterloo, Ontario: Wilfrid Laurier University Press).

Drezner, Daniel (2007), *All Politics Is Global: Explaining International Regulatory Regimes* (Princeton, NJ: Princeton University Press).

Fratianni, Michele, John Kirton, Alan Rugman and Paolo Savona, eds (2005), *New Perspectives on Global Governance: Why America Needs the G8* (Aldershot: Ashgate).

Hajnal, Peter (2007), *The G8 System and the G20: Evolution, Role and Documentation* (Aldershot: Ashgate).

Ikenberry, John (1993), "Salvaging the G7," *Foreign Affairs* 72 (Spring).

Ikenberry, John (2001), *After Victory: Strategic Restraint, and the Rebuilding of Order after Major Wars* (Princeton, NJ: Princeton University Press).

Kirton, John (1989), "Contemporary Concert Diplomacy: The Seven-Power Summit and the Management of International Order." Paper prepared for the annual meeting of the International Studies Association, 29 March–1 April. London. <www.g8.utoronto.ca/scholar/kirton198901>.

Kirton, John (2002), "The G8, the United Nations and Global Security Governance," in John Kirton and Junichi Takese, eds, *New Directions in Global Political Governance* (Aldershot: Ashgate).

Kirton, John, ed. (2009a), *Global Law* (Farnham: Ashgate).

Kirton, John, ed. (2009b), *International Organization* (Farnham: Ashgate).

Kirton, John and Madeline Koch, eds (2008), *G20: Growth, Innovation, Inclusion: The G20 at Ten* (London: Newsdesk).

Kirton, John and Madeline Koch, eds (2009), *G20: The London Summit: Growth, Stability and Jobs* (London: Newsdesk).

Kirton, John and Michael Trebilcock, eds (2004), *Hard Choices, Soft Law: Voluntary Standards in Global Trade, Environment and Social Governance* (Aldershot: Ashgate).

Payne, Anthony (2008), "The G8 in a Changing Global Economic Order," *International Affairs* 84(3): 519–33.

Putnam, Robert D., and Nicholas Bayne (1987), *Hanging Together: Cooperation and Conflict in the Seven Power Summits*, 2nd edn (Cambridge, MA: Harvard University Press).

PART II
Multilateral Organizations and the G8: Academic Analyses

Chapter 2
Multilateral Organizations and G8 Governance: A Framework for Analysis

John Kirton

How do international institutions, led by the formal, hard law bodies of the Bretton Woods–United Nations (UN) system, and informal plurilateral bodies, led by the Group of Eight (G8), help each other govern the world? More specifically, how have and can the world's many multilateral organizations (MOs) assist the G8 in enhancing its members' ability to consider, reach consensus on, commit to and comply with ambitious, appropriate agreements to address key global needs?

These questions are becoming increasingly important. The longstanding dissatisfaction with the 1944–45 MOs is reaching a critical peak, especially amidst the American-turned-global financial crisis of 2008–09. The G8 during the past decade has been making a growing number of commitments, of a more ambitious kind, over a broader range of issues. G8 governors have been assigning to the world's major established MOs as well as those in their own G8-centric system the responsibility for implementing the decisions that G8 leaders make collectively. G8 governments, civil society organizations and citizens agree that improved compliance and implementation are critical for improved G8 and global governance as a whole. Since 1996, G8 members have been increasingly involving MOs in the G8 system and summits to help with these tasks. In preparing and producing the 2006 St. Petersburg Summit, Russia, hosting a regular G8 summit for the first time but lacking full membership in all parts of the G8 system, relied on MOs to an unusually high degree. It invited as participants to the summit an abnormally large number of leaders of the MOs most relevant to that summit's work.

Yet little is known about how well, how, where, when and why MOs help or harm G8 governance, and which MOs can be counted on in particular situations to help the most. There is thus a very slender foundation for judging which international institutions should be invited to a summit, and how they should be involved in the overall summit process and system throughout the year. There is also little to guide outside analysts and G8 governors in assessing, selecting from and innovatively expanding the diverse array of recommendations about how the G8–MO connection can be improved.

To help build the analytical foundations for exploring and improving the MO–G8 connection, this chapter takes up five tasks. First, it briefly reviews the existing debate and evidence about the relationship between the MOs and G8, especially on the key dimension where compliance with G8 commitments is concerned. Second, it offers an analytical framework identifying the many ways in which MOs can help G8 implementation. Third, it presents hypotheses about why MOs assist the G8 with compliance and implementation. Fourth, it offers new evidence and analysis from the G8's recent compliance record to test some of these hypotheses. Fifth, it identifies the major policy questions that arise about the way MOs might better assist with G8 implementation.

This study identifies six major schools of thought on logical possibilities about the G8–MO relationship: G8 governance through, against and without the MOs, and MO governance through, with and without the G8. Using the level, timing and intentionality of the G8–MO connection as key criteria, it highlights 15 ways in which MOs can help the G8. It next offers nine hypotheses about the conditions under which these MO contributions will come. Using compliance with the commitments made at the G8's 2000, 2004 and 2005 summits as evidence, it shows how these hypotheses can be tested, and offers some support for G8 governance through, without and with the MOs. It concludes with several policy-relevant questions to guide future research.

Throughout this study, the emphasis is on compliance with the G8 summit's decisional commitments, within the broader array of governance functions that the G8 summit and system performs. The focus is on the first-order compliance of G8 members, rather than extended implementation through to solving the problem addressed. A further focus is on the one-way relationship flowing from G8 governance to MO responsiveness and support. The chapter generally does not deal directly with the equally important reciprocal relationship in which the G8 helps implement the MO's commitments and governance. However, it is hypothesized that the connection between the two is a synergistic, two-way street in which G8 support for MOs constitutes a cause of the MO's help for the G8 in its compliance, implementation and other tasks in return, in a relationship of both specific and diffuse reciprocity. Thus a full temporal spectrum is included in this analysis, running from the start of an annual G8 summit's preparatory process through to its implementation end, in order to examine comprehensively how MOs are involved at every stage. Such early and continuous involvement should, it is hypothesized, produce superior results compared to the alternative of the G8 involving MOs only immediately after the summit commitments are publicly produced, as a *fait accompli* from a *deus ex machina*-like directoire that then asks MOs out of the blue to help implement what the G8 has already decided all on its own to do.

The Multilateral Organization–G8 Connection: Arguments and Evidence

The Debate among Competing Schools of Thought

To date, the debate on the relationship between the G8 and MOs, especially in regard to the critical dimension of compliance and implementation, has centered on three major competing schools of thought.

G8 governance through multilateral organizations The first school, pioneered by Ella Kokotsis in her 1999 democratic institutionalist model of G8 performance, presents a vision of effective G8 governance through MOs (Kokotsis 1999).[1] It argues that the work of those MOs controlled by G7 members is an important cause of compliance with G8 commitments by G8 members when those organizations are directly relevant to the particular G8 commitments in question (Kokotsis 1999, Kokotsis and Daniels 1999). Thus, from 1988 to 1995, compliance with G7 commitments by the world's most powerful country, the United States, and the weakest member, Canada, was higher in those globally critical areas – assistance to the former Soviet Union and debt relief for the poorest – most relevant to the long-established, most powerful MOs – the International Monetary Fund (IMF) and World Bank – that were employed by the G7 as an implementing instrument, and controlled by the G7 members through their dominance of the institutions' executive boards. In contrast, compliance was lower in those equally critical global areas – climate change and biodiversity – where the relevant institutions – the 1972 United Nations Environment Programme (UNEP) and the 1992 secretariats of the United Nations framework conventions on climate change and biodiversity – were more recent, more fragmented, less organizationally powerful and less controlled by the G7.

Also relevant in causing compliance were institutional factors at the informal, G7-influenced plurilateral and the national levels. In the finance fields there had been a G7 ministerial forum since 1973 (which Canada and Italy joined in 1986) and strong coordinative centers within the US Treasury Department and Canadian Department of Finance. In the environmental field, a G7 ministerial meeting emerged only in 1992, and national coordinative centers – the US Environmental Protection Agency and Environment Canada – remained relatively weak. In all cases, however, compliance for both countries improved from 1992 on, when new multilateral and G7-centered institutions arose in finance, and especially in the environment field. Thus, the G8 could use the powerful MOs it controlled to help put G8 decisions into effect and, as a rational extension in emerging fields such as the environment, even help bring new MOs to life.

G8 governance against multilateral organizations The second, sharply contrasting, school, developed by John Kirton in his concert equality model, offers

---

1 In the seminal work prior to that of Kokotsis, George von Furstenberg and Joseph Daniels's conjectures ruled out the structural factor of member countries' relative capability as a relevant cause of compliance. Quan Li's (2001) subsequent analysis of their data set found that compliance with inflation control commitments correlated positively with the interstate-level variable of reciprocating behavior and negatively with the domestic-level variables of divided/coalition governments and uncertainty. International institutional variables were not addressed.

effective G8 governance against MOs (Kirton 2004).[2] It asserts that the G8, born of the great failure of the old MOs during the crises of the early 1970s, has increasingly moved from reinforcing, through reforming, to replacing the old MOs and their order with a fundamentally antithetical G8-centered global governance system of its own. This evolution was first seen in the newer "transnational/global" issues areas, such as energy, investment, competition, the environment, information, terrorism, crime and corruption, and drugs, where the old multilateral order had no serious, strong organizations of its own. Yet after the great failure of the G7 to reform the 1944 Bretton Woods and broader 1940s functional UN systems at the 1995 Halifax Summit, where institutional reform was the defining focus, the G7 moved to create a new generation of G8-centered institutions to govern the traditional economic fields where the IMF and World Bank had long reigned supreme. It did so most notably with the Group of 20 (G20) and Financial Stability Forum (FSF) for finance in a now globalized world and the African Personal Representatives, African Partnership Forum and a G8 meeting of ministers for development in a now rapidly democratizing one. This great transformation toward G8-led global governance extended into the political-security field, with the G8-led liberation of Kosovo and development of a G8 conflict prevention agenda and forums in 1999 (Kirton 2002). It also came to embrace functional fields such as health and education, where since the 1940s, strong UN bodies had been at work.

Across all domains, the established MOs are similarly not allies but adversaries in the G8's effort to ensure effective global governance in a fast-changing, globalizing, post-Cold War world. These organizations have at least obsolete and often antithetical mandates, management and governance arrangements and institutional cultures, and a record and reputation of failure. They have proven impervious to change by a determined G7 in 1995 at its most self-confident post-Cold War height. The failure of the UN to change its charter and Security Council at its September 2005 World Summit and the failure of the IMF and World Bank to fundamentally transform themselves with voices, votes, missions and mandates appropriate for the twenty-first century, and do so in ways that the now finance-surplus superpowers of Japan, China and other Asians accept, strongly suggests that the G8 can count even less on the old MOs in the years ahead.

---

2 Kirton's concert equality model, developed to explain the G8's governance performance overall, highlights member countries' relative vulnerability and capability, along with poor UN-based MO performance, the common purpose and constricted participation within the G8 summit, and the domestic political capital and control of G8 leaders at home. The model worked well almost everywhere, but failed to account for G8 compliance overall or in the trade and finance fields (Kirton 2004). Its failure in explaining compliance may have flowed from its neglect of the striking growth and operation of G8 sub-summit institutions in reinforcing compliance and of the way the leaders themselves mobilize their political capacities at the summit consciously to craft commitments that will bind their own and their partners' polities to comply for a longer time (Kirton 2006a, 2006b).

G8 governance without multilateral organizations The third school of thought, lying between the first two but with a tilt toward the second, points to G8 governance without MOs. Developed most explicitly by Nicholas Bayne, and elaborated in a detailed look at the G8's relationship with the Organisation for Economic Co-operation and Development (OECD), this view begins with the original frustration of G7 leaders with the inherited MOs and their poor performance in the crisis-ridden world of 1970–75. As Bayne (2000: 45) puts it:

> The OECD covered all the economic subjects of concern to the summits and included all the summit participants. But the political objectives of the leaders and their reaction against bureaucratic procedures made it difficult for the summits and the OECD to work together. Their relations were often tense or distant. The OECD, instead of being encouraged by the summits, at times came to feel threatened by them. While these tensions did not endure, the end of the Cold War and the advance of globalization shifted the summits' attention to institutions of wider membership.

Bayne added that as the G7's fourth cycle began, the connection between the G8 and the OECD withered too. His analysis suggests the relationship between the G8 and MOs is one of mutual co-existence and non-involvement when their agendas are different, but one of tension when they are the same. In the latter case, the central cause of such tension is the seminal anti-bureaucratic convictions of the leaders-driven G8, and implicitly the failure of most MOs to have an annual leaders-driven centerpiece similar to that of the G8.

The Missing Models: MO Governance without, through and with the G8

Beyond these three well-established competing schools there are, on logical grounds, additional possibilities that have not yet arisen or been featured in the G8–MO debate. One is that the formal multilateral system governs well without the G8, to effectively meet a growing array of global needs. A second is that the UN–Bretton Woods bodies primarily use as instruments a G8 system that has little autonomous impact of its own. A third is that MOs govern in equal partnership with the G8, with the two converging and cooperating by contributing what hard law multilateral bodies and soft law plurilateral ones respectively each do best, to produce a combination that provides better global governance overall (Kirton and Trebilcock 2004).

To be sure, there are many who claim that the G8 is irrelevant, ineffective or epiphenomenal. But none has claimed that this is because the multilateral system works so well on its own, or because the G8 merely bows to the UN's will, as opposed to the US's, capitalists' or market's.

The Available Evidence

The most recent attempts to analyze the course and causes of effective compliance with and implementation of G8 commitments across a wide array of issues areas and countries has yielded a rich repertoire of evidence for developing and testing hypotheses and guiding future empirical research (Kirton 2006a, 2006b, Kokotsis 2006, Panova 2006, Savić 2006, Scherrer 2006, Stephens 2006, Ullrich 2006). But it has as yet produced no compelling analysis to confirm which of the three major competing visions is most likely to be more correct.

The most recent systematic research, assessing G8 compliance since 1996 in the fields of finance and development, has focused on how G8 leaders themselves as autonomous agents can improve compliance by embedding different compliance catalysts in the commitments they craft or approve at the summit, and whether these are in turn assisted or driven by the work of their own G7/8 ministerial bodies or structural forces in the world as a whole (see Chapter 5). Here it seems that when leaders at their summit embed their finance and development commitments with a specific timetable to be met, and with priority placement in their declarations, greater compliance comes about (Kirton 2006a, 2006b). Explicitly referencing other international institutions has no such effect. Moreover, when their G7/8 finance ministers remember and repeat the same commitment in the year before and in the year after the summit, compliance rises as well. A combination of increasingly equal vulnerability and capability among the G8 members inspires finance ministers to remember and repeat such commitments, but does not directly increase compliance itself. These findings offer some support for the arguments of G8 governance against or without MOs. But they do not include a detailed examination of the impact of MOs beyond the G8 in the ensuing actions taken by member countries to put these commitments into effect (as distinct from references to them in the commitment itself).

An Analytic Framework of the G8–MO Relationship

In order to explore this largely missing ingredient of outside MO involvement as a cause of compliance and contribution to G8 governance, the first task is to develop an analytic framework that identifies in systematic fashion the multiple ways in which MOs are connected to the G8 system, and how they help or harm the G8's global governance tasks.

Here, three dimensions stand out.[3] The first is the level of connection. On the G8 side, this ranges from the leaders' summit and the personal representatives

3 Other analytic dimensions to be developed and incorporated in subsequent work are scope (issues of intra-G8 or global concern, following Bayne's analysis), function and coherence (especially given the inherent comprehensiveness and interconnectedness of the G8).

or "sherpas" preparing this annual event, through the many ministerial-level G8 and G8-centric bodies, to the dozens of official-level and increasingly multi-stakeholder bodies that the G8 has created since 1975 to assist its work. A similar hierarchical range applies to the MOs, with the important addition that they often have permanent secretariats and thus the full-time international civil servants (at many levels) that the G8 system deliberately lacks. It is in this respect that the G8 is unique, even among the now plentiful plurilateral summit institutions of potentially global relevance in the world.

However, a basic structural imbalance between the two sides should be noted. The G8 reliably meets face to face at the leaders' level at least once a year, whereas the MOs seldom do. The one organization that reliably beats the G8 in this regard, and has a vast international secretariat of its own as well – the European Union (EU) – is also a member of the G8. Together with the relatively small size and combined power of the G8, it is thus analytically sensible to begin the analysis by conceiving of the G8 as the world's inner cabinet or directoire for global governance, with the MOs constituting the civil servants required to implement what their popularly and democratically elected G8 political masters from the major powers direct them to do.[4]

The second dimension is the timing of the connection. Again with the G8 and its core institutional process as the referent, the relevant period extends from the pre-summit "preparatory" phase, which starts immediately after the previous year's summit is done, through the intra-summit "on-site" stage at the summit itself, to the post-summit "implementation" phase that starts immediately after the summit its over, when its decisions have just been released in its public documents and the tasks of compliance and implementation begin, to continue for at least the following year. While the contributions MOs make for each phase may extend into the others, each contribution can be best considered as making its greatest impact at a single phase.

A third dimension is the intentionality of the international institutions' contribution, on the part of the G8 and the relevant institution(s) alike. Taken together, in broadest terms, the combination of the two sides highlights the "reinforce, reform, replace" trilogy familiar from this author's work: are the two sides pulling together as allies (with support flowing both ways, if not in equal degrees)? Or are they competitive colleagues, each trying to do the same things differently and better to the same end, reforming the other to this same end, or each

4 The use of the term "directoire" will immediately inspire the objection, usually voiced by G8 co-founder France, that the G8 is not a directoire. It clearly is in the English-language sense of a board of directors for global governance. It has arguably become so in the seminal French-language sense of the *directoire* that decided who would live or die during the terror of the French Revolution. The G8 has often decided who would live or die by omission, in such cases as Darfur. It also has started doing so by commission, by initiating the war to liberate Kosovo in 1999, using the North Atlantic Treaty Organization (NATO) as its implementing MO of choice.

doing different things for the common cause, even in convergent fashion as ships passing in the night, with one serving (consciously or not and in a coordinated fashion or not) as the global governance gap filler for issue areas or functions that the other cannot do? Or are they adversaries, each acting against the other to govern the same fields through the same functions on a foundation of antithetical values and to essentially different ends, to bring about the very different vision of global order each holds dear?

Within this larger framework, the dimension of intentionality embraces three components on the side of both the G8 and the organizations. The first is awareness of what the other is doing, intends to do or wants done. The second is the willingness of each side to support, co-exist or compete with the other. The third is the ability of each side to put its will (including that elusive element of "political will") into effect, with the resources it has at hand or can readily raise. On the G8 side, the G8 may deliberately be aware of the MOs' work, seek to not duplicate, to respond to, and to support it, and craft its commitments to be compatible with those of the MOs or easily digestible and implemented by them.

Within this analytic framework, there are 15 major contributions MOs make to G8 governance, arranged along the temporal dimension identified above. While a specific contribution can run throughout and beyond all phases in the summit's year, each is considered to be most relevant to a particular stage, as identified below. In all cases a premium is placed on critical resources the MOs can offer that the G8 lacks entirely or has in short supply, and that the G8's member national governments (and even the quasi-national/quasi-international institutional EU) cannot easily provide. In no case is the sheer legalized formality of the MOs an essential or relevant element of the contribution they make.

Before the Summit: The Preparation Stage

Prior to the summit, during the preparation stage, MOs can make an important contribution. Their involvement can range from routinely providing, as a public good, services that the G8 can freely access, through to lobbying for G8 action on initiatives and resources preferred by the MOs (notably raising more money for them), through to adopting a full component of the G8's agenda and action plan on the G8's behalf (as with the World Bank and energy poverty for St. Petersburg in 2006). Whatever the directness and direction of the connection, several critical institutional contributions stand out at this stage.

Information The first is information, starting with the provision of statistics that provide reliable information on the state of global problems, causes, effects and responsive actions, including on the part of members of the G8. Here, the IMF's and OECD's regular forecasts of global and comparative country economic growth form the foundation for the G8's treatment of its "world economy" agenda (see Chapter 6). Such reliable information can aid the G8's deliberative agenda setting (what problems need to be addressed now), direction-setting (what new principles and norms are needed) and decision-making of several kinds (for example, by forming the base from which G8 commitments are calculated, as in doubling official development assistance [ODA] to Africa by 2010). MOs also serve as a permanent repository for information, and a convenient meeting place for facilitating the work of G8 bodies, such as the Financial Action Task Force (TATF).

Analysis MOs can assemble various streams of information into analysis that further helps the G8 identify what problems need to be addressed, by whom, and how soon. A classic case is the OECD's creation in the 1980s of a producer subsidy equivalent formula to measure agricultural subsidies. This formula was used by the G7 summit in its effort to control such subsidies and thus liberalize agricultural trade. The findings of the Intergovernmental Panel on Climate Change (IPCC) also importantly prompt and shape the G8's work.

Expertise MOs also offer, from their permanent staff or multi-stakeholder constituencies, professional and policy expertise that can not only analyze information, but also develop and recommend options as to how problems can best be addressed. Those with staff or stakeholders from many countries can offer broader and deeper expertise on specific issues than even the largest and most internationally deployed national bureaucracy of a G8 member government can. From these, full-fledged epistemic communities can emerge.

Consensus MOs can also generate analytically based policy and political consensus that form a foundation for G8 commitments to be created, complied with and implemented. At a minimum, they lower transaction costs by providing a continuous meeting place for contact and communication among members, especially when the MOs have G7/8 caucus groups, as the IMF and OECD do. The OECD and its ministerial meetings have long served as a convenient focal point where regular and special G8 sherpa and other gatherings are held. The MOs can share, compare, chose and approve best practices, facilitate the application of peer pressure and moral suasion, and promote or conduct more active forms of policy coordination as a foundation for, or on behalf of, the G8.

Catalytic support MOs can provide the pressure or support required to get the G8 to agree to create a commitment in a certain way, and do so with sufficient force to propel compliance with the commitment soon after it is announced. These are the commitments created by the MOs and adopted by the G8 as its own. Indeed there is a long tradition of the G8 explicitly endorsing, or adopting without explicit acknowledgment, commitments the MOs have already made. The UN's Millennium Development Goals (MDGs) are a contemporary case. They are thus the ones the MOs best understand, have bought into for the longest time, and are thus more likely to actively, and even enthusiastically, help put into effect.

At the Summit: The Commitment Stage

At and around the time of the summit, MOs can provide six more crucial contributions. This is especially the case if they are involved in the G8 leaders' discussions on site. But this can also be done by communication or public and private endorsements from afar.

Visibility The MOs can create greater awareness for G8 governance around the world in new constituencies. They carry awareness of G8 governance out to their own constituents and stakeholders and the wider world.

Sensitivity MOs can provide the G8 with superior intelligence about the problem being addressed, work already being done by others, including themselves, and the likely reaction of their broader membership to the G8's proposed deliberations, directions, decisions and development of new institutions. This intelligence can improve what the G8 leaders do on site. They can thus generate G8 commitments that are inherently more appealing to, and absorbable by, the outside world, even in the absence of further action on the MOs' part. Indeed, the G8 has not only invoked IMF information at the summit, but brought the IMF's Managing Director in to deliver an assessment, to point out the macroeconomic shortcomings of the US that no G8 leader was prepared to make to the US President on his or her own. It is even possible that an MO participant can tip the balance when the G8 is divided or uncertain about what to do.

Understanding The involvement of MOs at or during the summit can provide them with a better understanding of the intentions, context and political considerations behind G8 actions. It thus enables the MOs to reinforce and better implement G8 decisions and directions, assuming this enriched awareness is accompanied by a willingness to assist on the MOs' part.

Buy-in Involvement in the shaping of G8 actions can allow the MOs to "buy in" to them, by adopting them as their own and taking ownership of them. This moves the MOs from mere awareness to an embedded willingness to assist. Kofi Annan's willingness and success in getting the United Nations Security Council (UNSC) to adopt the G8's new Middle East roadmaps in 2006 is such a case.

Credibility Involvement by the MOs can give G8 actions greater credibility. Inside and outside constituencies will then know that these actions are grounded in, and backed by, the intellectual, bureaucratic, financial and legal resources that the MOs bring. For example, at Gleneagles in 2005, the G8 leaders in their communiqué explicitly relied on the OECD to define the figures for how much their ODA pledge would be worth, to give it greater credibility among those skeptical of the G8's self-generated arithmetic alone. This extends the MOs' contribution from awareness and willingness to the ability to assist.

Legitimacy Involvement by the MOs can confer greater legitimacy on G8 actions. It can do so regardless of the content of the commitments, by having them approved by, or associated with, bodies with a much broader membership (in terms of number of members and across all diversity dimensions, such as geographic region and class). Moreover, to the extent that the executive heads of MOs, such as the Secretary-General of the UN, have legitimacy in their own right, their involvement with the G8 can reinforce this legitimizing effect.

After the Summit: The Implementation Stage

After the summit, G8-aware MOs which are willing and able to assist can make further contributions in specific ways. They do so largely by bringing their critical resources of money, staff, secretariats, stakeholders and legal authority to bear. Among their many contributions at this stage, the following stand out.

Burden-sharing The first is broadened burden-sharing, as MOs add the money of the organizations themselves or their non-G8 members to that mobilized by the G8 to put G8 consensus and commitments into effect. Cases include donations to the G8-created Global Fund Against AIDS, Tuberculosis and Malaria, assistance packages to the former Soviet Union and Central and Eastern Europe, and debt cancellation for the poorest countries at Gleneagles in 2005.

Substitute secretariats MOs can serve as substitute secretariats for a G8 system that has none of its own and that is adamantly opposed to creating any for the particular G8-centered processes and institutions. One case is the World Health Organization (WHO) assuming the accounting and associated responsibilities for the Global Fund, which the G8 created along with the UN in 2001. Another is the OECD's provision of a platform for the Heiligendamm Process the G8 created with its Group of Five partners in 2007. One prospective case is the personal offer by Angel Gurria, head of the OECD, to have his organization formally assume the role of serving as the secretariat for the G8.

Training MOs, with their experience, permanent professional staff and associated resources, can provide training to those the G8 wants trained. One case is the role of the OECD's Development Assistance Committee (DAC) in training Africans about the process of peer review.

Compliance monitoring With their permanent professional staff and internal experience, MOs can perform compliance monitoring of, or for, the G8. They can do so by systematically assessing how much and how G8 members are complying with G8 commitments, especially those entrusted to the MOs to carry out. They could do so with or without the G8's permission, cooperation or even knowledge. They can extend this contribution to include evaluations of the effectiveness of G8 actions in actually solving the problems it addresses.

Hypotheses to Explain MO Assistance with G8 Compliance

Under what conditions will MOs make these contributions? The relevant conditions come from a wide range of domains. These embrace the nature of the MOs, the G8, and the relationship between them. Among the rich array of hypotheses that can be created across this wide range, the following stand out.

Participation

The more the MOs' agents participate in the G8's summit, ministerial meetings and official-level bodies, the greater the contribution the MOs will make in assisting with G8 governance, across all the components noted above (see Appendix 2A).

Communiqué Incorporation

The more G8 summit communiqués and their commitments explicitly reference MOs and different MOs, the more likely the MOs will do what the G8 wants (see Appendices 2B, 2C and 2D).

Mission Compatibility

The more the charter-encoded core constitutional mission of the institution coincides with the G8's foundational values of globally promoting open democracy, individual liberty and social advance, the more the MOs will effectively assist G8 governance.

Membership Overlap

The more G8 members (and their partners participating in their meetings) dominate the membership of the MOs, the more the MOs will effectively assist the G8. Thus the old OECD should help more than the new OECD with its expanded membership, and both much more than the virtually universal UN (see Appendices 2E and 2F).

Managerial Control

When G8 members and their participating partners dominate the management structure of the MOs, through voting shares, decision rules, membership on the inner management core or executive board, appointment of the executive head or location of the headquarters, greater assistance for G8 governance will come about.[5]

Mutual Experience

The more direct experience G8 leaders and sherpas (and their ministers and officials) have had or simultaneously have with MOs, and the more the MOs have had with the G8, the more the MOs will assist the G8 (see Appendix 2G).

Co-hosting Responsibility

When the G8 host simultaneously serves as the rotational head of an MO (such as the EU within the G8 system), then greater assistance from that MO will arise, as the host tries to coordinate its approach to global governance between the two. One case is Canada's hosting of the Commonwealth and La Francophonie summits in the Fall of 1987, in the lead-up to the G7 summit it hosted in Toronto in June 1988. Britain has also used the G8–Commonwealth combination to good effect.

Early Involvement

The more the MOs are involved in G8 governance and commitment creation at an early stage, and especially from the very start, the more the institutions will effectively assist the G8.

Government Coordination

When responsibility for G8 and MOs is combined in a single division/bureaucratic center in a G8 member's home government, implementation assistance increases, as coordinated strategies can more easily be mounted by the member states. For example, in the case of Canada's foreign ministry, at the divisional level, responsibility for the G8, OECD and Asia-Pacific Economic Cooperation (APEC) have been combined.

Country-Specific Hypotheses

In addition, a further set of country-specific hypotheses, building on those above, can be devised, along the following lines. A country's compliance with commitments that are assisted by an MO is likely to be greater when that country is an MO member, founder or board member (as all G8 members are in the IMF

5 Financial contributions from G8 members may not have the same effect. The difference between a high financial contribution and low managerial control may lead to unresponsiveness and frustrations, as with the United Nations Environmental, Scientific and Cultural Organization (UNESCO) and the US and UK.

and World Bank's Executive Board, but Japan, Germany, Italy and Canada are not in the UNSC's Permanent Five).

The Evidence from the G8 Compliance Record

An initial empirical assessment of how MOs enhance G8 governance in the critical component of compliance can be made, following the first hypothesis above, by seeing whether the G8 summits where the MOs participate generate priority commitments with higher compliance scores. Appendix 2B suggests that they do, especially when the MOs participate in the summit sessions themselves, rather than meeting with the G8 in add-on sessions at the summit's start or end.

A second assessment, following the second hypothesis above, can be made by considering the record on compliance with G8 priority commitments from 1996 to 2005 to determine whether high compliance is associated with the relevance and relationship of MOs in the commitment itself and in the compliance behavior which follows. In the commitment itself, attention is directed at the explicit presence or absence of a notation of an MO, the number of such MOs, the number of different MOs and the number of notations of a particular MO. In the latter case, the same dimensions would be measured for the behavior of all (and each) member countries, as identified in the research reports of G8 Research Group analysts who have assessed compliance with that commitment each year. On this foundation, attention can be then directed at particular combinations of issues, G8 members and MOs where compliance is particularly high (or low). A preliminary analysis yields the following results.[6]

Okinawa, 2000–01

At Okinawa in 2000, the highest complying summit in G7/8 history, more references to MOs and to different MOs did increase compliance. The commitments with the highest compliance contained the most references to the UN and the WTO, and to leading these MOs without offering support. This was even though no MOs were at the actual summit in Okinawa (but were just beforehand, in Tokyo) to participate.

Sea Island, 2004–05

Results only partly emerge with regard to the 2004 Sea Island Summit. More references to MOs and to different MOs do not increase compliance. Perhaps this is because of the particular MOs and G8 relationship selected. The G8 in its lowest complying commitments relied heavily on the virtually universal UN and on instructing (leading) it in what to do, rather than offering support. This

6 Detailed data are available from the author upon request.

approach came at a summit where, for the first time in four years, not a single MO (including the most frequent favorite, the UN) was invited to participate. Again, G8 reliance on MOs with smaller membership, rather than larger, seems to help compliance more. This striking difference in the two summits of 2000 and 2004, hosted by the G8's two most powerful countries, may be explained by systemic factors such as the 9/11 terrorist attacks that struck after Japan's hosting but before that of America under George W. Bush. However, it may also point to particular compliance-inducing combinations of the G8 host country (and its agenda and strategy) and the MOs specified as compliance instruments. Here a multilateralist, UN-committed Japan is juxtaposed against a unilateralist, UN-skeptical US.

Gleneagles, 2005–06

At Gleneagles in 2005, compliance tended to be higher when the commitments contained more references to MOs, mentioned a wider variety of MOs and (more tentatively) offered the MOs support rather than guidance. Those MOs featured uniquely in the high compliance commitments – the Middle East Quartet, the Paris Club and the African Development Bank (AFDB) – are those dominated by the G7/8 in membership and management (and financial contribution in the last case). These international institutions are also small, plurilateral bodies with restricted membership.

The Analytic Case for Policy Innovation

Further analysis along these lines should yield a richer empirical foundation for assessing the wisdom of the major policy recommendations offered to improve summit performance in general, and in the critical compliance domain in particular. The major questions with regard to these recommendations are as follows:

- Would making Russia a greater participant in, and full member of, the WTO, the OECD, the International Atomic Energy Agency (IEA) and similar institutions (as all other G8 members are) make G8 governance more effective?
- Should the OECD assume a stronger and more formal role of a particular sort as a "secretariat" for the G8, in some functions or overall?
- Should the OECD meet at the summit level, perhaps first to celebrate its fiftieth anniversary in 2010/11 and combine this summit with the work of the G8 summit that year? Should other international institutions such as the Commonwealth and la Francophonie move to match the G8 by having summits every year?
- Can MOs and their secretariats assist more directly in the systematic monitoring of G8 compliance and implementation?
- Would the greater involvement of civil society representatives in the G8

and the international institutions, and more openness, transparency and answerability from them, help?

- Given that the Secretary-General of the UN frequently attends G8 summits, should the host of the G8 each year attend all UNSC meetings as well?
- Would the creation of a G8 secretariat, to match and coordinate continuously with those of most other institutions, help compliance?

Bibliography

Abbott, Kenneth W., Robert Keohane, Andrew Moravcsik Anne-Marie Slaughter and Duncan Snidal (2000), "The Concept of Legalization," *International Organization* 54(3): 401–20.

Baliamoune, Mina (2000), "Economics of Summitry: An Empirical Assessment of the Economic Effects of Summits," *Empirica* 27: 295–314.

Bayne, Nicholas (1999), "Continuity and Leadership in an Age of Globalisation," in M.R. Hodges, J.J. Kirton and J.P. Daniels, eds, *The G8's Role in the New Millennium* (Aldershot: Ashgate), pp. 21–44.

Bayne, Nicholas (2000), *Hanging in There: The G7 and G8 Summit in Maturity and Renewal* (Aldershot: Ashgate).

Bergsten, C. Fred and C. Randall Henning (1996), *Global Economic Leadership and the Group of Seven* (Washington, DC: Institute for International Economics).

Buxton, G.V. (1992), "Sustainable Development and the Summit: A Canadian Perspective on Progress," *International Journal* XLVII(4) (Fall): 776–95.

Cooper, Andrew, John Kirton and Ted Schrecker, eds (2007), *Governing Global Health: Challenge, Response, Innovation* (Aldershot: Ashgate).

Daniels, Joseph (1993), *The Meaning and Reliability of Economic Summit Undertakings* (Hamden, CT: Garland Publishing).

Fratianni, Michele and Heejoon Kang (2005), "Borders and International Terrorism," in Michele Fratianni, John Kirton, Alan Rugman and Paolo Savona, eds, *New Perspectives on Global Governance: Why America Needs the G8* (Aldershot: Ashgate), pp. 119–35.

Fratianni, Michele, John Kirton, Alan Rugman and Paolo Savona (2005), "Conclusion," in Michele Fratianni, John Kirton, Alan Rugman and Paolo Savona, eds, *New Perspectives on Global Governance: Why America Needs the G8* (Aldershot: Ashgate).

Fratianni, Michele, Paolo Savona and John Kirton, eds (2003), *Sustaining Global Growth and Development: G7 and IMF Challenges and Contributions* (Aldershot: Ashgate).

G8 Research Group (1996–), "Compliance Assessment," available at <http://www.g8.utoronto.ca/compliance>.

Ikenberry, John (1988), "Market Solutions for State Problems: The International and Domestic Politics of American Oil Decontrol," *International Organization* 42 (Winter): 151–78.

Juricevic, Diana (2000a), "Compliance with G8 Commitments: Ascertaining the Degree of Compliance with Summit Debt and International Trade Commitments for Canada and the United States 1996–1999" (Toronto: University of Toronto G8 Information Centre), available at <http://www.g8.utoronto.ca/scholar/juricevic2000/index.html>.

Juricevic, Diana (2000b), "Controlling for Domestic-Level Commitments: An Analysis of the Authoritative National Commitments Made in Canada and the United States from 1995–2000" (Toronto: University of Toronto G8 Information Centre), available at <https://tspace.library.utoronto.ca/bitstream/1807/917/2/juricevic.pdf>.

Keohane, Robert and Joseph Nye (1977), *Power and Interdependence: World Politics in Transition* (Boston, MA: Little, Brown).

Kirton, John (1989), "Contemporary Concert Diplomacy: The Seven-Power Summit and the Management of International Order," paper prepared for the annual meeting of the International Studies Association, London, March 29–April 1, available at <http://www.g8.utoronto.ca/scholar/kirton198901>.

Kirton, John (1993), "The Seven Power Summits as a New Security Institution," in David Dewitt, David Haglund and John Kirton, eds, *Building a New Global Order: Emerging Trends in International Security* (Toronto: Oxford University Press), pp. 335–57.

Kirton, John (2002), "The G8, the United Nations and Global Security Governance," in John Kirton and Junichi Takese, eds, *New Directions in Global Political Governance: The G8 and International Order in the Twenty-First Century* (Aldershot: Ashgate), pp. 191–208.

Kirton, John (2004), "Explaining G8 Effectiveness: A Concert of Vulnerable Equals in a Globalizing World," paper prepared for the 45th Annual Convention of the International Studies Association, Montreal, March 17–20.

Kirton, John (2005), "Toward Multilateral Reform: The G20's Contribution," in Andrew Cooper, John English and Ramesh Thakur, eds, *Reforming from the Top: A Leaders' 20 Summit* (Tokyo: United Nations University Press), pp. 141–68.

Kirton, John (2006a), "Explaining Compliance with G8 Finance Commitments: Agency, Institutionalization and Structure," paper presented at a conference on "Perspectives on Monetary, Financial and Economic Integration" at the Kelley School of Business, Indiana University, Bloomington, IN, April 7–8.

Kirton, John (2006b), "Explaining Compliance with G8 Financial and Development Commitments: Agency, Institutionalization and Structure," paper presented at the Convention of the International Studies Association, March 22–25, San Diego, CA, available at <http://www.g8.utoronto.ca/scholar/kirton2006/kirton_060322.pdf>.

Kirton, John and Ella Kokotsis (2003), "Producing International Commitments and Compliance without Legalization: G7/8 Performance from 1975 to 2002," paper prepared for the Annual Convention of the International Studies Association, Portland, OR, March 1.

Kirton, John and Ella Kokotsis (2004), "Keeping Faith with Africa: Assessing Compliance with the G8's Commitments at Kananaskis and Evian," in Princeton Lyman and Robert Browne, eds, *Freedom, Prosperity and Security: The G8 Partnership with Africa* (New York: Council on Foreign Relations).

Kirton, John and Ella Kokotsis (2007), "Keeping Faith with Africa's Health: Catalyzing G8 Compliance," in Andrew Cooper, John Kirton and Ted Schrecker, eds, *Governing Global Health: Challenge, Response, Innovation* (Aldershot: Ashgate).

Kirton, John, Ella Kokotsis and Diana Juricevic (2002), "G7/G8 Commitments and Their Significance," in John Kirton, Michele Fratianni and Paola Savona, eds, *Governing Global Finance: New Challenges, G7 and IMF Contributions* (Aldershot: Ashgate), pp. 227–31.

Kirton, John, Ella Kokotsis and Diana Juricevic (2002), "Okinawa's Promises Kept: The 2001 G8 Compliance Report," in John Kirton and Junichi Takase, eds, *New Directions in Global Political Governance* (Aldershot: Ashgate), pp. 269–80.

Kirton, John, Ella Kokotsis, Gina Stevens with Diana Juricevic (2004), "The G8 and Conflict Prevention: Commitment, Compliance and Systemic Contribution," in *The G8, the United Nations and Conflict Prevention* (Aldershot: Ashgate), pp. 59–84.

Kirton, John and Michael Trebilcock, eds (2004), *Hard Choices, Soft Law: Voluntary Standards in Global Trade, Environment and Social Governance* (Aldershot: Ashgate).

Kokotsis, Ella (1995), "Keeping Sustainable Development Commitments: The Recent G7 Record," in John Kirton and Sarah Richardson, eds, *The Halifax Summit, Sustainable Development and International Institutional Reform* (Ottawa: National Round Table on the Environment and the Economy), pp. 117–33.

Kokotsis, Ella (1999), *Keeping International Commitments: Compliance, Credibility and the G7, 1988–1995* (New York: Garland).

Kokotsis, Ella (2004), "Explaining G8 Effectiveness: The Democratic Institutionalist Model of Compliance with G8 Commitments," paper prepared for the Annual Convention of the International Studies Association, Montreal, March 18.

Kokotsis, Ella (2006), "Explaining Compliance with G7/8 Sustainable Development Commitments, 1975–2005," paper presented at the 2006 Convention of the International Studies Association, March 22–25, San Diego, CA, available at <http://www.g8.utoronto.ca/scholar/kokotsis_060324.pdf>.

Kokotsis, Ella and Joseph Daniels (1999), "G8 Summits and Compliance," in Michael Hodges and John Kirton, eds, *The G8's Role in the New Millennium* (Aldershot: Ashgate), pp. 75–94.

Kokotsis, Ella and John Kirton (1997), "National Compliance with Environmental Regimes: The Case of the G7, 1988–1995," paper prepared for the Annual Convention of the International Studies Association, Toronto, March 18–22.

Labonte, Ronald and Ted Schrecker (2004), "Committed to Health For All? How the G7/G8 Rate," *Social Science and Medicine* 59(1): 661–76.

Labonte, Ronald and Ted Schrecker (2005), *The G8, Africa and Global Health: A Platform for Global Health Equity for the 2005 Summit.* London: Nuffield Trust, February 28, available at <http://www.nuffieldtrust.org.uk/members/download.aspx?f=/ecomm/files/G8+Book.pdf>.

Labonte, Ronald, David Sanders and Ted Schrecker (2002). "Health and development: How are the G7/G8 doing?" *Journal of Epidemiology and Community Health* 56(5): 322–3.

Labonte, Ronald, Ted Schrecker, David Sanders and W. Meeus (2004). *Fatal Indifference: The G8, Africa and Global Health* (Cape Town: University of Cape Town Press/IDRC Books).

Li, Quan (2001), "Commitment Compliance in G7 Summit Macroeconomic Policy Coordination," *Political Research Quarterly* 54 (June): 355–78.

Panova, Victoria (2006), "Explaining Compliance with International Energy Commitments: The G8 and the IEA," paper presented at the 2006 Convention of the International Studies Association, March 22–25, San Diego, CA, available at <http://www.g8.utoronto.ca/scholar/panova_060324.pdf>.

Putnam, Robert and Nicholas Bayne, eds (1987), *Hanging Together: Co-operation and Conflict in the Seven-Power Summit*, 2nd edn (London: Sage Publications).

Savić, Ivan (2006), "Explaining Compliance with International Commitments to Combat Financial Crisis: The IMF and the G7," paper presented at the Convention of the International Studies Association, March 22–25, San Diego, CA, available at <http://www.g8.utoronto.ca/scholar/savic.pdf>.

Scherrer, Amandine (2006), "Explaining Compliance with International Commitments to Combat Financial Crime: The G8 and FATF," paper presented at the Convention of the International Studies Association, March 22–25, San Diego, CA, available at <http://www.g8.utoronto.ca/scholar/scherrer.pdf>.

Stephens, Gina (2006), "G8 Institutionalization as a Cause of Compliance: The DOT Force Case," paper presented at the Convention of the International Studies Association, March 22–25, San Diego, CA, available at <http://www.g8.utoronto.ca/scholar/stephens_060326.pdf>.

Ullrich, Heidi (2006), "Explaining G7/8 Multilateral Trade Commitments: Is the G7/8 Still Relevant?" paper presented at the Convention of the International Studies Association, March 22–25, San Diego, CA, available at <http://www.g8.utoronto.ca/scholar/ullrich.pdf>.

Von Furstenberg, George and Joseph Daniels (1991), "Policy Undertakings by the Seven 'Summit' Countries: Ascertaining the Degree of Compliance," *Carnegie-Rochester Conference Series of Public Policy* 35: 267–308.

Von Furstenberg, George and Joseph Daniels (1992a), "Can You Trust G7 Promises?" *International Economic Insights* 3 (September/October): 24–7.

Von Furstenberg, George and Joseph Daniels (1992b), *Economic Summit Declarations, 1975–1989: Examining the Written Record of International Co-operation*, Princeton Studies in International Finance 72 (Princeton, NJ: Department of Economics).

Chapter 3

The New Partnership between Multilateral Organizations and the G8

Marina Larionova[1]

Contemporary challenges of global governance, global economic and financial unbalances and crises, climate change, poverty and global security generate growing pressure on both formal multilateral organizations (MOs) and informal, plurilateral institutions such as the G8. In the case of the G8, at its annual summit, this leads to a huge expansion of the agenda, the priority issues debated, the summit documents produced and the number of commitments made. The sixth and seventh series of the G8 summits shows a major growth in commitments, if not a compliance performance to match (Bayne 2005; see G8 Research Group 2006–, under 2007; see also Appendix 3A).[2]

The 2006 St. Petersburg Summit itself produced 14 summit documents plus a chair's summary. Together they contained 317 specific, concrete commitments. This confirmed the trend of rising commitments in the seventh series. It was the highest of any summit since they started in 1975. Of the 317 total, 216 commitments reflected decisions in the Russian Presidency's three priority issues: 114 on global energy security, 52 on the fight against infectious diseases and 50 on education for an innovative society in the twenty-first century.

---

1 The author would like to express her deepest appreciation for the ingenious and meticulous work of the HSE G8 Research Group members E. Gorbunova, E. Bylina, N. Churkina, M. Kaloshkina, A. Shadrikova and Y. Zaitzev, without whose contribution of data building the study would not have been possible. The author also wishes to express her special gratitude for the inspiration for the analysis to the leaders in independent analytical thinking on the G8 and global governance, Nicholas Bayne, John Kirton, Ella Kokotsis and Peter Hajnal.

2 A summit sequence refers to a run of seven (eight) summits; a summit series is a group of summits focused on a particular set of issues. The summit cycle denotes all the summits from Rambouillet to the present day. The assessment of compliance has been carried out by the G8 Research Group of the University of Toronto under the leadership of John Kirton and Ella Kokotsis since the 1996 Lyon Summit, and has continued on an annual basis. The report on the 2006 St. Petersburg Summit is available at <http://www.g8.utoronto.ca/evaluations/compliance>. The full text of commitments of all summits from 1975 to 2006 and compliance scores for the period (Annex 1) can be found at <http://www.g8.utoronto.ca/evaluations/G8_commitments.pdf>. The methodology and compliance coding manual are also available at <http://www.g8.utoronto.ca/compliance>.

However impressive the scope of the pledges, their viability depends on the members' commitment to their consistent implementation within a strategy of concerted actions. On compliance, the 2006 summit registered an average score of 45 percent, though it differed across countries and across issues. The highest average of 65 percent came in energy security and the lowest average of 33 percent in health (see Appendices 3B and 3C).[3]

Compliance studies suggest that higher compliance generally happens in cases where the G8 are members of existing regimes such as the International Monetary Fund (IMF) and the World Bank, where the G8 members are major shareholders, and are therefore able to exert their political and financial influence, set the agenda, and secure agreements on the implementation (G8 Research Group, Kokotsis 2006). Other factors offered to explain enhanced compliance are the leaders' personal involvement in an issue, the presence of dedicated domestic institutional structures, the increased number of level working and official bodies, the link of the commitment made with the domestic priorities of the member states, and the degree of consensus on the commitments and the mechanisms of their implementation.

Yet thus far there has been little systematic analysis of the actual causes of compliance with G8 commitments. This chapter takes up that task. It addresses in particular the role that MOs are asked by the G8 to play in the implementation of the G8's summit commitments. It does so by examining the G8's use in their summit communiqués of two cooperative models – acting in alliance with MOs and through them – and two conflictual models – acting without them or against them.

The analysis shows that there has been a steady increase in the G8's cooperation with MOs from 1998 to 2007. While acting through MOs remains the G8's dominant pattern, acting in alliance is slowly increasing, especially in development, security and health.

Hypotheses

The debate between competing schools of thought about the general effectiveness of G8 governance offers three central arguments on the link between the G8 and other MOs: G8 governance through MOs, G8 governance against MOs, and G8

3 The measure of compliance is assessed on a three-point scale: full or nearly full compliance with a commitment is assigned a score of +1; complete or nearly complete failure to implement a commitment is indicated by a score of -1; an "inability to commit" or a "work in progress" is given a score of 0. An "inability to commit" refers to factors outside of the executive branch that impede implementation. A "work in progress" refers to an initiative that has been launched by a government but has not yet been completed by the time of the next summit, and whose results therefore cannot be judged effectively.

governance without MOs (Hajnal 2007, Kirton 2006, 2007). The three are explored in detail by John Kirton in Chapter 2 of this volume.

To develop and arbitrate this debate, this chapter puts forward a fourth model based on two assumptions. The first, positivist, assumption is that the G8 and MOs in their diversity are there to serve a common cause, and thus should be natural allies. The second, constructivist, assumption is that given the challenges of global governance, the G8 members' choice of the mode of interaction with MOs will rationally tilt toward G8 governance in alliance with the multilateral organizations based on the democratic institutionalism and network of networks models (Larionova 2007, Kokotsis 1999, Kokotsis and Daniels 1999).

Together, these two assumptions serve as the foundation for a model of G8 governance in alliance with MOs. This model makes eight central claims, as follows:

1. The MOs' role in performing the functions of collective management and reconciling domestic and international pressures has been growing; whereas their role in achieving the objectives of collective leadership remains negligible.
2. The MOs' influence at the preparatory stage continues to grow as the result of MOs' aspiration for expansion of their mandates and authority to be "blessed" by the G8 commitments. However, this is also the result of the G8 constructivist approach to the specific contributions MOs can render at the three stages of summit preparation, commitment and implementation.
3. The G8–MO interaction modes and instruments can be classified as either common to all institutions or organization-specific.
4. The comprehensive nature of most of the commitments determines the need for action by several MOs and the need for their coordination.
5. The totality of the modes and tools of G8–MO interaction constitutes a multi-level governance system, containing elements of the open method of coordination and multilateral surveillance.
6. As the capacity for peer learning is dependent on the policy sphere in G8–MO cooperation, it is restricted by the political nature of the context of the open method of coordination and multilateral surveillance tools' application (Lodge 2005). The effect of their application also depends on the architecture and capacity of the organization networks (Radaelli 2004). MOs have accumulated sufficient capacity for assisting the cognitive processes and search for most effective resolution of the G8's common political and socio-economic problems.[4]
7. The bureaucratization of the G8 sub-summit apparatus can enhance the impact and effect of G8–MO interaction through the latter's early

4 One example is education, which has been emerging as a priority on the agenda. Examples of such organizations' institutional capacity-building for education include the OECD's Directorate for Education, which was created in July 2002, UNESCO's Institute

involvement and coordination, but can also diminish the effect if mutual disappointment and tensions lead to increasing distancing and self-reliance of the institutions.

8. Effective use of MOs' capacity for implementation of G8 commitments hinges on the member countries' G8 apparatus' experience with MOs, as well as on the international organizations staff expertise with the G8.[5]

The premise for testing "G8 governance in alliance with MOs" model includes several further suppositions: the intensity of G8–MO interaction steadily increases; the models described above are not mutually exclusive, but co-existing, and the G8 choice of models will differ across issues and across institutions; governance through and governance in alliance with MOs will be the two dominant models of G8 governance, whereas governance against and governance without will be less frequently used; the intensity and modality of the G8–MO engagement depend on the issue area; for security and development issues the intensity will be higher than for the other spheres; as an integrated approach to priority issues becomes more pronounced, it will be reflected in the modality of the G8–MO interaction, engaging several MOs in commitment implementation mechanisms; member state preferences can also influence the choice of the modality and intensity for G8–MO engagement.

Methodology and Evidence

An analytical framework developed to explore these hypotheses covers several dimensions, as follows.

The timeframe includes the sixth and seventh summit series (from 1998 to 2006), coinciding with the launch of the G8 cycle and its first sequence.

The policy spheres selected for analysis featured as priority issues on the summit agenda. Some belong to the traditional priorities, while others are new issues or issues acquiring new dimensions in response to the emerging challenges.

---

for Information Technologies in Education, established in 1997, the Regional Center for Higher Education in Latin America and the Caribbean (1978), which was transformed into the UNESCO International Institute for Higher Education in Latin America and the Caribbean in 1997, the International Institute for Capacity-Building in Africa, established in 1999, the UNESCO Institute for Statistics, established in 1999, the International Centre for Technical and Vocational Education and Training, established in 2002, and the World Bank Education Sector Strategy, adopted in 1999.

5 Thus, for Russia, so far not possessing extensive experience in the field (not being a member of the World Trade Organization (WTO) or the Organisation for Economic Co-operation and Development (OECD) and being relatively new to the G8), it is vital to develop and pursue consistent policies on education and exposure in this sphere. Ultimately, such an approach will ensure that Russia's future membership of the OECD and WTO will contribute to the effectiveness of G8–MO cooperation.

They are energy, development, education, security (including such issues as fighting terrorism, transnational crime, nuclear security, non-proliferation, conflict prevention and resolution in Afghanistan, Lebanon–Palestine–Israel, Iraq), information and communication (including the 2000 Information Society Okinawa Charter on Global Information Society) and innovation.

MOs include the major global and regional institutions with which the G8 has systemic relations (as founder, governing board member, sponsor or in other ways). The methodology uses a broad conception of international institutions, including multilateral processes, initiatives and conferences not yet formalized.

A content analysis was conducted of all summit documents for the period except bilateral leaders' statements or statements made on the outreach meetings outcomes. They were coded for the number of and the type of references to MOs and the modality of interaction indicated.

A list of verbal markers signaling the type of model referred to, assembled in the course of analysis, served as formal guidance in the classification of the references (Appendix 3D).

In counting the number of references to MOs made in the G8 documents several mentions of one organization were counted as one if made in a statement on one commitment (Appendix 3E). Mentions of several organizations in a statement on one commitment were accounted for separately.

In the coding, certain sub-structures of the organizations have been merged and accounted for as one entity (Appendix 3F). The UN Organization includes mentions of the Security Council, General Assembly and subsidiary bodies.

"UN programmes and funds" includes mention of the UN Conference on Trade and Development, the International Trade Centre, the UN Control Programme, the UN Environment Programme, the UN Children's Fund (UNICEF), the UN Development Programme (UNDP), the Office of the UN High Commissioner for Refugees, the World Food Programme, the UN Relief and Works Agency for Palestine Refugees in the Near East and the UN Human Settlements Programme.

"UN specialized agencies" are counted separately. They include the International Labor Organization, the Food and Agriculture Organization, the UN Educational, Scientific and Cultural Organization (UNESCO), the World Health Organization (WHO), the International Civil Aviation Organization, the World Intellectual Property Organization, International Fund for Agricultural Development, the UN Industrial Development Organization, the World Tourism Organization, the UN Industrial Development Association and the World Meteorological Organization.

Some of the departments and offices of the UN Secretariat most frequently referred to in the G8 documents also have been identified. These include: the Department for Disarmament Affairs, the Department of Peacekeeping Operations, the Office for the Coordination of Humanitarian Affairs, the Department of Economic and Social Affairs, the Department of Safety and Security, and the UN Office on Drugs and Crime.

The IMF and the World Bank were singled out, the latter including references to all World Bank Group entities including the International Bank for Reconstruction and Development, the International Development Association, the International Finance Corporation, the Multilateral Investment Guarantee Agency and the International Center for Settlement of Investment Disputes.

"UN-related organizations" such as the World Trade Organization, the World Customs Organization, the International Atomic Energy Agency (IAEA) and the Organization for the Prohibition of Chemical Weapons have also been counted as separate entities. All mentions of other UN structures have been included in the count of the UN.

Other organizations, entities, programs and initiatives include the European Union (although the EU is a collective member of the G8 and not an MO, where it was treated in the documents on a par with MOs it was counted in this category), the European Commission and the Organisation for Economic Co-operation and Development. Regional organizations include the Asia-Pacific Economic Cooperation, the Africa Partnership Forum, the African Union, the Council of Europe and the Organization for Security and Cooperation in Europe. Financial institutions and instruments include the Economic Community of West African States, the European Bank for Reconstruction and Development, the Financial Action Task Force on Money Laundering, the Financial Stability Forum, the Highly Indebted Poor Countries Initiative, the multilateral development banks (MDBs) (including regional development banks) and the Millennium Development Goals (MDGs). Education instruments and programs include: Education for All and the Fast Track Initiative. Development initiatives, instruments and programs include the New Partnership for Africa's Development (NEPAD). Health initiatives include the Global Fund to Fight AIDS, Tuberculosis and Malaria, the Global Polio Eradication Initiative, the Global Plan to Stop TB (Stop TB Partnership) and the UN Programme on HIV/AIDS. Energy initiatives include the Extractive Industries Transparency Initiative and the International Energy Agency. For climate and the environment, initiatives include: the UN Framework Convention on Climate Change and the Kyoto Protocol. Security initiatives include the Nuclear Non-Proliferation Treaty.

Key Findings: Toward Alliance

The empirical findings confirm the hypothesis of a trend toward "G8 governance in alliance with MOs" based on the democratic institutionalism and "network of networks" models.

The data highlight the steady increase in the intensity of G8–MO interaction. G8 governance through MOs remains the dominant model, averaging 56 percent of the total references. G8 governance in alliance with MOs is gaining, to constitute 32 percent of the total. Governance against and governance without MOs are resorted to less frequently. They amount to a combined 12 percent of the total references made. The models co-exist. The G8's choice of the engagement mode differs across issues and across institutions. In some summits there is a

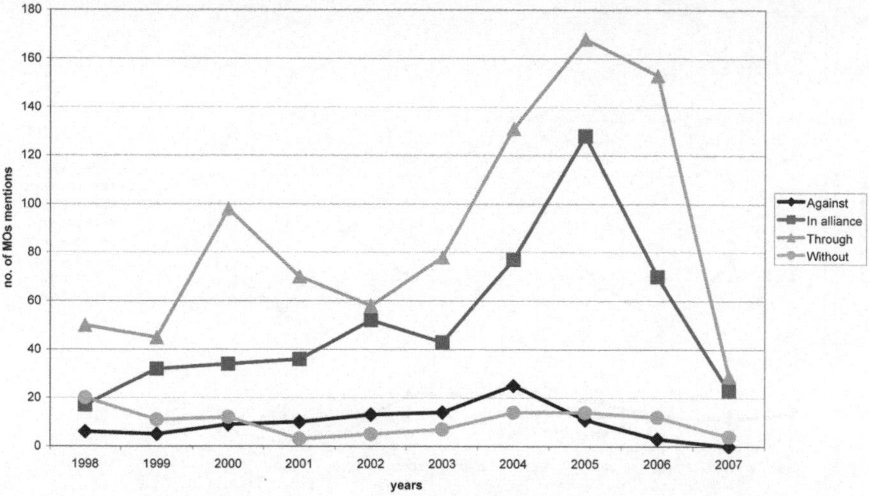

Figure 3.1 G8 and multilateral organizations, references in absolute numbers

convergence of the four models as in the cases of education and energy in 1999. In others there are peaks of the two dominant models, such as Gleneagles for energy and development and St. Petersburg for education and health. The G8 thus seems to need MOs to produce its priority themes.

Simultaneously, the number of governance initiatives undertaken by the G8 without and against MOs continues to accumulate, amounting to 115 actions against and 134 actions without MOs over the period 1998–2007. There is no obvious dependence on host country preference. However, the 1998 Birmingham Summit demonstrated the highest number of these types of modes as a percentage of the total number of references (28 percent). There was 17 percent in Cologne, leveling down to an average of 14 percent in the following years. The lowest were 8 percent and 5 percent for Gleneagles and St. Petersburg, respectively.

Peaks of 41 percent and 40 percent for the G8–MO alliance models occur in 2002 and 2005. They reflect the summits' emphasis on Africa and development.

Figure 3.1 represents the distribution of references on all issues in absolute numbers. It shows the trends for the G8's choice of patterns for engagement with MOs.

Figure 3.2 represents the distribution of references as a percentage of all mentions made on all issues generally. This confirms the above trends for the G8's choice of patterns of engagement with MOs.

The intensity and choice of modes of the G8–MO engagement depends on the issue area (Appendix 3F). For security and development, the intensity is higher than for the other spheres. In both, the two dominant modalities of through and with

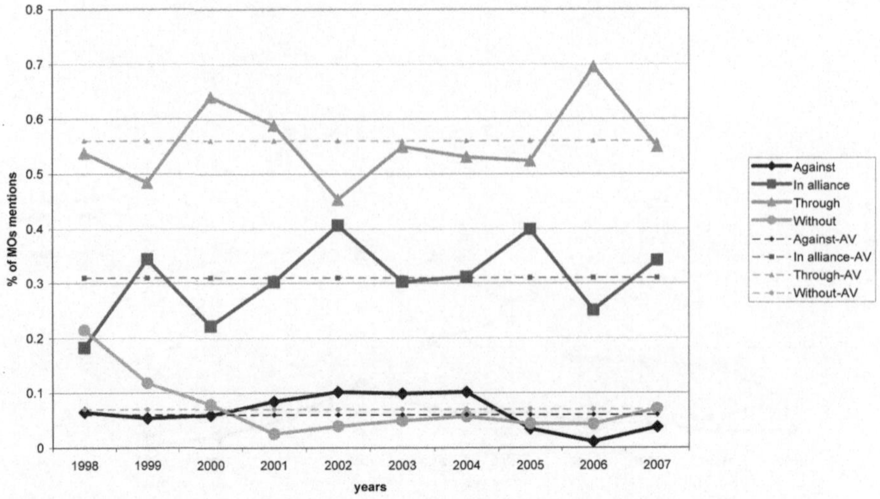

Figure 3.2 G8 and multilateral organizations, references as percentages

(alliance) are especially pronounced. However, in health, the G8 member states demonstrate the highest preference for alliance with the key organizations, namely the WHO, the World Bank, UNICEF, UNAIDS, the Global Fund and regional initiatives.

Development

In development, the trend for alliance with MOs steadily gains, bringing it to a level equal to that of the governing through MO pattern in Kananaskis in 2002 on renewing the focus on Education for All and debt relief for heavily indebted poor countries. Evian, Sea Island and Gleneagles fall slightly back to the traditional preference of through MOs. Heiligendamm's priority of growth and responsibility in Africa is enhanced by sharing the responsibility with other organizations rather than handing them the mandate to act on decisions made by the leaders. Figure 3.3 represents the distribution of references on development issues in absolute numbers, showing the trends for the G8's choice of pattern for engagement with MOs in the sphere.

Figure 3.4 represents the distribution of references made on development issues as a percentage of all mentions, showing the trends for the G8's choice of pattern for engagement with MOs in the sphere.

This percentage analysis changes the general trend for the choice of governing through the MO model. It shows its gradual decrease from 1998 to 2007, with the exception of the St. Petersburg Summit, where it peaks again at 66 percent. It also shows a steady trend for the choice of alliance with MOs. The three summits renowned for their commitments to development – Kananaskis, Gleneagles and Heiligendamm – demonstrate a common trend toward convergence of the two

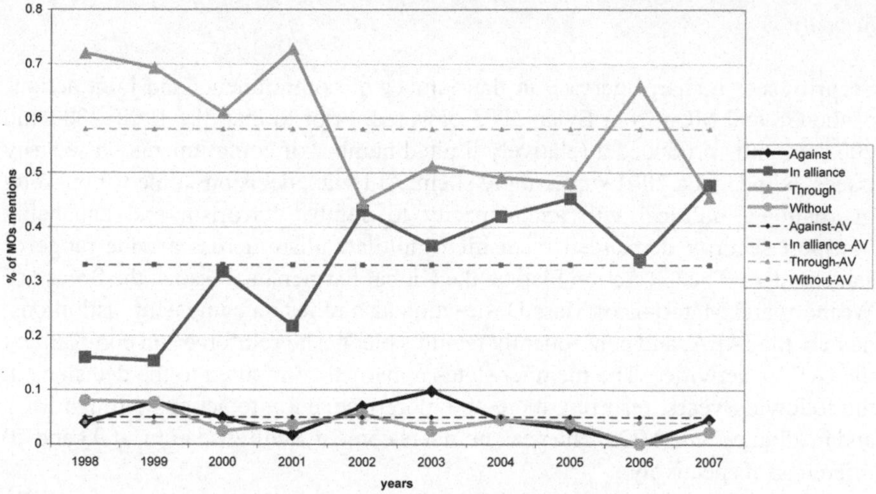

Figure 3.3 Development, references in absolute numbers

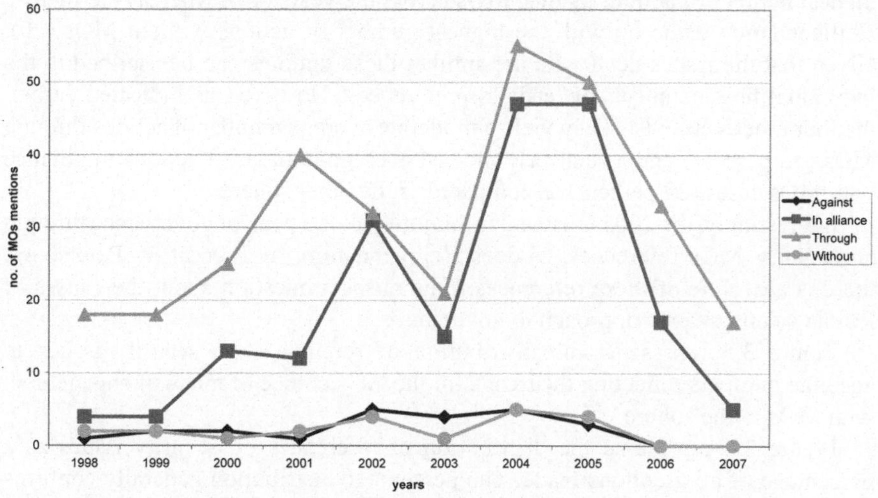

Figure 3.4 Development, references as percentages

modes of governance, with the number of actions in alliance increasing and the number of actions through MOs decreasing. The other two modes, however, do not wither away, again with the exception of the St. Petersburg Summit, where no actions were planned either against or without MOs. Russia as host relied heavily on working with the MOs.

Security

Security sees a sharp increase in the number of commitments and joint actions of the G8 and MOs from Evian 2003 onwards. Prior to that, the 1998–2000 and 2002 summits produced a relatively limited number of commitments on security issues, with Genoa 2001 surprisingly silent. At Evian, decisions aimed at building international political will and capacity to combat terrorism and enhancing transport security demanded intensified multilateralism across a wide range of stakeholders. The G8 Action Plan on the Global Partnership Against the Spread of Weapons and Materials of Mass Destruction also relies on competent institutions, namely the IAEA, and consequently features pledges to reinforce and complement the IAEA's activities. The member states remained committed to the decisions in the following years, resorting more and more frequently to actions through MOs and in alliance with MOs. The peak numbers come in Heiligendamm, at 93 and 70 references respectively.

The number of actions undertaken by the G8 without and against MOs also grows, though much more slowly. The two peaks of 21 in Sea Island and Heiligendamm relate to the G8 Global Partnership initiative and capacity building to counter terrorism. Sea Island, hosted by US President George Bush, produced the highest number of actions against MOs across the years (13), whereas Germany's Heiligendamm came up with the highest number of actions without MOs (20). Given that the issues dealt with are similar, these findings can be ascribed to the individual host country's or leader's preferences. However, as indicated earlier, the four modes co-exist. They yield a moderate average number of actions through MOs (55 percent) and a relatively modest average number of actions in alliance with MOs cases (29 percent) as compared to the other spheres.

Interestingly, the 2005 Gleneagles Summit yields a peak of governance through and against MOs references, as does Heiligendamm. In 2006 at St. Petersburg, there is a decline of these references. This raises a question about the causes of Russia's conservative approach to governance.

Figure 3.5 represents the distribution of references on security issues in absolute numbers reflecting the trends for the G8's choice of mode of engagement with MOs in the sphere.

Figure 3.6 represents the distribution of references on security issues as a percentage of all mentions made. The percentage distribution generally confirms the common tendency for a gradual rise of G8 actions through MOs, in alliance with MOs and to a lesser degree without MOs. The years 1998–2001 see significant fluctuations in G8 engagement with MOs on the two dominant modes, though with a tendency for a rise in governing against and a tendency for a decline in governing without. The Genoa 2001 peak on alliance is in fact a percentage frequency outlier, as the overall number of references was only four, all relating to the same type.

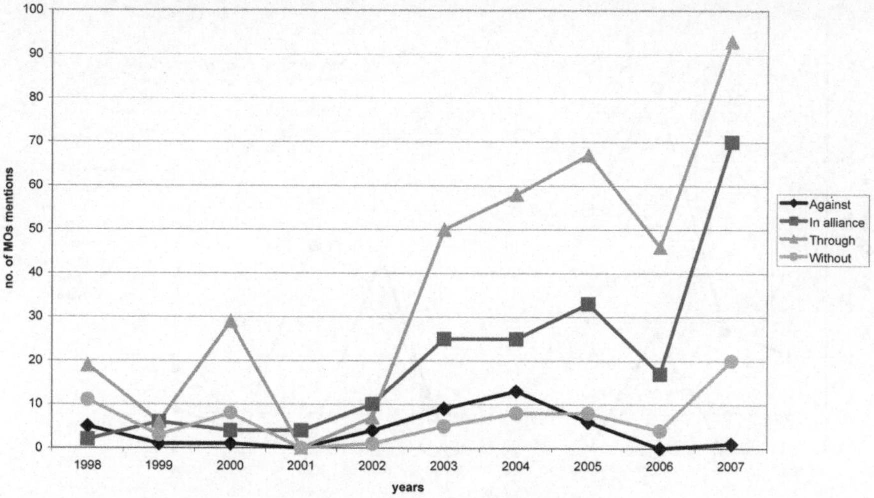

Figure 3.5 Security, references in absolute numbers

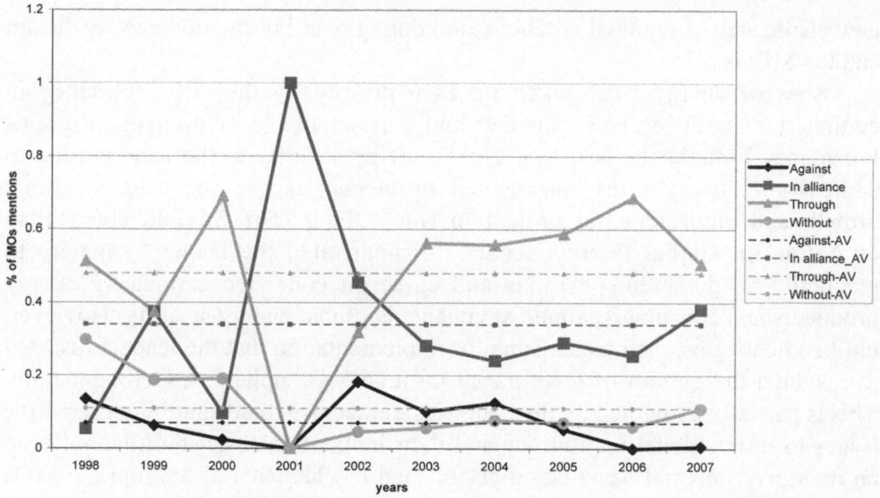

Figure 3.6 Security, references as percentages

Energy

Although energy has traditionally featured prominently on the G7/G8 agenda, over the years 1998–2004 it lingered behind the scenes, ceding the limelight to the

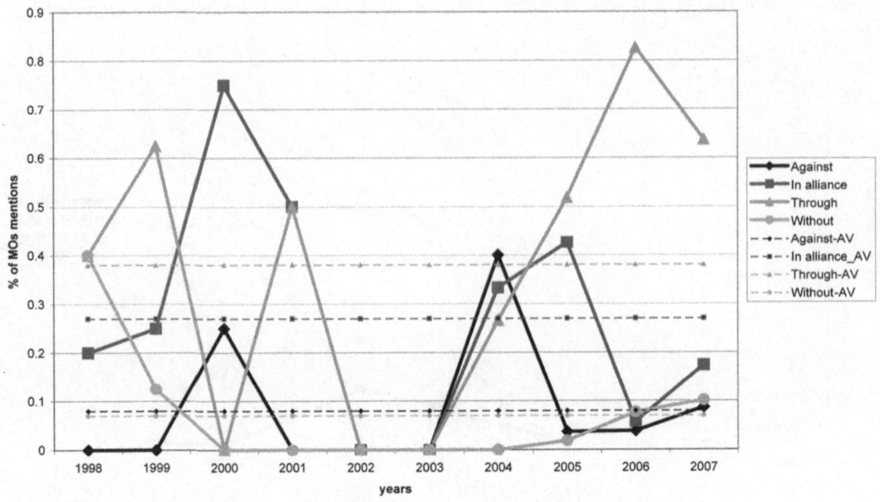

Figure 3.7 Energy, references in absolute numbers

new challenges of regional conflict resolution, global information society, health and the MDGs.

Issues of energy were taken up as a priority by the UK Presidency in conjunction with climate change and sustainable development. Russia's Presidency brought the issues of global energy security to the fore, aiming to address effectively three interrelated problems: energy security, economic growth and environmental protection (the "3Es"). The St. Petersburg Plan of Action on Global Energy Security demonstrated the leaders' capacity to reconcile the divergent positions and agree on concerted actions by energy producers and consumers, aimed at enhancing global energy security. However, unlike Gleneagles, the mechanisms for implementation that the leaders resorted to resumed the pattern of governance through MOs upheld at Heiligendamm. This is partially explained by the countries' reluctance to delegate such sensitive issues to international institutions and their inclination to act multilaterally on an intergovernmental basis using established mechanisms of appropriate MOs while retaining close control over the mandates handed to them. The causes of the Gleneagles breakaway are connected with the summit energy issues' immersion in the climate change and development agenda, as well as Prime Minister Tony Blair's ambitious stance on "a global alliance for global values" promoting a foreign policy of engagement (Blair 2005).

Figure 3.7 represents the distribution of references on energy issues in absolute numbers reflecting the trends for the G8's mode of engagement with MOs in the sphere.

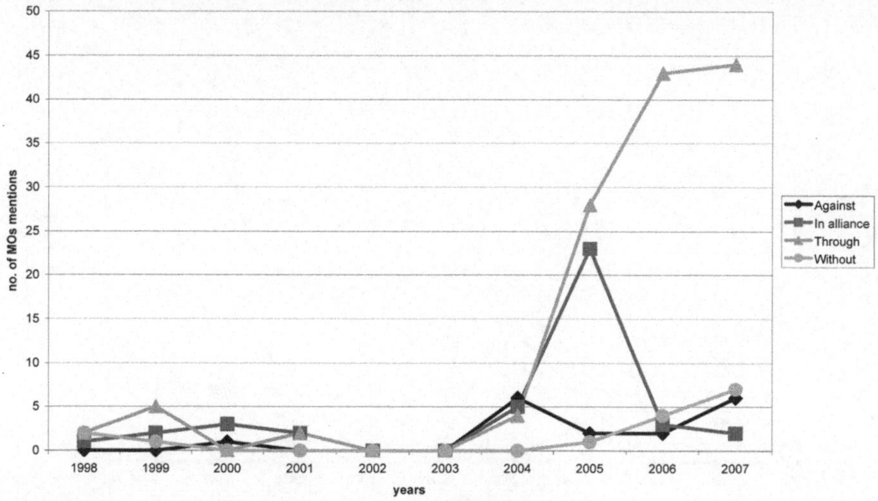

Figure 3.8 Energy, references as percentages

Figure 3.8 represents the distribution of references on energy issues as a percentage of all mentions made reflecting the trends for the G8's choice of mode for engagement with MOs in the sphere.

With the caveat that fluctuations from 1998 to 2003 are not representative due to a low number of (or no) commitments in energy which include MOs, the percentage distribution confirms the trend of the G8's enhanced use of MOs and acting in alliance with them, simultaneously with a general rise in G8 actions undertaken without the international organizations. Sea Island's performance gives another bit of evidence for the preference for acting against MOs on the issue under the Bush administration. St. Petersburg's outcomes confirm the earlier conclusions on the G8 member states' preference for retaining control over governance in this sensitive sphere.

Education

Education has been on the G8 agenda since the 1977 London Summit.[6] It has been regarded as a means to achieve the G8 objectives of growth and employment,

6 The analysis of the topic of education in the documents produced at the summits and meetings of the finance ministers provides evidence for distinguishing three periods in its evolution: 1975–83, when education issues are practically absent from the main G8 summit and finance ministers' documents; 1984–98, when education issues feature more frequently in the main G8 summit and finance ministers' documents, primarily in connection with the resolution of other priority problems, such as growth and employment, macroeconomic and structural reforms, social cohesion and inclusion, and development; and 1999–2006, when

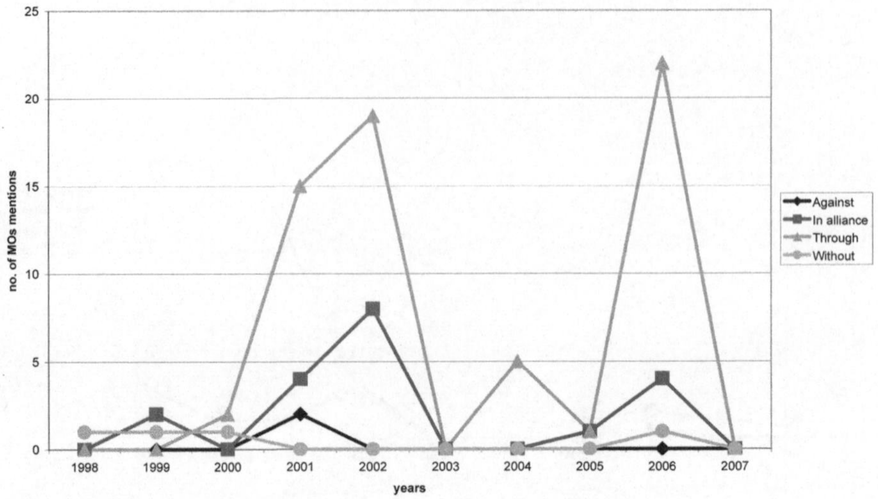

Figure 3.9 Education, references in absolute numbers

macroeconomic and structural reforms, social cohesion and inclusion, and development. Preliminary analysis indicates that the intensity and context of the education discussion reflect individual member states' priorities. The three countries raising education issues most consistently have been Britain, Germany and Japan.

In Genoa in 2001, the G8 pledged support to education as a central building block for growth and employment in Africa, reaffirming the G8 commitment to help developing countries meet the Dakar Framework for Education goals of universal primary education by 2015. The new element demanded that G8 members resort to new forms of partnership with the UN, UNESCO and the World Bank. Thus there was an increase in the number of references to these organizations, mostly in the through MOs mode.

Education remained a low priority from 2003 to 2005. But when it was selected as one of the three priorities by the Russian Presidency in 2006, there was a new high in the level of G8 engagement with MOs, including, in addition to those mentioned above, the OECD, UNDP and UNICEF.

Figure 3.9 represents the distribution of references on education issues in absolute numbers. Figure 3.10 represents the distribution of references on education issues as a percentage of all mentions made. The2re is a very clear general trend for a decline in the G8's actions without MOs, and a higher level of resort to MOs as instruments and partners in governance. This came as education

---

education becomes an issue in its own right, as well as a major instrument for achieving other G8 objectives in global governance and development.

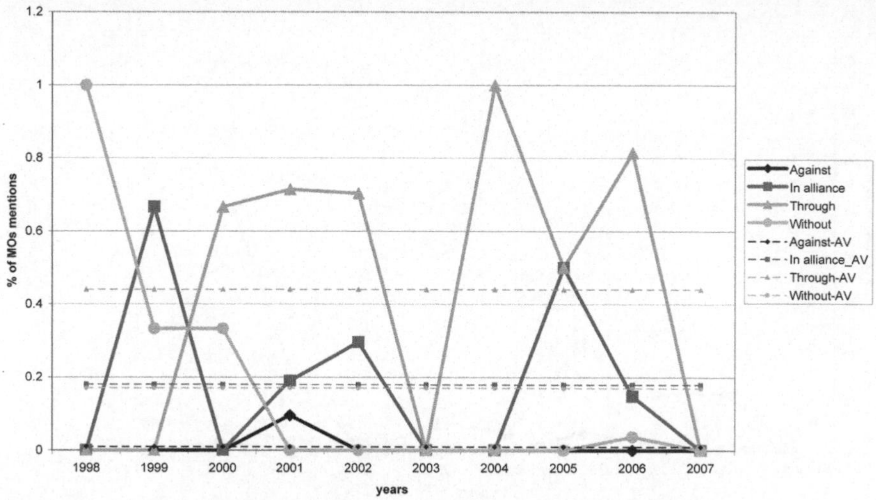

Figure 3.10 Education, references as percentages

featured more prominently as part of the development and growth for Africa agenda and, less so, for the G8 members' own agenda for employment and growth.

Health

Health is a relatively new issue on the G8 summit agenda. It is divided into core health and health-related issues. Core health considers a range of issues tackled directly by the G8, including infectious diseases (HIV/AIDS, malaria, tuberculosis (TB), polio and so on), medical research, the health care system, improved health as a function of development, health promotion, medicine and treatment, global collaboration and resource mobilization for health, the current global health organizations (WHO, UNAIDS, MDBs and so on) and more recent items such as bioterrorism. Health-related agenda items cover issues other than health that have a related effect on human health or health policies, such as debt relief for the benefit of health systems in developing countries, information and communications technology (ICT) to improve health care facilities or environmental issues that affect human health (Kirton and Sunderland 2005).

As a core issue, health emerged in the G8 1999 Communiqué, responding explicitly to rapid spread of diseases and pledging to work in alliance with the appropriate MOs. The 2000 Okinawa Communiqué committed G8 members to working in strengthened partnership with governments, the WHO and other MOs, industry (notably pharmaceutical companies), academic institutions, non-governmental organizations (NGOs) and other relevant actors in civil society to reduce the number of HIV/AIDS-infected young people by 25 percent by 2010, reduce TB deaths and prevalence of the disease by 50 percent by 2010 (WHO

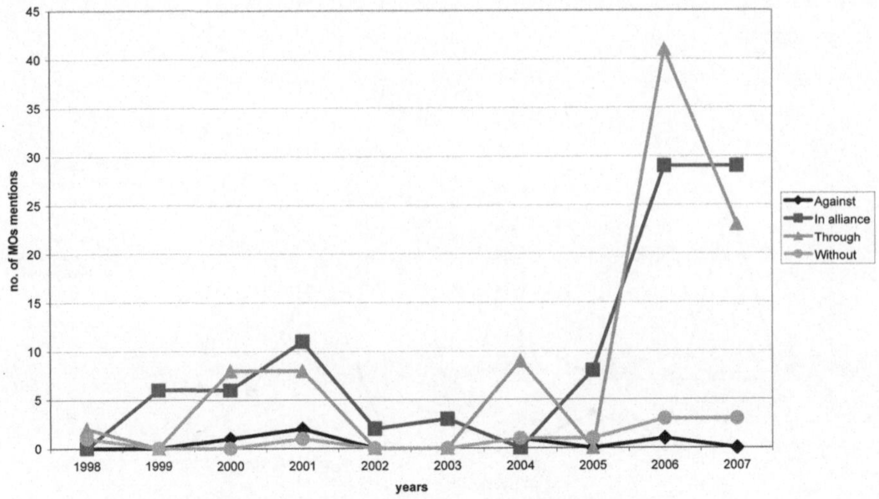

Figure 3.11 Health, references in absolute numbers

Stop TB Initiative) and reduce the burden of disease associated with malaria by 50 percent by 2010 (WHO Roll Back Malaria). Sea Island in 2004 reversed the trend for a gradual increase in alliance actions. It resorted to G8 working through MOs and acting without them in the G8 Commitment to Help Stop Polio Forever and the G8 Action to Endorse and Establish a Global HIV Vaccine Enterprise.

However, this Sea Island sabbatical did not overturn the general tendency for the G8 members to act in health with more reliance on the appropriate MOs and with the highest degree of alliances with them across all issues. Figure 3.11 represents the distribution of references on health in absolute numbers. Figure 3.12 represents the distribution of references to health as a percentage of all mentions. The percentage distribution vividly illustrates the 2004 reversal and the subsequent resumption of the alliance mode by the British Presidency, which remained during the 2006 Russian and 2007 German Presidencies.

Information and Communication Technologies

ICT as an issue has been part of the G8 agenda since the 2000 Okinawa Charter on Global Information Society. However, it has not been a major item, and G8 preferences in dealing with the issue have not been pronounced. Figure 3.13 represents the distribution of references to ICT in absolute numbers. The year 2000 leaps up, with the three modes used together. The next two years feature a G8 preference for actions against MOs. The years 2005 and 2006 indicate a G8 choice for the traditional action through MOs.

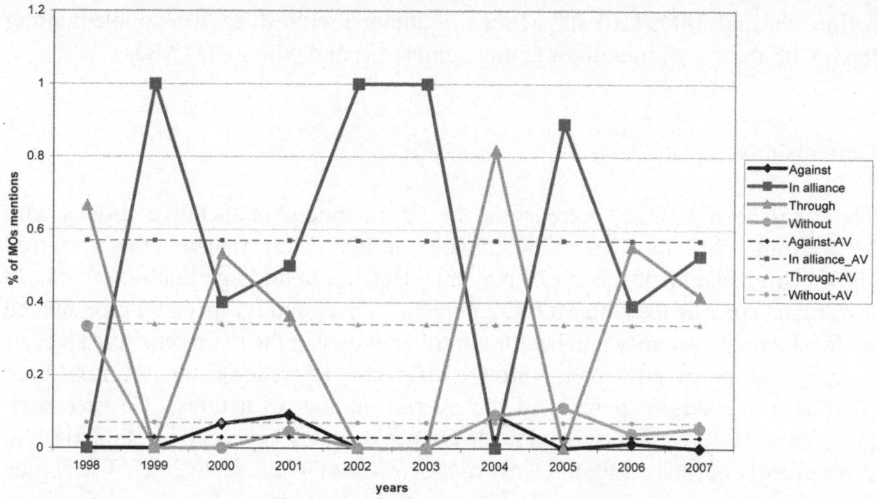

Figure 3.12 Health, references as percentages

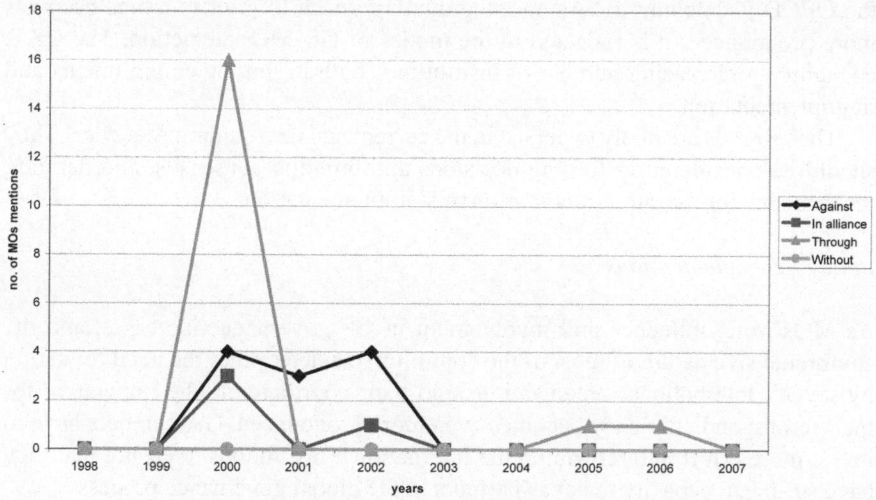

Figure 3.13 Information and communications technology, references in absolute numbers

Innovations

Innovation as a core issue featured for the first time in 2007. The G8 and the German Presidency came up with an integrated approach relying equally on actions through MOs (10) and actions in alliance with MOs (10), supplementing them with their own initiatives acting against (3) and without (1) MOs.

Conclusions

There has been a steady increase in the G8 members' cooperative actions with MOs from 1998 to 2007. Governance through MOs remains the preferred choice of engagement mode (56 percent). But the trend is gradually toward G8 governance in alliance with MOs (32 percent). This trend is especially pronounced in development, security and health. Simultaneously in the more sensitive areas of security and energy, governance through MOs remains predominant. Acting without MOs is decreasing (6 percent of the overall number of actions). G8 members' preference for governance without MOs peaked at 10 percent in 2002–04 and subsequently decreased significantly to the lowest of 4 percent in 2007. The choice of mode and intensity for G8 interaction with MOs is affected, but not defined, by the chair's preferences. The UN system remains the main partner the G8 engages with most intensely. In both cooperative models, the UN is the forerunner and the OECD is catching up. As an integrated approach to priority issues becomes more pronounced, it is reflected in the modes of G8–MO interaction. The G8 is engaging an increasing number of institutions, both in forging commitments and in implementation.

These trends are likely to persist in the current and next summit sequence. They should be considered in forging decisions and building consensus, and defining mechanisms for the summit commitments' implementation.

Policy Recommendations

As MOs' role, influence and involvement in G8 governance increases, and the comprehensive nature of most of the commitments determines the need for action by several international organizations and their coordination, the imperative for their reform and efficiency becomes even more pronounced. G8 members have to invest more effort into reforming the international institutions to ensure that they have sufficient capacity to act as partners in the global governance process.

G8 members need to enhance the impact and effectiveness of G8 engagement with the international organizations through the early involvement and coordination of the latter. The G8 should also build the capacity of their own G8 sub-summit apparatus to prevent or mitigate mutual disappointment and tensions in order to avoid increasing the distancing and self-reliance of the institutions.

To enhance the G8 member countries' experience with MOs, as well as MOs' staff expertise with the G8, it is important that members of G8 and MOs should put in place and pursue consistent policies on education and training. Building adequate capacity is especially vital for Russia. It has not accumulated extensive experience in the field, is not a member of the WTO and OECD, and is relatively new to the G8. Such an approach will ensure that Russia's future membership in the OECD and WTO will contribute to the effectiveness of G8–MO cooperation, as well as the effective membership of Russia in the OECD, WTO and G8.

Given that Russia's role and influence as well as the level of influence of the MOs on the global governance processes are different, Russia must invest intellectual, infrastructural and financial resources in MOs with a high level of global influence, where Russia can contribute to defining the rules and decisions and using its capacity to project and promote its vision and goals. The top priority for investment would be institutions satisfying both criteria, followed by institutions satisfying at least one criterion. The G8 is the top priority in meeting both criteria.

The role of the G8 as a mechanism for effective multilateral leadership for the implementation of Russia's strategic objective of strengthening multilateralism in international relations, accelerated integration into global economy, creation of external conditions conducive to socio-economic growth of the country and consolidating its sovereignty and democratic institutions will continue to grow (Review of the Russian Federation Foreign Policy 2007). The impact of Russia's G8 membership on global governance will depend, among other factors, on its capacity to provide organizational, financial, resource, expertise and informational support for its membership. Hence, it is essential to ensure long-term forecasts and calculations of costs involved and their planning and budgeting, as the reputational and political risks of ineffective membership and failures to comply are very high. Such risks can flow beyond the G8, spilling into other international institutions and regimes. Irrespective of the significant degree of political flexibility of G8 decisions stemming from the institution's special nature, participation in the forum implies sharing political responsibility among a limited number of actors. This imposes significant economic and political commitments.

Even though G8 expansion would presumably enhance its legitimacy and better reflect the distribution of economic power in the world, it may not necessarily lead to better governance. Expansion inevitably leads to widening the divisions of interests, visions and priorities between the members, and reducing the common denominator and trust, and hence the effectiveness of the G8. Thus, enhancing G8 effectiveness and legitimacy would be best achieved not through an expansion to G13 or G20, but through strengthening the new mode of partnership – alliance with the MOs – and deepening the structured cooperation with the Outreach Five in the Heiligendamm Dialogue Process.

Bibliography

Bayne, Nicholas (2005), *Staying Together: The G8 Summit Confronts the 21st Century* (Aldershot: Ashgate).

Blair, Tony (2005), "PM's Speech at World Economic Forum in Davos, Switzerland," January 26, available at <http://www.number-10.gov.uk/output/Page7006.asp>.

G8 Research Group (2006–), Annual Compliance Studies, available at <http://www.g8.utoronto.ca/compliance>.

Hajnal, Peter I. (2007), *The G8 System and the G20: Evolution, Role, and Documentation* (Aldershot: Ashgate).

Kirton, John (2006), "Implementing G8 Economic Commitments: How International Institutions Help," paper prepared for a 2006 G8 Pre-Summit Seminar "On the Road to St. Petersburg: The Role of International Organizations in Implementing G8 Commitments," June 30, available at <http://www.g8.utoronto.ca/scholar/kirton2006/kirton_institutions_060622.pdf>.

Kirton, John (2007), "Implementing G8 Economic Commitments: How International Institutions Help," in *Global Governance Issues: G8 and Multilateral International Institutions* (Moscow: Logos).

Kirton, John and Laura Sunderland (2005), "The G8 Summit Communiqués on Health, 1975–2005," <http://www.g8.utoronto.ca/references/health.pdf>.

Kokotsis, Ella (1999), *Keeping International Commitments: Compliance, Credibility and the G7, 1988–1995* (New York: Garland).

Kokotsis, Ella (2006), "Explaining Compliance with G7/8 Sustainable Development Commitments, 1975–2005," paper prepared for the Annual Convention of the International Studies Association, San Diego, CA, March 22–25, available at <http://www.g8.utoronto.ca/scholar/kokotsis_060324.pdf>.

Kokotsis, Ella and Joseph P. Daniels (1999), "G8 Summits and Compliance," in M.R. Hodges, J.J. Kirton and J.P. Daniels, eds, *The G8's Role in the New Millennium* (Aldershot: Ashgate), pp. 75–91.

Larionova, Marina (2007), "G8 Commitments in Education: Compliance Performance and the Role of International Institutions," in *Global Governance Issues: G8 and Multilateral International Institutions* (Moscow: Logos).

Lodge, Martin (2005), *Comparing New Modes of Governance in Action: The Open Method of Co-ordination in Pension and Information Society*, ESRC Seminar Series, Implementing the Lisbon Strategy: Policy Learning and the "Open" Method of Co-ordination (London: London School of Economics and Political Science), available at <http://www.law.qmul.ac.uk/lisbon/papers/Paper_doc/Lodge Paper.pdf>.

Radaelli, M. Claudio (2004), *Who Learns What? Policy Learning and the Open Method of Co-ordination*, ESRC Seminar Series, Implementing the Lisbon Strategy: Policy Learning and the "Open" Method of Co-ordination (Birmingham: ERI, University of Birmingham).

Review of the Russian Federation Foreign Policy (2007), Ministry of Foreign Affairs of the Russian Federation, 431-27-03-2007, March 27, available at <http://www.mid.ru/brp_4.nsf/0/3647DA97748A106BC32572AB002AC4DD>.

Chapter 4
Financial Crises, the International Monetary Fund and the G8

Ivan Savić

Financial crises have been an enduring problem for the international financial system. As financial markets have developed and become more sophisticated, numerous institutional arrangements have been devised to prevent the outbreak of financial crises. The world, however, is no closer to a crisis-free system. Indeed, given the complexity of international finance, it is hard to imagine any institutional setup which could completely eliminate this danger. Thus financial crisis response remains an essential part of maintaining international economic stability.

In Chapter 2, John Kirton offers three competing theoretical models of the relationship between multilateral-organizations and the G8:[1] Kokotsis's G8 Governance through Multilateral Organizations, his own G8 Governance against Multilateral Organizations and Bayne's G8 Governance without Multilateral Organizations. But, as he is careful to point out, these three schools do not exhaust the possible relationships between the G8 and hard law multilateral organizations, nor are they equally valid for all issue areas. Of these three models, Bayne's comes closest to capturing the relationship between the G8 and the International Monetary Fund (IMF) under normal circumstances: "mutual co-existence and non-involvement" when the IMF's and G8's agendas are different. However, when their agendas coincide, usually during a systemic crisis or during efforts to enact major reforms to the international financial architecture, their relationship is not as tension-prone as suggested by Bayne. Rather, in such cases the relationship more closely resembles the model suggested by Kokotsis: G8 leadership supported by the IMF.

Thus, since the 1970s a three-part division of labor has gradually developed between the IMF and the G8. The IMF acts as the primary monitor of the international financial system and deals with financial crises in low-and middle-income countries. The members of the G8 share information and coordinate policy to maintain stability at the core of the system. More serious challenges,

1 In the area of international financial and monetary policy, the work of the G8 is actually the product of three interlinked and evolving institutions: the G7, G8 and G20. Thus, unless specifically stated otherwise, this chapter will adopt the convention of using the term "G8" to refer to the coordinated operation of all three institutions. The exact relationship among these three is discussed in more detail below.

specifically systemic crises, are dealt with through the coordinated efforts of the G8, IMF and other international financial institutions (IFIs). While this institutional arrangement is not without its problems, it is an effective and essential buttress of the international monetary system. In fact, it is superior to all the arrangements that have existed since the emergence of the international monetary system in the late nineteenth century.

Financial Crises and the Need for Crisis Response

The term "financial crisis" encompasses a diverse set of problems. In simplest terms, a financial crisis can be defined as a sudden and dramatic fall in the price of a financial asset. However, this simple definition obscures the complexity and importance of the topic. The sudden collapse of a financial asset can produce ripple effects that are felt throughout the financial system and real economy. On average, the economic effects of a crisis are sharp but short-lived.[2] A financial collapse can affect prices and incomes, diminish investor and consumer confidence, and lead to recessions and even depressions.[3] Crises can also dramatically affect a government's ability to conduct fiscal and monetary policy and weaken its ability to provide social safety nets when they are needed most (Burnside et al. 2006).

The fallout from crises is not limited to the economy, however. In keeping with the logic of the political business cycle, financial crises can have important political effects.[4] This connection between economic and political crises is most often associated with the 1930s, but it is by no means limited to this period. Perhaps the most dramatic recent demonstrations of the political effects of financial crises are the cases of Indonesia in 1997 and Argentina in 2001. In both, a financial crisis, and the government's ineffectual response, led to massive demonstrations that brought down the government: in the former, an entrenched authoritarian regime, and in the latter a democratically elected one. In the case of Argentina, this led to prolonged instability and a succession of short-lived administrations.

With interconnected markets, these problems are amplified. A financial crisis in a globalizing economy can have the same impact that an infectious disease has

2 Eichengreen and Rose (2003) find that a currency crisis is followed by an economic loss equal to one year of economic growth or 3 percent of gross domestic product (GDP). Similarly, Bordo et al. (2001: 72–3) found that banking, currency and twin crises cause downturns which on average last two to three years and cost 5–10 percent of GDP.

3 Crises can also be preceded and triggered by economic slowdowns.

4 Frankel (2005) points out that currency devaluation in a developing country increases the probability of its leader being removed from power by 45 percent and doubles the chances of a change in the country's top leadership within the next six months. Of course, as with the relationship between crises and economic slowdowns, the converse can also happen: a political crisis can act as a catalyst for financial meltdowns; see Lebang (2003).

in a densely populated community. Money can leave the national economy as investors look for safe havens. This "flight to safety" can in turn trigger crises in other financial markets.[5] Even without direct financial contagion, the economic fallout from a crisis can affect other countries. A recession in one country will disrupt cross-border trade and investment, which can mean economic slowdown, even recession, for its trading partners. In the worst-case scenario, financial crises can take on pandemic proportions: destabilizing financial markets and causing or deepening worldwide recessions. As with most worst-case scenarios, financial crises on this scale are relatively rare. In the twentieth century there have only been four crises that approached this threshold: the banking and currency crises of 1930–31, which exacerbated the Great Depression, the collapse of the Bretton Woods system in the early 1970s, the debt crises of the late 1970s and early 1980s, and the Asian meltdown and the crises that followed in its wake from 1997 to 2001. Although rare, such crises tend to dominate the collective memories of markets, policymakers and ordinary citizens.

The Nature, Causes and Frequency of Financial Crises

According to the theory of perfect markets, the price of a good or service reflects all the information that is relevant for determining its value. Financial markets are the closest approximation of perfect markets because financial instruments are in essence promissory notes which have no intrinsic value aside from the issuer's ability to honor them. This means that the price of any financial instrument (for example, a unit of currency, a stock, bond or bank deposit) should reflect all the information that is relevant for determining the present value of the expected future income stream associated with that instrument. Therefore, prices should be automatically updated to reflect changes in these underlying "fundamentals" and financial crises should not occur.

However, the theory does not fully match reality, for a number of reasons. Even in the current "information age," access to information is imperfect. Financial markets are subject to local conditions that may be unknown or poorly understood by foreign investors. Standards for information disclosure can vary across markets and firms. Most important perhaps is the role played by human psychology, which "helps" investors fill the gaps in available information. It can even lead them to discount/ignore relevant information that does not fit their expectations. These factors can create a market bubble: dramatic price inflation not justified by underlying fundamentals. Unless the bubble is deflated by a market or policy mechanism,[6] it eventually bursts, producing a financial crisis: an equally dramatic price collapse, often below the fundamental value. Thus, markets are often said to

5 Whether this financial contagion is justified or is a result of irrational market panic is still controversial.

6 In such a case there will be "a soft landing" – the orderly realignment of the price with its fundamentals with minimal disruption to the financial system and real economy.

be driven by two basic emotions: greed and fear. Greed inflates bubbles and, once the price inflation becomes untenable, fear bursts them.

Governments can also impede the proper functioning of financial markets through reckless policy. Such behavior can be characterized under two broad headings: "sins of omission" and "sins of commission." Sins of omission occur when governments do not provide effective regulatory and legal frameworks. Without these frameworks, markets will not properly disseminate information. Sins of commission occur when government policy distorts market incentives. This leads to moral hazard problems, where investors act more recklessly than they would have without the government policy.

Thus there are two primary explanations for financial crises. For those who believe that financial markets function well, the main culprit is government failure: improper regulation, bad policies, inappropriate responses to shifts in fundamentals, corruption and so on.[7] For those who are more skeptical of markets, the main cause of crises is irrational or unscrupulous behavior by investors, which leads to the collapse of otherwise sound markets.[8] On balance, however, there is generally enough blame to go around.

Although all crises share these general characteristics, there is great variation between different types of crises and individual crises themselves.[9] The nature of a financial crisis is defined by parameters such as its origins, course, duration, spread and impact. Crises can take place in any financial market. The most common are debt, banking and currency crises.[10] A debt crisis occurs when debtors are unwilling or unable to meet their short-term and/or long-term debt obligations. Similarly, a banking crisis arises when banks find themselves facing liquidity and/or solvency problems. Both debt and banking crises can lead to a credit crunch, where lenders become unwilling to lend even to creditworthy borrowers. A currency crisis, on the other hand, happens when investors/speculators abandon a currency for fear that it might become devalued. It is also not uncommon to have a twin crisis: simultaneous crises in two different financial markets which feed off and exacerbate each other. The crises in Thailand, Indonesia and the Philippines in 1997–98 were all twin banking and currency crises.

7 This is sometimes referred to as the "first-generation" or "fundamentalist" view of financial crises. See, for example, Kaminsky and Reinhart (1998), Corsetti, Pesenti and Roubini (1999) and Horowitz and Heo (2001).

8 This is also referred to as the "second-generation" or "self-fulfilling" view of crises. See in particular Kindleberger (1978), Obstfeld (1996) and Morris and Shin (1998).

9 So much so that some have gone so far as to argue that the only common denominator all crises share is their heterogeneity (see Rose's (2001) discussion of Bordo et al. 2003: 75–7). But this issue is not unique to financial crises. Most social phenomena (such as wars, elections and so on) display levels of heterogeneity that raise similar questions.

10 Stock market crashes are also relatively common, but they tend to have a lesser impact, especially at the international level. The notable exception is the Wall Street Crash of 1929. However, even in this case the economic downturn was already under way almost a year before the crash; see Eichengreen (1998: 222–57).

A debate rages over whether and how crises spread.[11] The key question is when, and whether, a crisis in one country will trigger a crisis in another country. The contagion school argues that crises can spread to otherwise healthy financial markets. As a market in crisis collapses, investors in similar markets begin to fear that their investments are also in danger now. In response, they will pull out of these similar markets even if they are in fact sound, leading to a new crisis (Yusoff and Zulkhibri Abdul Majid 2000, Chang and Majnoni 2002). The vulnerability school, on the other hand, argues that contagion does not happen, and that financial crises will only spread to those markets that were vulnerable to a financial crisis in the first place (Simone 2002, Ellison et al. 2006). However, these two schools are not incompatible. A number of recent works have argued that the outbreak and spread of crises, in particular the Asian financial crisis, are characterized by both the presence of panic and a response to market deviations from fundamentals (Pesenti and Tille 2000, Berger and Wagner 2005).

In terms of the frequency and overall impact of crises, there are some general trends. A study by Bordo et al. (2001) which looked at the frequency and severity of international financial crises over the last 120 years found that currency, banking and twin crises are endemic to the international financial system. Since the collapse of the Bretton Woods system, the frequency of crises has grown compared to the pre-World War I and Bretton Woods periods, and is at a level similar to the crisis-prone interwar period. However, the severity of these crises and their impact on the real economy have not increased. International debt crises are also enduring phenomena. There have been regular periods of increasing lending from high- to low-income countries in the 1820s, 1880s, 1900–14, 1920s and 1974–82. Each of these lending booms was followed by defaults, credit crunches and debt crises (Eichengreen and Lindert 1989: 2–3).[12]

There is also a clear distinction between the "core" and the periphery (small and emerging financial systems) of the international system in terms of financial crises.[13] Throughout the last 150 years, financial crises have primarily been an emerging-market phenomenon. Over 75 percent of all financial crises before 1914 happened in the periphery, as did those in the post-1945 period (Bordo et al. 2001: 58). This was only reversed during the interwar period.[14] In addition to being more frequent, the impact of crises is also generally more severe in emerging markets.

---

11 Although there is still some disagreement over whether financial contagion actually takes place, there have been a number of studies that have shown that crises do spread, notably Botman and Jager (2002) and Edwards and Rigobon (2002).

12 What is remarkable about these episodes is that each generation reacts to its crisis as if it was historically unprecedented; see Fishlow (1985: 383).

13 Here, "core" refers to those countries that have large and diversified financial systems with strong ties to the global system, and "periphery" refers to countries whose financial systems are much less developed and connected.

14 See Bernanke and James (1991). Bordo et al. (2001: 58) confirm this finding, though they note that this reversal is partially the result of the reclassification of a number

This difference between core and periphery is primarily due to four factors. First, less-developed economies tend to also have less-developed financial and regulatory institutions. This makes them more vulnerable to crises in the first place. Second, they have less diversified financial systems. This means that financial problems in one firm or market are more likely to spread to other parts of the financial system and affect the real economy. Third, such countries are more vulnerable to short-term international capital flows (so-called "hot money"). That is, low- and middle-income countries are much more likely to face a massive capital flight during a financial crisis then are high-income countries. Thus, poorly developed financial and regulatory institutions, when combined with financial openness (lack of capital controls), are a particularly dangerous combination (Eichengreen 1998: 190–96). Finally, the smaller and less integrated a national financial system is, the less important it is to the overall stability of the international system. As a result, it is less likely to find international help during a crisis.

Crises Prevention and its Limits

A great deal of academic and policy work has focused on the reform of domestic and international financial institutions, in the hope that this will prevent the outbreak and spread of future crises. Such work is important. But it is doubtful that any reform could completely eliminate all possibility of financial crisis.

The problem is that creating a comprehensive reform proposal that is universally acceptable would be nearly impossible. Individual governments, international institutions, investors and citizens all have very different ideas about what needs to be done and which problems pose the greatest threat. Even if such an agreement could be reached, it would be impossible to ensure that it was consistently implemented through the entire financial system. This is particularly true as states vary greatly in their capacity and willingness to implement such reforms. Finally, no matter how well designed the financial architecture, it cannot ensure that policymakers or investors will not act recklessly at some point.

Another way of dealing with crises is to try to predict them before they happen, since it is easier and less costly to deal with a potential crisis than an actual one. Many public, private and international institutions devote much time and effort to monitoring the international monetary system. However, it is still very difficult to predict a crisis. Financial markets are constantly growing and evolving, creating new financial instruments and opportunities. This makes monitoring the system and reaching a consensus on the implications of the observed changes difficult. Even with the combined efforts of the G8 and the other IFIs, it is still impossible predict all problems.

Identifying a problem does not automatically mean one is able to fix it. The problems plaguing the Bretton Woods system were well known. However, this foreknowledge did not lead to a consensus on what needed to be done or how the

---

of economies from "developing" to "developed" after 1918.

cost of fixing the problem would be shared (James 1996: 175–204, Eichengreen 1998: 93–135). Even if a consensus can be reached, crisis prevention still faces substantial obstacles. The most serious problem is that while the policy measures needed to pre-empt a crisis are visible to both markets and citizens, their success may not be. That is, how does one show that the costs of crisis prevention are outweighed by the costs of a crisis that did not happen? What is worse, if the measures fail, the government will seem just as incompetent as if it had done nothing. Finally, if policymakers can predict a crisis, then chances are so can some private actors. Speculators will bet against government intervention if they think they can profit from it. If enough speculators act in this way, they can undermine crisis prevention efforts.

Crises Response at the Domestic Level

In the domestic sphere, the government, specifically the central bank, is primarily responsible for crisis response as lender of last resort (LOLR).[15] As noted above, a financial crisis is, in effect, a panicked response to the realization that the market value of an asset does not match its underlying, fundamental value. This panic puts significant downward pressure on prices, which dramatically decreases market liquidity.[16] This in turn can destabilize other financial markets and the real economy. Therefore, an effective crisis response entails a mix of three policies: immediate crisis response (to deal with the panic), a package of financial reforms (to deal with the underlying causes of the crisis) and the provision of economic stimulus (to counteract the negative impact on the real economy). Since the role of economic stimulus is self-evident, only the first two elements need elaboration.

Immediate crisis response restores stability to the distressed market by infusing both liquidity (supporting the price of the distressed asset) and confidence into the market. This provides temporary relief, which gives investors time to get over their initial panic and process information properly. In the case of a purely self-fulfilling crisis, this will be enough to restore the market. In the case of a crisis triggered by fundamental problems, the intervention will provide the market with a soft landing (an orderly adjustment of the new asset price).

The goal of reform efforts is to identify the underlying problems that have led to the crisis and create a policy package that will fix them. These reforms can pertain to market practices and institutions, regulation, government policy and so on. Thus, while immediate crisis response (and economic stimulus) is a stopgap, financial reforms are the longer-term solution to the crisis.

15 For an excellent overview of the issues surrounding the idea of a lender of last resort, see Goodhart and Illing (2002).

16 Market liquidity is the extent to which one can sell a financial asset (convert it to cash) without lowering its value. During a financial crisis, market liquidity diminishes rapidly.

The difficulty of creating an appropriate crisis response package lies in getting the mix of the three elements right. The right mix will depend on the characteristics of the crisis and on the economic and political environment that policymakers face. Any one of these three elements can encounter serious opposition from markets or powerful political groups. Such opposition can render crisis response ineffective.

Getting the mix right also means making sure that the various crisis response efforts do not interfere with one another. This is a potential problem because these three elements can effectively neutralize one another. Consider the case of a banking crisis that is the result of reckless lending practices. In the long run, reforms need to be made that will make sure that banks adopt sound lending practices, which in this context means adopting more conservative standards. However, in the short run the crisis makes banks very reluctant to extend credit. Thus, if lending reforms are imposed too early, they will exacerbate the credit crunch, which will in turn frustrate short-term financial and economic stabilization efforts.

But even successful crisis response can create long-term problems in the form of moral hazard. By bailing out investors and financial institutions, governments reward rather than punish reckless behavior. This effectively removes the downside of taking risks, which can lead to more reckless behavior. Some would even argue that in the long run it would be better to let markets feel the consequences of their actions, as this would lead to more market discipline. While this argument is valid, it is not without its dangers. This "tough love" approach is economically costly and politically risky. Therefore, one should not expect governments to be willing to consider this option lightly. A better solution would be to design crisis response efforts in such a way that they do not fully isolate market participants from the negative consequences of their actions. However, this is also not an easy thing to do.

Crises Response at the International Level

Crisis response at the international level poses the same dilemmas as it does at the domestic level. However, it is further complicated by the fact that there is no single authority to act as an international lender of last resort (ILOLR). There are three types of actors that could provide this public good: an IFI, a hegemonic state or a concert of financial powers. Each has its strengths and weaknesses.

Assigning this role to an IFI might seem the most appealing, since it is the kind of technical issue that is best left to international institutions. However, creating an institution that has the resources and influence to deal with crises in both low-income and high-income countries would entail such a concentration of power at the international level that is quite unfeasible. One need only consider the fact that the IMF has been underfunded from its inception (Eichengreen 1998: 49) and the problems over reforming IMF quotas (Broz and Hawes 2006) to appreciate how difficult it would be to create a true institutional ILOLR.

The idea of a hegemon playing this role has been around since the 1970s.[17] This is also theoretically appealing. But it has never operated the way its advocates have proposed. It requires a concentration of economic and political power, and a willingness to use it, that has rarely existed. The only true hegemon, as defined by this theory, that the world has ever had was the United States in the late 1940s and early 1950s. However, this does not mean that leadership by a pre-eminent financial power is not desirable. In fact, such leadership was an important element in both the pre-1914 system, where Britain played this role, and the post-1945 system, where it was played by the US.

The most common form that a quasi-ILOLR has taken is that of a concert of key financial powers. However, this setup is also not without its problems. For the concert to work, its members must be able to overcome collective action problems and reach a consensus on the problem they face and the solutions they need to adopt. Some level of institutionalization is desirable to overcome these problems. However, too much institutionalization may also decrease the main benefit of a concert, namely its adaptability. The second problem is the question of how inclusive the club should be. This requires a balance between the benefits of maximizing resources (increasing membership) and minimizing collective action problems (decreasing membership). The final, and perhaps most serious, problem is that this institutional setup is very effective at maintaining stability at the core of the system, but will not be effective at maintaining stability in the periphery. Put simply, unless a crisis in the periphery poses a systemic risk, it will not attract the attention of the concert.

The Evolution of International Crisis Response Mechanisms

Past Institutional Structures

The financial system of the late nineteenth century, known as the classic gold standard, lacked formal institutional structures. The closest that the system came to an institution was the consensus among central banks at the core of the system about the need for regular policy coordination and mutual aid in times of financial turmoil. This need arose from the fact that central banks were responsible both for defending their gold pegs and acting as national lenders of last resort in times of financial crises. The problem was that during a crisis, the unilateral use of discount rates and liquidity injections to help distressed markets compromised a central bank's ability to defend its gold peg. Thus, the only way to maintain stability was though coordinated interventions. But if the core of the system was stable,

17 Kindleberger (1978) was the first to argue that international economic stability depended on the existence of a hegemon which acted as an ILOLR and provided other international public goods. His argument would eventually be expanded into hegemonic stability theory.

countries in the periphery were not so fortunate. Since they could not expect the same kind of support, it was not uncommon for them to experience severe economic dislocation during a financial crisis (Eichengreen 1998: 35–8).

The political and economic fallout of World War I damaged the concert at the heart of the old gold standard. In the 1920s, some stability was provided by Anglo-American cooperation, often supported by the League of Nations (James 1996: 19–21). This period also saw the emergence of the first international financial institution. As early as the international conferences in Brussels (1920) and Genoa (1922), there were proposals for the creation of an international institution that would help central bankers share information and coordinate policy. However, not much was done until 1930, when the Bank for International Settlement (BIS) was established.

Unfortunately, in 1931 the system faced a series of financial crises whose complexity and magnitude parallel the Asian meltdown of 1997.[18] The BIS tried to organize a series of interventions to deal with the crisis, but it was not up to the task. It had not yet developed the capacity to deal with a crisis on this scale. Complicating matters further, in addition to its role as facilitator of central bank coordination, it was also charged with managing German reparations. This divided mandate hampered its effectiveness, since one of the main recipients of the bail-out package would be Germany. This made it hard to separate attempts to deal with the crises from the issues surrounding reparations. In addition, the active cooperation between London and New York that had supported the system in the 1920s was over by 1928.[19] The US Federal Reserve was not even a member of the BIS. This meant that US participation in crisis response efforts was *ad hoc*, and not very effective.

Thus, the 1930s lacked both a concert of the key financial players and formal institutional structures strong enough to deal with the problems facing the system. As a result of the financial crises and deepening depression, the gold exchange standard collapsed, leading to a hodgepodge of autarkic currency zones.

The experience of the interwar period largely informed the agenda and goals of the Bretton Woods Conference in 1944. The conference was the result of an Anglo-American consensus that the international system needed institutional

---

18 The crisis was preceded by a series of defaults by heavily indebted nations, many of them in Latin America. Like the peso crisis of 1994–95, these defaults made investors nervous about the safety of emerging markets. This greatly reduced international lending, especially from the US, which was a key source of capital in the 1920s. This decline in international lending and investor confidence led to concerns about the viability of national banking systems in Central Europe. As a result, Hungary, Austria and Germany experienced twin banking and currency crises similar to those experienced by Thailand, Indonesia and the Philippines during the Asian crisis. However, unlike the Asian crisis, the crisis of 1931 would eventually hit the City of London, the very core of the financial system.

19 The Anglo-American axis was based on the personal relationship between Montagu Norman (Governor of the Bank of England) and Benjamin Strong (Governor of the Federal Reserve Bank, New York). This ended with the death of Strong in 1928 (James 1996: 23).

supports. The IMF was created to regulate the dollar standard and provide support to countries with balance-of-payments problems. But it was also intended to be a forum in which countries could discuss common problems and coordinate their policy efforts. Despite these innovations, the post-war monetary system was not without problems, which would eventually lead to its demise.[20] However, the IMF, despite its shortcomings, proved useful and survived the collapse of Bretton Woods.

The creation of the IMF did not diminish the need for a concert of key financial powers. Without the US-British partnership, the Bretton Woods Conference could not have succeeded. However, Britain could not continue to play this role, due to its post-war economic difficulties. As a result, the US acted as a hegemon in the 1950s, supporting the international financial system and providing loans and aid for post-war reconstruction.[21] But as post-war recovery progressed, additional financial powers emerged. This led to the formation of the Group of Ten (G10) in 1962 under the auspices of the IMF.[22] This working group was created to help the IMF deal with the problems plaguing the dollar exchange system. Despite various initiatives, the most prominent of which was the Smithsonian Agreement of 1971, the G10 and IMF were unable to save the system. Despite its failure, the G10 became the model for subsequent groupings of financial powers that would eventually lead to the G8.

The Evolution of the G8

In 1975, the proto-G8 (in fact a G5) was little more than an *ad hoc* working group created to discuss the issues surrounding the collapse of Bretton Woods and the energy crisis. During the next fifteen years, the G7 leaders' summits helped shape the monetary and financial system. The emergence of the G8 created, for the first time in history, a regular forum of the world's key financial powers. As the global financial system has evolved, so has the G8, often in response to dramatic systemic

---

20 The most serious problems were the system's lack of flexibility and its inability to deal with persistence imbalances. The US suffered from the so-called "N-1 problem": because all currencies were pegged to the dollar and the dollar to gold, the US had no means of adjustment. In the minds of US policymakers, this placed an unfair burden on the US and robbed it of the flexibility enjoyed by other countries. On the other hand, although this was true in theory, in practice other nations did not enjoy much more flexibility in setting their pegs. Furthermore, as the 1960s wore on, many felt the central position of the US effectively gave it seniorage, which the US used to finance its increasingly unsustainable balance-of-payments deficits.

21 The Marshall Plan in fact dwarfed the funds available to both the IMF and the World Bank.

22 The G10 consisted of the future members of the G7 plus Belgium, the Netherlands and Sweden. Switzerland would join the group in 1964, despite not being a member of the IMF.

changes. The key constant in this evolution is the close working relationship the G8 maintains with the IMF.

The first development of the G7 happened in response to the dollar appreciation of the mid-1980s. This problem demonstrated that the post-Bretton Woods system would require policy coordination at its core. Since the problem was not immediately endangering the system (though it was causing friction), and since it was very technical in nature, it was not solved at the leaders' level. Instead, it was handled by finance ministers and central bank governors though *ad hoc* meetings which produced the Plaza (1985) and Louvre (1987) Accords.[23] After this success, the G7 finance ministers and central bank governors held a semi-annual forum for monitoring the international financial system and coordinating policy.

With the end of the Cold War, the new challenge was the political and economic integration of the former Soviet Bloc. This led to a working relationship with Russia and the eventual creation of the G8. Initially, this existed as a parallel forum to the G7, but gradually the two merged at the leaders' level. This, however, did not happen at the level of finance ministers, due to Russia's lack of financial capacity. As a result, the G7 finance ministers' meeting still exists as a separate forum.

The outbreak of the Asian crisis in the late 1990s dramatically demonstrated the downside of financial globalization and the increased vulnerability of the core to financial problems in the periphery. As a result, for the first time in history, there was a move to supplement the efforts of key financial powers with a broader forum that included key emerging market economies. Thus, the G20 finance ministerial grouping was created as a parallel to the G7. However, during its first decade, the G20 was not a particularly dramatic institutional innovation, as it largely supplemented rather than replaced the G7.

Another result of the Asian crisis was the creation of the Financial Stability Forum (FSF). This brought together 26 national financial authorities,[24] six IFIs,[25] seven international standard-setting, regulatory and supervisory groupings,[26] two committees of central bank experts[27] and the European Central Bank. The mandate

---

23 See Funabashi (1988). Not all members of the G7 participated in these conferences. At Plaza, only the G5 (France, Germany, Japan, the UK and US) participated, and at Louvre, though all G7 countries were invited, Italy chose not to attend.

24 From Australia, Canada, France, Germany, Hong King, Italy, Japan, the Netherlands, Singapore, Switzerland, the UK and the US.

25 Two each from the IMF and World Bank groups, and one each from the BIS and Organisation for Economic Co-operation and Development (OECD).

26 Two each from the Basel Committee on Banking Supervision (BCBS), the International Accounting Standards Board (IASB) and the International Association of Insurance Supervisors (IAIS), plus the International Organization of Securities Commissions (IOSCO).

27 The Committee on Payment and Settlement Systems (CPSS) and the Committee on the Global Financial System (CGFS).

of the FSF was to coordinate international financial surveillance efforts and act as a financial think tank for the G8.

Thus, in its role as watchdog of international financial stability, the G8 is currently an interlocking and mutually supporting web of international institutions with the original G7 still at its center. However, recent events point to a dramatic shift of the center from the G7 to the G20. Responses to the most recent financial crisis have taken place primarily at the G20 leaders' level rather than the G7 finance ministers' level. This is a dramatic change from the handling of the Asian crisis. In addition, the FSF has been transformed into the Financial Stability Board (FSB), which has a broader membership and mandate. It is still too early to judge the extent and implications of this shift.

The Structure of Current Institutional Arrangements

The relationship between the G8 and IMF is based on four key factors: the position of the G8 in international finance, its institutional ties with the IMF, and the division of labor and principle of non-interference that exist between the two.

The G8's Central Position in the International Financial System

The members of the G8 have at their command a unique set of resources that make them indispensable in dealing with crises. Increasingly, this is also true of the members of the G20, especially China and India.

The most obvious resource is the vast financial reserves at the disposal of the G8. If the IMF's resources, and those of other IFIs, prove inadequate to deal with a crisis, the G8 can step in to cover the shortfall relatively quickly. A better solution would be to give the IMF and other IFIs the resources to fulfill their roles. But this is difficult, for two reasons. First, such changes take a great deal of time and political will to enact, especially since they require the approval of domestic legislatures. Second, given the growth of financial markets, it usually does not take long for sizable reserves to become inadequate.

But the importance of the G8 is not limited to providing resources during a crisis. Crisis response is not simply a matter of throwing money at the problem. International markets today are simply too large and fast-moving to be managed with brute force. Instead, the key to stabilizing distressed markets is convincing investors that measures will be taken to correct the underlying problems. Thus, the G8's influence on financial markets is arguably as important as the material resources it commands. The G8 countries are home to the world's top financial centers and private financial institutions. They are also the largest source of international capital in the world. This makes the G8 incredibly influential in world markets. By supporting an IMF intervention, the G8 can enhance the recipient's credibility in the eyes of international investors. G8 governments can also use moral suasion to influence private financial institutions. This is often a more effective way of bringing stability to distressed markets, though it is not always easy to achieve. One notable case where it was is South Korea in 1998 (Kirton 2002).

Formal Institutional Relationships

The G8 and IMF have very strong ties with one another. Although the G8 is the senior partner in the relationship, the influence works both ways. The members of the G7 control 43.94 percent of the votes in the IMF Board of Governors.[28] With the members of the G20 added, this rises to 61.58 percent. Important decisions, such as amending member quotas or the Articles of Agreement, require 85 percent of votes to pass. This not only gives the G8 a veto, but also provides a strong basis for building coalitions to push through changes when necessary.[29] This also translates into a great deal of influence over the Executive Board of the IMF, which shapes IMF policy.[30] Finally, by tradition, the IMF's Managing Director is appointed by the Europeans. This means that the G8 has a great deal of influence over the IMF. In times of crisis, the G8 can use its influence to help the IMF adapt to the problem at hand. During the Asian financial crisis, a number of major changes to the IMF had to be enacted in this way.

It would be wrong, however, to conclude that the IMF is simply a puppet of the G8. Like all international institutions, it jealously guards its autonomy. Thus, while the G8 has a great deal of influence in shaping overall IMF policy, the IMF bureaucracy maintains a great deal of independence in the daily running of the IMF. In addition, the Managing Director of the IMF participates in all G8 and G20 finance ministers' forums and is regularly invited to the annual leaders' summits. This, along with the IMF's indispensable surveillance capacity, gives the IMF an influential voice in the G8.

Division of Labor

The advantage of small forums like the G7, G8 and G20 is that they bring together states that are best able to influence the overall development of the international financial system and deal with its most pressing problems. The limitation of such forums, even ones that are as inclusive as the G20, is that they do not have the means or the inclination to monitor and manage the financial system as a whole.

28 As of May 21, 2009: US (16.77 percent) – which gives the US an effective veto; Japan (6.02 percent); Germany (5.88 percent); France (4.86 percent); UK (4.86 percent); Italy (3.19 percent), and Canada (2.89 percent). Source: <http://www.imf.org/external/np/sec/memdir/members.htm#3>.

29 The G8's strong ties with the EU make creating such coalitions much easier.

30 Of the 24 members of this board, five seats automatically go to the members with the largest quotas (currently the US, Japan, Germany, France and the UK) and the rest are appointed on the basis of quotas and demand for national currencies.

Thus, they are less receptive to smaller, yet still serious, international financial problems. On the other hand, the IMF has the advantages of a large international institution: formal structures, a large bureaucracy and substantial independent resources. This means that the IMF can provide a much broader forum for discussion. It is better able to monitor the international financial system as a whole. Also, given its mandate and resources, the IMF is ready to provide assistance to individual countries in a much more effective way than the G8 could. In times of systemic crisis, these different capabilities can complement each other. Thus, the real advantage of the current system is that it builds on the strengths of these two different institutional structures and minimizes their individual shortcomings.

Non-interference

The principle of non-interference means that the two institutions will generally keep to the division of labor outlined above. In fact, even when responding to a systemic crisis, the efforts taken by the G8 and IMF form a coordinated and harmonized set of individual interventions, not a joint action plan.

This principle of non-interference holds especially true for the developed economies in the G20. The main reason for this is that these states are in a privileged position compared to the rest of the world: when they experience a crisis, they are largely able to deal with it on their own. This is because they have very large, complex and diversified financial markets. In such systems, difficulties with individual financial institutions or sectors are normally less likely to lead to a cascade that threatens the financial stability of the economy as a whole. These markets are usually also better regulated, making them more transparent, and are less vulnerable to the escalation of financial problems into full-blown crises. Moreover, during a financial crisis they do not experience the kind of "capital flight" that devastates small, open economies, especially less-developed ones. The result is that when difficulties arise, the problem can be more easily identified, isolated from the rest of the market and dealt with.

This is less true of the emerging economies in the G20, with the notable exception of China. However, even they have an advantage compared to other emerging economies, due to the strategic importance to the international financial system. Since financial problems in these countries pose a greater systemic risk to the system as a whole, they have more leverage when dealing with the IMF and the members of the G7.

Similarly, while the members of the G7 regularly supplement the efforts of the IMF, they never try to supplant them. This is true even when the crisis in question happens in a country with strong ties with a member of the G7. During the 1994–95 Mexican peso crisis, the US and Canada intervened to help their partner in the North American Free Trade Agreement (NAFTA), but did so in cooperation with the IMF. A similar response has been adopted recently by the European members of the G20 with respect to EU countries facing financial crises. Instead of directly bailing out their EU partners, they have opted to increase IMF resources so that it can deal with these problems as they arise. Thus, during a systemic crisis, the G8 supplements rather than circumvents the efforts of the IMF.

In part, this non-interference is a result of basic political and economic realities. The IMF and the G8 generally do not have the power to bully the individual members of the G8. For its part, the G8 is better off supporting rather then undermining the IMF, since in the long run it does not want to get into the business of dealing with every crisis. But maintaining this principle strengthens the ties between these institutions and makes cooperation more palatable.

The IMF and G8's Record in Dealing with Crises

The Effectiveness of this Arrangement

The G8 is seen as often slow to react to crisis, a critical problem in a globalizing financial system. Although there is some validity to this criticism, two things must be kept in mind. First, crises are complex and hard to predict. Second, a concert of powers, such as the G8, functions on the basis of consensus. Until a consensus is reached, cooperation cannot take place. This means that delays in international crisis response are inevitable. Despite this, the nature of the G8 goes a long way toward minimizing this problem. Of critical importance here are the formal and informal ties between the IMF and the G8 finance ministries and central banks.

However, it is the IMF which receives the bulk of criticism when it comes to international crisis response. A number of studies have highlighted, and given empirical evidence for, the negative economic impact of IMF programs. The evidence suggests that IMF programs are associated with weaker macroeconomic performance (Bordo and Schwartz 2000, Przeworski and Vreeland 2000, Dreher 2006). Similarly, IMF interventions are not followed by a restoration of investment inflows after a crisis (Bird and Rowlands 2002, Jensen 2004). However, despite these criticisms and the myriad reform proposals, there are no dramatic measures which could be taken to fix these problems. Rather, improving the performance of IMF lending is and will remain a slow work in progress.

The issue of IMF conditionality is perhaps the most controversial. Many have pointed out that IMF conditionality has grown to absurd and dangerous dimensions, becoming increasingly intrusive (Kapur 1998). This has raised concerns about the negative economic, social and even political consequences of IMF programs. The IMF has also been criticized for adopting a "one size fits all" model of conditionality. The seriousness of this problem is widely recognized, including by the IMF itself. In September 2002, the IMF's Executive Board approved the reform of conditionality guidelines according to five principles: parsimony, tailoring, coordination, clarity and ownership (Best 2007).

However, IMF conditionality does serve a very important purpose. Conditions are policy commitments that are intended to convince financial markets that the problems affecting the distressed market will be corrected. Without such policy commitments, IMF loans would at best only delay the collapse of a financial market.

Moreover, the IMF does not simply dictate terms to a recipient country. Rather, conditionality is the product of a complex set of explicit and tacit bargains between the various stakeholders. Despite its influence, the IMF cannot force the recipient government to implement any policies, nor can it perfectly monitor compliance (Kahler 1993). Also, since financial crises can lead to political crises, this gives domestic interest groups influence over IMF loan negotiations. There is only so far that the IMF can push a government before it triggers a political backlash. On the other hand, it is also not uncommon for a government to accept conditionality as a means of passing unpopular, but in their view necessary, reforms (MacIntyre 2001, Vreeland 2005). Others have pointed to the influence of powerful members of the IMF in influencing conditionality, especially when the IMF loans depend on supplementary financing (Gould 2003). Financial markets themselves play an important role, as the whole point of conditionality it to convince them that steps are being taken to end the crisis.

Finally, there is a danger in making IMF lending too painless. This could foster the kind of moral hazard problem that would lead governments to make bad policy choices in the future. Why should governments make painful, but necessary, policy choices if they can count on a relatively painless bail-out in the case of a crisis?

Cui Bono?

One of the key issues surrounding the activities of the G8 and the IMF is the question of whose interest these institutions serve. A common argument is that both organizations are primarily concerned with advancing their own interests and the interests of international investors (Thacker 1999, Wade 2002). However, it would be a mistake to think that the IMF is simply a tool of the G8 or US interests. One such case is an IMF loan given to Pakistan following the 9/11 terrorist attack. Many saw this as a reward from the US to its ally, and the US did try to take credit for it. But the evidence shows that this was just a coincidence, as the IMF was adamant in arguing (Vreeland 2002).

The argument is also made that IMF intervention is unjust because it favors international investors over governments and taxpayers. Thus, the burden is born by citizens of emerging economies who bear the brunt of conditionality and must ultimately repay IMF loans. In complete contrast, international investors, who are seen by many as the cause of financial crises, do not bear any such burdens and are the prime beneficiaries of IMF bail-outs. Although there is some merit in this argument, it is not the entire story. First, in many cases governments are as much to blame as markets for crises, and in some cases more so. Second, it is rarely the case that international investors escape from a crisis untouched. Finally, the burden of adjustment falling on governments and their citizens is not the result of the supposed favor shown by the IMF and the G8 to investors and markets. The fact is that the current levels and speed of capital mobility give financial markets a great deal of leverage. Whether this should be the case and whether government should try to change this are very different, and very difficult, questions.

The final question is whether the IMF and G7 (the US in particular) use their power to impose a particular political and economic model (the so-called "Washington consensus") on developing economies. The idea of an emerging Washington consensus was first identified by Williamson (1993), but the idea that the US was using the IMF as a means to advance the goals of the Washington consensus was most fully developed by Wade (2002). The Washington consensus was a very influential intellectual framework in the 1990s and had a great deal of influence on the IMF and World Bank. However, due to the fall of communism and the failure of state-centered development strategies, this framework also had a great deal of influence on many politicians, bureaucrats and economists in both the developing and developed worlds. Throughout the history of the international financial system, intellectual frameworks about how the international system does and should function have developed (Ruggie 1983). Some of these have been beneficial, while others produced very negative, even disastrous, results. It is a mistake to see the IMF and the G8 as incurably fixed ideological institutions. These institutions are co-evolving with the international financial system, as is their understanding of how the system works. The fact that the G8, G20 and IMF function as forums in which the key players of the financial system can exchange ideas is an important and beneficial feature of the current international financial architecture (Baker 2006).

G8 and Systemic Crises: The Asian Financial Crisis

Controversy still surrounds the causes, responses to and consequences of the Asian crisis. This section focuses only on the IMF and G8's contribution to crisis response.

Although there was a great deal of inter-country variation, there were three primary factors that led to this crisis. First, the region experienced a substantial inflow of short-term capital before the crisis. This made the region vulnerable to sudden capital flight. Second, there was declining confidence in the region's currency pegs, which made them much more vulnerable to speculative attacks. This decline in confidence was due to the experience of the Mexican peso crisis in 1994–95 and the fact that most countries in the region, particularly Thailand, Indonesia and South Korea, were running large current account deficits while setting their currency pegs too high. Finally, there were serious vulnerabilities in the region's banking systems: the banks were highly interconnected, lacked transparency and carried a substantial portion of bad loans on their books (often backed by government guarantees), and their balance sheets had serious currency mismatches (they borrowed short-term on foreign capital markets and lent long-term in local currency without adequately covering their exchange rate exposure). These circumstances led to a series of twin currency and banking crises.

The crisis spread very quickly from its initial outbreak in Thailand in the summer of 1997. It first hit the Philippines, which was forced to float the peso. From there it spread to Hong Kong and Taiwan, though these countries had more success in minimizing the impact of the crisis. Indonesia was hit next, followed by South Korea, whose commercial banks had close ties to Indonesia. In 1998, the crisis spread to countries outside the region, the most serious incidents occurring in Russia, Brazil and Argentina. Russia and Brazil would eventually manage to stabilize their problems with the help of the IMF, G8 and other IFIs. Argentina, on the other hand, experienced continued pressure, which culminated in a financial and political crisis. Even the members of the G8 were not immune to the crisis. Japan and the US in particular were seriously affected. In both cases, however, the crisis did not have nearly the same economic impact as in the other affected countries.

At first the G8, like most of the world, ignored the crisis. At the Denver Summit of 1997, the problem was completely absent from discussions, despite the fact that the 1995 Halifax Summit had been primarily focused on the creation of a new international financial architecture in the wake of the Mexican peso crisis. Similarly, the bulk of the discussion at the G7 finance ministers meeting that year focused on issues relating to international financial regulation. There was some talk about the events unfolding in Asia, but there was no urgency to the discussion. The G8 was more than happy to leave the issue to Asian countries, regional institutions and the IMF.

This changed dramatically at the next meeting, which coincided with Hong Kong's currency and stock market difficulties. But it was at the semi-annual IMF meeting that the first dramatic steps were taken. The G7 finance ministers agreed to increase IMF reserves by 45 percent and to amend the IMF's Articles of Agreement within the year. The three proposed amendments aimed to formally expand the IMF's responsibilities to include capital account liberalization, to strengthen its role in financial sector reform (with an emphasis on improving national governance and a reduction in corruption) and to expand the allocation of special drawing rights.

During the Fall of 1997, Japan and the US provided significant contributions to the "second line of defense" fund for Indonesia, in case the funding provided by the IMF and other IFIs proved inadequate. By November, the G8 formalized the "second line of defense" fund agreement and its members started working on obtaining legislative authority to contribute to it as the crisis progressed. In December, the G7 endorsed the $35 billion package the IMF and other IFIs had created for South Korea, and pledged to reinforce it if necessary. The specific pledges were as follows: Japan $10 billion; the US $5 billion; Germany, France, the UK and Italy $1.25 billion each; and Canada $1 billion. But more important than the monetary contribution was their influence on private bankers, who promised to roll over and reschedule their loans to South Korea (Kirton 2002). This, in addition to the pledges made by South Korea's newly elected government, stabilized investor confidence without drawing on the "second line of defense" funds.

The pressure on other governments was similarly decreasing in this period, with the notable exception of Indonesia, which refused to adopt IMF prescriptions. As a result, at the beginning of 1998 Germany and the US intervened, with the support of other G7 members. By mid-January, Indonesia negotiated a letter of intent with the IMF. Indonesia revised its economic targets and pledged far-reaching structural reforms. However, by April 1998 it became clear that both Indonesia and South Korea could not meet the pledges they had made to Thailand the previous summer. As a result, Canada assumed Indonesia's share in the first-line fund to deal with the crisis, which amounted to US$500 million. By this time, the crisis in Asia had stabilized. The crisis would eventually spread to Russia and Brazil, but further contagion was prevented through joint IMF-G7 actions. Finally, although the US and Japan would also experience direct financial problems as a result of the Asian financial crisis, they were still strong enough to deal with these on their own, while still being able to contribute a great deal to the G7's efforts to contain the crisis. Throughout this period the US was experiencing continuous Congressional opposition to any attempts to increase IMF quotas. However, the other G7 members successfully covered this shortfall in US support.

As one would expect with a crisis that did not initially affect the core of the system, the Asian crisis initially drew the attention of the IMF, but not the G8. However, once the extent of the danger was realized, the G8 played a decisive role in managing the crisis by providing necessary second-line funds to back up the loans arranged by the IMF and other IFIs, by helping to restore some confidence in international investors and by pushing reluctant countries into adopting the necessary steps to end the crisis.

There are two criticisms that can be leveled at the response efforts of both the IMF and G8. First, both institutions ignored important warning signs and reacted later than they should have. Second, the actions of both were seen as extremely harsh by the East Asian countries. One result is that since the crisis, countries in this region have accumulated excessive foreign currency reserves to ensure that they can deal with future crises without depending on international institutions.[31] While moral hazard problems mean that it is generally not a good idea to make international crisis lending too easy, this trend does indicate a danger that the IMF has developed a reputation for harshness that could limit its future usefulness.

The crisis was also significant because it created two new institutions: the G20 and the FSF. At the Vancouver APEC conference in November 1997, US President Bill Clinton announced the creation of a temporary committee called the G22 (also

31 There is an interesting irony here. Before the crisis, there were suggestions for the creation of an Asian Monetary Fund (AMF) which would be more in tune with the political and business culture of the region. At the time, the crisis seemed to kill this idea. However, ten years later, although there is no formal AMF, the policies adopted by the central banks in the region have in effect created an informal AMF.

known as the "Willard Group"), which would be a broader G7-like forum. It first met on April 16, 1998, in Washington. It was quickly superseded by the G33 in early 1999, and then by the G20 later that year. The FSF was based on a study the G7 finance ministers commissioned to propose improvements to the international financial architecture (Hajnal 2007). The G7 formally founded this institution in February 1999. However, although the Asian crisis created these institutions, it was the crisis that erupted ten years later that would breathe life into them.

Ten Years Later: Current Financial Problems and Their Implications

There is always a danger in discussing an ongoing crisis. Even today, after years of analysis and scholarly debate, controversy still surrounds not just the Asian crisis, but much older crises such as the Great Depression. None the less, while it is too early to evaluate the effectiveness of current efforts, it is important to consider the extent to which the G8/G20 and IMF have facilitated cooperation so far, and the institutional shift that has taken place over this period and its possible long-term implications.

One can divide recent crisis response into two periods: August 2007 (when the first serious symptoms of the crisis appeared) to October 2008 (when the crisis intensified), and November 2008 (when crisis response shifted to the G20) to April 2009 (the G20 leaders' summit in London). During the first period, response mainly took place at the level of the G7 finance ministers; they focused primarily on immediate crisis response, and were on the whole low-key. During the second period, the focus shifted to the G20 leaders (an institution created in response to the crisis); there was more of a focus on economic stimulus and reform efforts, and these efforts had a much higher profile.

The current crisis constitutes a much more serous challenge than the Asian financial crises because it originated in, and has serious implications for, the very core of the international financial system. It began with the collapse of the US sub-prime mortgage market, which placed a severe strain on the US banking system, as well as numerous financial institutions around the world. The US mortgage market began attracting increasing investor attention after the collapse of the dot.com bubble in the early 2000s. This boom in real estate, along with poor regulation, government policy and unscrupulous and in some cases illegal behavior by lenders, played a role in expanding mortgage investment. When prices in the real-estate market began to deflate, mortgage holders, many of whom were overextended, began defaulting. A similar crisis also developed independently in the UK due to similar trends in its housing and banking sectors.

However, what increased the toxicity of this crisis was the securitization of the US mortgage market ("What Went Wrong: Wall Street's Crisis" 2008). By creating mortgage-backed securities Wall Street not only increased its own exposure to the crisis but also made this a truly global crisis, as these securities were bought by a diverse set of international investors. Even worse, these "toxic assets" obscured the connections between the original mortgage holders and final investors. This created a great deal of uncertainty, as borrowers and lenders could not easily determine their exposure. This uncertainty helped fuel the crisis and resulting credit crunch.

The first signs of trouble began appearing in the summer of 2007, though the crisis would not reach a critical mass until a year later. In the period August 2007–August 2008 there were numerous efforts to try to deal with the crisis. First, there was a series of short-term interventions (open market operations and interest rate cuts) aimed at preventing a credit crunch. These efforts demonstrated a high level of coordination among G7 central banks. Second, there was a series of direct government bail-outs to help distressed banks. Of these, the most prominent were the Bank of England's nationalization of Northern Rock Bank and the US government's bail-out of Fannie Mae, Freddie Mac and AIG. Third, there were more general attempts to stimulate the economy and thus avoid or minimize the coming recession. The most prominent of these was the Economic Stimulus Act of 2008 passed in the US by the Bush administration.

In addition to these short-term and largely *ad hoc* efforts, the G7 finance ministers were adopting more long-term solutions. At their October meeting in 2007, the G7 finance ministers commissioned the FSF to create a plan for dealing with crises. On April 12, 2007, the FSF proposed a series of reforms which emphasized strengthening prudential oversight, enhancing transparency, changing the role and use of credit ratings, strengthening responsiveness to risks and producing robust arrangements for dealing with stresses in the financial system.

While these efforts were well coordinated, they only delayed the credit crunch and downturn in the real economy. By September 2009 it was clear to both the US and UK that a more comprehensive approach was necessary. After a protracted legislative process, both governments passed rescue packages that would provide substantial resources and a set of guidelines for fixing problems in their respective banking systems. The US Troubled Asset Relief Program (TARP) amounted to $700 billion, and the UK bank rescue package amounted to £500 billion (or approximately $850 billion). Other governments would follow with packages of their own.

In the Fall of 2008, the finance ministers meetings of both the G7 (October 27) and G20 (November 7–8) were dominated by the financial crisis. However, the leaders of the G20 decided that the crisis was too serious to be left to these forums. They decided to meet for the first time at the special Leaders' Summit in Washington on November 14–15. At this meeting the G20 leaders decided that the G20 should coordinate its continuing crisis response, make provisions for minimizing the impact of the crisis on emerging markets and begin the process of reforms to the international financial system. In order to help emerging markets, they agreed to increase funding for the IMF, World Bank and regional development banks to help with crisis response and maintain trade and capital flows to the least-developed countries (LDCs). The reform proposals largely followed the earlier recommendations of the FSF, with a focus on transparency, improved regulation, coordination and the reform of IFIs. Perhaps the most important long-term decision taken at Washington was that the G20 leaders would meet again on April 2, 2009, in London.

At the London conference, the G20 increased IFI resources by $1.1 trillion through member contributions, the creation of new special drawing rights and the sale of IMF gold. The G20 also agreed on the transformation of the FSF into the Financial Stability Board (FSB). Substantial changes to the international financial system were proposed, including the extension of regulation to all financial markets and institutions (including hedge funds and, for the first time, credit agencies), the creation of new and internationally consistent capital requirements and accounting standards, and the promise of harsh measures against non-cooperative jurisdictions (tax havens and secrecy in off-shore banking). There were also pledges to reform IFIs. The most significant pertained to the IMF: increased transparency of top leadership appointments, increasing the voice of LDCs, and more oversight and transparency in IMF lending and conditionality. Although there was some disagreement among the members of the G20 over the need for more economic stimulus (stressed primarily by the US and UK) and the need for immediate financial reforms (stressed primarily by the other European members), the extent and coordination of efforts on both fronts were substantial.

The Pittsburgh Summit of September 24–25, 2009, has continued this work in three important ways. It outlined the "Framework for Strong, Sustainable and Balanced Growth," which should aid future economic policy coordination. It proposed further changes to financial regulations. Most importantly, it made major reforms to global financial governance: institutionalizing the G20 as an annual summit and pledging substantial quota/vote changes in the IMF as well as development banks.

Conclusion

On the whole, the G8 and IMF contribute significantly to maintaining international financial stability. Although one can argue about the focus and effectiveness of their efforts, the members of the G20 have shown remarkable solidarity and a willingness to coordinate policy despite serious disagreements and problems. Recent cooperation has been as good as it was during the heyday of the classic gold standard. However, unlike the late nineteenth century, much more attention has been paid to the effects of the crisis on the periphery.

The 2008 crisis has also brought major institutional transformations. The G20 has been strengthened, and the G20 leaders forum has emerged as a new center of economic governance. Similarly the FSB has, at least on paper, been given substantial new responsibilities for monitoring and reforming the international financial system. However, just how permanent these institutional changes will be remains to be seen. During the G20 summits in Washington and in London, some used the terms "Bretton Woods moment" and "Bretton Woods II" to capture the importance of these events. However, this is premature and raises unrealistic expectations. It is appropriate to recall that the Nixon administration heralded the 1971 Smithsonian Agreement as "the most significant reform of the international economic system," and yet just two years later the Bretton Woods System collapsed. In fact, even the Bretton Woods conference in 1944 was not really the "Bretton Woods moment" many imagine. In practice, the system that it created did not function the way its designers envisioned, and it was riddled by the many structural flaws that would eventually lead to its collapse.

Financial crises are simply an unavoidable cost of an integrated international financial system. While much work has been done to improve the international financial architecture, no reform effort can prevent all future crises. The current division of labor between the G8 and the IMF is not perfect. But it is an important improvement over past institutional arrangements, both formal and informal. Global financial governance, like all global governance, is a work in progress.

Bibliography

Baker, A. (2006), *The Group of Seven: Finance Ministries, Central Banks and Global Financial Governance* (London: Routledge).

Berger, W. and H. Wagner (2005), "Interdependent Expectations and the Spread of Currency Crises," *IMF Staff Papers* 52(1): 41–54.

Bernanke, B. and H. James (1991), "The Gold Standard, Deflation and Financial Crises in the Great Depression: An International Comparison," in R.G. Hubbard, ed., *Financial Markets and Financial Crises* (Chicago, IL: University of Chicago Press).

Best, J. (2007), "Legitimacy Dilemmas: The IMF's Pursuit of Country Ownership," *Third World Quarterly* 28(3): 477.

Bird, G. and D. Rowlands (2002), "Do IMF Programmes Have a Catalytic Effect on Other International Capital Flows?" *Oxford Development Studies* 30(3): 229–49.

Bordo, M. and A. Schwartz (2000), "Measuring Real Economic Effects of Bailouts: Historical Perspectives on How Countries in Financial Distress Have Fared With and Without Bailouts," National Bureau of Economic Research Working Paper (May): 7,701.

Bordo, M., B. Eichengreen, D. Klingebiel and M.S. Martinez-Peria (2001), "Is the Crisis Problem Growing More Severe?" *Economic Policy* 16(32): 51–82.

Botman, D. and H. Jager (2002), "Coordination of Speculation," *Journal of International Economics* 58(1): 159–75.

Broz, L. and M.B. Hawes (2006), "Congressional Politics of Financing the International Monetary Fund," *International Organization* 60(2): 367–99.

Burnside, C., M. Eichenbaum and S. Rebelo (2006), "Government Finance in the Wake of Currency Crises," *Journal of Monetary Economics* 53(3): 401–40.

Chang, R. and G. Majnoni (2002), "Fundamentals, Beliefs and Financial Contagion," *European Economic Review* 46(4–5): 801–8.

Corsetti, G., P.A. Pesenti and N. Roubini (1999), "What Caused the Asian Currency and Financial Crisis?" *Japan and the World Economy* 11(3): 305–73.

Dreher, A. (2006), "IMF and Economic Growth: The Effects of Programs, Loans and Compliance with Conditionality," *World Development* 34(5): 769–88.

Edwards, S. and R. Rigobon (2002), "Currency Crises and Contagion: An Introduction," *Journal of Development Economics* 69(2): 307–13

Eichengreen, B. (1998), *Globalizing Capital: A History of the International Monetary System* (Princeton, NJ: Princeton University Press).

Eichengreen, B. and P.H. Lindert (1989), "Overview," in B. Eichengreen and P.H. Lindert, eds, *The International Debt Crisis in Historical Perspective* (Cambridge, MA: MIT Press), pp. 1–11.

Eichengreen, B. and A.K. Rose (2003), "Does It Pay to Defend against a Speculative Attack?," in M.P. Dooley and J.A. Frankel, eds, *Managing Currency Crises in Emerging Markets* (Chicago, IL: National Bureau of Economic Research), pp. 61–88.

Ellison, M., L. Graham and J. Vilmunen (2006), "Strong Contagion with Weak Spillovers," *Review of Economic Dynamics* 9(2): 263–83.

Fishlow, A. (1985), "Lessons from the Past: Capital Markets During the 19th Century and the Interwar Period," *International Organization* 39(3): 383–439.

Frankel, J.A. (2005), "Contractionary Currency Crashes in Developing Countries," *IMF Staff Papers* 52(2): 149–92.

Funabashi, Y. (1988), *Managing the Dollar: From the Plaza to the Louvre* (Washington, DC: Institute for International Economics).

Goodhart, C. and G. Illing, eds (2002), *Financial Crises, Contagion and the Lender of Last Resort: A Reader* (Oxford: Oxford University Press).

Gould, E. (2003), "Money Talks: Supplementary Financiers and International Monetary Fund Conditionality," *International Organization* 57(3): 551–86.

Hajnal, P. (2007), *The G8 System and the G20: Evolution, Role and Documentation* (Aldershot: Ashgate).

Horowitz, S.A. and U. Heo, eds (2001), *The Political Economy of International Financial Crisis: Interest Groups, Ideologies and Institutions* (Lanham, MD: Rowman & Littlefield).

James, H. (1996), *International Monetary Cooperation Since Bretton Woods* (New York and Oxford: IMF and Oxford University Press).

Jensen, N.M. (2004), "Crisis, Conditions and Capital: The Effect of International Monetary Fund Agreements on Foreign Direct Investment Inflows," *Journal of Conflict Resolution* 48(2): 194–210.

Kahler, M. (1993), "Bargaining with the IMF: Two-Level Strategies and Developing Countries," in P. Evans, H. Jacobson and R. Putnam, eds, *Double-edged Diplomacy: International Bargaining and Domestic Politics* (Berkeley and Los Angeles, CA: University of California Press), pp. 363–94.

Kaminsky, G. and C. Reinhart (1998), "The Twin Crises: The Causes of Banking and Balance of Payment Problems," *American Economic Review* 89(3): 473–500.

Kapur, D. (1998), "The IMF: A Cure or a Curse?" *Foreign Policy* 111 (Summer): 114–29.

Kindleberger, C.P. (1978), *Manias, Panics and Crashes: A History of Financial Crises* (New York: John Wiley & Sons).

Kirton, J. (2002), "Consensus and Coherence in G7 Financial Governance," in M. Fratrianni, P. Savona and J. Kirton, eds, *Governing Global Finance: New Challenges, G7 and IMF Contribution* (Aldershot: Ashgate), pp. 45–74.

Lebang, D.A. (2003), "To Devalue or Defend? The Political Economy of Exchange Rate Policy," *International Studies Quarterly* 47: 533–59.

MacIntyre, A. (2001), "Institutions and Investors: The Politics of the Economic Crisis in Southeast Asia," *International Organization*, 55(1): 81–122.

Morris, S. and H.S. Shin (1998), "Unique Equilibrium in a Model of Self-fulfilling Currency Attacks," *American Economic Review* 88(3): 587–97.

Obstfeld, M. (1996), "Models of Currency Crisis with Self-Fulfilling Features," *European Economic Review* 40(3): 1,037–47.

Pesenti, P. and Tille, C. (2000), "The Economics of Currency Crises and Contagion: An Introduction," *Economic Policy Review, Federal Reserve Bank of New York* 6(3): 3–16.

Przeworski, A. and J. Vreeland (2000), "The Effect of IMF Programs on Economic Growth," *Journal of Development Economics* 62(2): 385–421.

Rose, A.K. (2001), "Discussion," *Economic Policy* 16(32): 75–7

Ruggie, J.G. (1983), "International Regimes, Transaction and Change: Embedded Liberalism in the Postwar Economic Order," in S.D. Krasner, ed., *International Regimes* (Ithaca, NY: Cornell University Press).

Simone, A. (2002), *Essays on Contagion of Financial Crises* (Los Angeles, CA: University of California Press).

Thacker, S. (1999), "The High Politics of IMF Lending," *World Politics* 52(1): 38–75.

Vreeland, J.R. (2002), "Pakistan's Debt of Gratitude," *Foreign Policy* (129): 72–3

Vreeland, J.R. (2005), "The International and Domestic Politics of IMF Programs," working paper (Hartford, CT: Department of Political Science, Yale University).

Wade, R.H. (2002), "US Hegemony and the World Bank: The Fight over People and Ideas," *Review of International Political Economy* 9(2): 215–28.

"What Went Wrong: Wall Street's Crisis" (2002), Special Report on the Financial Crisis. *The Economist* March 22–28.

Williamson, J. (1993), "Democracy and the 'Washington Consensus,'" *World Development* 21(8): 1,329–36.

Yusoff, M. and M. Zulkhibri Abdul Majid (2000), "ASEAN Currency Crises and Contagion Effects," *Asia Pacific Journal of Economics and Business* 4(2): 22–34.

Chapter 5
Finance and Development Compliance in the G8: The IMF and World Bank Role

John Kirton, Nikolai Roudev and Laura Sunderland

Do the world's major powers keep the international commitments they make? This central question of international relations has long been met with skeptical answers on many fronts. Realist scholars of international relations since Thucydides have argued that in an anarchic international system, where the strong do what they want while the weak do what they must, international institutions and commitments are only instruments through which the smart and the strong bind the stupid and the weak. Liberal institutionalist scholars, especially in their recent "legalization" phase, argue that international regimes and their principles, norms, rules and decision-making procedures do make an autonomous difference in how relative power relationships are converted into the behavior of even strong states, particularly when those regimes and their commitments are equipped with high levels of precision, obligation and delegation (Krasner 1983, Abbott et al. 2000, Ikenberry 2001). They look at the Group of Seven (G7) and now Eight (G8) Summit of major market democracies as having the lowest levels of possible precisions, obligations and delegations, implying that promises made there are unlikely to become promises kept (Abbott et al. 2000). They thus join a great array of G8 watchers and governors who claim that the G8 is merely a "photo op," a global "hot tub party" or a "country club," and certainly not a directoire that makes decisions that its members subsequently put into effect. A more recent generation of constructivist scholars, however, suggests that such intense direct communication among members of a small elite club can make a difference in how the otherwise isolated and individual members change and construct their conceptions of interests, and even their identity itself (Wendt 1999).

The evidence suggests that G8 governance does make a difference for its members, and thus for the global community as a whole. Since its 1975 start, the G7/8's global governance performance has embraced not just the photo op function of domestic political management by the leaders for their audiences back home, nor only the global hot tub party or country club function of deliberation to increase information, transparency, trust and the avoidance of accidental conflicts that no one wants. Rather, it has extended to the directional function of setting new principles and norms, the decisional function of collectively creating new rules or commitments, delivering on these commitments through the compliance of its members and creating new decision making procedures by developing G8-centered global governance through G8 institutions of its own. Indeed, as Appendix 5A indicates, the number of commitments made at the annual summit has risen from a mere 14 at the first such gathering (among the original six members) in 1975 to 329 at the 2007 Heiligendamm Summit (among the nine members, including the European Union [EU]). Equally striking, over these 34 years, members' compliance with these commitments has also risen, both for the group overall and for its most powerful member, the United States (see Appendices 5A, 5B and 5C).

What explains this rising compliance with commitments crafted in such an informal institution that has no legal charter or secretariat, that meets only once a year, and that was co-founded by and contains the United States, which was thought by many to have become even more hyper-hegemonic and unilateralist in the post-Cold War, rapidly globalizing, post-September 11 world? Despite a wealth of analysis over the past decade and a half, scholars of the G8 have no convincing solution to this puzzle. The founding generation of G8 compliance scholars, George von Furstenberg and Joseph Daniels, offered only causal conjectures rather than conclusions (von Furstenberg 1995, von Furstenberg and Daniels 1991, 1992b, Daniels 1993). Ella Kokotsis later offered a "democratic institutionalist" model, but it arose only from an analysis of the compliance behavior of two countries, the US and Canada, over four issue areas during the eight years from 1988 to 1995 (Kokotsis 1999, Kokotsis and Daniels 1999). Subsequently, the G8 Research Group's data bank of member compliance with the G7/8's priority commitments from 1996 onward has been analyzed by John Kirton and his colleagues through the "concert equality" model constructed to explain the G8's governance performance overall (Kirton and Kokotsis 2003, 2004, Kirton, Kokotsis and Juricevic 2002, 2003, Kirton et al. 2004). But while the model satisfactorily explains most dimensions of G8 performance, it fails to explain compliance equally well.

One possible cause of this failure is that the concert equality model concentrates on structural variables from the international system while extending to international institutional features of the G8 and domestic political forces within the member states. It omits the individual agency of G8 leaders themselves, acting face to face at their annual summits. This is an important omission for an international institution that not only generates commitments in the name of the leaders, but also publicly issues and approves them by leaders directly at their annual summits. These commitments are often crafted by leaders, with varying degrees of engagement, in face-to-face diplomacy during their summits, as well as by their deliberately named "personal representatives" (or sherpas) during the year before. This particular leader-delivered and directed decision-making procedure is central to an international institution that was created by and for leaders who rejected the highly legalized, hard law, multilateral organizations (MOs) replete with charters and secretariats that had all failed so spectacularly in the crisis-ridden world of 1970–75 (Putnam and Bayne 1984, 1987).

To explain G8 compliance satisfactorily, this chapter addresses this "absent agency" omission by constructing and testing a more comprehensive, multi-level model of the causes of G8 compliance. It begins with agency, examining how the G8 leaders at their summit deliberatively craft their commitments in ways that embed "compliance catalysts" designed to improve the chances that the commitment will be complied with in the following year. It then explores how a particular institutional characteristic of the G8 – the presence of a G8-centered ministerial institution – may reinforce the leaders' commitments and improve compliance with them as a result. It finally adds systemic structure – in the form of both vulnerability and capability – to determine whether agency and institutional forces act autonomously, or are overwhelmed by systemic structure, in causing G8 promises made to become G8 promises kept.

The analysis focuses on the field of finance and development, which most see as the core agenda and very *raison d'être* of the G7/8 summit. In this field, there has been a dedicated ministerial institution which has operated from even before the start of the summits, and where individual government agents can be expected to make little autonomous difference in a market-driven domain. This is especially the case in the rapidly globalizing world since 1996, where finance outcomes have been left to flourishing market forces while governments have concentrated on the rising terrorist threat. Finance and its development-related matters are thus a "hard" test of the importance of agency and institutions in explaining rising G8 compliance since 1996.

This analysis concludes that agency matters, and that institution and structure do too. More specifically, when leaders at their summit embed their finance commitments with a specific timetable – a deadline for completion, and with a priority placement – placing the commitment front and center in their declaration, greater compliance is likely to arise. Pre-summit year commitment (when the ministers make the commitment first and the leaders later reconfirm it) and post-summit year reaffirmation (when ministers reaffirm their intention to keep their leaders' commitment) by G7/8 finance ministers raises compliance too. However, structural changes in vulnerability and capability by themselves do not.

In order to generate these conclusions, this chapter first charts the record of rising member compliance with G7/8 summit commitments from 1975 to 2008, examining the record by year, by country and by issue area. It then explores the results of the existing efforts to explain compliance, from von Furstenberg and Daniels, through Kokotsis, to Kirton. It constructs a multi-level model of agency, institutional and structural factors, and tests it against the G7/8's members' compliance with 42 finance and development commitments from 1996 to 2006. It concludes by identifying important paths for future research and policy change.

The Record of Rising G7/8 Compliance with G8 Commitments

From 1975 to 2008, the G7 and now G8 summits have become increasingly effective in constraining the actions of their members, including the most powerful United States, as judged by the performance of the members in complying with the major concrete, future-oriented commitments they collectively encode in the annual summit statements, declarations and communiqués. Although direct comparisons over time are difficult to make due to the different conceptions of compliance and methodologies employed, the overall pattern is clear.[1]

The Initial Record of 1975–89

The original study by George von Furstenberg and Joseph Daniels was based on the G7's 209 communiqué-encoded economic and energy commitments from 1975 to 1989. Three findings stand out.[2]

First, commitments matter, even if not very much. As Daniels puts it: "Testing the hypothesis of zero average credibility for all 209 commitments together shows that the undertakings had some predictive content. However, the summit undertakings fall well short of complete or full compliance, with an average score of only .310" (Daniels 1993: 276). However, an achievement of +31 percent, on the 200-point compliance scale ranging from -100 percent to +100 percent, makes summits worth doing. Still, as Appendices 5A and 5B show, there is little trend toward rising compliance over these years. The highest scores calculated by von Furstenberg and Daniels came in 1979 (+82 percent) and in 1987 (+93 percent) and the lowest in 1988 (-48 percent).

Second, compliance varies widely by issue area, as shown in Appendix 5D. It ranges from +73 percent for trade to -70 percent for foreign exchange rates. The classic finance and related development areas are those where the least compliance comes. From an inductive perspective, at the ministerial level compliance thus seems to be harmed by the G5 (France, Germany, Japan, the UK and the US) finance ministers' forum operating from 1973 to 1986 (when it became the G7), but helped by the advent of the stand-alone trade ministers' quadrilateral in 1982.

Third, compliance also varies widely by participating country, as shown too in Appendix 5D. Britain and Canada lead the list as high compliers, while the US and especially France stand at the bottom. None the less, the compliance of all country members comes in the positive range. Inductively, two potential causes of compliance variation arise. Realist scholars of international relations would note

1 In addition to the three major compliance studies discussed herein, assessments of compliance with G8 commitments include Baliamoune (2000), Barnes (1994), Buxton (1992), US Climate Action Network and Climate Network Europe (1995), Ikenberry (1988), Labonte and Schrecker (2004, 2005), Labonte et al. (2002, 2004, 2005a, 2005b), Schrecker and Labonte (2007) and Halifax Initiative (1996).

2 In evaluating these findings, several points are worth keeping in mind. First, it may take longer than a year to comply for some kinds of governments and with some kinds of commitments. Second, some countries might comply in advance. Third, it may be easier for some countries if they get the commitments they want or have already complied with. Fourth, this assumes a decisional summit (per Putnam and Bayne 1987) with hard if fuzzy decisions. On compliance with international commitments in general, see Chayes and Chayes (1993, 1995), Chayes and Mitchell (1995) and Koremenos (1996).

that the strongest member, the US, complies the second least, while the weakest, Canada, complies the second most. Scholars of comparative politics would note that the presidential systems of the US and France comply the least, and the classic parliamentary systems of Canada and Britain the most.

The Rising Record of 1988–95

The second generation of G7/8 compliance studies come from Ella Kokotsis. She examined the compliance of the US and Canada with G7 leaders' commitments in the areas of the environment (climate change and biodiversity) and finance and development (financial assistance to the former Soviet Union and debt relief of the poorest) between 1988 and 1995. Three patterns stand out.

First, compliance was generally positive, with an overall compliance score of +39.3 percent (Kokotsis 1999, Kokotsis and Kirton 1997). This is a notable rise from the +31 percent of the earlier period. Moreover, compliance varied by year, but with a sharp rising trend over the seven years. The steady rise from -50 percent in 1989 to +100 percent in 1995 suggested that the advent of post-Cold War "unipolarity" and early globalization had a strong compliance-inducing effect.

Second, compliance varied by issue area. There were very high levels of compliance in assistance to the former Soviet Union. High compliance also came in debt relief for the poorest. It was lower for the environmental issue areas of climate change and biodiversity. In a striking reversal of the 1975–89 pattern, compliance in the formerly high energy-related area of climate change was low, but in the formerly low area of finance, compliance was now high. This reversal points to the potential potency of structural vulnerabilities and shocks – the energy shocks of 1973 and 1979 versus the invisible cumulative onset of climate change, and the surprising, dramatic, sharp collapse of the USSR. It also implies that an institutional variable – the common purpose of global democratization – may have some causal force.

Third, compliance again varied by country, with Canada at +53 percent and the US at +34 percent. This is a particularly high level for Canada, and a sharp rise in US compliance from the previous era. The US rise, and thus Canadian–US convergence at a higher level, is particularly strong in the field of finance. Here, across both the previously prevailing East–West (the former Soviet Union) and North–South (debt relief) divides, the G7 was now generating commitments that counted and constrained the US administrations (of Republican George W. Bush and Democrat Bill Clinton alike).

The Rapidly Rising Record of 1996–2005

Evidence for the most recent period since 1996 comes from the University of Toronto's G8 Research Group (see Appendix 5D). It has assessed for each of these years the compliance record of the G7/8 members with the priority commitments identified in the summit documents, using the Kokotsis methodology employed from 1988 to 1995. Again, three major patterns stand out.

First, overall annual average compliance between 1996 and 2008 averaged +47.2 percent. This is higher than the +39.3 percent from 1988 to 1995, and rises across all countries and issue areas. Moreover, as Appendices 5A and 5B show, all these annual summits score in the positive range, as they have since 1990. Moreover, there is a notable twenty-first-century rise, with all summits since 2000 (save for 2002) coming in above the average (as they had from 1992 to 1995).

Second, compliance varied widely by issue area. For the 1996–2000 summits taken together, even before the shock of 9/11, compliance was highest in the political-security domain at +67 percent (including traditional East–West relations, terrorism, arms control, regional security and conflict prevention). This is followed by the core economic sector at +37 percent, which is followed by global/transnational issues at +34 percent. At the bottom comes global governance (focused on reform of the United Nations) at +14 percent. From 1996 to 2008, in the old field of energy, compliance averaged +79 percent. From 1998 to 2006, in the newer field of health, it averaged +54 percent.

Third, from 1996 to 2008, compliance also varied widely by country. Canada continued to lead with +66 percent and Britain came in second with +65 percent. The EU came in third with +57 percent, and the US in fourth with +56 percent. Germany was fifth with +51 percent, followed by France with +49 percent and Japan with +41 percent. Falling below the G8 average were Italy with +28 percent and Russia with +19 percent. From 2003 onward, as the US moved into, through and from its hosting at Sea Island in 2004, US relative compliance rose to first place in 2007. This suggests that George W. Bush's allegedly unilateralist, "hyper-hegemonic" America was being constrained by the G8 and the particular institutional force of serving as its host. And the tentative evidence suggests this is not because the annual G8 summit commits to whatever the US wants and announces in its State of the Union address at the start of a summit year (Juricevic 2000a, 2000b).

Causes of G8 Compliance: The Existing Explanations

What explains this composite pattern of generally rising compliance with G8 commitments since 1989, across all issue areas and countries, including the most powerful United States? None of the existing explanations offers a convincing or even adequate account.

Von Furstenberg and Daniels offered only conjectures rather than a casual model to interpret their data, but in doing so ruled out the realist relative capability as a relevant cause. Subsequent analysis of their data set by Quan Li (2001) found that compliance with inflation control commitments was correlated positively with the interstate-level variable of reciprocating behavior (as rationalist scholars of international relations would predict) and negatively with the domestic level variables of divided/coalition governments and uncertainty.

To interpret her data from 1985 to 1995, and subsequently beyond, Ella Kokotsis offered a democratic institutionalist model (Kokotsis 1995, 1999, 2004, Kokotsis and Kirton 1997, Kirton and Kokotsis 2001). To account for high US and Canadian compliance in the finance field, Kokotsis examined one international institutional cause – the strong MOs of the International Monetary Fund (IMF) and World Bank (where both countries are permanent members of an Executive Board collectively controlled by the G7) – and several domestic-level factors. Those factors include strong and G7-focused ministers of finance; and the domestic popularity, political control and personal commitment of democratically elected leaders to the G8 as an institution and the particular commitments it generates. Yet many of these individual causes have been weak, even as compliance performance generally climbed from 1989.

Moreover, the democratic institutionalist model was silent on two critical causes. The first, from the realm of individual agency, is how leaders consciously use their existing political capital and personal commitments at the summit to "lock in" their own and other countries' compliance with those commitments during the subsequent year(s). They do so knowing that their own political popularity/capital and control might evaporate and domestic institutional barriers might arise to overwhelm their summit political will. The second, from the realm of international institutions, is how the G8 focus – and even the interdepartmental intra-governmental power of finance ministries (in an era of intense globalization) – is reinforced by their international institutionalization in informal, exclusive, equal clubs of G8 peers. Notable among those groups are the G7/8 finance ministers' forum (meeting three or more times a year since 1998), the G7 deputies, and the larger G20 of systematically significant countries since 1999 (Kirton 2005a, 2005b).

Kirton, subsequently supported by his colleagues, has developed and applied a concert equality model, aimed at explaining G8 governance performance overall (Kirton 1989). The model highlights the structural variables of members' relative vulnerability and capability, the international institutional variables of poor UN-based MO performance, the common purpose and constructed participation of the G8 summit, and the domestic-level variables of political capital and control of G8 leaders at home.

It shared the same two basic deficits as the Kokotsis democratic institutionalist model. First, it did not account convincingly or adequately for G8 compliance, either overall or in the trade field, where von Furstenberg and Daniels discovered very high compliance from 1975 to 1989 (Kirton 2004).

Second, it ignored how the existing growth and operation of G8 sub-summit institutions, both overall and in specific fields, served not just as a part of high G8 governance performance at a single summit, but also as a cause of that performance in subsequent years. Similarly, it ignored how leaders mobilize their political capacities at the summit consciously to craft commitments that will bind them and their partners' polities to comply.

The Record of Compliance with G8 Finance Commitments, 1996–2008

How well and how do these missing causes of leaders' conscious collective agency at the G8 summit itself and their creation, acceptance and use of sub-summit-level G8 institutions help them secure the collective compliance they presumably want? To answer this question, in the light of the G7/8's generally rising compliance record over its 35-year life, it is useful to focus on the post-1996 finance and related development field, where compliance was very low from 1975 to 1989, but rose sharply from 1988 to 1995.

The Record of G8 Compliance with Finance and Related Development Commitments, 1996–2005

To conduct this analysis, a data set of 42 finance-related commitments, for which compliance scores exist, was assembled largely from the G8 Research Group's data bank of compliance assessments on priority commitments assembled from 1996 to 2004 (see Appendix 5F). The issue area was defined broadly as including all commitments where core G7 finance ministers' competences were involved. It thus also embraced (at least some) commitments on exchange rates, macroeconomics, microeconomics, debt relief, development, international financial institutions (IFI) and UN reform, health, terrorism (for terrorist finance), Africa, economic growth, world economy, crime and drugs (money laundering and Financial Action Task Force), but not trade.[3] Several compliance scores were assembled for commitments from each of the nine years from 1996 to 2004, as follows: 1996 = 6, 1997 = 2, 1998 = 2, 1999 = 4, 2000 = 3, 2001 = 5, 2002 = 4, 2003 = 7 and 2004 = 9. The compliance scores ranged from a low of -100 percent (for three) to a high of +100 percent (for eight), with an overall average for the 42 commitments of +48 percent (as against an overall average G8 average, across all issue areas for these years of +43 percent). Over the ten years, the data show a rising trend of +18 percent from 1996 to 2000, +32 percent in 2001 and +43 percent from 2002 to 2004 (perhaps reflecting the effect of the financial and terrorist shocks of 1997–2001).

In 2005, at the Gleneagles Summit on July 6–8, a further ten finance commitments were produced. Their interim (sixth-month) compliance scores range from 0 percent (for HIPC debt relief) to +100 percent for peace in the Middle East. The average interim score for these ten is +42 percent.

3 More formally, finance includes all commitments with references to international financial institutions, development, economic growth, official development assistance, debt relief and heavily indebted poor countries (HIPCs), any time money is committed, and any time finance or finance ministers are mentioned.

To construct the dependant variable of financial compliance in a way that best captures the concept of conscious compliance, the compliance scores of the 42 finance commitments from 1996 to 2004 were converted into "adjusted compliance" scores that represent the difference between compliance with an individual finance commitment and the summit's overall priority commitment compliance score for that year. Here it is assumed that overall forces cause overall compliance, whereas what is of interest, and needs to be isolated, is how conscious finance-focused agency and international institutional behavior drive compliance with finance commitments above or below that summit's compliance norm. This adjustment highlights the Okinawa 2000 anomaly, for while that summit had very high compliance overall, its finance compliance was unusually low. One inductive conjecture for why this may be the case points to the institutionalization of the broader G20 finance ministers forum, which started mobilizing in the Fall of 1999 and sprang into sustained life at Montreal in the Fall of 2000. Another, structural-based, conjecture from the realm of the new vulnerability is the dot.com-fuelled stock market crash that began at the start of 2001.

Causes of Compliance with G8 Finance Commitments: Agency Assessed

Are these rising and high finance compliance scores caused at all by the conscious action of the agents who write them – the leaders at the summit itself and their personal representatives who work over the previous year to craft them in their leaders' names? Recent work suggests that leaders can embed "compliance catalysts" in their health commitments in ways that lead to the desired higher compliance over the following year (Kirton and Kokotsis 2007). But beyond the newer G8 field of health, can they do so in the field of finance, where private markets allegedly dominate at least the leaders' assumptions in determining outcomes in the intensely globalizing years since 1996 (Bergsten and Henning 1996)?

To answer this question, each of the 42 finance compliance cases was coded to see whether its commitment contained one or more of the eight compliance catalysts that G8 leaders at the summit can consciously embed into their commitment in order to increase its chances of compliance success (see Appendix 5F).

Of these eight, a linear multiple regression analysis suggests that two have an impact in the desired way. First, an estimate of the full unrestricted model showed that setting a timetable for completion had a strong positive effect (significant at the 95 percent confidence level), improving compliance by 0.42 points. The optimal restricted model, with only a timetable and a control for the 2000 anomaly noted above, explained more than 29 percent of the variation in compliance. Second, priority placement also had a strong effect (significant at the 90 percent confidence level) in improving compliance in the full unrestricted model. But in a restricted model controlling for the 2000 anomaly, it accounted for only 8 percent of the variation in the dependent variable.

One further finding deserves comment. In the unrestricted model, the presence of a G8 body had a negative impact on compliance (significant at the 90 percent confidence level). To be sure, this result disappears when the 2000 anomaly is removed. But it raises the suspicion, long held by skeptics of the institutionalization of the summit, that the creation of sub-summit bodies distracts from G8 summit performance, presumably by allowing leaders to count on someone other than themselves to ensure that their previous public summit promises are actually kept.

Causes of Compliance with G8 Finance Commitments: International Institutionalization Investigated

Can leaders or their finance ministers improve compliance, not by merely creating G8 sub-summit institutions, but by actively employing them each year to assist with compliance with the summit commitments the leaders create?

To answer this hitherto empirically unexplored question, each finance commitment was coded to determine whether and how often it was repeated by G7/8 finance ministers as a commitment in essentially the same form in the year surrounding the summit itself. Three forms of "repeated commitment" were coded. The first, recommitment, covers the calendar year within which the summit occurred (usually at the summer mid-point). This allows ministers to assist their leaders in that summit's preparation and implementation phase. The second is pre-commitment, covering the full chronological year prior to the summit, during which ministers can take ownership of, ripen and shape, or even create a commitment for the leaders to merely endorse (at times without any conscious action or attention) at the summit itself. The third is post-affirmation, covering the full chronological year after the summit, during which ministers, through reaffirmation, reinforce the pressures for compliance, ride in to rescue commitments where compliance is in trouble, or politely repeat as a ritual their leader's mantra as a courtesy while they proceed to do their own thing in a fast-changing world.

None of these repeated commitments appears to have a significant impact on the standard compliance scores. A stepwise selection of the best-nested restricted model (using the AIC for optimization) did suggest that the more general measure of the number of ministerial documents in the year of and after the summit (noting essentially the same commitment) were slightly significant in improving compliance scores, but not at standard social science confidence levels.

However, the use of mean-adjusted compliance as the dependent variable (again with the use of an AIC-based stepwise selection of the best restricted model) produced several strong results. All six institutional causes, as specific repeated commitments or more general documentary mentions, are significant, although both recommitments and re-documents have negative effects on compliance. The latter findings suggest that same-year ministerial repetition may have more of a rescue and ritual function than a reinforcement one. The message seems to be that if G8 finance ministers want to boost compliance with their leaders' finance commitments at the summit, they should start to prepare them very early, immediately after the previous summit, and act to complement them very late – as compliers of last resort – in the six months before the subsequent summit takes place.

When the agency and institutional causal candidates are considered together, there are several strong results. With mean-adjusted compliance as the dependent variable, and again using an AIC-based objective stepwise selection procedure for the best nested model, agency and institutional causes together account for more than 32 percent of the variance in mean-adjusted financial commitment compliance. In contrast, a restricted agency-only model explained just 18 percent of the variance. Its institutionalization-only equivalent accounted for a little under 20 percent of the variation in mean-adjusted compliance.

In some composite models that were attempted, all five regressors (save for the control variables of total catalysts and re-documents) are significant at or above the 95 percent confidence level. In the realm of agency, the presence of a priority placement catalyst in a finance commitment increases compliance, all else equal, by 0.5132 points. Its timetable equivalent does so by 0.6381 points. Institutional causes emerge even more strongly: the effects of the pre-commitment, post-affirmation and recommitment variables on mean-adjusted compliance are +1.74599, +1.5507 and -2.0910 points, respectively.

The overall message is clear. To improve compliance with their summit financial commitments, leaders should give them priority placement and set a timetable for their completion, while finance ministers should act supportively during the six months before and six months after the summit year, but leave the leaders alone to do their own thing during the summit year itself.

Causes of Compliance with G8 Finance Commitments: System Structure Surveyed

How well do these conclusions and the supporting evidence survive when changes in the structure of the international system are taken into account? While leaders' conscious action as agents and that of their supporting ministers through their G7/8 institutions seem to control their own delivery destiny, at least partly during the past decade, in doing so are they merely responding unknowingly to more powerful forces from the structure of the international system? And can the leaders at the summit, and their ministers before and after, act amidst alternative structural configurations to secure the compliance they seek?

To address these questions, six structural causal candidates were added to the regression model. Three were for the vulnerability that creates a demand for G8 domestic political management, deliberation, direction-setting, decision making (commitment), delivery (compliance) and the development of G8 governance (institutionalization). They include the "old" intended, targeted state-to-state vulnerability (Keohane and Nye 1977) and the "new" often unintended, undirected, transnational but still deadly and threatening vulnerabilities which the onset of globalization has fuelled (Kirton 1993).

Three variables are for supply-side capability, centered on the realists' reliable concept of relative capability among the major powers. The focus is on both overall capability and issue structure (Keohane and Nye 1977). In both cases, in keeping with the concert equality model and its evidence of why the G8 succeeds in all but the compliance function, attention is directed at the equalizing relative capability among individual G8 members and the collective predominance of the G8 collectively, relative to the international system as a whole.

To transform the annual variations in vulnerability and capability into commitment-specific data, the scores for the chronological year following the summit were assembled for each of the structural variables in a panel matrix (see Appendix 5G). The three most relevant structural variables were selected for each commitment, and the average score of the structural variables selected for each commitment was then converted into a single commitment-specific composite structural score.

Three major conclusions emerged from the analysis of the effect of this structural data. First, a decrease in US relative capability and/or an increase in common G7/8 vulnerability increases pre-commitment scores. That is, a combination of growing vulnerability of the G8 collectively and/or equalizing capability among members within the G8 inspires G8 finance ministers to pre-commit in support of their heads. G8 ministers thus act rationally (and presciently) as the first responders in reacting to changes in financial vulnerability and capability in the world. In the bivariate regression model with pre-commitment scores as the dependent variable, the effects of the US relative capability and common G7/8 vulnerability variables are strong and statistically significant at the standard 95 percent social science confidence levels. Second, structural vulnerability and capability similarly increase recommitment scores, once again in a strong and statistically significant way. G8 finance ministers thus retain their reinforcing rational first responder role throughout the summit year.

Third, and most important, is the conclusion that the introduction of these structural variables into the restricted and unrestricted catalyst models discussed above does not alter the findings in any significant way. That is, changes in structural vulnerability and capability by themselves have no direct impact on compliance. Only agency and institutionalization do. Structure matters only (albeit strongly) in spurring pre-commitment and recommitment. And, as seen above, of these, only pre-commitment (along with post-affirmation operating autonomously) directly connects with compliance, and does so in a positive way. Thus compliance is largely endogenous to the G8; it is driven by agency and institutionalization, and is not affected directly by global structural change.

Conclusion

As seen in previous studies, changes in structural vulnerability and capability have a powerful direct effect on driving high G8 performance in the deliberative, direction-setting and decisional domains, just as the concert equality model of G8 governance predicts. But these strong structural forces and the concert equality model that starts with them uniquely fail in driving the G8 system to deliver on those decisions the year after they are made. It is now clear why.

Structural forces at the international level do not directly push the complex, historically embedded political systems of G8 members to comply with the commitments that are produced at the annual summit. Only the individual leaders and finance ministers (in each case acting collectively and consciously) can do that. G8 agency and institutionalization cause compliance. Structural forces matter only in inspiring one of several compliance-creating institutional factors (pre-commitment) to increase. In short, increasing vulnerability and internal equality may cause G8 leaders to make promises at their summit. But only they alone, with help from their finance ministers, can transform them into promises kept.

These findings point to a rich agenda for future research. The first task is to add these agency and institutionalization variables to the concert equality, democratic institutionalism and other models to see if they improve their power in explaining G8 performance across all six functional domains. The second is to explore whether iteration – the leaders' own recommitment at successive summits – increases compliance, as some claim (Bayne 1999). A third task is to delve deeper into the murky world of sub-summit institutions to see whether repeated commitment or other actions by G8 official-level bodies have the same compliance-inducing effect as the ministerial-level body does. The fourth is to see whether these findings in the finance field apply to other issue areas, and to the G8's compliance performance overall.

In the mean time, G8 leaders can work, alone and together, to increase their compliance through several means. At the summits, leaders can inject more priority placement and timetables into their finance commitments, rather than shying away from the subject altogether, as they have tended to do in recent years. G8 finance ministers can recognize their role as starters and closers, and leave the middle innings (spanning the summit year) to the leaders themselves. And both leaders and ministers can work together to find better ways to use the structural forces that cause G8 finance ministers to recommit in reinforcing ways during the summit year. The leaders can also work to craft commitments in meaningful ways at the summit, as it is their agency alone that causes compliance during the summit year. The Birmingham formula of separating finance ministers from their leaders at the summit, and having G7/8 finance ministers meet largely on the margins of the International Monetary Fund and World Bank gatherings, could well require a rethink. It may even be appropriate to welcome the initiative of the Russians in adding a stand-alone G8 finance ministers meeting in early January, designed for no other purpose than to prepare the summit itself.

Bibliography

Abbott, Kenneth W., Robert Keohane, Andrew Moravcsik, Anne-Marie Slaughter and Duncan Snidal (2000), "The Concept of Legalization," *International Organization* 54(3): 401–20.

Baliamoune, Mina (2000), "Economics of Summitry: An Empirical Assessment of the Economic Effects of Summits," *Empirica* 27: 295–314.

Barnes, James (1994), *Promise, Promises: A Review – G7 Economic Summit Declarations on Environment and Development* (Washington, DC: Friends of the Earth).

Bayne, Nicholas (1999), "Continuity and Leadership in an Age of Globalisation," in M.R. Hodges, J.J. Kirton and J.P. Daniels, eds, *The G8's Role in the New Millennium* (Aldershot: Ashgate), pp. 21–44.

Bergsten, C. Fred and C. Randall Henning (1996), *Global Economic Leadership and the Group of Seven* (Washington, DC: Institute for International Economics).

Buxton, G.V. (1992), "Sustainable Development and the Summit: A Canadian Perspective on Progress," *International Journal* XLVII(4) (Fall): 776–95.

Chayes, Abram and Antonia Handler Chayes (1993), "On Compliance," *International Organization* 47 (Spring): 175–205.

Chayes, Abram and Antonia Handler Chayes (1995), *The New Sovereignty: Compliance with International Regulatory Agreements* (Cambridge, MA: Harvard University Press).

Chayes, Abram and Ronald. B. Mitchell (1995), "Improving Compliance with the Climate Change Treaty," in Henry Lee, ed., *Shaping National Responses to Climate Change: A Post-Rio Guide* (Washington, DC: Island Press).

Daniels, Joseph (1993), *The Meaning and Reliability of Economic Summit Undertakings* (Hamden, CT: Garland Publishing).

G8 Research Group (1996–), Annual Compliance Studies, available at <http://www.g8.utoronto.ca/compliance/>.

Halifax Initiative (1996), *First Annual G7 Report Card on Bretton Woods Reform: Report on the Commitments Made by the G7 Leaders at the Halifax Summit, June 1995* (Ottawa: Canadian Coalition for Global Economic Democracy).

Ikenberry, John (1988), "Market Solutions for State Problems: The International and Domestic Politics of American Oil Decontrol," *International Organization* 42 (Winter): 151–78.

Ikenberry, John (2001), *After Victory: Institutions, Strategic Restraint and the Rebuilding of Order after Major Wars* (Princeton, NJ: Princeton University Press).

Juricevic, Diana (2000a), *Compliance with G8 Commitments: Ascertaining the Degree of Compliance with Summit Debt and International Trade Commitments for Canada and the United States 1996–1999*, available at <http://www.g8.utoronto.ca/scholar/juricevic2000/index.html>.

Juricevic, Diana (2000b), *Controlling for Domestic-Level Commitments: An Analysis of the Authoritative National Commitments Made in Canada and the United States from 1995–2000*, available at <http://www.g87.utoronto.ca/scholar/juricevic2000/juricevic.pdf>.

Keohane, Robert and Joseph Nye (1977), *Power and Interdependence: World Politics in Transition* (Boston, MA: Little, Brown).

Kirton, John (1989), "Contemporary Concert Diplomacy: The Seven-Power Summit and the Management of International Order," paper prepared for the Annual Meeting of the International Studies Association, London, available at <http://www.g8.utoronto.ca/scholar/kirton198901>.

Kirton, John (1993), "The Seven Power Summits as a New Security Institution," in D. Dewitt, D. Haglund and J.J. Kirton, eds, *Building a New Global Order: Emerging Trends in International Security* (Toronto: Oxford University Press), pp. 335–57.

Kirton, John (2004), "Explaining G8 Effectiveness: A Concert of Vulnerable Equals in a Globalizing World," paper prepared for the 45th Annual Convention of the International Studies Association, Montreal, available at <http://www.g8.utoronto.ca/scholar/kirton2004/kirton_isa_040304.pdf>.

Kirton, John (2005a), "From G7 to G20: Capacity, Leadership and Normative Diffusion in Global Financial Governance," paper prepared for a panel on "Expanding Capacity and Leadership in Global Financial Governance: From G7 to G20," at the International Studies Association Annual Convention, Hawaii, available at <http://www.g8.utoronto.ca/scholar/kirton2005/kirton_isa2005.pdf>.

Kirton, John (2005b), "Toward Multilateral Reform: The G20's Contribution," in Andrew F. Cooper, John English and Ramesh Thakur, eds, *Reforming from the Top: A Leaders 20 Summit* (Tokyo: United Nations University Press), pp. 141–68.

Kirton, John (2006), "Explaining Compliance with G8 Finance Commitments: Agency, Institutionalization and Structure," *Open Economies Review* 17 (November): 459–75.

Kirton, John, ed. (2009a), *Global Finance* (Aldershot: Ashgate).

Kirton, John, ed. (2009b), *International Law* (Aldershot: Ashgate).

Kirton, John, ed. (2009c), *International Organization* (Aldershot: Ashgate).

Kirton, John and Ella Kokotsis (2001), "Compliance with G8 Commitments: The Peace and Security and Conflict Prevention Agenda, Okinawa-Genoa," paper prepared for the Department of Foreign Affairs and International Trade's Policy Planning Division in Preparation for the Canadian Presidency of the G8 Foreign Ministers' Process in 2002.

Kirton, John and Ella Kokotsis (2003), "Producing International Commitments and Compliance without Legalization: G7/8 Performance from 1975 to 2002," paper prepared for the Annual Convention of the International Studies Association, Portland, OR, available at <http://www.g8.utoronto.ca/scholar/kirton2003/KirtonPortland2003.pdf>.

Kirton, John and Ella Kokotsis (2004), "Keeping Faith with Africa: Assessing Compliance with the G8's Commitments at Kananaskis and Evian," in

Princeton Lyman and Robert Browne, eds, *Freedom, Prosperity and Security: The G8 Partnership with Africa* (New York: Council on Foreign Relations).
Kirton, John and Ella Kokotsis (2007), "Keeping Faith with Africa's Health: Catalyzing G8 Compliance," in John Kirton, Andrew Cooper and Ted Schrecker, eds, *Governing Global Health: Challenge, Response, Innovation* (Aldershot: Ashgate).
Kirton, John, Ella Kokotsis and Diana Juricevic (2002), "Okinawa's Promises Kept: The 2001 G8 Compliance Report," in John Kirton and Junichi Takase, eds, *New Directions in Global Political Governance* (Aldershot: Ashgate), pp. 269–80.
Kirton, John, Ella Kokotsis and Diana Juricevic (2003), "G7/G8 Commitments and Their Significance," in John Kirton, Michele Fratianni and Paola Savona, eds, *Governing Global Finance: New Challenges, G7 and IMF Contributions* (Aldershot: Ashgate), pp. 227–31.
Kirton, John, Ella Kokotsis, Gina Stevens with Diana Juricevic (2004), "The G8 and Conflict Prevention: Commitment, Compliance and Systemic Contribution," in *The G8, the United Nations and Conflict Prevention* (Aldershot: Ashgate), pp. 59–84.
Kirton, John, Nick Roudev and Laura Sunderland (2007), "Making Major Powers Deliver: Explaining Compliance with G8 Health Commitments, 1996–2006," *Bulletin of the World Health Organization* 85: 192–9.
Kokotsis, Ella (1995), "Keeping Sustainable Development Commitments: The Recent G7 Record," in John Kirton and Sarah Richardson, eds, *The Halifax Summit, Sustainable Development and International Institutional Reform* (Ottawa: National Round Table on the Environment and the Economy), pp. 117–33.
Kokotsis, Ella (1999), *Keeping International Commitments: Compliance, Credibility and the G7, 1988–1995* (New York: Garland).
Kokotsis, Ella (2004), "Explaining G8 Effectiveness: The Democratic Institutionalist Model of Compliance with G8 Commitments," paper prepared for the Annual Convention of the International Studies Association, Montreal, available at <http://www.g8.utoronto.ca/scholar/kokotsis_isa2004.pdf>.
Kokotsis, Ella and Joseph Daniels (1999), "G8 Summits and Compliance," in Michael Hodges and John Kirton, *The G8's Role in the New Millennium* (Aldershot: Ashgate), pp. 75–94.
Kokotsis, Ella and John Kirton (1997), "National Compliance with Environmental Regimes: The Case of the G7, 1988–1995," paper prepared for the Annual Convention of the International Studies Association, Toronto, March 18–22.
Koremenos, Barbara (1996), "On the Duration and Renegotiation of International Agreements," paper prepared for the Annual Convention of the International Studies Association, San Diego, CA, April.
Krasner, Stephen D. (1983), *International Regimes* (Ithaca, NY: Cornell University Press).

Labonte, Ronald and Ted Schrecker (2004), "Committed to Health for All? How the G7/G8 Rate," *Social Science and Medicine* 59: 1,661–76.

Labonte, Ronald and Ted Schrecker (2005), *The G8, Africa and Global Health: A Platform for Global Health Equity for the 2005 Summit* (London: Nuffield Trust), available at <http://www.nuffieldtrust.org.uk/members/download.aspx?f=/ecomm/files/G8+Book.pdf>.

Labonte, Ronald, David Sanders and Ted Schrecker (2002), "Health and Development: How Are the G7/G8 Doing?" *Journal of Epidemiology and Community Health* 56(5): 322, available at <http://www.pubmedcentral.nih.gov/picrender.fcgi?artid=1732149&blobtype=pdf>.

Labonte, Ronald, Ted Schrecker and A. Sen Gupta (2005a), "A Global Health Equity Agenda for the G8 Summit," *British Medical Journal* 330(7490): 533–6.

Labonte, Ronald, Ted Schrecker and D. McCoy (2005b), "Health and HIV/AIDS: Fine Words and Fatal Indifference," in G. Hubbard and D. Miller, eds, *Arguments Against G8* (London: Pluto Press), pp. 182–97.

Labonte, Ronald, Ted Schrecker, David Sanders and W. Meeus (2004), *Fatal Indifference: The G8, Africa and Global Health* (Cape Town: University of Cape Town Press/IDRC Books).

Li, Quan (2001), "Commitment Compliance in G7 Summit Macroeconomic Policy Coordination," *Political Research Quarterly* 54 (June): 355–78.

Payne, Anthony (2008), "The G8 in a Changing Global Economic Order," *International Affairs* 84(3): 519–33.

Putnam, Robert and Nicholas Bayne (1984), *Hanging Together: Co-operation and Conflict in the Seven-Power Summit*, 1st edn (Cambridge MA: Harvard University Press).

Putnam, Robert and Nicholas Bayne, eds (1987), *Hanging Together: Co-operation and Conflict in the Seven-Power Summit*, 2nd edn (London: Sage Publications).

Scherrer, Amandine (2009), *G8 against Transnational Organized Crime* (Aldershot: Ashgate).

Schrecker, Ted and Ronald Labonte (2007), "What's Politics Got to Do with It? Health, the G8 and the Global Economy," in I. Kawachi and S. Wamala, eds, *Globalization and Health* (Oxford: Oxford University Press).

US Climate Action Network and Climate Network Europe (1995), *Independent NGO Evaluations of National Plans for Climate Change Mitigation: G7 Countries – Summit Meeting, Halifax, June 1995*, report coordinated by the United States Climate Action Network and Climate Network Europe.

Von Furstenberg, George (1995), "Accountability and a Metric for Credibility and Compliance," *Journal of Institutional and Theoretical Economics* 151 (June): 304–25.

Von Furstenberg, George and Joseph Daniels (1991), "Policy Undertakings by the Seven 'Summit' Countries: Ascertaining the Degree of Compliance," *Carnegie-Rochester Conference Series of Public Policy* 35: 267–308.

Von Furstenberg, George and Joseph Daniels (1992a), "Can You Trust G7 Promises?" *International Economic Insights* 3 (September/October): 24–7.

Von Furstenberg, George and Joseph Daniels (1992b), *Economic Summit Declarations, 1975–1989: Examining the Written Record of International Co-operation*, Princeton Studies in International Finance 72 (Princeton, NJ: Department of Economics, Princeton University).

Wallace, William (1984), "Political Issues at the Summits: A New Concert of Powers?" in C. Merlini, ed., *Economic Summits and Western Decisionmaking* (London: St. Martin's Press).

Wendt, Alexander (1999), *Social Theory of International Politics* (Cambridge: Cambridge University Press).

PART III
Multilateral Organizations and the G8: Practitioners' Perspectives

Chapter 6

Finance, Macroeconomics and the Multilateral Organization–G8 Connection

Robert Fauver

Since the first Group of Eight (G8) summit in Rambouillet in 1975, there have been significant changes in the substance, style and process of the annual leaders' summits. In the beginning, the annual summits were referred to as "economic summits" by the media and most commentators. That was a fairly accurate description. Now they are no longer focused mainly on economic issues and problems. Summits now include a considerable consideration of non-economic issues. And the membership has grown. What started as an offshoot of the "Library Group" of the Group of Five (G5) finance ministers has now grown to eight plus the European Union (EU), to make the G8 now a group of nine. Foreign ministers and finance ministers are now no longer direct participants in the leaders' meetings.

Various types of communiqués have been issued by the heads of state and government at the annual summits. In some years, the leaders' statements and communiqués have discussed the general state of the world economy. In some years, the leaders have determined that it was appropriate to include in their communiqués specific commitments to change policies at home. Sometimes they have focused on implementing their joint efforts through changes in multilateral organizations (MOs), particularly the financial institutions of the International Monetary Fund (IMF) and the World Bank. In some years, the leaders have chosen a mixture of general statements and specific commitments. And in earlier times, finance and foreign ministers sometimes issued separate statements with specific commitments to change as well.

Over the many years that the summits have been held, one of the most frequently asked questions has been: "Do these summits matter?" An offshoot of this questioning is a consideration of whether or not the leaders follow through on their commitments. One of the most interesting questions about the annual economic summits thus focuses on compliance.

This chapter centers on the role of international institutions in implementing G7/8 commitments. It looks at the role of the IMF and World Bank in implementing the commitments of the G8 summits. It also addresses the more philosophical question of whether or not there should be a role for the MOs. Should the G8 summits task them to take action of any kind? Should the G8 play the role of a directoire for the MOs?

The Early Years

In the early 1970s, the US Treasury Department initiated a project to forecast short-term developments in the world economy. At that time, the IMF had not yet started its annual global forecasts. The project focused on macroeconomic developments – real growth, inflation, unemployment and balance of payments. The global outlook discussion was broken down into individual industrial economies – essentially those of the Organisation for Economic Co-operation and Development (OECD), major individual and some regional groupings of the less-developed countries (LDCs) and the rest of the world (the planned economies of the Soviet Union and China). Group averages were calculated with a focus on the relative performance of the different groups. By studying the individual forecasts and group outlooks, it became possible to judge the consistency of the individual projections. For example, if all individual projections suggested current account surpluses, it became obvious that there were inconsistency of problems in the global outlook.

After considerable effort, the first edition of the Treasury's World Economic Outlook was circulated in the late summer of 1973. It was just in time for the preparations for the Fall IMF meetings. Then, in October 1973, the first oil crisis began, with the embargo of the US and a quadrupling of oil prices by the Organization of Petroleum Exporting Countries (OPEC). It was clear that on this basic function, a better job was needed. The IMF joined the US in the forecasting game.

At the beginning of the G7/8 summit process, the focus was on economic issues. The primary cause of the summit evolved from the recognized need to change the world's foreign exchange regime in the early 1970s. The important devaluing of the dollar following the US abandonment of the dollar's link to gold in August 1971 and the huge instabilities in the international monetary system brought about by the first oil crisis of 1973–74 led to the need for a change in the international monetary system. The shift from the fixed exchange rate regime of the post-war period was legitimized by the G7's Rambouillet Communiqué in 1975. That communiqué set the stage for the formal revision of the Articles of Agreement of the IMF. The revisions allowed for the possibility of flexible or floating exchange rates among the major currencies of the world.

So, at its very beginning, the first summit set out a commitment to revise the rules of operation of the IMF, and hence the international monetary system. Since the IMF undertook the assignment and created through its Interim Committee a revision of the Articles of Agreement, the MOs perfectly implemented the commitments of the summit.

If the first summit was successful and the MOs followed through and implemented the original commitments so perfectly, then the future was destined to go downhill. Complete success cannot be sustained.

What sort of control do the G8 members have over the MOs? To answer, it is useful to remember the operating rules of the IMF. The management of the organization is run on a day-to-day basis by the Executive Board, led by the Managing Director. The executive directors represent "constituencies" of members according to voting shares. Some executive directors represent only one country, such as the US or Japan. The majority of votes are controlled by the major members of the IMF. The original G5 nations control roughly 38 percent of the voting power of the IMF. They thus maintain veto power over major changes in the Articles of Agreement of the body. While they do not control veto power over day-to-day management, they maintain a controlling interest in the organization. Hence, obtaining the IMF's agreement to implement a commitment of the economic summit should be relatively straightforward. The World Bank voting arrangements are virtually identical to those of the IMF, with the G5 nations controlling 37 percent of the voting shares.

While the G8 members do not possess sufficient voting power in the IMF or World Bank to force issues or changes through the institutions, they do carry much weight in the process. And they are able to put items on the agenda for the two executive boards.

The important question to ask about potential implementation is: "do the finance ministries or treasuries support the summit initiative of the leaders?" If the finance ministries do not support the initiative, as is sometimes the case, then very little will come to pass in terms of implementation or compliance.

One such case arose in 1994. The Naples Summit in 1994 set forth a commitment by leaders in the communiqué of which finance ministries were not supportive. The communiqué asked what framework of institutions will be required to meet these challenges in the twenty-first century. How can existing institutions adapt and new institutions be built to ensure the future prosperity and security of our everyone.

This language was not negotiated in advance of the leaders' meetings. Finance ministries did not approve it before the meetings. The language was inserted into the communiqué at the last minute by the leaders themselves. The US Treasury Department and other finance ministries did not want their governments focusing on the international financial institutions (IFIs). Finance ministries felt that the IFIs were within their individual purview and did not want other government agencies involved in a review of their structure or framework. They thus quickly moved to have the IFIs establish committees to study themselves. This was like having a fox in the chicken coop. It was no surprise that the committees of both the IMF and the World Bank found little need for change or for restructuring themselves.

This highlights one of the problems facing the IFIs. How can they adjust to the changing world environment if their management and career staff are heavily vested in the current institutional structures? If the finance ministries of the major industrial countries continue to be bound by the existing institutional models, who will lead a serious review or study of the adequacy of the institutions? It should be obvious that some outside group would be required. But what will be the impetus for the creation of such an outside group?

In general, the IFIs have supported the various commitments stated in various G8 leaders' communiqués. In most cases, the institutions were consulted prior to the communiqué drafting sessions. Hence, they were able to affect the outcome of the summit requests for institutional support.

But there are cases when the institutions have not been particularly cooperative. In the May 1986 leaders' meeting in Tokyo, considerable discussion focused on the relative performance of member economies. During this period, when significant adjustment of bilateral exchange rates was being pursued by the major economies, the need for consistent domestic policies was recognized. The G5 finance ministers' Communiqué at the Plaza Accord in 1985 had highlighted the need for changes in domestic macroeconomic policies to support the desired movement in relative exchange rates. The Tokyo Summit recognized the need for increased multilateral surveillance of macroeconomic policies and the need to assure policy consistency across countries. In support of this conclusion, the Tokyo Economic Declaration called on the IMF and the Group of Ten in particular to create a series of economic indicators which could be helpful in assigning responsibility for policy change to member countries. It was envisioned that the IMF would construct the desired economic data and create the appropriate economic indicators. The data would then provide the basis for future policy discussions, both within the IMF and in the summit process. Twenty years later, the IMF had yet to fulfill the assignment.

It is important to ask: "What should be the role of the IFIs in implementing G8 summit commitments?" Many members of the IFIs who are not participants in the annual summit process resent having the institutions being "assigned" jobs by the summits. Since 1997, there has been a growing resentment on the part of emerging market economies over their role in global trade negotiations. They have started to adopt a unified blocking position on a number of key issues.

This unity will spread to the financial institutions. Since they have different views on the role of capital markets and regulations on inflows and outflows, the emerging market economies resist taking direction from the major industrial nations – both bilaterally and multilaterally. The 1997 Asian financial crisis is a key case where the emerging nations rejected – when possible – the urgings of the IMF. Led by Malaysia, emerging nations now play with the role of capital control "speed bumps" to reduce the vulnerability of capital markets to outside speculative pressures.

Conclusion

Rather than provide impetus for change through the summit channel, the major industrial nations would have greater success if they worked inside the MOs to build consensus before announcing the changes they want to see in the financial institutions.

Overall, the G8 summit process is successful in securing international institutional support for implementing its commitments when the issues being examined are ready for action. That is the time when the institutions themselves and a significant majority of their members have already come to the conclusion that come sort of institutional change is warranted. Then the impetus added by the summit focus helps the process along. On the other hand, if the membership – or importantly, the organization itself – is not ready for change or does not believe that change is needed, the summit process builds ill will within the body. The directoire concept is not well loved.

Chapter 7
Development, the Commonwealth and the G8

Ade Adefuye

Since 1975, the heads of state and government of the world's industrial democracies have met annually to deal with the major economic and political issues facing their domestic societies and the international community as a whole. Collectively known as the Group of Eight (G8) since Russia joined fully in 1998, the summit has consistently dealt with macroeconomic management, international change and relations with developing countries. The annual G8 summit has acquired the reputation of giving direction to the international community by setting priorities, determining new issues and providing guidance to established international institutions. Because of the gravitas which the leaders in their personal capacities and the nations over which they preside command, the G8 meetings have over the years become the defining moment in the annual global economic and political calendar.

In recent times, Africa has attracted the attention of the international community because of the realization that the present state of affairs on the continent, if allowed to continue, will eventually have unpleasant effects on the global economic and political order. There is an increasing awareness that allowing Africa to remain a scar on the conscience of the world will one day make progress and success in the developed world rather meaningless.

This is why the G8 has been focused on issues of importance to Africa at every summit since the late 1990s. At Kananaskis in 2002, the G8 adopted an Africa Action Plan in response to the New Partnership for Africa's Development (NEPAD) (Lyman 2007). Three years later, 2005 was described as Africa's year because the continent was at the heart of several global initiatives. There was the Make Poverty History project, the Live 8 Concert, the Commission for Africa Report and the G8 Summit in Gleneagles, which put Africa on top of its agenda (Wickstead 2007). All attest to a renewed commitment on the part of the international community to improve living standards on the continent and combat poverty and disease (Cooper, Kirton and Shrecker 2007).

This chapter reviews the G8 commitments to Africa arising from G8 summits from Kananaskis in 2002 through every year during which the G8 has since received African leaders in its meetings to discuss the political and economic affairs of the continent with a view to offering assistance that will enable it to achieve the Millennium Development Goals (MDGs) and improve living standards. It explores the extent to which commitments made at these meetings have been translated into action, and how much progress has been made in lifting Africa out of poverty, disease and political instability as a result. It identifies areas in which the results have fallen below expectations and suggests what could be done to translate the dreams to realities, with the assistance of international organizations such as the Commonwealth.

This chapter concludes that the Commonwealth can pressure the G8 to deal with development and African issues, use its extensive contacts in Africa to help the G8 implement its commitments and help hold the G8 accountable, especially as it lacks a secretariat of its own. The G8 has worked effectively with the Commonwealth and other multinational organizations (MOs) on peace and security, good governance, debt relief, economic growth and sustainable development. Further G8–Commonwealth cooperation can do even more.

The Commonwealth and Africa

The Commonwealth is made of up of 53 countries which were formerly part of the British Empire but which, after their independence, decided to retain the links inherited during colonial days as a basis for consultation and cooperation in the interests of their people. The organization sees itself as complementing the United Nations (UN) in the pursuit of global peace, sustainable development and the promotion of consensus on international economic and political issues. Out of the 53 member countries of the Commonwealth, 18 are from Africa. The Commonwealth has been at the forefront of the pursuit of political stability and sustainable economic development in Africa. It has also established a good track record of cooperating and collaborating with MOs that pursue similar objectives.

The Commonwealth has established memoranda of understanding with a number of reputable MOs. It has also been involved in joint projects and co-funded programs with many MOs. Two Commonwealth countries, Britain and Canada, are also members of the G8. The Commission for Africa had within its membership a number of Africans from Commonwealth countries, including President Ben Mkapa of Tanzania. A series of memoranda were submitted by Commonwealth Secretariat divisions to the Commission. The Commonwealth has also offered to assist in whatever way in the implementation of the Commission's conclusions. Commonwealth finance ministers during their meetings have presented proposals for dealing with the debt problems of African countries. Initiatives such as the Trinidad and Tobago terms and the Clarke Initiative were forerunners of schemes for easing the debt burden on Commonwealth countries, as the Commonwealth finance ministers' calls had been at the start of the G7's action on debt relief for the poorest in 1988. Indeed, the Heavily Indebted Poor Country (HIPC) Intiative was initiated by the Commonwealth. Through Britain and Canada, and by using the influence of its members in other MOs, the Commonwealth has exerted tremendous pressure on the G8 countries to ease the debt burden of Commonwealth developing countries, especially those in Africa.

The G8 and Africa

An important aspect of G8 concern with the global economic and political situation is the challenge of Africa. The G8 has been concerned with political stability and economic development in the whole of the African continent (Adefuye 2007). Indeed, so much has the broader international community been concerned with the situation in Africa that 2005 featured many activities devoted to calling attention to the situation on the continent. That year was described as "Africa's year." It was a year in which concrete steps were taken to free the continent from poverty, disease and unemployment. It had become clear that the continent was the least likely to achieve the MDGs. At that time, over 2,000 children under the age of five died every day from malaria. Over 6,000 people died each day from HIV/AIDS. The pandemic continued to undermine the political, economic and social fabric of many African societies. Over 250 million people did not have access to safe drinking water. Over 40 million children were still not in school. Conflict in countries such as the Democratic Republic of Congo, Sudan and Uganda resulted in tens of thousands of people dying each month and millions displaced. Without much faster progress, by 2015, 247 million people could still be living on less than $1 a day and 45 million children could have died.

It is possible that such a situation can be attributed in part to the lingering effects of slavery and colonialism, which at independence bequeathed weak states and weak economies to the first generation of African leaders. The situation was, however, aggravated by poor leadership, corruption and bad governance, leading to some African countries being classified as failed states. But African leaders have recently realized the need to put their own house in order. The transformation of the Organisation for African Unity (OAU) to the African Union (AU) and the adoption of NEPAD signify the commitment by African leaders to consolidate democracy, adopt sound economic management and promote peace, security and people-centered development. African leaders have formally undertaken to hold each other accountable for their achievements. They have emphasized good governance and human rights as a necessary precondition for Africa's recovery.

There has since been noticeable progress in Africa. The transformation of the OAU into the AU has resulted in the replacement of the principle of non-interference in the internal affairs of other countries by one of non-indifference to violations of human rights, good governance and accountable government. By 2006, 23 African countries had signed up to the African Peer Review Mechanism (APRM), where countries submit their political, economic, corporate and social governance to peer review. Of these countries, 18 were Commonwealth members. The African countries established the AU Peace and Security Council, which led to AU missions in Darfur and the Central African Republic. As a result, conflict in Africa has continued to decline. Political stability and democracy have been strengthened in many countries. From 2000 to 2006, about two-thirds of countries in sub-Saharan Africa held multi-party elections. Governance indicators improved at least as fast as in any developing region. Primary school enrolment increased rapidly. Political commitment to tackle HIV/AIDS increased. The International Monetary Fund (IMF) projected economic growth for Africa at over 5.3 percent for 2005, and an average inflation of 9.9 percent, compared with 41 percent 20 years before. This is partly a result of economic reform and business climate improvements by African governments to spur the private sector. The international community, including the G8, embraced this new commitment by African leaders. The G8 promised to support Africa's effort. The G8 signified its intention to build on Africa's own efforts as set out in the AU and NEPAD's strategies and programs. The G8 demonstrated its determination to focus on Africa so that it would go as far as possible in meeting the MDGs by 2015.

For this reason, since 2001, African leaders have been present at each G8 summit. At the 2001 Genoa Summit, G8 leaders appointed the Africa personal representatives (APRs) to produce the Africa Action Plan, to support NEPAD. The Evian Summit in 2003 established the Africa Partnership Forum (APF) to develop the relationship further. The APF meets twice a year with representatives from the G8, African countries, MOs and Organisation for Economic Co-operation and Development (OECD) donors who give over $100 million to Africa in official development assistance (ODA) each year. At Gleneagles in 2005, APRs reviewed progress against the Africa Action Plan. Individual G8 members produced bilateral progress reports. Past G8 commitments relevant to Africa's development include plans to support African and global peacekeeping capacity, action plans on water and health, an action plan on fighting famine in Africa and an action plan on how entrepreneurship could help to fight poverty.

Implementing the Commitments

The G8, in partnership with Africa, has made some progress on the Africa Action Plan. But as Africa continues to face similar challenges, more G8 support for Africa will be needed. The scope of the G8 commitment to Africa is very wide. But the following issues stand out: peacekeeping and capacity building for peace and security, strengthening institutions and governance, economic growth and sustainable development, and debt relief.

Peacekeeping and Capacity Building for Peace and Security

With the active support of the G8, the AU is establishing itself as the prime interlocutor on peace and security on the continent. The establishment of the AU's Peace and Security Council is an important step. G8 members have provided core support to the new Peace and Security Director, as well as significant support to AU peace and security operations. There has been encouraging progress in the area of peace and development. From 2004 to 2006, there was some reduction in the number of violent conflicts in Africa. Further implementation of the plan to support peace and security in Africa has come in the area of providing expertise, equipment, training and logistics for institutions dealing with conflict prevention and resolution. With the active support of G8 members, UN peace support operations in Africa have increased. With the establishment of a mission in Sudan, by 2006 there were eight UN peacekeeping operations in Africa involving the deployment of over 51,000 military and police personnel, with civilian support from G8 members. Africa accounted for two-thirds of the total number of peacekeepers deployed in UN missions world-wide.

The G8 record in the area of promoting peace and security in Africa is fairly good. But more can be done. Too often, responses to conflict in Africa have been reactive and focused on large-scale crisis, with limited attention to sub-national conflicts. At the local level, many people continue to face chronic insecurity. More attention should be given to the prevention of state fragility and conflicts that are caused by structural weaknesses such as unaccountable governance, social exclusion and inequality. There should be more focus on conflict prevention and better preparedness to respond to different kinds of crises such as natural disasters, financial crisis and pandemics. The international community should support early warning systems of partner countries and regional as well as sub-regional organizations in Africa.

Here, the Commonwealth can help. Because of its style of a soft, non-threatening approach, the organization has been able to win the confidence of member countries in such a manner that matters that used to be regarded as internal can now be dealt with using Commonwealth institutions, such as the Good Offices of the Commonwealth Secretary-General, with the active support of eminent Commonwealth citizens.

There should be progress in implementing the concept of African stand-by forces. There should be more coordinated support for the system of post-conflict reconstruction so that once settled, conflicts will not reoccur. The Commonwealth has earned a reputation of working effectively with regional organizations. It is in a good position to support the implementation of G8 plans for security in Africa.

Strengthening Institutions and Governance

Since the 2003 Evian Summit, the AU and NEPAD have made progress in strengthening institutions and governance. Apart from 23 countries signing the APRM, the first country reports for Ghana and Rwanda were considered by the APRM Forum on June 19, 2005. The implementation plans from Ghana and Rwanda were presented to the next forum in August 2006. The AU also established the Pan African Parliament and a Peace and Security Council in 2004. Fifteen African countries scored well in World Bank indicators of policy and institutions in 2003, compared to only ten in 2002. Democracy and transparency are growing and government accountability to people is improving. Many G8 members have provided support to parliamentary institutions at the national and regional level. They have also supported the NEPAD contact group of pan-

African parliamentarians and the pan-African network of civil society focused on anti-corruption measures. The G8 Evian and Sea Island Summits both included G8 commitments on transparency and accountability. The Evian Declaration "Fighting Corruption and Improving Transparency" sets out areas for action. At Sea Island, "Transparency Compacts" were established with four countries, including Nigeria. One of Nigeria's priorities is the implementation of the Extractive Industries Transparency Initiative (EITI), begun in 2002 and endorsed in the Evian Declaration. G8 member countries have also provided support for African organizations such as the African Regional Commission, sub-regional anti-money laundering groups and African-led research on economic governance, trade and gender issues through the UN Economic Commission for Africa (UNECA). However, many African countries continue to face serious challenges in fighting corruption and institutionalizing transparency and accountability. The problem of the transfer outside Africa of illicitly acquired assets requires action both in Africa and by G8 members, amongst others. The Commonwealth at its summit in Abuja in 2003 established a commission to examine the issue of stolen assets in Africa and their recovery. The report was submitted to the Malta Summit in 2005.

Some key recommendations were made. Commonwealth countries should sign, ratify and implement the United Nations Convention Against Corruption as a matter of urgency. Commonwealth heads of state and government, ministers and other public officials should not have immunity from prosecution in domestic courts for alleged criminal activity. Heads of government should commit themselves to take active steps to ensure the removal of these immunities. Commonwealth countries that have yet to do so should promptly put in place strong and comprehensive legislation and procedures for criminal conviction-based asset confiscation. This should include the power to confiscate in circumstances where the accused has absconded or died. Commonwealth countries should also put in place comprehensive laws and procedures for non-conviction-based asset confiscation. Commonwealth countries should provide by law, either through a judicial process or executive discretion, for the return of funds minus reasonable expenses to a requesting country, in cases of misappropriation or other unlawful taking of public funds, or the laundering thereof, where the requesting country reasonably establishes its prior ownership of confiscated property, or when the requested country recognizes damage to the requesting country.

Discussions on the matter did not show sufficient commitment on the part of developed countries to assist in the recovery of these assets and their repatriation to their countries of origin. Legislation was cited as a constitutional hindrance to the return of these assets. For a number of countries in Africa, Nigeria in particular, the return of these assets constitutes an important contribution to their economy. There must be stronger political will on the part of the G8 to assist. The G8 countries should adopt and assist in the implementation of the recommendations of the Commonwealth group.

Debt Relief

The G8 has been instrumental in achieving progress on debt relief in Africa. A full 22 of the poorest countries in Africa have benefited from the $32 billion in debt relief under the Heavily Indebted Poor Countries (HIPCs) Initiative. After the Evian Summit, seven African countries had completed the HIPC Initiative, receiving irrevocable debt reduction. Individual G7 countries provided HIPCs with up to 100 percent relief on bilateral debt. Niger, Ethiopia and Rwanda also received substantial topping-up in order to bring their debts back down to the HIPC threshold. The 2005 Gleneagles Summit became famous for the debt relief it granted to several African countries. On this issue, the G8 record is quite good. What should be done now is to separate debt relief from development assistance. There is an allegation that in calculating the amount of aids and grants to Africa, money granted as debt relief is calculated as part of the assistance. This should be separated.

The British non-governmental Oxfam organization alleged that increases in aid from the world's richest countries were not enough to meet the promises they made at the Gleneagles Summit in 2005. It concluded that debt write-off was added into the total development figure to make it appear better. Although the raw data showed a $2 billion increase in development spending in 2005 over 2004, 80 percent of that figure came in one cancellation of debt to Nigeria along with debt cancellation for Iraq. It is true that debt cancellation and other measures have made a real difference by allowing millions of dollars to be directed to fight poverty. Yet the procedure of adding debt cancellation to total figures of aid may allow the G8 to take its foot off the accelerator in increasing the real volume of aid.

The second of NEPAD's primary objectives is to place African countries, both individually and collectively, on a path of sustainable growth and development. In 2006, there were encouraging signs that prospects for overall economic growth in Africa were improving. In 2004, economic performance was the best since 1998 in sub-Saharan Africa, with 14 countries exceeding 5 percent growth (up from 10 in 2002) and 13 growing at a rate of 3–5 percent.

Despite progress, current longer-term growth trends in many African countries are too low to produce sufficient resources for poverty reduction. The Africa Action Plan underlined the importance of the G8 helping Africa attract investment from within the continent and abroad. The G8 must therefore intensify its efforts to support Africa in harnessing the potential of private sector growth and developing the capacity of Africa to trade. In general, foreign direct investment (FDI) in Africa remains minimal outside a few sectors, such as telecommunications, oil and gas. Domestic savings rates and investment are still low. At Sea Island in 2004, the G8 endorsed the action plan on "Applying the Power of Entrepreneurship to the Eradication of Poverty" to assist developing countries in Africa and elsewhere in creating better conditions for private sector growth.

G8 members support many initiatives to improve the climate for private sector investment and support programs to encourage investment such as the OECD/NEPAD Investment Initiative, Investment for Development Project and Middle

East and North Africa/OECD Initiatives. Many support the Common Market for Eastern and Southern Africa (COMESA) and the Southern African Development Community (SADC) to undertake initiatives at the regional level on areas such as competition policy. Canada launched the Canada Investment Fund for Africa, a public-private initiative that provides risk capital for private investments in Africa. The Canadian government pledged to contribute up to CA$100 million on a matching basis with other investors.

Trade is at the heart of achieving NEPAD's third primary objective of enhancing Africa's full and beneficial integration into the global economy. At Evian in 2003, the G8 committed to completing the Doha round of trade talks by January 1, 2005. Unfortunately, such progress was not possible. However, the World Trade Organization (WTO) framework agreements reached in Geneva in July 2004 offered a good basis to move forward and achieve progress for the poorest developing countries. WTO members agreed to negotiate an end date for the elimination of all forms of agricultural export subsidies, as well as to achieve substantial reduction in trade-distorting domestic support and substantial improvements in market access.

G8 members have made progress in reducing trade-distorting agricultural subsidies and domestic support. Progress is also being made to promote increased trade among and between developing countries and to increase market access. However, the G8, working with all WTO members, can and should do more to enable African producers to exploit the comparative advantage they have in agricultural production by achieving agreed ambitious results in the Doha negotiations.

There is a need for stronger political will on the part of the G8 to implement fully the commitment to increase the capacity of African countries to trade. Some believe that after the Seattle 1999, Cancun 2003 and Hong Kong 2005 ministerial meetings of the WTO, all that has happened is the promise to abandon farm subsidies by 2013. This ought to have been done earlier. By mid-2006, the so-called special and preferential treatment in applying WTO rules had resulted in just five out of 200 such requests being adopted since Seattle. The EU kept insisting on implementing a 39 percent cut in agricultural tariff instead of the 54 percent which the developing countries demanded. Rich country support for agriculture was worth $280 billion a year, which amounts to ten times the aid to Africa. The World Bank clearly stated that increased trade liberalization, especially market access, would benefit African countries.

The Commonwealth has been using its connections to impress on the rich countries the need to effectively implement the program on trade liberalization and improved market access. The organization is not party to the WTO talks in its own right. But it has been using its influence, derived from the fact that many member countries are involved in the negotiations, to promote international consensus on the issue. At the meeting of Commonwealth Heads of Government Meeting in Malta in 2005, the organization issued the Valetta Statement, by which leaders agreed on a set of key principles to guide their trade ministers. The organization has been facilitating the process and supporting member states, especially those that have capacity constraints. The Secretariat runs a program called the Hub and Spoke jointly with the EU to make experts available to guide regional and national trade negotiating teams in the WTO.

In their Valletta Statement on Multilateral Trade concluded at Malta the Commonwealth leaders reaffirmed their abiding commitment to the objectives of the WTO's Doha Development Agenda. It provides an unprecedented opportunity to cement a rules-based and equitable international trading system.

Commonwealth leaders also recalled their Aso Rock Statement on Multilateral Trade in December 2003, and welcomed the progress achieved in the Doha round since that time. They expressed their deep concern about the pace of negotiations, and pledged their global influence to ensure that the outcome of the Doha round is based on higher ambitions than had been evident to date.

They also called on all developed countries to demonstrate the political courage and will to give more than they received in this round, particularly in the negotiations on agriculture and market access, as their own longer-term prosperity depends on such an approach. They recognized that developing countries must also demonstrate flexibility and commitment to ensure a successful outcome to the round.

Commonwealth leaders continued to call for the WTO to reach agreement on the elimination of all forms of export subsidies, and on time-bound commitments for substantial reductions in trade-distorting domestic support and significant improvements in market access.

They applauded the "Aid for Trade" initiative endorsed by the G8 as a vehicle for meaningful market access. They called for adequately funded and structured assistance to developing countries in this area to enable them to participate more effectively in the multilateral trading system.

Conclusions

Greater political will on the part of the G8 is needed to achieve the objectives and fulfill the commitments which have been made to Africa. But this is more likely if there is serious and consistent pressure on G8 governments to act differently, and if G8 governments are held properly and publicly to account for the impact of their policies on Africa. MOs such as the Commonwealth can do much in this regard. Through its activities such as the Valletta Statement, the Report of the Task Force on Asset Repatriation, institutional support for NEPAD and pressure on the members of the G8, the Commonwealth has been complementing the activities of the G8 on Africa.

African countries are properly being urged to be accountable and being made to subject their policy performance to external evaluation through the APRM and the UNECA Report. But there is no truly comparable process for the G8. The Director General of the World Bank's Evaluation Report noted that no integrated effort is under way to evaluate the developmental effect of G8 policies, particularly on Africa.

In recent years, there have been several proposals to address policy on the way forward in Africa. The central concern is that the G8 should not take with the left hand what it has given to Africa with the right hand. All countries in the G8 and Africa are legitimately trying to maximize the opportunities for their countries in an increasingly globalized environment. Therefore, no one expects the G8 to accept policies that will not be in the long-term interests of its members. But in the emerging global village, it is of mutual advantage if the vested interests are removed. Apart from the accepted notion that progress in Africa would make the world a better place, Africa and the G8 would in the long run specifically benefit eventually from phasing out agricultural subsidies and increasing market access.

Real obstacles to more coherent G8 policies on Africa are not technical, but political. It is necessary to push African matters to the fore of the international agenda. If 2005 was Africa's year, the impetus developed then should not be allowed to subside.

G8 countries should now do three things. The first is to establish a new G8/Africa Forum bringing together political leaders from the G8 and Africa, as well as the UN Secretary-General, and the heads of the international financial institutions and the African Development Bank – and make this a permanent part of the G8. The second is to make the UNECA/OECD biennial report – a checklist of commitments made to Africa and of progress in implementing them – a central focus of discussions at the G8/Africa Forum, and to respond in detail to the report. The third is to subject important areas of government policy – including trade, investment and arms exports – to a comprehensive "development audit."

Bibliography

Adefuye, Ade (2007), "Africa and the G8: Political Aspects," in Michele Fratianni, John Kirton and Paolo Savona, eds, *Financing Development: The G8 and UN Contribution* (Aldershot: Ashgate), pp. 143–54.

Cooper, Andrew, John Kirton and Ted Schrecker, eds (2007), *Governing Global Health: Challenge, Response, Innovation* (Aldershot: Ashgate).

Lyman, Princeton (2007), "The G8 Africa Action Plan: How Much a Partnership?" in Michele Fratianni, John Kirton and Paolo Savona, eds, *Financing Development: The G8 and UN Contribution* (Aldershot: Ashgate), pp. 121–32.

Wickstead, Myles (2007), "The Commission for Africa: Accomplishments and Unfinished Business," in Michele Fratianni, John Kirton and Paolo Savona, eds, *Financing Development: The G8 and UN Contribution* (Aldershot: Ashgate), pp. 133–42.

Chapter 8
Trade, the World Trade Organization and the Doha Development Agenda

Roy MacLaren

The Group of Eight (G8) countries – or, more accurately, the Group of Seven (G7) countries, since Russia is not yet a member of the World Trade Organization (WTO) – have at their annual summits repeatedly urged the early and comprehensive conclusion of the Doha round of trade negotiations of the WTO. But to whom are these repeated exhortations addressed? In fact, to themselves. It is they, the G7 countries themselves, who can make a success or failure of the Doha round. Many of the fundamental multilateral trade issues at stake arise largely from their own domestic policies. Yet the same seven governments have, year after year, issued hortatory statements addressed to unidentified countries, and even to the WTO itself, as if it had some substance beyond its members' wishes. It is disingenuous to "punt" the problem back to the WTO negotiations when in essence it remains a transatlantic issue.

The onus for the success of the Doha round hinges on a political, not a technical, decision. It is up to the G7 countries themselves to make the Doha round a success. But to do so, they must be willing to institute profound changes in their domestic policies, particularly agriculture. The WTO cannot make trade policy. It is, to a greater degree than most international organizations, a collectivity of its member states. If the United States and the European Union (EU) do not, for domestic reasons, choose to reduce sharply or to eliminate their various barriers to international trade in agriculture, despite their own exhortations at the annual G8 meetings, there is nothing that the WTO itself can do.

International Economic Organizations, the G8 and Globalization

The same ultimate responsibility for policy coherence in other international economic organizations also resides with the G8 governments. The WTO, the World Bank, the International Bank for Reconstruction and Development (IBRD), and the International Monetary Fund (IMF) largely have the same members. Yet the G8 countries pursue contradictory policies across the several institutions. The same G8 governments that contemplate in the IBRD and IMF debt relief for the poorest countries defend in the WTO their restrictions on market access that make debt relief of limited or transient value. At home, within national governments, development assistance programs follow one route while trade policy follows another. Policy coherence is not to be found in multilateral organizations. It is in national capitals, especially G8 capitals, that coherence must first be attained.

The G8 countries, in their annual communiqués, still refer to globalization as if it were somehow a centrally controllable phenomenon, controllable at least by multilateral agreement. But no one controls globalization. No single country or international institution can. What should be possible in global trade and investment is a binding, rules-based system, with a review procedure, so that all benefit. But that will happen only when national governments accept that global rules rather than narrow domestic priorities must govern world trade. They must eschew their domestic protectionist programs in return for open markets everywhere.

The Trade System

The Uruguay round of the General Agreement on Tariffs and Trade (GATT) finally succeeded in reducing significantly or eliminating most tariff and other trade barriers applied at borders. What the Uruguay round could not do, and what the Doha round has so far failed to do, is to win agreement on an elimination of a whole range of domestic practices that are now the principal obstacles to global free trade. Such obscurantism has only been compounded by the naming of the Doha round a "development round," without any real understanding of what a development round might be (Page 2007, Ostry 2007).

Against this background, the Doha round has missed successive deadlines for conclusion, despite the annual exhortations of the very countries that could make it a success. Presumably, the G8 countries, meeting at their future summits, will again call for a prompt and comprehensive conclusion of what is still described as a negotiation vital to the further expansion of the global economy.

Perhaps in the Doha round enough can yet be cobbled together for the G8 countries to declare victory. Some sort of papering over of the vast differences remaining among G8 states, especially in agricultural trade policy, may still be possible. Some will no doubt argue that one-tenth of a deal is better than no deal at all. But who will really care when the agreed trade liberalization is so minimal? Another option might be to set yet another Doha deadline, this time a date when the US President Barack Obama will presumably obtain fast-track negotiating authority. But that too would be a tacit admission that rounds no longer work. And the option of delay simply puts back by several years the basic question of the future of the WTO.

Beyond Rounds to Reviews

The Uruguay round, having called into being the WTO, should have marked the conclusion of the long series of post-war trade negotiating rounds. The new WTO, a very different organization, should itself have been recognized for what it is: a place for the negotiation of trade issues with a review and dispute mechanism provided.

Furthermore, the WTO could have been – and still can be – the place where bilateral or regional free trade agreements can be carefully assessed for their impact on enhancing trade. Given the current multilateral difficulties in addressing domestic protectionist practices, it is hardly surprising that the urge to liberalization has recently taken the form of a myriad of bilateral and regional agreements. Even G8 countries themselves, notably the US and the EU, have now mounted the bilateral bandwagon. Yet the WTO is not permitted by its members to police such agreements effectively. This is despite the evaluation of Article 24 of the GATT and the trade policy reviews that the WTO inherited from the GATT.

Beyond the G8

Additional restraints on the current effectiveness of the WTO result from the failure of the G8 countries to digest the fact that India, Brazil and China, to name but the three most evident, have now become major players on the world trade scene. The implications of the advent of China in particular are far from comprehended among the WTO membership. For its part, Brazil is no less wary of trade liberalization *vis-à-vis* China than G8 countries. India can be counted upon to drag its feet, especially over agriculture.

Conclusion: Beyond Doha

In mid-July 2006 at St. Petersburg, the G8 issued yet another collective exhortation about the Doha round. This exhortation they should have instead addressed to themselves singly, since the Doha round cannot be allowed to fail. It is too late for that. If such G8 appeals eventually prove successful, then the G8 could turn to the more promising if daunting prospect of collaborating to make the WTO that which at the conclusion of the Uruguay round in 1994 it was widely intended to be. The goal then was a non-stop negotiating forum of trade rules, underpinned by an effective dispute settlement mechanism, capable of monitoring the rapidly increasing numbers of regional and bilateral free trade agreements, all to be seen as stepping stones on the way to global free trade and sustainable development.

The Doha round remains in a very real sense a test of the value of the G8 itself. For more than 30 years, the G7 – and now the G8 – has met annually and consulted between annual gatherings to resolve such fundamental issues as trade and investment. If now, at the 11th hour, the G8 still cannot offer some resolution to the Doha dilemma, it is the efficacy of the G8 itself and its ability to shape a healthy trade and investment system for the next generation that will be called into question, not the efficacy of the WTO. What are the costs of failure? It is not the economic costs that are most worrisome – although these are potentially high – it is the systemic ones: the blow that would be delivered to the WTO and to multilateralism in trade. Failure would give a further impetus to bilateralism and weaken the credibility of WTO rules. Globalization and the current economic expansion will not end overnight if Doha fails. But the world economy will be left significantly weaker, perhaps weaker than anyone can foresee today.

Bibliography

Ostry, Sylvia (2007), "Asymmetry in the Post-Doha Trading System," in M. Fratianni, P. Savona and J.J. Kirton, eds, *Financing Development: The G8 and UN Contribution* (Aldershot: Ashgate), pp. 219–34.

Page, Sheila (2007), "Doing Doha for Development: A Development Perspective,'" in M. Fratianni, P. Savona and J.J. Kirton, eds, *Financing Development: The G8 and UN Contribution* (Aldershot: Ashgate), pp. 201–18.

PART IV
The St. Petersburg Priorities: Energy, Education, Information and Health

Chapter 9
Energy Security and Sustainable Development: The WTO and the Energy Charter Treaty

Sylvia Ostry

The trade–environment linkage – or sustainable development, as it is called – has been uneasy and unclear. "Sustainable development" is now firmly lodged in the World Trade Organization (WTO) – at least in words. And in a rule-based system, words matter. But the present arrangements in the WTO are ill-suited to cope with the formidable challenges of environmental deterioration, growing inequality and the central issue of energy security itself.

This chapter first traces the trade and environment issue as it evolved into sustainable development in the global trading system. It provides a brief review of the Energy Charter Treaty. It next explores some options for policy cooperation between the two institutions. After all, policy coherence is part of the historical legacy of another institution – the G8 summit itself.

Trade and the Environment

There was no explicit reference to the environment in the General Agreement on Tariffs and Trade (GATT) when it was established in 1948. But as the issue became prominent in international circles, the GATT was pressured to pay attention. In the early 1970s, along with the 1972 Stockholm Conference on the Human Environment, the GATT Group on Environmental Measures and International Trade (EMIT) was formed. It did not meet until November 1991, in advance of the 1992 Rio Summit on Environment and Development. By and large, the mainstream view in the trade community was that environmental policies could spur protectionism – a kind of "Baptist-Bootlegger" approach. And environmental non-governmental organizations (ENGOs) were far more interested in lobbying the World Bank than the GATT.

But everything changed in the early 1990s after a GATT dispute panel ruled in favor of Mexico's challenge to the American embargo on tuna caught in a fashion harming dolphins. This mobilized a massive attack on the GATT and the ongoing Uruguay round. Posters of "Gatzilla" were plastered on streets in Geneva and Washington. The new slogan was "GATT – Guaranteeing a Toxic Tomorrow."

The ENGOs were very effective at the end of the Uruguay round in pressuring the US government to ensure that a reference to sustainable development was included in the preamble of the document establishing the WTO.[1] This was an enormous victory for the greens. Unlike the tuna and dolphin failure, in a challenge to the US concerning shrimps the WTO's Appellate Body in 1998 cited the WTO's preamble. Sea turtles were viewed as a non-renewable resource, and the substance of WTO rules in effect amended. The role of the Dispute Settlement Mechanism (especially the Appellate Body) was launched – the rule of law and the rule of lawyers (Weiler 2001). Did developing countries in Marrakesh understand the implications of the WTO preamble? How much expertise did they possess regarding constructive ambiguity?

There was a favorite joke in the 1990s about drafting communiqués. After grueling all-night sessions, the final draft was produced and the question was put: is there anyone here who believes that this communiqué can be fully understood in his (or her) nation's capital? If no hands went up, it was time to release it. The outcome was a masterpiece of creative ambiguity. The definition of sustainable development must have been achieved in the same way. In 1987, the United Nations (UN) Brundtland Commission report *Our Common Future* defined the term "sustainable development" as follows: "development that meets the needs of the present without compromising the ability of future generations to meet their own needs" (World Commission on Environment and Development 1987). Since then, there have been many definitions. But the most famous one might be termed "destructive ambiguity."

There were, and to some extent still are, wide differences between the economists and the environmentalists that were not created, but were catalyzed by events in the 1990s. The differences are complex, but often expressed in a right–left debate. Furthermore, there was a serious North–South cleavage reflecting fundamentally different priorities. The South favored growth, not the post-materialism of many ENGOs from rich countries. American ENGOs in particular have been mainly concerned with wildlife protection and landscape protection. As one Southern ambassador at the WTO remarked: "If only we were elephants, developed countries might be more concerned about us" (Shaffer 2001).

The ambiguity was an attempt to gloss over these deep divides. The conventional wisdom cited the "Three Es" – efficiency, equity and ecology – enshrined in sustainable development. This was win-win-win. But how? What are the policies, and how are they connected? How does one measure sustainable development? What are the costs and benefits? Who pays for what? How is this related to trade?

These and other issues remain to be analyzed and debated. But it is important to recognize that while left–right and North–South conflict remains, there is a far greater willingness today than in the 1990s to discuss the linkages between trade and development and environmental concerns. A WTO Committee on Trade

1 Personal communication from Mark Halle, International Institute for Sustainable Development, Geneva.

and the Environment (CTE) and on Trade and Development (CTD) have been established. This change was reflected in the Doha agenda.

The Doha Round and Sustainable Development

The Doha round, or the Doha Development Agenda as it is often termed, was the first in the trading system to include issues related to trade and environment. These included the relationship between WTO rules and specific trade obligations in multilateral environmental agreement (MEA) (to be limited in scope to parties to the MEA in question), procedures for information exchange between MEAs and relevant WTO committees and on the criteria for the granting of observer status, and negotiations on the reduction or elimination of tariff and non-tariff barriers to environmental goods and services. A cautionary note was added that the outcome of these negotiations must not alter the balance of WTO members' rights and obligations under existing agreements.

In addition, the CTE was mandated to review a number of other trade-related environment issues including the effect of environmental measures on market access for developing countries and the effects of trade liberalization on the environment. These issues were included at the founding of the CTE in Marrakesh. Nothing much has emerged since.

Another, potentially very important, issue on the Doha Development Agenda was "to clarify and improve WTO disciplines on fisheries subsidies, taking into account the importance of this sector to developing countries." This was the first proposal that dealt directly with an environmental issue *per se.* It was included because of effective lobbying by ENGOs. It is not being negotiated in the CTE, but is included in the Group on Rules.

It is not difficult to summarize the outcome at the WTO's Hong Kong multilateral meeting. One word will do: nothing. Given the fear that the whole round would collapse – as in Cancun – this may not have been surprising. Sustainable development was not a hot ticket item for the WTO. It is not now.

The Doha round is still in a comatose state. Yet the issue of sustainable development – and, more broadly climate change – is becoming more and more important, Doha or not. Yet, more by accident than design, the WTO houses a wide range of agreements and handles numerous disputes that are related to sustainable development. This transformation was the result of the Uruguay round, which shifted the focus of the trading system from border barriers to major areas of domestic policy and institutional infrastructure. Gary Sampson (2005) provides a comprehensive review of the substantive links between WTO provisions and sustainable development. These include the complex and sophisticated regulations and the technical mandatory standards to protect public health, safety and the environment (the agreements on Technical Barriers to Trade (TBT) and on the Application of Sanitary and Phytosanitary Measures (SPS)). They embrace the intellectual property issues in the Agreement on Trade-Related Aspects of

Intellectual Property (TRIPS) concerning biotechnology that arouse enormous anger and friction both across the Atlantic, such as genetically modified organisms (GMOs) and "Frankenfoods," as well as North and South, such as access to essential medicines, and within the environment community, such as biodiversity. Surely the issue of reducing trade distorting agricultural and other subsidies should take into account the environmental and distributional impacts for win-win-win policies. So even if the Doha Agenda on sustainable development were completed by the end of the round, this would hardly scratch the surface of the WTO and sustainable development.

Moreover, the "development" part of sustainable development is important. Another unintended consequence of the Uruguay round was systemic asymmetry, a profound manifestation of inequity. In the global trading system, one crucial aspect is complexity. Knowledge, advanced and sophisticated, is essential. Complexity requires knowledge, and knowledge enhances power. The strong are stronger because of their store of knowledge, and the weak are weaker because of their poverty of knowledge. So the system has endogenized asymmetry. The knowledge trap feeds the poverty trap. And this is well documented by a growing number of case studies by the World Bank that demonstrate the capacity deficit. Many concern the TBT and SPS. Furthermore, the asymmetry is not offset, but rather reinforced by the legalization of the system, as a number of recent studies show (Ostry 2007).

What is at stake in the Doha round is not a negotiation on trade, but the survival of the rules-based multilateral trading system. The alternative is very apparent – fragmentation by an increasing proliferation of preferential agreements led by American "competitive liberalization" based on power and episodic ad hocery. This fragmentation is exacerbated by the recent mushrooming of regional trade and other agreements involving developing countries. These reflect the "New Geography" already apparent at Cancun in 2003, and the decline in attraction of the WTO (Antkiewicz and Whalley 2006). They also reflect the ongoing shift in the balance of power from the West to the East and Russia.

WTO Reform

Whatever the final outcome of Doha, it would be both possible and very desirable (not to say urgent) for the WTO member countries to launch some serious reform. First, on environmental issues, the Doha Development Agenda, paragraph 51, explicitly calls on the CTE and the CTD to "act as a forum within which the environmental and developmental aspects of the negotiations can be debated in order to achieve the objective of sustainable development." There is little likelihood that there could be a serious and informed debate on this subject if it is tied to negotiations. That would completely constrain the participants. What is required is a WTO policy forum – recommended by the Sutherland Consultation Board among others – to be accompanied by an increase in research resources.

There was one in the GATT – the Consultative Group of 18 – involving senior officials from capitals. It was immensely important in the launch of the Uruguay round. The forum should include knowledge networking with non-governmental organizations (NGOs), intergovernmental organizations (IGOs), MEAs and others. It should begin to explore the main dimensions of sustainable development.

This is a formidable challenge. The trading system thrived on reciprocity often derided as mercantilism by policy purists. The environmental issues are *au fond* intrinsic to public goods. The trade-offs are complex: costs now, and uncertain benefits over an uncertain time frame. Reciprocity is not on the table. The system of national accounts was created as an offspring of Lord Keynes's General Theory. Measurement is key to the policy process. But despite myriad efforts, there is no generally accepted definition or set of data on sustainability. These are but a few of the agenda items to be tackled.

But as noted, the most stupendous item is global warming. And the widening chasm between the US government and the EU is narrowing with President Barack Obama's energy policy initiative. US states, and even cities, are adopting sustainable development policies. There has been a proliferation of codes of corporate social responsibility by American multinationals, although a review of these measures by David Vogel suggests that the impact on environmental degradation will be modest in the absence of government policy (Vogel 2005). So a policy forum is essential to engage a wide range of actors, and not just countries. It would not likely be approved by many WTO members. But a coalition of the willing could play a catalytic role.

In addition to the policy forum, the Aid for Trade project announced in Hong Kong requires cooperation between the WTO and development institutions such as the World Bank. Here, a precedent is the integrated framework launched in 1997 as a demonstration of the improved "international coherence" promised in the Uruguay round. This was designed to include only the WTO and the Bretton Woods twins. The idea of cooperation with institutions covering issues such as the environment or energy security would not have occurred to anyone at that time. The debate over the EU's Energy Charter Treaty shows how important these issues have become.

Energy Security

The issue of energy security has been a high priority for the EU for many years as the history of the Energy Charter shows. That was hardly the case in the US – except during the 1970s and the oil crises.

Coincidentally or not, the 2006 G8 summit hosted by Russia put energy security at the top of the agenda. This was a complex and contentious issue, especially in regard to the Energy Charter that has become involved.

The roots of the Energy Charter date back to the early 1990s. It was launched by the EU as a project to enhance cooperation between East and West and facilitate the transition to market economies of the former socialist countries. It was a kind of "grand bargain" investment for Eastern energy supplies. The scope has broadened considerably since 1991, when the European Energy Charter was established. In 1998, the Energy Charter Treaty entered into legal force. As well as European countries, a number of Asian countries have joined. But the US and Canada have not. Russia has refused to ratify.

The treaty is an enormously complex and ambitious regime. First, it incorporates the rules of the WTO, even for non-members. The most essential feature of the Charter concerns investment. The rules for investment are divided into two sections: one covers pre-establishment and the other post-establishment. The latter are based on the North American Free Trade Agreement (NAFTA) and include investor–state dispute settlement by arbitration (*à la* NAFTA Chapter 11). The pre-establishment rules remain "soft law," and do not cover vital issues such as most-favored nations and national treatments. The same is true of other issues such as environmental regulation and competition policy.

The Energy Charter Treaty is, however, the first broadly multilateral agreement that covers investment, albeit in one sector. This is path-breaking, and a first step in establishing clear and transparent rules to reduce risk and encourage financial support for energy supply. However, the efforts to extend the provisions concerning investment access (pre-establishment) have so far failed. Similarly, another key factor on the supply side – transit infrastructure – is still not agreed. Despite lengthy negotiations for a protocol, it remains subject to serious disputes, especially with Russia. Indeed, the most serious deficiency in the Charter is the refusal of Russia to ratify the treaty. Energy security without Russia is akin to *Hamlet* without the Prince.

The G8's Contribution

Clearly, the most significant achievement for the G8 summit in the issue of energy security would be for the United States and Canada to ratify the Energy Charter so that the G7 could persuade Russia to do so too. But that seems unlikely. Even the definition of "energy security" could be agreed upon.[2]

Maybe it would be wiser to recognize that the Energy Treaty Charter is far too ambitious in today's geopolitical ambience. Instead of reaching to build a bridge too far, the G8 should initiate a step-by-step passage for a long journey, even though the destination is not fully agreed.

The heart of the Treaty concerns foreign investment. After the failure of the OECD's Multilateral Agreement on Investment (MAI) and rejection of the European proposal to include investment in the WTO at Cancun, the main route to

2 A neat way of summing this was presented by President Vladmir Putin before the 2006 summit: you want security of supply and we want security of demand. But that is just one way of covering up a vast and complex set of disagreements.

investment rules remains bilateral agreements "designed" for the most part by the powerful, especially the US and EU (Rugman 1999). The only exception has been NAFTA (Rugman, Kirton and Soloway 1999). And, indeed, NAFTA established the template for the Energy Treaty investment regime.

The NGO attacks on the Multilateral Agreement on Investment (MAI) and NAFTA were founded in a fundamental concern over "state sovereignty." They centered mainly on the investor–state dispute mechanism. But there were also disputes concerning differences among legal systems. For example, although the US and Canada are both common-law countries, Canada does not include property rights in its constitution. It has different jurisprudence in the area of "regulatory takings." This has raised a political firestorm in several challenges by American companies. But in the case of Mexico, the differences in legal systems were so great that NAFTA required fundamental change in laws, regulations and administrative law procedures. How this has provided credible implementation has not been examined so far.

Significant differences among countries in legal and regulatory system are of fundamental importance of the effectiveness of the Treaty and more broadly. The G8 should launch a project on analysis of the legal and regulatory systems with respect to foreign investment in energy, both in its pre- and post-establishment domains. It would be very important, in addition to legal experts and multinational corporations, to include the WTO Secretariat to discuss trade-related investment measures as well as intellectual property measures. A review of the MAI experience provided by the Organisation for Economic Co-operation and Development (OECD) would also be immensely useful.

The legal and regulatory differences will be significant. A study will provide information essential to the understanding of how effectively they could be monitored in regards to implementation. This would be useful both to members and to those considering membership. Clearly, there is no single benchmark. But this would facilitate a reasoned discussion on the key issue: what is energy security, and how can it be established via an investment regime?

This would be a useful project to launch as a continuing process. A special forum should be established by the Charter, open to members and non-members. There should be an agreed list of issues presented to members for discussion and debate. There should be a recognition that the situation is urgent. Energy security is not just about the market, but part of an ongoing (and dangerous) geopolitical game. Thinking about that could clear the mind. The world needs energy security to foster sustainable development. This is international coherence writ large.

Bibliography

Antkiewicz, Agata and John Whalley (2006), "The Sustainability of Growth in the B(R)ICSAM Countries," paper presented at the 2nd annual Conference on International Governance Innovation. Waterloo, Ontario.

Ostry, Sylvia (2007), "Asymmetry in the Post-Doha Trading System," in Michael Hodges, John Kirton and Joseph Daniels, eds, *Financing Development: The G8 and UN Contribution* (Aldershot: Ashgate), pp. 219–34.

Rugman, Alan (1999), *Negotiating Multilateral Rules to Promote Investment*, in Michael Hodges, John Kirton and Joseph Daniels, eds, *The G8's Role in the New Millennium* (Aldershot: Ashgate).

Rugman, Alan M., John Kirton and Julie A. Soloway (1999), *Environmental Regulations and Corporate Strategy: A NAFTA Perspective* (Oxford: Oxford University Press).

Sampson, Gary (2005), *The WTO and Sustainable Development* (Tokyo: United Nations University Press).

Shaffer, Gregory C. (2001), "The World Trade Organization under Challenge: Democracy and the Law and Politics of the WTO's Treatment of Trade and Environment Matters," *Harvard Environmental Law Review* 2: 88.

Vogel, David (2005), *The Market for Virtue* (Washington, DC: Bookings Institution Press).

Weiler, Joseph H.H. (2001), "The Rule of Lawyers and the Ethos of Diplomatic Reflections on WTO Dispute Settlement," in Roger Porter et al., eds, *Efficiency, Equity, Legitimacy* (Washington, DC: Brookings Institution Press).

World Commission on Environment and Development (1987), *Our Common Future* (Oxford: Oxford University Press).

Chapter 10
Energy Security: Russia, the European Union and the G8

Nodari A. Simonia

From the very beginning of January 2006, when Russia became the G8 Chair, accompanied by noisy disputes about price increases for Russian gas to Ukraine, energy security was clearly the issue of the year. Gazprom's demands and claims on its Ukrainian counterpart were fair. But their implementation was so clumsy, ill-conceived and immaturely unskillful that it simplified the task of developing a mass psychological attack on Russia and its leadership by anti-Russian politicians and by almost the entire Western mass media. Thick and fast came accusations that big Russia with reviving imperial ambitions was harming a small Ukraine, that the Russian leadership was using its energy truncheon for political purposes, and that Russia was an unreliable partner for Europe (in spite of 40 years of a stainless reputation in energy cooperation with Europe, even in the most complicated years for Russia). The tone was set by high-ranking American politicians and the press, though many Europeans were not far behind.

None explained to their countries' public that it was Ukraine, not Russia, which was stealing Russian gas meant for European countries. Nobody blamed Ukrainian leaders, who allowed "unsanctioned gas extraction" from the main gas pipeline. It is difficult to believe that those critics sincerely supposed that Russia was obliged to subsidize the economic development of independent post-Soviet states. They had previously blamed Russia's leadership for the fact that due to a difficult economic situation, it had delivered gas to its own enterprises at low prices. Meanwhile, Ukraine, unlike countries in the European Union (EU), was able to buy Russian gas for a price two or three times lower than the world price. This was clearly a politicization of the energy problem.

Russia's leadership thus seemed not too sophisticated in the Machiavellian geopolitical public merrymakings related to the summit energy agenda proposed by Russia. But it cannot be blamed for a lack of common sense and logic. To live according to European standards means paying European prices. And if the US Administration wanted to stimulate the implantation of Western values in Ukraine, Georgia or Moldavia, it should subsidize their economy and cover their energy bills. To demand from Russia that it should subsidize openly anti-Russian policy is already cynical. Such things seldom took place even at the height of the Cold War.

As the St. Petersburg Summit approached, tensions around the energy problem continued to grow. Some US senators stood for expulsion of Russia from the G8, and recommended that President George W. Bush refuse to participate in the summit. G7 leaders could hardly take those recommendations seriously. But an impression was forming that some of them were ready to play the part of the "good cop" in the "good cop, bad cop" game, and to use all the uproar as an additional lever to get considerable concessions from Russia in the energy sphere.

Differences in Energy Security Concepts

In preparing the St. Petersburg Summit's final documents, the most stubborn arguments up to the last day concerned the interpretation of the very idea of "energy security." A majority of Western representatives insisted on a one-sided understanding of this term as a supply guarantee – that is, security for consumers. Russia insisted that guarantees for supply ought to be supplemented with guarantees for demand, and that the governments and businesses of consumer countries must share responsibility and risks with producing countries.

From the point of view of "pure market" theory, the position of Western consumers looked logical: if there is demand, their problem boils down to the provision of guarantees on deliveries. The pure market approach, however, does not work in energy security, especially under modern circumstances. Oil and gas are not ordinary goods. They are not shoes or shirts that can be produced practically anywhere in the world, where the differences will be only in quality and fashion, while demand in the market will itself determine the production scale and delivery price. Hydrocarbons are different. First, they are non-renewable raw materials. Second, their location around the globe is quite uneven. Countries are divided into haves, have-nots, and those which have little and are forced to import increasing amounts. Third, all the main traditional oil and natural gas deposits have entered a productivity decline, while new ones are difficult to access (ocean shelf, deep water or Arctic deposits) and require new, expensive technologies and equipment. That is why producing countries demand that importing ones share the business risks connected with these factors. They also insist that demand guarantees should be fixed in long-term contracts, protecting both producing countries and consumers from volatility and the unpredictability of the spot market, as well as speculative fluctuations in futures auctions.

Experts managed to find compromise formulas. These allowed the St. Petersburg Summit to adopt a joint declaration and the plan of action for the provision of global energy security. They affirmed producers' and consumers' mutual responsibility for sustainable and stable development of world energy. However, unsettled problems remained behind the framework of the compromise formula. The dispute around them flared up with new force soon after the summit, and especially on the threshold of the Russia–EU Summit in November 2006, where negotiations on a new partnership and cooperation agreement were scheduled to start. Not long before the planned summit, EU Energy commissioner Andris Piebalgs, in his interview with *Kommersant GUIDE*, recounted, in ways typical of Brussels' bureaucracy, his understanding of the interconnection between demand and supply within the framework of Russia–EU energy cooperation. Asked whether energy security is a similar problem for Europe and Russia, he answered:

> I must give a good prognosis for Russian producers regarding market development, i.e., the amount of gas Europe is going to consume. It's not a plan, of course, but it's a quite exact prognosis. For Russia it means that she may calmly decide whether she ought to invest in new production or not .... Inner consumption of the European Union is based on market mechanisms, and it might always happen that a new technology appears which will be so much more comfortable and cheaper, that it will impetuously enter the market, and will change the situation in gas consumption. Besides, nobody knows how the price on oil and gas will change. That is, if gas is very expensive, people would use more coal. ... I, for instance, believe the free market economy to be correct, but Russia decides itself which system is more comfortable for her. We would like to have no stoppages with deliveries.[1]

Piebalgs did not say a word about guarantees for producers or long-term contracts. He presented only his own consumption prognosis, on the basis of which Russia must "calmly" invest in development of new deposits. However, Piebalgs immediately negated the importance of this prognosis, having permitted the possibility of radical demand reduction due to unpredictable technological and other changes on free energy markets.

Which reputable financial institution will extend large multibillion-dollar credits against such a "prognosis" of a Brussels official? What will happen to those tens of billions of dollars of investments that Russia, having believed this prognosis, would invest in new projects, in *force majeure* circumstances or if another official proposes a different prognosis? Europe is clearly worried only about one energy security component – "for there to be no stoppages in deliveries."

A similarly asymmetrical and egoistical approach to energy security was expressed by the EU leadership on the issue of the Energy Charter's ratification by Russia. The Charter, according to the EU's idea, is to provide security of hydrocarbon raw material deliveries from Russia, the Caspian region and Central Asia. This Charter was written and signed in 1994, when Russia was in a deep economic crisis, extremely weakened by mass corruption among top bureaucratic echelons ready for paltry bribes to sign agreements, including those in energy, causing enormous damage to Russia's sovereignty and national interests. The Energy Charter is only one such case. For Russia, the main negative aspect in this Charter's contents lies in the demands by third parties for free access to Russian upstream resources, and free energy resource transit from other regions

1 *Kommersant GUIDE* 213 (November 15, 2006): 33.

via Russian territory and along Russian pipelines. The question concerns a loss of sovereignty in the sphere, which today is the main source of the means necessary for restoration and modernization of the whole Russian economy. And powerful permanent pressure on Russia was exerted by Brussels, which demanded ratification of this Charter as a manifestation of nostalgia for the "god-sent" Yeltsin era, with a delusive hope for a return to the time when Russia was gradually turning into an EU raw material appendage.

The most curious aspect was that the Brussels bureaucracy tried to subordinate Russia to an order which it had not managed to install inside the European Union itself. All the years of stage-by-stage realization of EU electric and gas directives aimed at liberalization and the formation of a single European energy market were filled with frictions and contradictions between the Brussels bureaucracy on the one hand, and national governments and large corporations of European countries on the other. National governments did not much enjoy the EU's constant interference in their home "energy kitchen." Indeed, an official directive in force made formation of national energy mixes the prerogative of national governments. They used it, in spite of persistent efforts by Brussels to arrange them into a "joint anti-Russian front." In fact, realization of the directives was carried out half-heartedly, with delays and energetic efforts of certain national governments and private corporations to indirectly bypass the European Commission's antitrust directives. Recent years have seen re-groupings, asset reshuffles, and hostile and friendly mergers and acquisitions. Instead of former national, vertically integrated companies being forced to undergo a split of functions (marked by the term "unbundling") inside their countries in the common European space (and even beyond its limits), now new, much larger, vertically integrated transnational corporations were being formed. Many Western experts believe that soon only several (from five to eight) oligopolical groups will dominate the whole EU territory. Such are the real results of "Brussels-style" liberalization. The Brussels bureaucracy thus tries to win back favor through another onslaught on Russia, hence raising its rating not so high, and perhaps obtaining desirable additional authorities.

An assessment of the Brussels bureaucracy's goals and actions was given by Alexander Rahr, of Germany's Council for Foreign Relations: "The Energy Charter is the EU's attempt to decoy Russia into quite a large trap to force it play according to the European rules."[2] Approximately two years before that, Timophei Bordachev, a Russian scholar specializing in Russian–European relations, warned: "Automatic proliferation of even a part of EU legislation will increase its actual dependence upon Brussels with the remaining isolation from its decision-making mechanism." In this, one should not include European legislation in general and the measures of civilization that have been worked out for ages, have made invaluable contributions in the development of humanity, and include many moments and ideas that Russia has been drawing on, and will continue to do so, in

2 *Vremya Novostei*, December 13, 2006.

its development. Rather, it should include those rules worked out by the Brussels bureaucracy which unilaterally protect only EU countries' interests. For Russia, a country that is at a different socio-economic development stage and is developing along the "catching-up model," implementation objectively causes damage to its national interests, depriving it of a chance to be in command of its own favorable natural factors for modernization of its economy, and of equal rights to participation in the European and even contribute to international division of labor.

The Brussels bureaucracy's plans did not come to fruition. In recent years, the consolidation of Russia's statehood and strengthening of the state's regulatory role in energy took place. These developments did not mean a return to state monopolies. Russia was merely taking the same steps as most countries, both producers and consumers. In Norway, two state companies, Stat Oil and Hydro, have always dominated oil and gas. In late 2006, they were merged into one holding to compete in external markets more successfully. Meanwhile, Norway was one of the three most important natural gas suppliers to EU countries. At the same time, Algeria (the second largest natural gas supplier to Europe, both through pipelines and liquefied natural gas [LNG]) decided to bring the state share in joint oil and gas projects up to 51 percent from the former 30 percent. Neither in the EU nor anywhere else in the world did such actions cause mass indignation or condemnation similar to that of the anti-Russian campaigns held so regularly.

Russian President Vladimir Putin repeatedly explained Russia's energy strategy as follows:

- Russia is ready in deeds, not merely in words, to actively participate in the provision of global energy security. That is why the Russian leader submitted this problem as the main subject at the St. Petersburg G8 Summit.
- Russia is ready to cooperate with foreign corporations – both state and private – only on equal and mutually beneficial terms.
- In exchange for access to its upstream resources, Russia wants to obtain the appropriate share of foreign midstream and downstream assets. However, for strategically important deposits, Russia will reserve control over a minimum 51 percent of shares.
- Russia believes that the mutual exchange of equities between Russian and European companies is the best route to close cooperation, and even economic integration. Nevertheless, Russia no longer intends to grant licenses for new deposits to foreign companies only to have them increase their reserves and international ratings, and for years to come (sometimes for even more than a decade) fail to observe the deposit development terms fixed in these license agreements, or more than double project costs in the final stages of a deposit's development (bearing in mind that in practice, the inevitable cost increases fluctuate within a range of 15–20 percent).[3]

3 Even the liberally minded UK several years ago considerably cut down the period between a company receiving a license and beginning to develop a new deposit, and, if

Russia's energy policy thus does not go beyond the framework of generally accepted global practice. But only toward Russia, which made up its mind to put its house in order, is the reaction exceedingly nervous. Is the West still hoping to return to the "order" ("disorder," to be more exact) of the Yeltsin era? Perhaps to put an end to such hopes that prevent fruitful, mutually beneficial and equal cooperation in energy sphere, President Putin firmly declared during the November 2006 Russia–EU Summit in Helsinki that Russia would never ratify the Energy Charter in its present state without the reconsideration of some of its provisions touching upon Russia's national interests, and without the introduction of appropriate amendments. The European Commission's "legal capacity" was illustrated by the fact that only one new European Union member, Poland, pursuing its own narrow, selfish interests, managed to derail the beginning of summit negotiations on a new partnership and cooperation agreement with Russia – an agreement touching upon vital interests of all 24 members of the Union.[4]

The diversification of energy sources is under consideration in the EU as a main panacea for addressing imminent energy threats. For a number of years, the European Commission's leaders and experts and the US administration have spoken of the need to diversify oil and gas sources to eliminate the monopolistic dependence on Russian deliveries. The idea of such diversification seems sensible for the countries dependant on imports. But how does one try to realize this diversification, and at what cost? The US and Brussels were ready to diversify at any cost, ignoring a project's economic reasonability, profitability, the ecological threats connected with its realization and even pure common sense.

One of the first cases of such diversification was the US administration's proposal to construct the Baku–Tbilisi–Ceikhan (BTC) oil pipeline. When it initially appeared in the US in the early 1990s, some oil majors pointed out that at that time, the project was unreasonable. The US administration, however, persistently pushed that project, pursuing its own geopolitical objects – primarily to isolate Russia from a number of post-Soviet republics. In Summer 2006, the pipeline was put into operation. However, by that time Azerbaijan did not have as much oil as was necessary to fill the pipe to full capacity. High-ranking US officials (including former US Defense Minister Donald Rumsfeld) began to talk Kazakhstan into joining the BTC pipeline. Ignoring the ecology and relations

the company acts otherwise, threatened to revoke the license. Recently, the Chamber of Accounts calculated that according to the practically ruinous conditions of the "production-sharing" agreement on the Sakhalin-2 project, and the recent decision of the project's operator, Sakhalin Energy, to double its cost, Russia as a result will get only about 10 percent of the extracted energy resources of that richest deposit. See: *Kommersant GUIDE* 213: 31.

4 See *International Herald Tribune*, November 24, 2006; *Wall Street Journal*, November 24–26, 2006.

with other Caspian states, it proposed to build a trans-Caspian pipeline and join it to the BTC. To attain his goal, Rumsfeld discovered the presence of democracy in Kazakhstan, in contrast to Russia. Nevertheless, Kazakhstan refused to participate in the construction of a pipeline, but agreed to partially fill the BTC pipe using tanker oil transportation from a new deposit to be put in operation in 2008. Thus, for several more years, the BTC project sometime would be unprofitable. The US is thus the top-ranking state in energy politicization, an offense of which it doggedly accuses Russia. Thanks to the BTC project, the US succeeded, if not in solving the energy problem, then in creating a special anti-Russian group of states on the territory of the Commonwealth of Independent States (CIS), similar to the case when, under their influence, a group of "new Europe" countries appeared inside the EU.

At the end of October 2006, the US Secretary of State on the Caucasus and South Europe, Mathew Brize, in an interview with the *Financial Times Deutschland*, declared that the Nord Stream gas pipeline (formerly called the North European Gas Pipeline) would increase Germany's dependence on Russian gas, which might lead to a repetition of the situation with Ukraine on German land. Construction of the Nord Stream pipeline was intended precisely to avoid any repetition of "the situation with Ukraine" (or with Belorussia), to avoid an energy threat for Germany and other EU countries. The Russian Foreign Ministry understandably responded:

> Unfortunately, the impression is formed that behind the US opposition at first to the "Blue Stream" and now to the North-European gas pipeline, there is no concern about Europe's energy security, but the principle professed by some American officials that good gas pipelines are those which bypass Russia.[5]

Russia's efforts to "untie" certain "transit knots" by constructing, together with consumer countries, gas pipelines directly connecting suppliers and consumers are by no means a threat to these consumers. If Russia was fomenting such plans, why would it get involved in large-scale investments, and even allow companies from consumer countries access to joint development of new deposits in its territory? Such mutually beneficial cooperation does not suit the EU's ally-competitor, the US, for which the strengthening of such an independent pole of influence as the EU is undesirable. For other reasons, expansion of "old Europe's" direct energy cooperation with Russia did not suit certain "new European" countries. And this was not only because Russia refused to deliver gas to them to satisfy their internal demands, as Russia confirmed all its obligations to them, and was ready to take new ones upon itself. The reasons are that first, these countries would have forfeited the chance to blackmail Russia (as they have repeatedly done) by stopping the transit or by "non-sanctioned extraction" of somebody else's gas; second, they would lose the chance to earn more on an increase of transit services; and third,

5 *Vremya Novostei*, November 3, 2006.

they wished to demonstrate once again their loyalty to the US, or to satisfy their ambitions and the urge for revenge for their "common Soviet past."

The EU leadership's claims about Russia do not show great consistency. It accuses Russia of an urge toward monopolization of European energy markets and of imposing its political domination. To prevent such developments, it proclaims its adherence to a free energy market (free of long-term contracts with Russia) and calls on its countries to diversify their import sources. But when Russia says that if the mutually beneficial and equal long-term partnership does not suit the EU, and Russia may thus use its legal right to diversify the consumers of its hydrocarbon resources, the EU protests that these resources are not enough for everyone, and that Russia is blackmailing the EU. What is preferable for the Brussels bureaucracy – stability and security of energy deliveries, or a phantom freedom of energy markets under conditions where the world is becoming more and more global and interconnected?

The Realism of Depoliticizing Energy Cooperation

The general course of energy cooperation between Russia and the EU shows a certain duplicity. On one level – political, diplomatic and bureaucratic – an endless duel is under way, with exchanges of blows, mutual accusations, threats and politicized diversification. But on a second, lower, level there is real cooperation between corporations of both parties with measured, diligent work in creating joint enterprises, exchanges of assets, rendering of services, and bilateral and multilateral agreements. Here, businesses are operating, contrary to the wishful thinking of an ideologized and politicized bureaucracy in Brussels, guided by pragmatism and realism. At the October 2006 EU Gas Summit:

> On the supply side, companies were surprisingly less worried than politicians about the short and medium term but were more interested in solving the technical hurdles to uninterrupted supply. They were concerned about the political turn the market has been taking and its impact on the implementation of the huge investments that will be needed to sustain and develop production and transport infrastructure. They also were in favor of stronger partnership, dialogue, and even interdependence with gas-producing countries.[6]

Probably proceeding from this business realism, the Russian leadership, and especially President Putin, permanently and directly supervising energy policy, reacted surprisingly calmly to all the political complications raised in the West. It kept its belief in common sense, in peoples', as well as European and Russian businesses', mutual interest in intensification of equal energy cooperation aimed at the abolition of threats to energy security. Russia's leaders and Gazprom were,

6 *Oil and Gas Journal* (November 13, 2006): 23.

step by step, developing structures for mutually beneficial energy cooperation with European business. This presented a sharp contrast to the political level, where many European Commission top officials set themselves the task of forming a "common energy policy" – a united front against Russia. Real achievements in Russia – European business energy cooperation – continue unpublicized.

Nord Stream

One such initiative is Nord Stream (formerly known as the North European Gas Pipeline). The model of mutually beneficial cooperation connected with this project deserves special attention. Initially, this was born as a Russian–German project. Gazprom and its old partner in cooperation, with 16 years' experience, German Wintershall (a 100 percent BASF subsidiary), came to an agreement on the joint construction of gas pipeline on the Baltic seabed for 1,200 kilometers connecting terminals on Russia's coast (in the suburbs of Vyborg) and Germany (in the Greifsvald region). The experience acquired in the course of cooperation between Gazprom and Wintershall included creation of the Wingas joint venture, through which Gazprom executed its partial participation in downstream sphere in some German lands, as well as another joint venture, Achimgaz, which had already begun to extract natural gas from the Achimovsky deposits in the Urengoy region. Soon Germany's largest energy corporation, E.On, joined Nord Stream. Together, they founded the Nord Stream AG corporation, where 51 percent of shares belonged to Gazprom, and 49 percent were divided into equal parts between BASF and E.On. Another project participant important for Gazprom then appeared on the stage – the Dutch corporation Gasunie, which received 9 percent from BASF and E.On's shares in equal proportion. In exchange for the above, Gazprom received a 9 percent share in the Balgazand Bacton Line, connecting the continent with the UK. It would allow Gazprom's affiliate in Northern Europe, Gazprom Marketing Trading, to increase its deliveries to the UK from 4 billion cubic meters (m^3) in 2005 to 10 billion m^3 in 2010. The UK, the largest gas market in Europe, had until then been carefully safeguarding its downstream from Gazprom. Gazprom received access to other gas transportation and gas storing in the Gasunie infrastructure, the largest in Europe, which can render services up to 100 billion m^3 of natural gas flows.

The Nord Stream project envisages construction of two gas pipelines. The first was due to begin construction in January 2008 and be completed by 2010 (together with a service platform in the Gotland island region of Sweden). Its throughput capacity will total 27.5 billion m^3. The second, parallel, gas pipeline will be put into operation in October 2013, and its aggregate capacity will then reach 55 billion m^3. It will cost €5.5 billion and provide up to a 25 percent increase in the EU's natural gas demand by 2015.[7]

7 *Petroleum Economist* (November 2006): 37.

In the middle of July 2006, E.On and Gazprom signed a framework agreement on the south Russian deposit, under which, up to 2009, the German concern would pay €1.2 billion for the acquisition of 25 percent minus one share in this deposit's development project. Gazprom would get 50 percent minus one share in Hungarian E.On Foldgaz Storage and E.On Foldgaz Trade, and 25 percent plus one share in E.On Hungarian, plus additional compensation. Thanks to the active cooperation between Ruhrgas and Gazprom in the past, E.On (which Ruhrgas became part of after the takeover) thus possessed 6.5 percent of Gazprom's shares.[8]

On November 13, 2006, Nord Stream AG participants E.On Ruhrgas, Wintershall and Gazprom submitted a claim to create this holding. In a month's time they received approval from Germany's anti-monopoly agencies. On November 14 they presented all the documents on the project to appropriate Russian, Finnish, Swedish, Dutch and German state bodies, whose exclusive economic zones and/or territorial waters would be crossed by the Nord Stream gas pipeline route. Official notification was also received by countries whose waters would not be touched by the gas pipeline's construction: Estonia, Lithuania, Latvia and Poland.[9]

Sweden, which had expressed its intention to join in natural gas deliveries via an offshoot from the future main gas pipeline, expressed worries regarding the ecological aspects of building the project. A majority of experts, however, connected its position with forthcoming parliamentary elections. In December 2006, Finland decided to join Nord Stream and to build a branch. This was to be carried out by the Gazum company, which distributes gas in the country. The gas pipeline branch would go underground in the region of the Karelia isthmus, which, if necessary, would simplify the link-up with the Finnish gas pipeline system. Finland has already offered its ecological expertise to the project.[10] All those countries that stood out in opposition to the Nord Stream project had traditionally played the role of transit states. Especially loud was the voice of Poland. As a result, in January 2007 the European Investment Bank declared that it would be unable to finance the Nord Stream gas pipeline's construction.[11]

Such a large project with such reputable participants did not depend on credit from the European Investment Bank. However, this action once again demonstrated the lack of a joint and clear strategy in the EU necessary to provide energy security, and the predominance of private, poorly grounded claims over common European interests. The *Petroleum Economist* pointed out that Poland's negative stance, as a traditional transit state, was determined by the fact that the Nord Stream pipeline was "removing an important bargaining chip with Moscow."[12]

The Nord Stream gas pipeline project shows that in some cases it is not the diversification of energy sources, but the diversification of natural gas delivery

8 *Kommersant*, December 15, 2006.

9 *Vremya Novostei*, November 15, 2006; *Kommersant*, December 22, 2006.

10 *Vremya Novostei*, December 12, 2006.

11 *Vedomosti*, January 10, 2006.

12 *Petroleum Economist* (November 2006): 37.

routes that is important. Indeed, if a supplier of energy resources has for dozens of years, notwithstanding political factors (such as the Cold War) been proving its reliability, and has never ever broken its commitments, why change the source? If new, unreliable transit countries appear between the consumer country and the supplier country, it is necessary to react to the challenge jointly and in unity, not occupy a formally neutral position, as some European politicians did in early 2007 during the short-term Russian–Belorussian gas–oil crisis. Energy security is too serious an issue to allow oneself such "neutrality."

Nabucco and Nabucco-2

The Nabucco project appeared as a result of the EU's aspiration to find an alternative to Gazprom at any cost. With European Commission financing, the Austrian corporation OMV carried out preliminary development of this project, which EU Energy Commissioner Andris Piebalgs characterized as the EU's "most important gas supply project."[13] The Nabucco agreement was signed in June 2006 in Brussels by Commissioner Piebalgs and the foreign ministers of Turkey, Bulgaria, Romania, Hungary and Austria. Each of the five consortium participants would have 20 percent of the shares, while the overall cost of the project would be $5.8–6 billion. It was expected that up to 70 percent of financing would be allocated by the European Investment Bank. The construction would be carried out by Austrian OMV, Turkish Botas, Hungarian MOL, Bulgarian Bulgargaz and Rumanian Transgaz.[14]

Initially, it was planned that natural gas would be delivered from Iran and Azerbaijan via Turkey. By 2010, a minimum of 8 billion m^3 would have to pass through the pipeline, while by 2020 the volume of gas would be increased to 31 billion m^3. Half was meant for transit countries, while the rest would continue to a supply nexus at Baumgarten, Austria, where the gas could enter the Austrian, German and Italian markets. But from the very beginning the project faced serious difficulties. The planned timing for the beginning of the construction had to be changed from 2008 to 2011.

The main reason was the conceptual approach of Brussels. European Commission officials were obsessed less with providing energy security and stable natural gas deliveries to appropriate EU countries than with getting rid by any means of the much disliked "energy interdependence" between the EU and Russia. This hostility toward Russia, and Gazprom in particular, prevented a sensible assessment of the most important aspect of the project: how secure were the alternative natural gas sources proposed by them? It was soon discovered that Azerbaijan's reserves were not large enough to provide the volume necessary for the pipeline. Then Brussels turned to Iran and Egypt. Nevertheless, as the *Petroleum Economist* magazine put it, "the EU's hopes that Egypt or Iran will

13 Ibid.: 20.

14 *Kommersant GUIDE* 213: 28.

make up the difference betray either naivety in Brussels or ignorance about the domestic politics of both these countries."[15] Iran was well and widely known for it tough opposition to the US and any cooperation with its allies. The generally unstable situation in Iran and the unsettled nuclear problem made the aggravation of tension between Gazprom and the Ukranian–Belorussian partners look like child's play. As for Egypt, natural gas consumption in the country grew rapidly against the background of a growth slowdown in extraction.

Gazprom, with the main advantages before the initial variant of the Nabucco project, began a broadened version of Nabucco, a sort of Nabucco-2, or the Southern European Gas project (a southern equivalent of Nord Stream). This project envisaged extending the existing Blue Stream pipeline, which crosses the Black Sea from Russia into Turkey, and from there stretches north and west into Bulgaria, Romania and Hungary. The present Blue Stream capacity exceeds Turkish demand in natural gas. Gazprom has agreed in principle with Turkey about the possibility of re-export and transit of this "surplus" potential gas to third countries. Moreover, Gazprom was already negotiating with Italian Eni (the firm that had done contract work for Russia on the Blue Stream project) on construction of the second gas pipeline – Blue Stream-2.

In 2006, Gazprom held negotiation rounds both with official Nabucco project participants and with some other countries – potential members of a wider project – on construction of a South European gas pipeline, and concluded agreements on further development of economic and energy cooperation.

In Hungary, in Summer 2006 Gazprom signed an agreement with the MOL company on construction of a new gas pipeline to supply Russian gas to Hungary, which was already 70 percent dependent on Russian natural gas deliveries. The agreement also envisaged construction of gas storage in western Hungary for Gazprom's possible deliveries of natural gas to nearby markets. Gazprom's aspiration to turn Hungary into a hub for deliveries to Central European countries looked more realistic against the background of Gazprom's agreements with E.On, according to which the latter agreed to swap some of its Hungarian assets for a share in the Yuzhno-Russky gas field development. These concrete Gazprom proposals and agreements were preferable for Hungary compared to the Nabucco project, which was still in the stages of planning, negotiating and harmonizing among its participants. For the majority of the project's participants, it became obvious that it would be practically impossible to fill the planned Nabucco gas pipeline without Russian gas. In October 2006, in an interview with *Petroleum Economist* magazine, Wolfgang Ruttenstorfer, the Chief Executive of OMV (participating since the very beginning of Nabucco in 2004), admitted there could be "synergies" between the Nabucco line and another pipeline following a similar route that Gazprom said it would build. "We are open," said Ruttenstorfer. "If there are synergies, let's use them." Very soon, an OMV spokesman confirmed this, saying: "We always said that there would be one or two strategic partners. We don't rule

15 *Petroleum Economist* (November 2006): 20.

out Gazprom."[16] Agreements were signed earlier in Spring of the same year, as a result of which Gazprom's direct presence in Austria (in 2005 it accounted for 68 percent of this country's natural gas imports) strengthened through the prolongation of the Austrian EconGas company's (of OMV group) contract with Gazprom for gas imports amounting to 7 billion m^3 up to 2027. At the same time, Gazprom delivered additional gas to Austria, which was distributed by the Gwh company – a joint venture of Gasexport (50 percent of shares), OMV (25.1 percent) and Centrex Europe Energy & Gas AG (29.9 percent). The latter heads a group of companies controlled by Gazprom with the help of a chain of financial companies spread between Cyprus and Luxemburg.[17]

Important agreements were reached in December 2006 between Gazprom and Bulgaria. The state company Bulgargaz signed documents with Gazprom on the further development of Russian–Bulgarian relations over the delivery and transit of Russian natural gas. Gazprom is the only natural gas exporter to Bulgaria. In 2005, it delivered 3.2 billion m^3 of gas and, in 2006, 4 billion. Gazprom has a large share in the downstream sphere – 73.8 percent in 2005. AO Overseas Inc., where Gazprom owns 50 percent, participates in 32 trading companies and is majority owner of 26 gas-distributing companies. Bulgaria is also an important transit link, through which natural gas from Russia travels to Turkey, Greece and Macedonia. Under the agreement reached in Sophia, Bulgaria agreed to give up the old (Ukrainian) barter payment for its transit scheme before the appointed time, which was connected with a special price for gas delivered to Bulgaria itself, and to move to monetary payment. At the same time, the parties agreed to prolong to 2030 the transit agreement which had been in force until 2010. Gazprom, in turn, agreed to a regime of stage-by-stage (for six years, 2007–12) price increases for gas delivered to Bulgaria from the current $91 per thousand m^3 to $245, with transit volumes to be increased from 12 billion to 17.8 billion m^3, instead of $785 million. In 2006, Bulgargaz will get a guaranteed long-term profit of up to $3 billion by 2012, and $5 billion by 2030.[18]

At the end of 2006 Gazprom Export, the Serbian government and state company Srbijagas signed a memorandum on construction of part of the South European gas pipeline on the countries' territory. The capacity of the 400 kilometer-long gas pipeline toconnect Serbia with Bulgaria and Croatia will be 20 billion m^3 a year, while the cost of the project would be more than $1 billion. This gas pipeline would be part of the South European Gas Pipeline Project, along which Russian gas would pass via Turkey to Bulgaria, Serbia and Croatia, to the north of Italy, and to Austria.[19]

---

16 Ibid.

17 *Il Sole 24 Ore*, November 19, 2006.

18 *Kommersant*, December 19, 2006; *Vedomosti*, December 18, 2006; *ROSBALT*), available at <http://www.rosbalt.ru/2006/12/18/279352/html> (in Russian).

19 *Vremy Novostei* and *Kommersant*, December 21, 2006.

December 2006 saw many Gazprom management trips for negotiations in European countries. In Greece, the possibility of direct gas deliveries via an alternative distributor, Prometheus Gas SA, was discussed. At the time, the main buyer of Russian gas in Greece was the state corporation DEPA. In 2005, Gazprom Export delivered to Greece about 2.4 billion m^3. Up to 2016, deliveries of 3.1 billion m^3 a year were planned, while after 2016, up to about 7 billion. German RWE AG (its affiliate company RWE Transgas is the monopoly gas supplier to the Czech market) extended its contract with Gazprom for natural gas deliveries to the Czech Republic up to 2025. The volume of annual deliveries would total 9 billion m^3 per year.[20]

Significant successes were achieved in Gazprom's protracted negotiations with such large players in EC energy markets as Italy's Eni Corporation and France's Gaz de France. Following almost 18 months of negotiations, on November 16, 2006, in Moscow, the head of Eni, Paolo Scaroni, signed an agreement with Gazprom on a strategic partnership. Under it, as of 2007, Gazprom was given the chance to perform direct deliveries of Russian gas to Italy. Before that, Gazprom sold all the gas destined for Italy on the Slovakian-Austrian border. In 2005, the volume of these deliveries amounted to 23.33 billion m^3, taking second place in Russian gas deliveries to the EU after Germany, and also second place in overall Italian imports of gas via pipeline after Algeria.[21] The volume of deliveries ceded by Eni was comparatively small – initially about 2 billion m^3, with further gradual increases bringing them up to 3 billion m^3 by 2010 – approximately 14 percent from the gas volumes sold by the Russian company to its Italian partner before. The term of the current contracts for delivery of Russian gas to Italy is extended from 2017 to 2035.

For Gazprom, this agreement is of principal importance. Italy is the second large EU country where, in defiance of EU officials' resistance, Gazprom has obtained access to the downstream sphere. In turn, the Italian company nurtured plans for participation within the framework of this strategic partnership in contract work on the Blue Stream-2 gas pipeline construction, sharing its new technology with Gazprom. The technology allows an increase in pressure in gas pipelines up to 140 atmospheres, which makes it possible to double the transported gas volume.[22] The agreement also envisages the possibility of exchange of assets. Both sides discussed the question of an acquisition by Italian Eni S.p.A. of 19.4 percent of NOVATEK shares (Russia's largest independent gas-extracting company), which in September of 2006 was obtained by Gazprom's German company, Gazprom Germania GmbH. On November 1, during his visit to London, Eni director general Paolo Scaroni proclaimed that his corporation was ready to spend €10 billion for an acquisition together with Gazprom of two gas assets in Russia, and that cooperation with Gazprom was "the guarantee of

20 *Kommersant*, December 22, 2006.

21 *BP Statistical Review of World Energy* (June 2006): 30.

22 *Expert* 43 (November 20–26, 2006): 8; *Vremya Novostei*, November 17, 2006.

success."[23] Characterizing the importance of the partnership between the two energy corporations, Italian Prime Minister Romano Prodi stressed that the agreement was "preparation for closer cooperation between Eni and Gazprom, and between Italy and Russia in general."[24]

During the meeting in early December of 2006, Gazprom, Eni and TNK-BP leaders discussed creating Eni's joint venture with Rospan (the affiliated company of TNK-BP which owns the license for development of the Achomovski gas pools of the Urengoy deposit) with Gazprom as mediator. In turn, Gazprom was interested in securing from Eni 40 percent of the shares of the Enipower energy company, uniting seven electricity stations, to participate in development of the Lyban Elephant deposit, and a plant producing LNG in Egypt's Dammiette.[25]

As for Gaz de France, the agreement signed on December 19, 2006 with Gazprom envisaged extension of the contract on gas deliveries from Russia to 2030. Gaz de France would buy from Gazprom 12 billion m^3 a year. The French also contracted for 2.5 billion m^3 with deliveries via the future Nord Stream gas pipeline as of 2010. In turn, Gazprom received a chance for direct deliveries to French consumers of up to 1.5 billion m^3 per year. On November 24, Gazprom established Gazprom Marketing & Trading France, and in the next several years planned to deliver up to 2 billion m^3 of gas via it directly to around one thousand consumers. Gazprom also carried out, together with Gaz de France (by swap), a trade of LNG. Gaz de France was engaged in a merger with the Franco-Belgian company Suez. EU anti-monopoly agencies approved the deal, but on condition that "superfluous" assets be sold. The new corporation would have to part with Belgian gas companies and a heat network in France. Gazprom had a good chance to participate in the acquisition of these assets, given Gaz de France management's favorable attitude.[26]

Conclusion

This overview of Russia's relations with the EU in the field of energy shows a sharp contrast between the real cooperation between Russian and European business, and the noisy, sometimes exaggerated, panicked reaction of European Commission officials to any Russian step toward integration in the European economic space on equal and mutually beneficial terms, as was called for by the St. Petersburg Summit. In the US Administration's behavior, one can find the logic

23 *Vedomosti* and *Kommersant*, December 4, 2006.

24 *Expert* 43: 8.

25 *Vremya Novostei*, November 3, 2006; *Il Sole 24 Ore*, November 19, 2006; *Kommersant*, December 6, 2006.

26 *ROSBALT*, December 19, 2006, available at <http://www.rosbalt.ru/2006/12/19/279491/html> (in Russian); *Oil and Gas Journal* (December 4, 2006): 8; *Vremya Novostei* and *Kommersant*, December 20, 2006.

of a competitor. But logic can barely be found in the behavior of some European Commission officials. Efforts toward mutually dependant cooperation cannot and should not be depicted as Russia's insidious actions aimed at establishing its own energy monopoly and political dominance.

Bibliography

Bordachev, T. (2004). "Russia and the European Union: To End and Begin Anew." Carnegie Endowment for International Peace Briefing Papers, 6(10). Available at <www.carnegie.ru/en/pubs/briefings/71436.htm>.

Chapter 11

Energy Security: The International Energy Agency and the G8

Victoria V. Panova

Energy and related issues have been the focus of the leading industrial countries since the first G7 summit in 1975. Indeed, one of the main reasons for setting up the G7/8 was the energy crisis, along with the economic crisis that came in its wake.

The intensive development of capitalist economies after the end of World War II led to considerably increased consumption of energy resources. From 1954 to 1974, crude oil production grew more than fourfold, from nearly 700 million tonnes to 2.9 billion tonnes, an annual increase of almost 8 percent. But the energy crisis of the 1970s and the recession in the world economy politically and economically motivated the members of the Organization for Petroleum Exporting Countries (OPEC) to reduce oil production so that extraction reached a peak of 3.2 billion tonnes in 1979 and a minimum of 2.8 billion tonnes in 1983.

In the middle of the 1970s, the leading Western countries recognized the vulnerability of their economies and their dependence on energy supply, the main flows of which were from the Middle East. The cause was the 1973 Arab–Israeli war, which started with an attack on Israel by Egypt and Syria during Yom Kippur. Within ten days of the end of the war, partly thanks to the insistence of Egypt's Anwar Sadat, Saudi Arabia induced OPEC members to raise crude oil prices by 70 percent (from $3 to $5 per barrel). Thus, it was decided to reduce oil extraction by 5 percent and continue with a 5 percent reduction per month until the desired political results were achieved. Some countries reduced extraction by 10 percent. The oil embargo was lifted on March 18, 1974. Although this occurred over a short period, developed countries economies nevertheless suffered a serious blow.

The second crisis of 1979–81 led to the oil price reaching $37.29 per barrel, thus attracting further interest in alternative energy sources and energy-saving economic models.

These two shocks led to several actions on the part of the industrialized countries. One step was to establish the International Energy Agency (IEA) in Paris within the framework of the Organisation for Economic Co-operation and Development (OECD) on November 15, 1974. The other step a year later was the establishment at Rambouillet of the informal mechanism for cooperation among six leading industrial countries, with Canada joining a year later – the G7.

Energy Issues in the G7/G8 Since its Inception

There are five phases of G7/8 activities in the realm of energy. During the two energy crises of 1970s and the early 1980s, issues relating to energy security were prominent on the G7 agenda. Later, during the period of much lower prices and sustainable excess of supply over demand, this issue was mentioned only within the context of the environment. At the end of the 1980s and early 1990s, after the demise of the Soviet Union and the socialist bloc, the G7 leaders shifted to focus on the problem of nuclear security. This focus extended beyond being an environmental issue after the Chernobyl nuclear accident in 1986, as well as in light of the growing risks of proliferation of nuclear materials and technologies. After 2000, energy security in its own right recaptured the attention of G8 countries. Yet another phase, with economic crises introducing new realms within the issue of energy security, closely intertwined with the issue of climate change. Thus priority was given to the expansion of environmentally friendly energy renewables and alternative sources of energy.

The G7 as a Rapid Reaction Force: From 1975 to the Early 1980s

The 1975 Rambouillet Declaration can, with certain reservations, be called the charter of the G7, as it outlined the main reasons for the establishment of the group and its agenda.

The leaders acknowledged that changes in the modern world led to increased vulnerability. In order to achieve the aims outlined in the declaration – to promote the well-being of the world economy and to acknowledge the responsibility of governing an open, democratic society dedicated to individual liberty and social advancement – they decided to "play their own full part and strengthen their efforts for closer international cooperation and constructive dialogue among all countries, transcending differences in stages of economic development, degrees of resource endowment and political and social systems" (G7 1975). Since "world economic growth is clearly linked to the increasing availability of energy sources," the leaders decided to undertake actions in order to secure "the energy sources needed for [the] growth" of their economies. Their common interests required that they "continue to cooperate in order to reduce their dependence on imported energy through conservation and the development of alternative sources."

At the following summit in San Juan, Puerto Rico, in 1976, the leaders pledged to continue their efforts to develop, conserve and use rationally different energy resources, as well as assist developing countries.[1]

1 There was, however, one energy-related decision taken by a G7 country: the Energy Policy and Conservation Act took effect in February 1976 and authorized the establishment of the Strategic Petroleum Reserve, participation in International Energy Program and oil price regulation.

The 1977 London Summit, however, saw a much wider and detailed consideration of the issue. It was mentioned not only in the communiqué, but also in the appendix to the Declaration of the Downing Street Summit Conference. The summit put further stress on conservation and diversification of energy production, in order to reduce Western countries' dependence on oil. In particular, with the decision to launch appropriate research, it was agreed to increase the share of nuclear power, with parallel commitments to reduce the risks of nuclear proliferation (G7 1977).

Energy issues were included in the communiqué issued at the 1978 Bonn Summit. In the introduction, the leaders agreed to "a comprehensive strategy covering growth, employment and inflation, international monetary policy, energy, trade and other issues of particular interest to developing countries" (G7 1978). Paragraphs 4–16 were devoted exclusively to energy problems. Specifically, the worsening political situation in Iran posed a danger, and an oil pipeline fire in October reduced Iraqi oil production considerably. The document outlined specific actions taken by all G7 participants. Thus, the volume of oil imported in 1978 and 1979 was supposed to be lower than that imported in 1977. In order to discourage excessive consumption of oil and to encourage a move toward coal, the United States was determined that the prices paid for oil should rise to the world level by the end of 1980 (G7 1978). In January 1979, the US distributed its first Crude Oil Buy-Sell Program allocations.[2]

At Bonn, the G7 countries also agreed to review their national energy programs over the long term. Private and public investment was underlined as effective instruments of more efficient energy use, thus leading to economic growth. For the first time, the G7 leaders noted that within energy development, it was important to pay specific attention to environmental protection and population security in energy development. A main reason lay in the largest crude oil spill to date, in March, when the *Amoco Cadiz* tanker ran aground off the coast of France, spilling 1.6 million barrels of crude oil.

From the start, the G7 acted as a mechanism of global governance, assuming coordination and other functions with regard to the developed countries, as well to the developing world. The OECD and the World Bank were vested with the responsibility to undertake specific actions (G8 1978).

The next year marked a new oil crisis, with OPEC decisions to further raise oil prices. The worsening political situation in Iran, following the revolution and the hostage-taking incident at the US embassy on November 4, 1979, led the Carter administration to order a stop to Iranian exports to the US and, subsequently, to Iran canceling all contracts with US oil companies.

These developments led to a stronger and more specific text in the communiqué released at the G7 Tokyo Summit in 1979. Inflation, which had previously been decreasing, regained momentum in most countries. Rising oil prices reduced the

2 This program existed from 1974 to 1981 to control petroleum prices. Buyers had to be small or independent refiners, whereas sellers were limited to the 15 largest refiners.

room for maneuver in the economic policy of G7 countries. Consequently, oil shortages and high prices damaged not only developed countries, but also, more significantly, developing countries.

The G7 also called for steps to bring into the open the working of oil markets by means of a "register of international oil transactions." It added the "feasibility of requiring that at the time of unloading crude oil cargoes, documents be presented indicating the purchase price as certified by the producer country," along with more information "on the profit situation of oil companies and on the use of the funds available" to them (G7 1979). It also decided to minimize and finally abolish administrative action that could put upward pressure on oil prices.[3]

The G7 reiterated the desirability of increasing the use of coal and nuclear energy, with the key role given to the International Atomic Energy Agency (IAEA). In the context of further assistance to the developing countries, G7 leaders called for the expansion of the World Bank's program on the use of hydrocarbon resources.

The key element in energy discussions was the recognition of the central role of new technologies, and the need for large public and private investment to reduce dependency on fossil fuels over the long term. The G7 decided to establish the International Energy Technology Group (IETG), linked to the OECD, the IEA and other appropriate multilateral organizations (G7 1979).

At the 1980 Venice Summit, the issue of energy prices and supply took central place. A substantial amount of criticism was directed toward OPEC countries, because continuing prices increases were not determined by market mechanisms. OPEC was never a unified body, however, with disagreement from the very start between the moderates and the "hawks." Thus, in December 1980, OPEC's pricing structure collapsed when Saudi Arabia used $32 per barrel as a marker and others used $36 per barrel. Moreover, rising tensions between Iraq and Iran over the Shatt al-Arab waterway further increased instability in the Middle East.

The G7 countries believed that their primary task was to "break the existing link between economic growth and consumption of oil" within a decade, with a maximum "reliance placed on the price mechanism," coordination between domestic and world oil prices, and "effective fiscal incentives and administrative measures" (G7 1980).

To increase the supply and use of energy resources other than oil during the next decade to the equivalent of 1,520 million barrels per day, the G7 leaders agreed to double coal production by the beginning of 1990s, asking the International Coal Industry Advisory Board to prepare the necessary recommendations. The International Nuclear Fuel Cycle Evaluation Group findings were noted as an important contribution to the nuclear energy issue, mostly in regard to "increasing predictable supplies; the most effective utilization of uranium sources, including

3 Nevertheless, national interests prevailed over the group interests, even within the G7 club. In October 1979, Canada eliminated light crude oil exports to US refiners, except for those exports required by operational constraints of pipelines.

the development of advanced technologies; and the minimization of proliferation risks, including support of International Atomic Energy Agency (IAEA) safeguards" (G7 1980).

Strong support was shown for the IETG recommendations, which allow for the commercial introduction of new energy technologies within a short time. The G7 leaders also agreed to create an international team of interested countries on specific projects, to be reviewed regularly by high-level representatives.

The G7 leaders affirmed their responsibility together with the exporting countries and socialist bloc for the fate of the developing countries (G7 1980). The main problem faced by developing countries was payment imbalances. The primary mechanism for adjustment was identified as the international capital market. The G7 leaders also supported the "work in progress by their monetary authorities and the Bank for International Settlements (BIS) designed to improve the supervision and security of the international banking system," with possible useful input by private banks.

The 1981 G7 Ottawa Summit at Montebello did not constitute a breakthrough in energy. Part of the G7 leaders' discussion on the energy issues faced by developing countries reviewed previous decisions and initiatives. Practical steps on renewables (solar, geothermal energy and biomass) were to be discussed at the subsequent United Nations Conference on New and Renewable Sources of Energy (G7 1981).

The low profile of energy issues is partly due to the fact that oil prices started to fall and the peak of the crisis passed. In 1981, Saudi Arabia flooded the market with inexpensive oil, forcing unprecedented price cuts by OPEC members. In October, all 13 OPEC members compromised on $32 per barrel. Later, the benchmark price was maintained, but differentials were adjusted.

The common perception of energy security derived from the conclusion that markets were ineffective and reacted to price fluctuations and supply disruptions too quickly. Many believed that the state should intervene to protect the consumer. The criteria for the G7 in 1970s and 1980s included maximizing the use of the members' own energy resources, increasing energy efficiency through taxation and legislation, reducing energy consumption, diversifying energy sources with the aim to lower the proportion of oil, and reducing oil imports, especially from the Middle East.

The main lesson of this stage of G7 activities, which was characteristic of overregulation and governmental intervention, was the discovery that energy security can be achieved only within the framework of effective market mechanisms functioning inside and outside the G7 countries.

Problem Solved? The 1980s

The liberalization of the oil market, a drop in prices and reduced oil demand in the mid-1980s contributed to the global economic recovery. Moreover, the growth of oil extraction outside OPEC countries was exceeding forecasts.

High oil prices led to changes in the energy sector, with new technologies for insulating buildings, increasing energy efficiency for business, and reducing fuel use by automobiles. All these factors led to declining prices.

Between 1982 and 1985, OPEC countries tried to stabilize prices, establishing low production quotas. In June 1985, OPEC output fell to a 20-year low of 13.7 million barrels per day, but this led to a further loss of customers in favor of cheaper North Sea oil. Thus, by mid-1986, crude oil prices dropped by 50 percent – below $10 per barrel.

Adding to the gloomy situation for the Arab countries was the start of the "tanker war" in March 1984. Over the next nine months, 44 ships, including Iranian, Iraqi, Saudi Arabian and Kuwaiti tankers, were attacked by Iraqi or Iranian warplanes or damaged by mines.

The crude oil price went up for a short time in 1990, influenced by the Iraqi invasion of Kuwait. But after the Persian Gulf War, its price steadily decreased until 1994, when it reached its lowest level since 1973. By the early 1990s, however, oil prices had returned to pre-crisis levels. With oil demand resuming, it became clear that a number of key energy security issues had lost their relevance.

The issue of dependency on oil imports was practically absent from the G7 agenda for a long time as it concentrated increasingly on environmental protection, and from the second half of the 1980s, on nuclear safety.

Apart from further oil price reductions, which caused few energy problems compared to other issues discussed by the G7 leaders, the early 1980s became the turning point as the agenda focused more on political rather than the original economic issues. This transition was primarily the effect of a change of power in most G7 countries. The newly elected conservative Ronald Reagan of the United States, Margaret Thatcher of the United Kingdom, Helmut Kohl of Germany and Yasuhiro Nakasone of Japan emphasized military and political cooperation inside the Western bloc, in response to what they perceived the socialist bloc as having. In the early 1980s, the Cold War recaptured its dynamics when Reagan announced the Strategic Defense Initiative Program, more commonly called "Star Wars." At the G7 Ottawa-Montebello Summit in 1981, East–West relations assumed what would become a permanent place on the G7 agenda. The following year, at the Versailles Summit, the leaders announced that it was possible to limit credit lines to socialist countries.

Energy problems at the first summit of the second cycle, at Versailles in 1982, featured only in one short paragraph. Devoted to developing countries, it stated the need for "special temporary arrangements to overcome funding problems for IDA [International Development Association] VI, and for an early start to consideration of IDA VII," with an emphasis on the increase of "food and energy production in developing countries which have to import these essentials, and to programs to address the implications of population growth" (G7 1982). During the same summit, the US was unsuccessful in convincing its European partners to reject the deal to start construction of the Druzhba pipeline, which would allow a mass supply of Soviet natural gas to Europe.

The 1983 Williamsburg Summit was notable for different reasons. For the first time in the history of the G7 forum, a political declaration was issued on security issues. The leaders acknowledged that security for their countries was indivisible and should be maintained on a global basis, with support for the deployment of US cruise missiles and Pershing-2 missiles in Western Europe (in response to the Soviet SS-20 missiles). This integrated Japan's Nakasone government into the common Western security strategy. The only passage in the final communiqué that related to energy was an agreement that oil price reductions should not lead to cessation of energy conservation efforts, the development of alternative sources of energy and an improvement in constructive dialogue between oil-exporting and oil-importing countries (G7 1983).

Energy was not a key component of the 1984 G7 London Summit's Final Communiqué. Reference to energy was short and insubstantive, emphasizing previous commitments. However, the G7 leaders decided to activate the Common Fund for Commodities (G7 1984a). There was also concern over the stability of international oil supplies in connection with Iran–Iraq War (G7 1984b).

The 1985 Bonn Summit made no reference to energy issues. Further reductions in oil prices allowed industrial countries to boost non-inflationary growth and increase international trade volumes. The G7 leaders were primarily concerned with the economic difficulties experienced by oil-exporting countries, such as high unemployment, significant internal and external imbalances, exchange rate volatility and protectionism, as well as economic hardships in developing countries and uncertainty over energy resource price levels. A reduction in oil prices was achieved by the coordinated G7 policies, and the leaders called for a continuation of energy market security. The existing situation of the oil market allowed for an increase in production levels.

On April 26, 1986, the Chernobyl nuclear disaster occurred. It had catastrophic consequences for the Soviet Union and neighboring countries, and it was on the agenda at the 1986 Tokyo Summit. The leaders issued a separate statement on the "Implications of the Chernobyl Nuclear Accident," in which they expressed sympathy for those affected by the incident, and a readiness to provide medical and technical assistance (G7 1986). The G7 criticized the USSR for not providing prompt, detailed and complete information on nuclear accidents, especially those with potential transboundary consequences. The Soviet Union would receive a positive assessment of its willingness to cooperate on the issue with the IAEA. It is worth noting that the Chernobyl accident remains on the global agenda: recent related questions refer to the shield construction for the atomic station, whether the reactor station should be shut down, and how to re-evaluate the consequences and effects of such a disaster on the environment and the population.

Environmental Security: Late 1980s to 1990s

In the second half of the 1980s, the G7 viewed energy security through the prism of environmental security. Considerable parts of the documents issued by the

1987 Venice Summit, the 1989 Paris Summit, and the 1990 Houston Summit were devoted to strengthening international cooperation in secure nuclear energy use.[4] At the London Summit in 1991, the leaders announced their support of the European Community initiative on the creation of the European Energy Charter. Full participation in the charter was considered important for promoting free and unhindered energy resources trade, strengthening the security of supply, ensuring environmental protection, and furthering economic reforms in Central and Eastern Europe and the Soviet Union by establishing an open, non-discriminatory regime of commercial investments in the energy sector.[5]

Energy problems have always been closely intertwined with economic and political issues. At the Venice Summit in 1987, the issue of oil supply was considered necessary for military security. The continued Persian Gulf War and the Iranian Ayatollah Khomeini's threat to block the strategically important Strait of Ormuz required the G7 to deliver a serious warning to the warring parties about the inadmissibility of such actions. Although the US had taken concrete actions to prevent such developments, the consolidated position of the rest of the G7 partners to a great extent strengthened these steps and demonstrated a unified front.

At the 1989 Paris Summit, the leaders emphasized the importance of cooperation with hard law organizations, namely with the International Maritime Organization to improve measures to prevent oil spills. The G7 also raised the issue of ocean pollution in 1989. Even during accident-free oil transportation, spills occur during stowage and offloading and from the discharge of bilge water. Indeed, huge spillovers during tanker accidents are not rare, although they account for only 5–6 percent of total oil pollution. On March 25, 1989, the tanker *Exxon Valdez* ran aground, spilling 11 million gallons of crude oil into the waters of Prince William Sound. Oil prices increased as a result of both the spill and potential shortages on the US West Coast caused by refinery fires. Exxon spent $1.4 billion on cleaning up the accident, but even this has not restored the area's full ecological balance. This was at a time when G7 leaders had reached a consensus on the environmental implications of greenhouse gases and the necessity of strengthening energy-saving measures to emissions (G7 1990).

Energy problems came to the forefront of G7 discussions once again due to a political crisis, this time Iraq's aggression against Kuwait. Immediately, crude and product prices soared; exchange markets also reacted with uncertainty and jet fuel prices rose due to increased defense demand. In late August, OPEC failed to revive attempts to organize a formal meeting to discuss the crisis and production strategies. Informal meetings resulted in record price falls. Conflicting reports of promises to increase OPEC output to compensate for the embargoed Iraqi and

---

4 At Houston, due to Washington's traditional interest in security issues, apart from environmental aspect, nuclear non-proliferation was given a large amount of attention.

5 Soon after, on December 17, 1991, the European Energy Charter was signed in the Hague by most European states, the European Community, Australia, Canada, Turkey, the US and Japan.

Kuwaiti oil further compounded market uncertainties. The strategic position of Kuwait, primarily due to its oil-reach capacities, played against Saddam Hussein: his aggression provoked an immediate response from an international coalition led by the US with the consent of the United Nations. One reason for such a surprising global consensus, in addition to the illegitimacy of Saddam's actions against this small country, was the weakened role of the Soviet Union and Mikhail Gorbachev's desire to support his Western colleagues. Gorbachev was motivated by political reasons – the ideology of his "new thinking" – and economic reasons – to make the most of possible Western aid to the Soviet Union.

The Persian Gulf crisis showed that oil supplies and prices remained vulnerable to political crises, although they could be contained to a certain extent by effective market mechanisms, expanded supply by several exporting countries and coordinated action by the IEA, especially with regard to oil reserves. The IEA system can be activated in cases of supply scarcity to one or several members if their consumption exceeds 7 percent. During the 1990–91 Gulf War, the IEA supplied oil globally and, together with other measures, managed to satisfy demand, working in part with Saudi Arabia. The threshold of oil scarcity was not passed.[6] The overall positive outcome of the crisis was the improved relationship between producers and consumers of hydrocarbon resources, which allowed for further promotion of information exchange, transparency and effective functioning of the market. Nevertheless, the war led to certain economic difficulties in a number of countries. At the 1991 London Summit, the Gulf Crisis Financial Co-ordination Group mobilized $16 billion for direct aid to those countries affected by the crisis (G7 1991). Another positive development, supported by the G7 leaders, was the creation of the Gulf Development Fund. After the conclusion of the counter-Iraqi operation, the world experienced the danger of the use of oil as a weapon – this time, not through an embargo, but through the burning of oil wells, which also had serious environmental consequences.

With the demise of the Soviet Union, the focus of the G7 leaders shifted to nuclear security. It was proclaimed that each country bears individual responsibility for the security of its nuclear energy facilities. At the 1992 Munich Summit, the leaders created an additional multilateral mechanism to provide for and elaborate on measures of operational and technical security, as well as to strengthen regulative regimes not yet existing in bilateral programs. Facilities that did not comply with existing standards were deemed to require modernization or closed, with such tasks passed on to the IEA and the World Bank.

A breakthrough could be considered at the Moscow Summit on Nuclear Security held under the co-presidency of the Russian President Boris Yeltsin and French President Jacques Chirac in April 1996. The regular G7 summit, now with Russia, was held a year later in Lyon. The Moscow Summit went beyond the narrow issue

6 The Gulf War was not the only reason for the reduced supply of oil on the market. In October 1991, the Soviet Union suspended petroleum product exports as its fuel shortages grew.

of nuclear security.[7] The eight leaders noted that the security of civilian nuclear reactors was an unquestionable priority, and that there was a need for a "culture of efficient nuclear security" in each country. One of the most serious steps in this direction was the adoption of Nuclear Security Convention, which called for all states to sign and which would come into force by the end of 1996. There was also a decision to convene a meeting of relevant nuclear and energy experts, which happened in October in Paris (G7 Plus Russia 1996).

Nuclear safety, although a component of the energy field, still holds an independent place on the G7/8 agenda because it involves issues such as non-proliferation and the reduction of weapons of mass destruction. Since 1996, it has featured prominently in various areas. There has been cooperation on a bilateral basis or within other international structures. In 2005, the US–Russian High-Level Task Force on Nuclear Security in Washington, created by the Russian President Vladimir Putin and US President George W. Bush in Bratislava, aimed to achieve a reduction of stockpiles and a guarantee of the secure storage of nuclear materials. Bilateral cooperation has taken place with the Asian component of the G8 – Japan – which adopted a program for diagnosing mechanical problems with training nuclear stations in 1992.

At the end of the twentieth century, the G7/G8 interest returned to more traditional energy issues. The first meeting of the G8 energy ministers occurred in Moscow on March 31–April 1, 1998, with a focus on global energy development. It was acknowledged that G8 countries are traditionally the key players in the international arena.[8] The consultative meetings that followed between the international business community and academic circles ensured the effectiveness of the G8: the results included the Joint Oil Data Initiative (JODI) on market transparency and increasing competitiveness. Other issues included nuclear security, energy transportation and environmental protection.[9] It was not formally decided to hold such meetings in the future, but ministers agreed to continue dealing with problems bilaterally or within existing international mechanisms. The ministerial recommendations were approved at the 1998 G8 Birmingham Summit.

7 Several reasons can be found for holding a special summit in Russia: it was the tenth anniversary of the Chernobyl accident, Boris Yeltsin was extremely unpopular in the run-up to the presidential elections, and the G7 leaders wanted to support their Russian colleague.

8 G8 members produce 39 percent of world energy, consume 48 percent of primary fuel resources and have a considerable share of energy resources trade.

9 It was only in 1998 that a fifty-year moratorium on mining and oil exploration in the Antarctic came into force. A protocol for the protection of the area was adopted by 26 countries in 1991, but could not be implemented until Japan's ratification cleared the way a month before its coming into effect. Antarctica contains 70 percent of the world's freshwater.

The G8 leaders also noted the success of cooperation on the pilot project of the International Thermonuclear Experimental Reactor, a promising trend in energy development. After diplomatic and political debates between Tokyo and Paris, it was decided that the experimental reactor was to be built in France. The Japanese government agreed, after receiving a guarantee that the first full-scale reactor would be built in Japan.

The New as Well as the Forgotten Old: The Twenty-First Century

The next phase of G8 energy-related activities started in 2000. This was to a great extent determined by changing oil prices and the development of the topic at the G8 summits in Genoa in 2001, Kananaskis in 2002, Sea Island in 2004 and Gleneagles in 2005, with intensive contacts among the G8 countries. The increase in oil prices was preceded by a less dramatic decrease, which to a certain degree could be explained by the cyclical nature of the economy and energy prices. The surge in prices could be determined mostly by temporary factors, some of them speculative in nature, such as economic growth, governmental decisions about greenhouse gas emissions and other environmental standards, and biofuels production and the development of unconventional renewable energy sources. Special attention was given to low hydrocarbon prices over the previous period, which left the oil sector with insufficient investments, and eventually led to its unpreparedness for demand growth on the part of the most vibrant world economies. This can also be explained by the cyclical nature of the economy (International Sustainable Energy Development Centre 2009).

In 2000, the G8 leaders again had to deal with surging price and a changing energy situation. Oil prices had fallen in 1998 by as much as 50 percent after OPEC decided to raise the production of oil by 10 percent in November 1997. Other factors led to a considerable excess of oil supply over demand, including the UN decision to allow for exports of large amounts of Iraqi oil; the diplomatic compromise on the Iraq, which precluded the US and the UK from carrying out air strikes; the 1997–98 financial crisis in Asia and Russia, which decreased demand for energy resources; and the unusually warm winter of 1997–98. This situation did not last for long, however, since the economic crisis had a limited geographic scope, and the global economy achieved better growth rates. With two cold winters in a row and a well-coordinated OPEC response, by the second half of 2000, oil prices had increased to \$27–32 per barrel, from \$10–11 per barrel in late 1998.

One of the main achievements of the 2000 Okinawa Summit was the establishment of the Renewable Energy Task Force, with the invitation extended to all the parties concerned – public officials, the private sector and non-governmental organizations (NGOs) in addition to the G8 countries. The task force was headed by former Shell President Sir Mark Moody-Stewart. Among other initiatives supported by the G8 were the 1992 Convention on Civil Liability for Oil Pollution Damage and the 1992 International Oil Pollution Compensation Convention (G8 2000). In 1992, Russia was not yet established as a full-scale G8 member. In some aspects, this exclusion was justified, but on discussions of crude oil markets, it was not clear why one of the biggest global producers would not be at the table. The G7 reaffirmed the need to strengthen the "stability of oil markets in order to provide for sustainable growth and prosperity in both, oil producers and consumers" (G7 2000).

The 2001 G8 Summit in Genoa showed that countries had many differences over environmental issues. This became especially evident after the US dropped out of the Kyoto Protocol. Not much was achieved on energy security issues either: the Renewable Energy Task Force presented its report, which included recommendations to change the structure of subsidizing energy projects in developing countries, in favor of turning down support for traditional energy resource suppliers, with this strategy being able to lead to growth of renewables from 2 percent to 7 percent by 2003 (G8 2001).

In separate discussions, the G7 once again raised the issue of oil prices. It was stated that "high and volatile oil prices" constituted a danger for the world economy, especially for the most vulnerable developing countries. It was reaffirmed that there was a need to "increase and diversify energy supply, energy efficiency build up, infrastructure development and stable oil markets." At the same time, the G7 noted the importance of complete and permanent closure of the Chernobyl nuclear reactor on December 15, 2000 (G7 2001).

The second energy ministerial took place in May 2002 in Detroit, co-chaired by the Canadian and US ministers. This meeting once again dealt with the issue of improving information exchange systems, which would be further considered at the eighth International Energy Forum in Osaka. Other points of concern included nuclear security issues, cooperation with developing countries, and the elaboration and use of new technologies. This time, a decision was made on regular formats; however, it would never be realized.

The 2002 Kananaskis Summit was notable because Russia fully participated in the group, and the Global Partnership against the Proliferation of Materials and Weapons of Mass Destruction was formed. This issue was indirectly connected to energy security through the use of nuclear energy, but took an autonomous and specific place.

The 2003 G8 Evian Summit shifted the focus to oil tanker transport security. There was a bid by the G8 to establish a new global regulatory regime of double hulls for oil tankers. Japanese resistance did not allow for a consensus among the G8 leaders. Nevertheless, this trend was firmly under way, with standards introduced by the European Union. Other energy initiatives were also undertaken, such as the creation of the G8 Nuclear Safety and Security Group, which included the core principles necessary to promote safe and secure use of civilian nuclear technology.

A stronger focus on energy security issues by G8 partners was reflected in the way the issue was viewed at the Sea Island Summit in 2004. G8 leaders were conscious of the way terrorist threats could hinder economic growth or recovery, influence energy prices and add to global political uncertainty. It remains uncertain whether this awareness enabled G8 leaders to overcome their divergence over the 2003 US invasion of Iraq, since not all G8 countries believed Saddam Hussein presented a real terrorist threat.

The next G8 summit took place at Gleneagles in 2005. The first working day was devoted to questions of climate change, clean energy and sustainable development, alongside the rest of the political agenda. The issue of climate change was contentious from the outset, particularly between the US and the Europeans. Climate change had been a source of division among G8 countries and their civil society stakeholders since 1997, but was not yet a high-profile issue for the public in all G8 countries. There was also speculation in the media a few days before the summit that the issue of climate change would result in a showdown between the G7 and the US or that there would be no agreement at all.[10] The Europeans argued from the start that the draft document was not as ambitious as it should have been, but it was not accepted by the US and Russia, and Japan had reservations. In the end, the declaration did not contain specific commitments, and was rather ambiguous. Nevertheless Nicholas Bayne (2005) argues that all energy accomplishments fully benefited from iteration and contributed to institutionalization, both key factors for summit success.

At Gleneagles, in addition to the leaders' declaration on climate change, clean energy and sustainable development, a plan of action was adopted with formulas to allow each G8 country to interpret the problem individually. No less then four-fifths of the plan was devoted to energy issues, the priority topic of the next year's G8 summit hosted by Russia. It was stressed that there was an urgent need to develop new technologies, as well as to reduce carbon dioxide emissions. Developing countries declared support for these ideas if they would not hinder economic development. Rich industrialized countries were to assist and share technologies with developing countries. A document on the global economic situation and the international oil market was released, which included one page with non-contradictory and non-obligatory formulas. A large part of the discussions at Gleneagles was devoted to the need to invest in alternative energy sources, mostly for automotive engine research. It was also agreed that outreach sessions with the five fastest-growing economies – the so-called Outreach Five (O5) countries of China, India, Mexico, Brazil and South Africa – would take place and require flexibility.

The topic of energy security was chosen by the Russian presidency as one of its three priorities for the 2006 St. Petersburg Summit, the first to be hosted by Russia. Choosing such a priority topic was a natural choice for Russia, being the second largest energy exporter in the world. An energy ministerial meeting

10 No G8 member would allow for a crackdown and disagreements to prevail and thus discredit the united Western front on the international arena. If there were profound divisions within the club, the issue would either be dropped altogether or (which happens most of the time) a document with no substance and only general wording would be released.

was held with the G8 plus the O5 plus the World Bank, OPEC and the IAEA. In the final documents, ministers supported three positions, pushed primarily by Moscow: the need for mutual and fair access to energy markets, the validity of diversification of supply and the right of other countries to develop nuclear energy. Participants also agreed to increase the market transparency of world energy and introduce clean energy technologies. They concluded that nuclear energy should take a more prominent place in the future world energy balance.

In December 2005, Germany had proposed an action plan to stabilize world oil markets by increasing investments in prospecting and extracting, upgrading transparency and introducing a new JODI within the framework of the IEA. Russia proposed improving existing statistical elements and introducing new ones in order to be able to follow the whole chain. Other initiatives embraced energy efficiency, ecological components and the harmonization of taxation, many of which had been addressed by the British presidency the year before. None the less, the St. Petersburg Summit reflected Russia's idea of establishing a new energy security architecture that allowed for the interests of all parties – an idea still promoted by the Russian Federation.

Environmental concerns, such as climate change, have come to the forefront of G8 discussions. Specifically, the issues of bioenergy, "clean coal" power plant technology based on coal and natural gas, carbon sequestration and storage, energy efficiency in buildings and fuel cells, hydrogen and energy storage have been discussed at the summits. Other topics have included energy efficiency in the industrial and commercial sector, nuclear fission, renewable energy technologies other than biomass and photovoltaic – including wind, especially offshore, and solar thermal heating and cooling, concentrating solar power, hydropower, geothermal and ocean energy.

The most important achievement of the 2007 G8 summit in Heiligendamm and the 2008 Toyako-Hokkaido summit was the agreement of all members that climate change negotiations should stay within the United Nations Framework Convention on Climate Change (UNFCCC), with a target of 50 percent reduction of greenhouse gas emissions by 2050, given common but differentiated responsibilities and capabilities. The G8 leaders agreed to promote innovative low-carbon technologies and energy efficiency, including 25 IEA recommendations with the use of market mechanisms such as an emissions trading system and tax incentives, plus the creation of the International Partnership for Energy Efficiency Co-operation (IPEEC). One key element of successful climate change mitigation is the promotion of clean energy, which the leaders at Toyako agreed should be achieved through "setting national goals and formulating action plans followed by appropriate monitoring" (G8 2008). The same applied to the role of renewable energy, including biofuel production and use, as with the Global Bioenergy Partnership.

Further actions were agreed upon by the G8 to assist the least-developed countries to adapt to energy development strategies, including the early start of the UNFCCC Adaptation Fund, the Climate Investment Funds, the Clean Technology

Fund and the Strategic Climate Fund under the auspices of the World Bank, Approximately $6 billion was allocated as a contribution of official development assistance, and IEA activities in the development of roadmaps for innovative technologies and cooperation between existing and new partnerships were supported. G8 leaders also pledged $10 billion annually in direct government-funded research and development (R&D).

A new framework was established at the 2007 G8 summit called the Heiligendamm Dialogue Process (HDP), which institutionalized a co-operative process with the O5. Among the topics selected for the agenda were climate change and clean energy. The HDP has dealt mainly with energy policy issues, with the key objectives being to achieve inclusive, green and sustainable development, which requires a predictable climate for investors, and the development of and access to modern technologies. The HDP allowed members to benefit from sharing experiences and good practices in the energy sphere, as well as identify specific steps and suitable stimulus packages for their economies. Another achievement was the creation of the Sustainable Buildings Network (SBN), aimed at building and maintaining a central database on new technologies and policies, disseminating best-practice examples and providing policy advice. The SBN and its support unit were to be created within the framework of the IPEEC, with the appropriate institutional links between the two to be launched at a high-level conference in 2009.

The promotion of renewable energy fits in with overall global strategic development. Taking into account the considerable slowdown in investments in the renewable and non-traditional energy sectors, G8 countries thought it vital to promote renewables by including them in economic stimulus plans of more than $100 billion over a three-year period. This would support a "green" economic recovery, investment in R&D and efforts to attract new institutional investors into these sectors by introducing a comprehensive policy framework. It would also help address non-economic barriers, such as integration into the grid, modern electricity market design, full access to technology, information and training, and issues of cultural and social acceptance.

The current phase of energy security and climate change negotiations has started in the wake of the global economic and financial crisis, and it is influencing all other sectors of human activities. The brand-new club of the G20 at the leaders' level met in November 2008 and April and September 2009. The G20 leaders have not paid much attention to the topic of energy, concentrating instead on resolving from economic turmoil. Thus, it is up to the G8 to undertake the task of further elaborating the global energy governance system and finding further compromises to mitigate the impact of climate change.

Conclusion

In the realm of energy, G7/8 activities, along with the work of other international organizations such as IEA, have contributed significantly to countering energy shocks generated by military, political and structural risks. The policies of the leading industrial countries have led to an overall stabilization. Countries have effectively implemented technologies that produce high energy savings and allow for rapid economic development (or recovery). Changing the world energy balance not only helps to achieve economic ends, but also plays a major role in achieving environmentally sustainable development (including moving to clean and alternative energy sources). Actions taken to diversify energy supply and demand and to create and increase oil reserves substantially reduce the risk of energy crises recurring in the future.

In general terms, G8 discussions on energy issues reveal basic priorities of a future energy strategy focused on adopting measures to stabilize world markets, creating new infrastructure capacities, rendering assistance to the poorest countries (both energy producers and consumers) and setting up rapid reaction systems for international energy security threats. Moreover, much attention is given to neutralizing the negative environmental implications of current energy development and elaborating new energy technologies, including alternative energy sources.

Such a framework leads to several tendencies for G8 measures that are currently being worked out. It primarily concerns the stabilization of the global energy market, with the price situation the top priority. Natural factors of energy resources supply could be evaluated today. An energy crisis as such is less dangerous for a world energy order than it was in the 1970s, because today oil and gas exporters constitute an organic element of the globalized economy.

Nevertheless, the G8 countries should take steps to increase the predictability of the global energy market, promote transparency flows, take preventive measures on infrastructure development, and coordinate exporting and importing countries' interests, taking into account their current and prospective place in the world economy.

In addition to the military protection of unstable oil-exporting regions, there are more aspects of international energy security: protection against short-term shocks (in this regard, the G8 actively supports the strategy of increasing strategic oil reserves in line with other international organizations (for example, the IEA or the EU) and the possibility of directing funds allocated for exploration directly to the world energy resource centers.

The problem with the first component lies in the fact that developing countries usually do not possess such reserves. Those countries may be among the fastest-growing economies, but they could suffer a huge blow as a result of a short-term shock (thus the possibility for assistance lies with the G8 and the OECD). With regard to the second component, there are possibilities for G8 action in examining ways to improve legislation for international investments in the energy sector, since many regions that are rich in oil suffer from bad governance that hinders foreign investment flows.

Thus, despite rather substantial progress, there still exist plenty of dangers for further sustainable world energy and economic development, which leaves a major role for the G8, the IEA, the International Energy Forum and others to play in future.

Bibliography

Bayne, Nicholas (2000), *Hanging in There: The G7 and G8 Summit in Maturity and Renewal* (Aldershot: Ashgate).

Bayne, Nicholas (2002), "Impressions of the Genoa Summit, 20–22 July, 2001," in Michele Fratianni, Paolo Savona and John Kirton, eds, *Governing Global Finance: New Challenges, G7 and IMF Contributions* (Aldershot: Ashgate).

Bayne, Nicholas (2003), "Impressions of the Kananaskis Summit," in Michele Fratianni, Paolo Savona and John Kirton, eds, *Sustaining Global Growth and Development: G7 and IMF Contributions and Challenges* (Aldershot: Ashgate).

Bayne, Nicholas (2005), "Overcoming Evil with Good: Impressions of the Gleneagles Summit, 6–8 July 2005" (Toronto: G8 Research Group, University of Toronto), available at <http://www.g8.utoronto.ca/evaluations/2005gleneagles/bayne2005-0718.html>.

G7 (1975), "Declaration of Rambouillet," November 17, Rambouillet, available at <http://www.g8.utoronto.ca/summit/1975rambouillet/communique.html>.

G7 (1977), "Declaration: Downing Street Summit Conference," available at <http://www.g8.utoronto.ca/summit/1977london/communique.html>.

G7 (1978), "Declaration," July 17, Bonn, available at <http://www.g8.utoronto.ca/summit/1978bonn/communique.html>.

G7 (1979), "Declaration," June 29, Tokyo, available at <http://www.g8.utoronto.ca/summit/1979tokyo/communique.html>.

G7 (1980), "Declaration," June 23, Venice, available at <http://www.g8.utoronto.ca /summit/1980venice/communique>.

G7 (1981), "Declaration of the Ottawa Summit," July 21, Ottawa, available at <http://www.g8.utoronto.ca/summit/1981ottawa/communique>.

G7 (1982), "Declaration of the Seven Heads of State and Government and Representatives of the European Communities," June 6, Versailles, available at <http://www.g8.utoronto.ca/summit/1982versailles/communique.html>.

G7 (1983), "Williamsburg Declaration on Economic Recovery," May 30, Williamsburg, available at <http://www.g8.utoronto.ca /summit/1983williamsburg/communique.html>.

G7 (1984a), "London Economic Declaration," June 9, London, available at <http://www.g8.utoronto.ca/summit/1984london/communique.html>.

G7 (1984b), "Statement by the Chair: The Iran–Iraq Conflict," June 8, London, available at <http://www.g8.utoronto.ca/summit/1984london/iraq.html>.

G7 (1986), "Statement on the Implications of the Chernobyl Nuclear Accident," May 5, Tokyo, available at <http://www.g8.utoronto.ca/summit/1986tokyo/chernobyl.html>.

G7 (1990), "Houston Economic Declaration," July 11, Houston, available at <http://www.g8.utoronto.ca/summit/1990houston/declaration.html>.

G7 (1991), "Economic Declaration of the G7 Summit," July 17, London, available at <http://www.g8.utoronto.ca/summit/1991london/communique>.

G7 (2000), "G7 Statement," July 21, Okinawa, available at <http://www.g8.utoronto.ca/summit/2000okinawa/statement.htm>.

G7 (2001), "G7 Statement," July 20, Genoa, available at <http://www.g8.utoronto.ca/g7/summit/2001genoa/g7statement.html>.

G7 plus Russia (1996), "Moscow Nuclear Safety and Security Summit Declaration," April 20, available at <http://www.g8.utoronto.ca/summit/1996moscow/declaration.html>.

G8 (2000), "G8 Communiqué Okinawa 2000," July 23, Okinawa, available at <http://www.g8.utoronto.ca/summit/2000okinawa/finalcom.htm>.

G8 (2001), "Communiqué," July 22, Genoa, available at <http://www.g8.utoronto.ca/summit/2001genoa/finalcommunique.html>.

G8 (2008), "Environment and Climate Change," July 8, Hokkaido, available at <http://www.g8.utoronto.ca/summit/2008hokkaido/2008-climate.html>.

Ikenberry, John (2001), *After Victory: Institutions, Strategic Restraint and the Rebuilding of Order after Major Wars* (Princeton, NJ: Princeton University Press).

International Sustainable Energy Development Centre (2009), "Global Energy and Sustainable Development," White Paper (Moscow: ISEDC).

Kalicki, Jan H. and David L. Goldwyn, eds (2005), *Energy and Security: Toward a New Foreign Policy Strategy* (Washington, DC: Woodrow Wilson Center Press).

Kirton, John (2005), "Toward Multilateral Reform: The G20's Contribution," in Andrew Cooper, John English and Ramesh Thakur, eds, *Reforming Multilateral Institutions from the Top: A Leaders 20 Summit* (Tokyo: United Nations University Press).

Kirton, John and Ella Kokotsis (2003a), "Producing International Commitments and Compliance without Legalization: The G7/8's Trade Performance from 1975–2002," paper presented on a panel on "Global Trade and the Role of Informal Institutions" at the Annual Conference of the International Studies Association, Portland, OR, February 23–March 3, available at <http://www.g8.utoronto.ca/scholar/kirton2003/KirtonPortland2003.pdf>.

Kirton, John and Ella Kokotsis (2003b), "The G7/8 Contribution at Kananaskis and Beyond," in Michele Fratianni, Paolo Savona and John Kirton, eds, *Sustaining Global Growth and Development: G7 and IMF Governance* (Aldershot: Ashgate).

Mitchell, John, Peter Beck and Michael Grubb (1996), *The New Geopolitics of Energy* (London: Royal Institute of International Affairs).

Morse, Edward L. and James Richard (2002), "The Battle for Energy Dominance," *Foreign Affairs* 2 (March/April).

Sokolsky, Richard., Stuart Johnson and F. Stephen Larrabee, eds (2001), *Persian Gulf Security: Improving Allied Military Contributions* (Santa Monica, CA: RAND).

Putnam, Robert and Nicolas Bayne (1984), *Hanging Together: The Seven Power Summits* 1st Edition (Cambridge, MA: Harvard University Press).

Putnam, Robert and Nicholas Bayne (1987), *Hanging Together: Cooperation and Conflict in the Seven-Power Summits* 2nd Edition (Cambridge, MA: Harvard University Press).

Rugman, Alan (2005), "U.S. Energy Security and Regional Business," in Michele Fratianni, John Kirton and Paolo Savona, eds, *New Perspectives on Global Governance: Why America Needs the G8* (Aldershot: Ashgate).

Chapter 12
Education, the G8 and UNESCO

John Kirton, Laura Sunderland and Jenilee Guebert

As an international institution founded in 1975 to globally promote the values of open democracy, individual liberty and social advance, the Group of Eight (G8) major market democracies has had, since its start, a potential interest in governing global education. As early as 1977, the then Group of Seven (G7) proclaimed: "we shall promote the training of young people in order to build a skilled and flexible labor force so that they can be ready to take advantage of the upturn in economic activity as it develops." Yet it was not until 1984, after the G7 summit turned its focus to micro-economics, technology and research and development as the foundations for economic growth and social advance, that education became a regular and rising G8 concern. At the dawn of the twenty-first century, education moved to center stage, with Japan hosting the first G8 meeting of ministers of education in 2000 and Russia choosing education as a priority theme for the St. Petersburg Summit in 2006.

Introduction

How has the G8 governed global education, and why has it performed in the way it has? The still limited analysis on this subject contains several competing schools of thought.

The first school sees the G8 as a civil society-driven success. Nicholas Bayne argues that the modern G8 in 1998 and 1999, due to the Jubilee 2000 civil society campaign, delivered debt relief so the poorest countries could spend more on education and health (Bayne 2000: 181–84). Jeffrey Hart similarly sees the G8's governance of cyberspace as successful in the domestic political management task of countering the claims of anti-globalization critics, deliberating on the growing digital divide and developing global governance by creating the multi-stakeholder Digital Opportunity Task Force (DOT Force) in 2000. This success was driven by civil society, the democratic principles of the G8, the shock of September 11, the inability of established international organizations to include non-state stakeholders and the G8's constricted "heads-only" participation (Hart 2005).

A second school sees successful G8 governance of cyberspace flowing from the novelty of the subject and the G8's institutionalization and specialization through top-down working groups. Gina Stephens, inspired by constructivist insights, argues that the dynamics of the DOT Force in particular induced its individual multi-stakeholder members to alter their conceptions of interests and identities to increase G8 cooperation and compliance across the growing North–South divide (Stephens 2006).

A third school sees the G8 as a slow-moving success in governing the new knowledge economy, as a result of US leadership, Japanese support and their accommodation with a distinctive EU. Tom Lawton argues that the new Internet-driven business models privileging openness and knowledge require the coordinated support of G8 governments if they are to prevail globally over strong, conflicting national and regional regimes (Lawton 2001). This slowly happened, as the "world's third dominant economic power, Japan, supports the same governance agenda as the US and the EU and strongly advocates international policy consensus and regulatory harmonization for e-commerce" (Lawton 2001: 56).

A fourth school emphasizes the G8's failure to deliver its sound educational commitments, because it did not recognize the underlying social and economic causes of poor educational performance in Africa and did not provide the necessary policy paradigm and funds. Ronald Labonte and Ted Schrecker argue that G8 members have been reluctant to provide the required levels of official development assistance (ODA) to meet the educational objectives of the Millennium Development Goals (MDGs) (Labonte et al. and Schrecker 2004: 79–95). They note that the G8 has endorsed the Dakar Framework for Education or "Education for All" (EFA) at its 2000, 2001 and 2002 summits, focused on the two goals of universal primary education and gender equality, and inspired the US, Japan, the UK and Canada to increase aid for basic education, especially in Africa, after the Kananaskis Summit of 2002. However, according to the United Nations Educational, Scientific and Cultural Organization (UNESCO), more than ten times more money is needed to meet the university primary education and gender equality goals, and to stop the growing number of developing countries from falling further behind.

A fifth school sees a deeper failure in direction-setting, due to the predominant power of a neo-hegemonic, neo-liberal United States. Michele Mastroeni argues that the G8 pioneered a regime for cyberspace governance, based on the principles of no taxation and open trade, which eroded the resources necessary for financing public education (Mastroeni 2001). While a social democratic Europe and its labor and political party supporters mounted a vibrant opposition to this thrust since the G7 meeting in Brussels in February 1995, the prevailing preferences were those of a US that by 1998 controlled 70 percent of the world's websites and generated 85 percent of the world's revenues from the emerging e-commerce field. Similarly, Chris Alden (2003: 457) argues that the G8's 2000 program to bridge the digital divide was misconceived, and "served to distort development priorities away from core issues like debt and poverty alleviation towards the pursuit of a 'virtual panacea for Africa's deep-rooted problems.'" The cause was structural inequalities between North and South and "the shortcomings of established mechanisms of global governance."

Amidst their many differences, these analyses share a common shortcoming. None adequately accounts for the great leap forward in the G8's governance of education at the Japanese-hosted 2000 Summit, across a wide range of traditional and electronic subjects, with an egalitarian emphasis on closing the North–South digital divide, and by pioneering the differently designed DOT Force and a new set of principles for a changing world. This great leap forward, which set the path for the G8's twenty-first-century global educational governance, took place when the US was at the height of its dot.com-fuelled relative capability and neo-liberal rise, and came before the terrorist shock of September 11, 2001, reminded all of the pre-eminent security need for state-delivered public goods. Accounting for this particular path of G8 global education governance requires a far more systematic and detailed analysis than those provided thus far.

This study conducts such an analysis. It argues that the G8 is shifting to become an effective institution of global education governance, due to the rising vulnerability and declining relative capability of a US now forced to look to its increasingly capable G8 colleagues for help. As a global education governor, the G8 first took a regular interest in education-related subjects in the mid-1980s with the emergence of the knowledge economy, and has deliberated continuously, comprehensively and robustly on core education issues since 1999. At Okinawa in 2000, it soared into sustained high performance across all of its domestic political management, deliberative, direction-setting, decision making, delivery and development of global governance tasks.

This great leap into effective global education governance has been driven by several forces. The first is a once-dominant US's declining level of educational achievement and ability to attract foreign post-secondary students after September 11, despite the US's leading public expenditure on education and teachers' salaries and the long years its students are formally enrolled in school. An ill-equipped US found little multilateral help from a poorly performing UNESCO, a United Nations Children's Fund (UNICEF) with a partial mandate, and an Organisation for Economic Co-operation and Development (OECD) with a partial membership. In contrast, the highly capable countries, gathered in a G8 devoted to the global promotion of open democracy, individual liberty and social advance, found it easy to take up the tasks of educating an Asia where the free flow of information is still censored, an aging G8 citizenry whose lifelong learning and multicultural openness has become critical for future economic and social success, and a rapidly democratizing but not developing Africa across an emerging North–South digital divide. A new generation of G8 leaders dedicated to education as a domestic priority, led first by the UK's Tony Blair and then the US's governor-turned-president George Bush, brought the topic to a G8 summit that they and their domestically popular colleagues had virtually all attended for an unprecedented five years in a row, starting in 2001. The new 1998 summit format left them with more time alone to deal freely and flexibly with the domestic issues that personally preoccupied them, and thus helped drive their summit to success in the field.

The G8's Education Issue Area Defined and Analyzed

Within the G8, the field of education encompasses all levels of public and private instruction, from primary through university into lifelong learning. It includes technical, vocational and professional training and mobility, employment and the labor market, productivity, innovation and competitiveness in the knowledge economy, and the governance of cyberspace. It further embraces social and political subjects, such as gender equality in education, education to prevent the spread of disease, education as a MDG, access to education in developing countries, literacy and free information flows.

To explore how the G8 has governed this wide-ranging but bounded set of subjects, this study begins with a systematic overview of G8 performance in the area of education since 1975, both overall and in its major governance functions of domestic political management, deliberation, direction-setting, decision making, delivery and the development of global governance. It next reviews the treatment of education at successive summits, detailing the dynamics at those where the greatest innovation on education has taken place. It finally examines the key causes of G8 education governance, exploring in turn the components of the proven concert equality model of G8 governance: common vulnerability, equalizing capability, multilateral organizational failure, common democratic principles, domestic political capital and controlled constricted participation.

An Overview of the G8's Education Performance, 1977–2005

There are several ways to assess the G8's performance in the field of education on a summit-by-summit basis, both through overall assessments and through a detailed examination of the individual governance functions that the G8 summit performs (see Appendix 12A).

Overall Assessments of G8 Education Performance

The G8's overall performance on education has been measured in two major ways. The first employs Nicholas Bayne's G8 summit grading methodology, first pioneered in his classic work with Robert Putnam (Putnam and Bayne 1987). Using the Bayne methodology, G8 effectiveness in education-related governance (in the fields of debt relief, information technology and Africa) has generally been on the rise since education first appeared on the summit agenda in 1984 as a component of debt relief. The 1984 London II and 1988 Toronto Summits' central achievements, according to Bayne, were debt relief, for which the summits were both accorded scores of C-. The 1989 Paris and 1996 Lyon Summits, which also led on debt, had scores of B+ and B respectively. Africa was the main achievement at the 1997 Denver Summit, which dipped down to a C-, before rising at Cologne in 1999 to a B+ for debt. Information technology earned a grade of B at the 2000

Okinawa Summit. At Genoa in 2001 and Kananaskis in 2002, achievements on Africa received a B and B+, respectively (Bayne 2005). Thus, there has generally been an increase in the grades received for education-related issues. However, core education was never the central focus of a Bayne grade, but only an element related to other subjects.

The second way of measuring education performance is through the summit performance assessments conducted by the University of Toronto's G8 Research Group's performance assessments since 1996 (see Appendix 12B). At the 1997 Denver Summit, the 1994 OECD Job Strategy scored a B and the global information society a C. At Birmingham in 1998, employability earned a grade of A-. At Cologne in 1999, education and human capital both received a B-. Okinawa in 2000 saw information technology get an A- and education an A. In 2001 at Genoa, the DOT Force received an A and the Africa Action Plan's education component an A-. However, Genoa also generated the lowest education grade on record, scoring a D+ on universal primary education, in a failure that extends to the 164 countries that agreed upon this goal in the Dakar Framework for Education at the UNESCO World Education Forum in April 2000. At Sea Island in 2004, the Broader Middle East Initiative received a respectable B+. In 2006 at the St. Petersburg Summit, education received a B. The 2007 Heiligendamm Summit gave a B- for the G8's efforts on education in the context of African development. And at the 2008 Hokkaido Toyako Summit, Africa and education were awarded an A. Thus, the trend in overall performance has generally been high and rising, especially since 2000.

Domestic Political Management

The first component of G8 governance is domestic political management – the degree to which the summit helps G8 leaders manage their policy, political and electoral priorities back home – which allows leaders to demonstrate to their publics that the G8 is helping them to do what their people want.

In practice, G8 leaders have occasionally referred to the G8's relevance in the formal national policy addresses they give annually at fixed dates to declare authoritatively to their citizens what their overall domestic priorities are. Since 1999, there has been a major, sustained jump in such references, which have appeared in at least one of the G8 members' speeches every year. For example, in the US's State of the Union address, on January 31, 2006, President Bush referred to education in seven paragraphs, energy in six, and health in four (these were the three priority areas for the 2006 summit). His one reference to the G8, however, came in relation to energy, in an indirect form.

Deliberation

The G8's deliberative or agenda-setting performance on education has generally been rising. As Appendices 12C and 12D show, core education subjects (where education is the central target) and education-related subjects (where education is a means or instrument to achieving other ends) received sporadic attention during the first summit cycle from 1975 to 1981, regular attention at every summit since 1983, and particularly vigorous attention from 2000 on. Core education, however, has sometimes fallen off the agenda completely. The education-related agenda is where deliberative performance has most consistently come.

Attention to education rose to high levels in 1999, 2000, 2002, 2004 and 2006. These peaks came during summits which focused on Africa, such as the 1999 Cologne Charter on Lifelong Learning, the 2002 *New Focus on Education for All* and G8 Education Task Force. They also came during the Okinawa Summit in 2000, which focused on the Global Information Society (GIS) and information communications technology (ICT), as well as the 2004 Sea Island Summit, in the context of broader Middle Eastern educational reform, and the 2006 St. Petersburg Summit, where education itself was an overarching theme.

The G8 summit has traditionally treated education as a means to an end, rather than an end in itself. The first reference, at London in 1977, came in the form of promoting training in order to develop a flexible labor force. This "education for job training" phase lasted until Venice in 1987, when "education for health" arose, in the form of education as a tool to stop the spread of AIDS in the Chairman's Statement on AIDS. In 1991, "education for development" arose when the London Summit first stated that education was a priority development issue.

In 1999 came the great reversal to "development for education," as education became an end in its own right. The Cologne Debt Initiative instructed several multilateral organizations (MOs) – the International Monetary Fund (IMF), the World Bank and the Paris Club – to provide funding for the Heavily Indebted Poor Country (HIPC) Initiative so that developing countries could divert adequate resources toward the attainment of social goals such as education (Bayne 2005: 52). The Cologne Summit also produced the Cologne Charter on Lifelong Learning, which set out specific targets for education, including international exchange programs, information and communications technology and distance learning as a supplement to traditional education systems (Bayne 2005: 53). It thus featured G8 governance through the MOs.

At the Okinawa Summit in 2000 came "information technology for education." The Okinawa Charter on Global Information Society dealt with closing the digital divide, providing equal global access to information, and education in general. The Final Communiqué at Okinawa discussed the importance of the Dakar Framework for Education, which included the ambitious goal of Education fFor All. The leaders committed themselves to "strengthen efforts bilaterally and together with international organizations and private sector donors to achieve the goals of universal primary education by 2015 and gender equality in schooling by 2005" (Okinawa G8 Summit 2000a). G8 governance with the MOs was the emphasis here.

The 2001 Genoa Summit generated the Genoa Plan for Africa. It promised G8 help to the least developed countries (LDCs) on various development initiatives, including human development, education and information technology. The Italian presidency produced a summit document entitled "Debt Relief and Beyond," which dealt extensively with the issue of education. The DOT Force released its first report just prior to the Genoa Summit. It concluded that action should be taken to build human capacity through a range of training and education initiatives. The report also stated that information technology and knowledge-sharing can help to achieve broad development goals. The G8 Final Communiqué reiterated the Debt Relief and Beyond sentiment of supporting education. In particular, the leaders reaffirmed their commitment to meet the goal of universal primary education by 2015, support gender equality in education, improve teacher training, build on the work of the DOT Force and use information communications technology to strengthen educational strategies.

At Kananaskis in 2002, the G8 Education Task Force established at Genoa released its report, *A New Focus on Education for All*. It was devoted to education and improving its delivery throughout the world. The goals of achieving universal primary education and promoting gender equality in education by increasing bilateral assistance to developing countries were reiterated by the leaders in the Kananaskis Summit Chair's Summary. Gender equality in education, or "education for girls," thus became a direct G8 goal. Following the Kananaskis Summit, leaders from the US, Japan, the UK and Canada were inspired to increase aid for basic education, especially in Africa.

The Sea Island Summit in 2004 added the Broader Middle East to Africa as a target of the G8's educational concern. The Broader Middle East G8 Plan of Support for Reform emphasized political aspects of reform, such as the Democracy Assistance Dialogue. But it included several social goals, such as education, increased literacy and training for employment. Education, in its broader definition embracing training, was also a component of the G8 Action Plan on Expanding Global Capability for Peace Support Operations, which aimed to train 75,000 troops for peacekeeping operations in Africa by 2010.

The 2005 Gleneagles Summit again focused on universal primary education in Africa, with references to this issue in both the Chair's Summary and the document on Africa. Following up on progress made at Sea Island, Gleneagles referred to education and educational reform in its document Partnership for Progress and a Common Future with the broader Middle East and North African Region. Both Africa and the broader Middle East had thus become continuing geographic parts of the G8's education concern.

The 2006 St. Petersburg Summit raised the profile of education by making it one of the three priorities of the summit. The leaders released a separate document, entitled "Education for Innovative Societies in the 21st Century." It focused on developing a Global Innovation Society, building skills for life and work through quality education, Education for All and development, and advancing social cohesion and immigrant integration through education.

In 2007 at Heiligendamm, the focus on education returned to Africa. The leaders reiterated their commitment to accelerate the delivery of universal primary education as an instrument for sustainable development in Africa. They noted that "education is a fundamental driver for national development and economic growth," thus suggesting they were interested in providing African countries with the tools (which included education) they needed to boost their economies.

The 2008 Hokkaido Toyako Summit's education goals were similar to that of 2007. The leaders again focused on education as a development imperative for Africa, but they also raised the issues in an environment context. Here, the G8 highlighted the importance of education for sustainable environmental development.

Direction-Setting

In its direction-setting function of defining dominant global principles and norms, the G8's education performance has been moderately high since the late 1980s. This has been true of all the three components of principles (statements of fact, causation and rectitude) and the prescriptions and proscriptions that constitute norms (Krasner 1983).

The annual G8 summit first made education a priority at the Okinawa Summit in 2000, and has consistently done so since 2002. It did this by including the subject in the preamble to the Final Communiqué, or as part of the separate Chair's Statement that has been a staple of the summit system since 2002. Information and communications technology appeared in the preamble to the 2000 Okinawa Summit. In 2002, the Kananaskis Chair's Summary addressed both the DOT Force's Genoa Plan of Action, and achieving universal primary education and equal access for girls. In 2003, the Evian Chair's Summary affirmed the leaders' commitment to raise productivity through education, lifelong learning and investing in knowledge and innovation. In 2004, the Sea Island Chair's Summary mentioned the G8 Plan of Support for Reform, and made commitments to support initiatives for literacy and vocational training. In 2005, the Gleneagles Chair's Summary reaffirmed the leaders' commitment to Africa and universal primary education. In 2006, the St. Petersburg Chair's Summary contained a record number of paragraphs on education. In 2007, the Heiligendamm Chair's Summary reiterated the G8's commitment to universal primary education. In 2008, the Hokkaido Toyako Chair's Summary referred to environmental education, the MDGs and Africa. And the leaders promised to issue a report on their education commitments at the next Summit in 2009.

In the realm of causation, from its first mention in 1977 until 1983, education was discussed by the G8 only in terms of training for employment and labor flexibility. Since 1983, the G8 has done much to connect the issue of education to many other core concerns. Education, since 1986, has been presented as an instrument for preventing the spread of AIDS, as a requirement for economic growth, for the management of agriculture and biotechnology systems, for development, for the environment, for preventing drug usage, for law enforcement, peacekeeping or other specific skills, for the Global Information Society, and for humanitarian purposes such as investing in people. It has also become the object of a growing array of other instruments, as in the Cologne Charter, the Education for All initiative, and debt relief or official development assistance for education. It has thus acquired a comprehensive causal relevance, as both a cause and an effect.

Decision Making

The G8 has also made many significant collective decisions, in the form of specific, future-oriented public commitments, in the field of education. These peaked with the 50 education commitments in 2006. Thus the summits' high twenty-first-century deliberative attention to education has often carried through into the decisional domain (see Appendix 12E). The 1999 Cologne Charter yielded no decisions, while Okinawa in 2000 produced some. Deliberative spikes in attention in 2002, 2004 and 2006 corresponded to similarly high levels of decisions. The twenty-first-century decisional surge has not been sustained every year. The ratio of education commitments to total commitments reached at the summit peaked at Genoa in 2001. It has generally declined since that time, with a particularly notable dip in 2003 and a significant rise in 2006. Driving deliberation and direction-setting into decisions is possible, but by no means guaranteed.

Delivery

The delivery of those decisions has also been generally good in the twenty-first century, but again by no means guaranteed. Since 1996, the limited available evidence from the G8 Research Group's annual compliance studies shows that compliance with the education commitments have been complied with, or delivered by, G8 member countries at medium to high levels. As Appendix 12F shows, on a scale ranging from -100 percent to +100 percent, education commitments have averaged +53 percent overall.

Although final compliance has never been in the negative range, there have been fluctuations. Lyon 1996 and Okinawa 2000 both had perfect scores of +100 percent. Across the component education issues, the digital divide and the DOT Force did very well in both 2000 and 2001, yielding an average score of +88 percent. Lower performance came from employment at Denver in 1997 (+38 percent), Education For All at Sea Island in 2005 (+33 percent), gender disparities at St. Petersburg in 2006 (22 percent) and sexual and reproductive education at Heiligendamm in 2007 (+33 percent).

The universal primary education or EFA initiative received an overall average score of +48 percent. It moved from a high of +58 percent in 2001 down to a low of +33 percent in 2005, and then back up slightly in 2007 to +44 percent.

There are thus periods of high and low compliance, fluctuating over time and not necessarily corresponding to the degree of attention that the leaders have paid to the education topic. The Okinawa Summit had concerted attention to education by the leaders and perfect education compliance. In contrast, the Kananaskis and St. Petersburg Summits also focused attention on education, but produced compliance of only +57 percent and +33 percent, respectively.

Development of Global Governance

During the twenty-first century, the G8 has also done much to develop institutions of its own for global education governance. In earlier years, many of the G7's ministerial and official-level bodies had dealt with individual education topics. The year 1995 saw the creation of ministerial meetings and supporting bodies of the Global Information Society. GIS ministerial meetings took place on February 25–26, 1995, in Brussels and May 13–15, 1996 in Midrand, South Africa. But only in 2000 did a more focused and frequent institutionalization of education come about.

In early 2000, during the lead-up to the Okinawa Summit, the G8 education ministers met for the first time, in Okinawa on April 1–2, 2000. This fulfilled a promise made in the 1999 Cologne Communiqué under the leadership of German Chancellor Gerhard Schroeder (Bayne 2005, 80). The 2001 Genoa Communiqué committed to creating a G8 Task Force of senior officials to advise them on how to pursue the Dakar Framework for Education goals, and requested that the task force provide the leaders with recommendations before their next summit. Thus, the work of the Task Force on Primary Education fed directly into the preparations for the 2002 Kananaskis Summit. There were no further moves to hold a G8 ministers of education meeting until the Russian hosts scheduled one for early June 2006.

When compared with the G8's overall ministerial-level institutionalization, education has been a lagging field, despite its increasing importance at the leaders' level. Stand-alone, at least annual, G8 ministerial forums began for trade in 1982, foreign affairs in 1984, finance in 1986 (and 1973 as the G5), environment in 1992–94, employment/labor in 1992, terrorism in 1995, and justice/interior in 1997. Other ministerial forums that met less frequently also emerged for crime and development.

At the official level, education has been the focus of several G8 institutions. These began with the Working Group on Technology, Growth and Employment from 1982 to 1986. The DOT Force, was established by the G8 in 2000 in order to recommend global action to bridge the international information and knowledge divide. The DOT Force released its report prior to the 2001 Genoa Summit. The G8 Task Force on Education was created at the 2001 Genoa Summit to advise G8 leaders on how to best pursue the Dakar goals. The Task Force's report, *A New Focus on Education for All*, was released at the 2002 Kananaskis Summit (see Appendix 12G).

The G8's Education Diplomacy: Critical Cases

A more detailed examination of individual summits where the G8's education governance has been importantly advanced again shows the leap forward into the twenty-first century, and points to why certain successes were achieved.

London 1977

Education as a subject was first introduced during the 1977 London Summit. One of the Final Communiqué's paragraphs read:

> We are particularly concerned about the problem of unemployment among young people. Therefore we shall promote the training of young people in order to build a skilled and flexible labor force so that they can be ready to take advantage of the upturn in economic activity as it develops.

The immediate cause of this concern was soaring unemployment in Europe. It had risen from 4.7 million at the time of the Rambouillet Summit in 1975 to 7 million as 1977 came to an end (Putnam and Bayne 1984: 82). The passage reflected a successful compromise between the US and UK on the one hand, who wanted Keynesian macroeconomic stimulus to create jobs, and Germany and Japan on the other, who resisted becoming macroeconomic locomotives with defined national growth targets to pull their lagging partners ahead. The Germans, supported by the French, prevailed by having the summit endorse the new principle that, in the words of France's proposed text, "inflation does not reduce employment. On the contrary it is one of its major causes." With this direction-setting initiative achieved, the summit was induced to turn to microeconomic causes and solutions for the unemployment dilemma, and so addressed education.

Tokyo 1986

The Tokyo Summit's Declaration in 1986 moved away from the notion of education for job training to approach education in a more philosophical and political way. It stated: "We have a solemn responsibility so to educate the next generation so as to endow them with the creativity befitting the twenty-first century and to convey to them the value of living in freedom and dignity."

This passage introduced into the summit the value of education, not merely for instrumental economic purposes, but as a means to broader political and social goals. Its emphasis on "creativity" can be taken as a G8 *gaitsu*, or pressure to reform Japan's tradition-bound education system, in the direction of that of its G8 peers. But it also introduced the broader principle of "education for freedom." It thus mobilized the G8's core common purpose of open democracy and individual liberty to drive G8 education performance, as the Cold War began to end and glasnost came in. And its explicit focus on the twenty-first century very much set the stage for the educational great leap forward when Japan hosted fourteen years later at Okinawa, as the twenty-first century began.

Venice 1987

The 1987 Summit took a new approach to education by forging its first link with health. It suggested that in the absence of a medical cure, educating the public was the best way to combat and prevent the spread of HIV/AIDS. This emphasis on prevention reflected the US origins, with support from the UK, behind the summit's treatment of AIDS. It flowed from a US interest in combating drug use.

Toronto 1988

For the Toronto 1988 Summit, the leaders moved to craft an agenda that for the first time dealt broadly with education as an end in its own right and included classic education issues such as literacy. They innovatively included in the summit a session for themselves alone where they could discuss in free-wheeling, unscripted fashion any subject they wanted, including those emerging on the spot. For the second time in summit history, they came to a university campus, holding this session at the University of Toronto's Hart House.

As the summit approached, the leaders and their sherpas began to consider in earnest what topics this session should include. The leading suggestions were aging populations, the environment and drugs. Host Prime Minister Brian Mulroney, however, wished to include literacy, a subject of personal domestic interest. It was related to aging populations, as older workers had lower literacy levels than the younger generations. The major impetus for education as a topic in its own right came from British Prime Minister Margaret Thatcher. She drew on her knowledge as a former education minister in the British cabinet.

The intention had been to focus on demography, social security and education. The United Kingdom was very strong on demography and the European Community on education. The United States did not know what it wanted at the session. Despite earlier promises from US officials, the Canadians as hosts had been unable to get Ronald Reagan to focus on the substance of the session. He was more interested in discussing the successes of his administration.

On June 20, the second day of the summit, at their informal session or mini-retreat at Hart House, the leaders held a relaxed discussion on the long-term issues of education, technology and training. The open, friendly and largely spontaneous exchange on education was dominated by Reagan, Francis François Mitterrand, Thatcher and Mulroney. Reagan led off the session, saying that the world was moving to the post-Reagan era. Mitterrand and then Thatcher spoke. Both had structured interventions, unlike Reagan, Italy's Ciriaco de Mita, Nobura Takeshita and Mulroney. These structured interventions took time, and rather overwhelmed the discussion. Mulroney then said a few words on illiteracy – a subject of great concern to him. The leaders spoke with no worry that a communiqué or a press conference would reveal their thoughts to the world. The leaders' discussion on this subject, an area of provincial jurisdiction which Quebec jealously guarded in Canada (and all other Hart House items, save the environment), were not carried over into any of the deliberately short Toronto declarations.

London 1991

Employment and training remained a central component of all education discussions at the leaders' level until the 1991 London Summit. In the London Communiqué, the leaders added education as part of their discussion on development, stating: "Additional aid efforts are required, to enhance both the quantity and the quality of our support for priority development issues. These include alleviating poverty, improving health, education and training and enhancing the environmental quality of our aid." Education became a priority path to development success.

Naples 1994

At Naples, education was broadened to encompass investing in people, and "developing a culture of lifetime learning." However, the centerpiece subject was the summit's endorsement of an US initiative on the new "information highway." This included a proposal to subsequently hold a separate ministerial meeting on the subject. President Bill Clinton proposed such a conference hosted by the US, but the EU's Jacques Delors succeeded in securing it for Brussels. The conference was duly held on February 25–26, 2005, as the G7 Information Society Ministerial Conference.

Denver 1997

The 1997 Summit connected education with both environmental protection and drug-use prevention. It also marked the start of the G8's interest in Africa on the education front. Here, the US began with a narrow trade and investment focus for its African agenda. However, other countries such as Canada pressed successfully for Africa to be dealt with in a much broader fashion. This put political issues such as peace-building and social policy items such as education on the agenda as well.

Cologne 1999

The year 1999 was important for expanding the G8's interest in education, both in a development context and as an issue in its own right. The Cologne Debt Initiative instructed the International Monetary Fund (IMF), the World Bank and the Paris Club to fund the HIPC program so that developing countries could divert adequate resources toward the attainment of social goals such as education (Bayne 2005: 52). Under the leadership of the new German Chancellor and G8 host Gerhard

Schroeder, the Cologne Summit also produced the Cologne Charter on Lifelong Learning. It set out specific targets for education, including using exchange programs, information and communications technology and distance learning to supplement traditional education systems (Bayne 2005: 53).

Okinawa 2000

The Okinawa Summit in 2000 marked a great leap forward, both by delivering what had been initiated at Cologne and by adding many new dimensions of its own (Kirton and Takashe 2002). On April 1–2, G8 education ministers met for the first time, as had been promised by the Cologne Communiqué (Bayne 2005: 80). On July 8, in Fukuoka, G8 finance ministers followed with a communiqué on the "Impact of the IT Revolution on the Economy and Finance." On July 21–23, the summit itself produced the Okinawa Charter on the Global Information Society, dealing with closing the digital divide, access to information and education. In it, the leaders recognized the need to develop, through education, the human resources needed to respond to the demands of the information technology age. The leaders at Okinawa, in their main summit communiqué, also discussed social development, committing to "follow up vigorously the conclusions of the recent Dakar Conference on Education by ensuring that additional resources are made available for basic education" (Okinawa G8 Summit 2000a).

These developments came about because Japan and its G8 partners transformed an early US interest in addressing information technology in a neo-liberal economic and democratizing political context into a much broader treatment emphasizing North–South equality and adding the new subject of cultural diversity to the summit's work (Alden 2003).

As its second subject, the summit dealt with information technology's role in transforming the world of the twenty-first century. Here, the emerging G8 consensus focused on "the revolutionary role of information technology for greater prosperity." This was seen as a multifaceted and positive revolution that did or could help all people. In this discussion, the leaders dealt with the remnants of an earlier US proposal to have Okinawa produce a liberalization package offering "four electronic freedoms." It consisted of, first, extending the existing moratorium on the taxation of international e-commerce indefinitely and ensuring that other barriers did not arise to obstruct free trade through this new medium; second, giving consumers and businesses abroad the freedom to enjoy this liberated e-commerce behind the border, through an agreement to deregulate telecommunications in G8 countries in ways that eliminated the monopolies and the ensuing high connection charges that impeded the use of e-commerce in countries such as Japan; third, liberalizing air cargo services so that consumers ordering seamlessly and inexpensively via the Internet from abroad could have their orders fulfilled without the delays and often large proportional expenses incurred in delivery, freight forwarding and customs clearance; and fourth, enhancing the way information technology (IT) could spread education, cultural exchange and democratic values, by first reaffirming and extending existing commitments entrenched in United Nations-based organizations for the free flow of ideas and information across international boundaries.

Okinawa delivered little of this US-inspired agenda. Within the G7 countries, state and other sub-federal authorities affirmed the principle of neutrality of taxation and worried that any further moratorium on taxing e-commerce would leave them to shoulder the burden of spending more money on IT education, and thus generate more electronic business, while their needed tax revenues disappeared. Nor did they agree on further action on ending customs clearance.

Much greater emphasis emerged on the Japanese-favored theme of bridging the digital divide on a North–South basis, even as the digital divide within G8 countries was acknowledged. Despite some US reluctance, the Okinawa leaders confronted the absence of international mechanisms to secure coherence in the approach to the digital divide. The summit established a new governance mechanism – the DOT Force – to bring relevant institutions such as the World Trade Organization (WTO), the UN Economic and Social Council (ECOSOC), the World Intellectual Property Organization (WIPO) and other stakeholders together. This mechanism was to operate for a few years, under the direction of the G8 chair each year. Its membership embraced G8 countries and those from international organizations, developing countries and, innovatively, from the NGO community. It thus gave concrete expression to Okinawa's new direction of embracing developing countries and civil society more fully in twenty-first-century governance.

The Japanese further succeeded in having the Okinawa leaders go beyond the digital divide – seen by some in the Japanese team as a negative phrase – to address the broader "knowledge divide." As conceived by Japan as host, development was about improving the lives of ordinary citizens in each individual country. As this required the ability to think, read, write and calculate, education was key. The G8's role was to give life to the existing United Nations agreement that there should be universal education by 2015. Ensuring Africans could receive primary and secondary education in their native languages was a valuable step in overcoming the "knowledge divide."

A further Japanese innovation, personally injected into the summit agenda by Japanese Prime Minister Keizo Obuchi, was cultural diversity. It arose in response to concerns, especially in Asia, that globalization was obliterating distinctive cultures in favor of a homogenized Americanism. The issue survived Obuchi's sudden death, thanks in part to the sympathies of Canada and France, and over the skepticism of Obuchi's successor, Prime Minister Yoshiri Mori. Mori felt, as a former trade minister, that this concept might serve merely as a refuge for trade protectionism everywhere. In the twenty-first century, as G8 education ministers recognized in April, and as leaders had acknowledged in the Cologne Charter, people needed to know one another, to avoid the vices bred by ignorance. Moreover, as President Clinton highlighted, Silicon Valley showed that "multi-ethnicity" was now the source of US economic dynamism.

Thus, the G8, meeting on the soil of its most monocultural member, emphasized the need for mutual understanding across different cultures, in part through the instruments of education and IT. The G8 moved from offering easier access to IT to providing and preserving richer content and expanding UNESCO's programs to protect the world's intangible heritage. Each G8 country was to develop a program for preserving its intangible heritage, such as minority languages and traditional songs.

Genoa 2001

At Genoa in 2001, "education for development" was the focus. The DOT Force's report, released just prior to the summit, concluded that IT and knowledge-sharing could lead to development, and that action should be taken to build human capacity through training and education. The Italian presidency's document, *Debt Relief and Beyond*, dealt extensively with education. The Genoa Final Communiqué reiterated the "beyond debt relief" sentiment for supporting education. The summit also generated a forward-looking *Genoa Plan for Africa*. It promised G8 help on various development initiatives, including human development, education and information technology.

Education for All received a major boost from Genoa. In April 2000, delegates from 164 countries had met in Dakar, Senegal for the UNESCO World Education Forum. They produced the 2,000-word Dakar Framework for Education, "Education for All: Meeting Our Collective Commitments." It stated: "we … commit ourselves to the achievement of education for all (EFA) goals and targets for every citizen and for every society" (UNESCO Education for All 2000). At Genoa, the leaders reaffirmed their commitment to meet the goal of universal primary education by 2015, to support gender equality in education, to improve teacher training, to build on the work of the DOT Force, and to use information and communications technology to strengthen educational strategies.

Genoa also developed G8-centered education governance at the official level for the second year in a row. The leaders created a G8 task force of senior officials to advise leaders on how to pursue the Dakar Framework, requesting recommendations before their next summit. At Genoa, the G8 supported the MO's work on education in a major way.

Kananaskis 2002

In the lead-up to the 2002 Kananaskis Summit, the task force consulted with developed and developing countries, MOs and civil society. All interested parties were invited to publicize their views on the appropriate role of the G8 in advancing the EFA process through an e-consultation between February 8 and April 5, 2002. In support, the World Bank established an "Education for All Fast Track" and called on the G8 to provide an additional US$4 billion per annum in order to achieve the EFA goals by 2015 (G8 Research Group 2002).

At Kananaskis, the G8 Education Task Force released its report entitled *A New Focus on Education for All*. It was devoted exclusively to education and improving its delivery throughout the world. The main recommendations included the need for a strong political commitment in developing countries, adequate resources supplied by increased, effective aid, and an improved monitoring system to assess progress. The Task Force also referred to the World Bank's list of Education for All Fast Track Initiative (FTI) countries. The leaders welcomed the report of the Task Force and endorsed its recommendations. The goals of achieving universal primary education and promoting gender equality in education by increasing bilateral assistance to developing countries were reiterated by the leaders through its priority placement in the Kananaskis Summit Chair's Summary. But there were no specific monetary commitments, nor was there any plan to work out donor commitments in the future.

Because of the relatively weak commitments, the financing needs for the universal primary education objectives were not met. The G8 Research Group noted:

> Given the crescendo of activity before the Kananaskis Summit, what the G8 needed to do, in Kananaskis, in order to fully comply with their commitment to "help countries meet the Dakar Framework for Education" was to agree to a well-specified increase of bilateral and/or multilateral aid. (G8 Research Group 2002)

The *New Focus on Education for All* document did not provide a consolidated package to ensure that those countries highlighted by the World Bank's FTI could meet their universal primary education goals (G8 Research Group 2002). The Africa Action Plan represented a missed opportunity for advancing assistance to LDCs to meet their Dakar universal primary education goal. The leaders' most forceful commitment in terms of aid to Africa for education reads: "in aggregate half or more of our new development assistance could be directed to African nations."

Sea Island 2004

The Sea Island Summit in 2004 shifted the G8's education focus away from Africa toward the Middle East, as part of the Broader Middle East G8 Plan of Support for Reform. The document referenced the literacy goal of the January 2004 UNESCO Conference on EFA National Action Plans which was held in Beirut, Lebanon. The G8's Broader Middle East agenda focused on political aspects, such as the Democracy Assistance Dialogue, and on several social goals, including education, increased literacy and training for employment. Education in the realm of training was also a component of the G8 Action Plan on Expanding Global Capability for Peace Support Operations. It aimed to train 75,000 troops for peacekeeping operations in Africa by 2010. While the G8 supported the MOs, G8 education governance without an MO was the central thrust, with George Bush's US as host.

Gleneagles 2005

The 2005 Gleneagles Summit turned the G8 leaders' attention back to Africa, and to primary education for all. It included references to this issue in both the Chair's Summary and the document on Africa. Following up on Sea Island, there were also references to education and educational reform in the Partnership for Progress and a Common Future with the Broader Middle East and North African Region.

St. Petersburg 2006

The St. Petersburg Summit was a first for the Russian hosts and for education. It was the first time ever that education had served as one of the main themes for a G8 summit. This was reflected in the overall commitments and references made to education, which far exceeded the G8's average. The G8 education ministers met for the second time ever in the lead-up to the summit. Education dominated much of the G8's overall discussions. The G8 discussed education in the related areas of health, energy and security, and also in a core "education" context. The leaders focused not only on primary education and education as a development imperative, but also on its role in contributing to prosperous economies and to improving the standard of living. They emphasized the importance of the innovation triangle – education, research and innovation – and focused on the overall theme of "education for innovative societies in the twenty-first century." The rationale for this theme was to promote an integrated approach, linking the pressing issues inherent to the different levels of education in both developing and developed countries. Overall, the education agenda was very ambitious. But while the ambitions of the Russian hosts and their G8 partners were commendable, the shift in focus did little to improve the G8's delivery on education promises.

Heiligendamm 2007

In 2007, the prominence of education fell far from the level of the preceding year, but it was still present in a significant way. The G8 discussed the importance of education as a social service. It reiterated the important correlation between higher education and sustainable growth, and discussed education in the context of intellectual property rights, the environment and in raising awareness on issues of corruption. It highlighted its commitment to the EFA strategy and to providing better education in Africa.

Hokkaido Toyako 2008

At the 2008 Hokkaido Toyako Summit, the references to education slightly increased from the year before, but were still nowhere near as high as 2006. The main thrust of the discussions on education focused on education in Africa, with commitments on improving the number, quality and training of teachers in the region, improving access to education for females, achieving EFA and working toward remedying FTI shortfalls. The leaders also indicated that they would monitor their progress on meeting their FTI shortfalls more closely, and would deliver a report on the topic at the 2009 Italian-hosted summit.

Causes of G8 Education Performance

This twenty-first-century increase in effective G8 global education governance has been driven by six forces, as the concert equality model of G8 governance highlights. First, after September 11, the US experienced declining levels of education achievement and inflows of post-secondary students from abroad compared to its G8 and OECD peers. Second, this decline was despite the US's leading public expenditures on education and teacher salaries and the long years its students were formally enrolled in school, suggesting that its G8 partners had critical specialized capabilities that worked. Third, a US that was ill-equipped for the Internet-dependent knowledge economy of the twenty-first century found little multilateral help from a poorly performing UNESCO or a narrowly focused UNICEF. Fourth, in notable contrast, a G8 devoted to the global promotion of open democracy, individual liberty and social advance found it easy to take up the task of educating an Asia where the free flow of information was still censored, an aging G8 citizenry whose lifelong learning and multicultural welcome had become critical for future economic and social success, and a rapidly democratizing Africa across the new digital divide. Fifth, a new generation of G8 leaders dedicated to education as a domestic priority, led first by the UK's Blair and then the US's Bush, brought the topic to a G8 summit that they and their equally popular colleagues virtually all attended for an unprecedented five years in a row from 2001 to 2005. Sixth, the new 1998 summit format allowed leaders themselves to deal more freely and flexibly with the often domestic issues, such as education, that they personally cared most about.

Vulnerabilities

The first cause of the G8's twenty-first-century effectiveness in governing global education is US vulnerability, caused not by shocks, but by a gradual decline in US performance in the output of quality human capital, regardless of the money and teachers flowing through its educational system. This vulnerability gained speed and visibility in 2000, accompanied by widespread fears of "the millennium bug" and a potential technological crash. The emerging importance of IT, aggregated by the dot.com boom at the turn of the century, suggested that IT was the wave of the future and the key to economic prosperity. Those countries that did not embrace IT would undoubtedly be left behind, and concern about the growing digital divide increased. The DOT Force, created at the 2000 Okinawa Summit, was a direct recognition of the new realities of an IT world (Stephens 2006). The G8 countries were fearful of being left behind, but they also knew that Africa was at far higher risk than the G8.

In the new knowledge economy of the twenty-first century, lagging educational performance of G8 states, most notably the US superpower and the relatively weaker Italy, stood out as a vulnerability. The US and Italy were the lowest-scoring countries both in terms of problem-solving and math skills. The 2000 host, Japan, was home to the students who ranked the highest among G8 countries on the PISA test. Canada, the G8's overall weakest power, came in second.

As the twenty-first century unfolded, the US became significantly less attractive to international students as a destination for higher learning. The September 11 terrorist attacks in New York, and the stringent national security measures undertaken in the US immediately in their wake, made it more difficult for foreigners to enter and study in the US. The US was losing its ability to attract a new generation of the best global human capital to its shores and its once highly desirable campuses. Germany also saw a small decline in its foreign student population. But the UK, France, Japan and Italy all saw increases, clearly at the expense of the US's universities and colleges, and to a lesser extent Germany.

Capabilities

The second cause of G8 performance on education is the G8's global collective predominance and internal equality in educational capability. The G8 countries as a group have higher adult educational attainment in terms of the number of years in formal schooling received than the average of four emerging G20 economies (Australia, Mexico, South Korea and Turkey), and also higher than the OECD mean. While this should stand out as a capability, it does not seem to translate into a higher level of human capital.

Similarly, G8 countries spend much more public money on their educational systems as a percentage of their gross domestic product (GDP). The United States in particular stands out among the G8 countries as spending the most on education as a percentage of GDP and as a percentage of total public expenditure in 2002. It is important to note that the US also has a larger, more robust economy producing public spending money, and that US President George W. Bush was a big spender. Moreover, the US has large amounts of private money being spent on the educational system, which is not taken into account. But again, despite a high proportion of GDP being allocated to public education spending, the education results in these countries, particularly the US, lag behind.

Teachers in the US and Germany have the highest starting salaries among G8 countries, along with the third and second highest possible salaries respectively within the pay scale (after Japan, which has the highest possible G8 teachers' salaries). G8 teachers' salaries are significantly higher on average than those of the G20, with the exception of Australia, which has similar salary scales to the G8 countries, and even more notably South Korea, which has a maximum teaching salary that is some $15,000 more than the highest G8 salary. But despite the fact that G8 countries pay their teachers well, education performance within the G8 lags.

Multilateral Organizational Performance

The third cause of high G8 education performance is poor MO performance. In the face of US educational vulnerabilities, the major MOs have largely failed to develop an adequate response. UNESCO was founded at the outset of the UN in 1945 to deal with development and education in a broad sense. UNICEF was set up one year later to meet the emergency needs of children in post-war Europe. It broadened its mandate in 1950 to address the long-term needs of women and children in developing countries. UNESCO and UNICEF are the two central multilateral organizations dealing with global educational governance. UNESCO has been criticized for being obsolescent and archaic. And while UNICEF performs better in terms of providing the international system with educational governance, it operates on only one component in the field.

Common Principles

The fourth cause of G8 education performance is common principles. Education is central to the G8's founding mission, which is to promote open democracy and social advance. The most obvious case of this is the Sea Island 2004 Broader Middle East G8 Plan of Support for Reform, which focused on both the political aspects of reform, such as the Democracy Assistance Dialogue, and the social goals of reform, such as education, literacy and employment training.

Domestic Political Capital

The fifth cause of high G8 education performance is the large domestic political capital of experienced G8 leaders who care. In 1988, Canada's Brian Mulroney was personally committed to literacy in relation to older workers and sufficiently popular to win a second majority mandate in the general election he called shortly after his Toronto Summit came to a successful conclusion. During these years, Margaret Thatcher had a personal interest in education as a former education minister, and was a domestically popular, successfully re-elected politician too.

For the twenty-first-century great leap forward, the personally committed, domestically popular and repeatedly electorally successful Tony Blair in the UK and George Bush in the US took the education lead. At Kananaskis in 2002, the lead on education for Africa came from Canadian Prime Minister Jean Chrétien, having won his third majority government electoral success in a row and supported by a sherpa who had served as an educator in Africa as a young man.

At Sea Island in 2004, the host, US President George W. Bush, was a firm believer in education. He supported the Head Start program in the US, an early childhood education program designed to help children succeed in the formal education system. During his first term in office and at the Sea Island Summit, President Bush had high political capital. The strong, focused commitments on education in the Middle East and the high compliance with these commitments at the Sea Island Summit reflects the use of this capital. Despite a second-term decline in political capital, President Bush's personal dedication to the education agenda remained strong.

Constricted and Controlled Participation

The sixth and final cause of G8 education performance is the controlled and constricted participation in the G8 club. Its small size, and legally and organizationally unconstrained assembly of procedural equals made it easier for flexible, innovative, leaders-initiated deliberations, directions and decisions to be forged.

Here, the first component is a constricted membership among procedurally equal major powers that produces a broad and balanced agenda brought by all, reduced transaction costs and vetoes, and ease of understanding and agreement between member states. Although the G8 expanded from six to nine members over three decades, it did so very slowly, and retained the small size necessary for a K-group to efficiently work. When Canada and the European Union joined the G8 in 1976 and 1977 respectively, they brought with them myriad diverse educational experiences and practices that did not immediately translate into concerted education attention. However, the 1998 entry into the G8 of Russia, with its traditionally strong educational capabilities and performance, coincided with the great leap forward in the G8's education governance. A mere year after Russia arrived as a full G8 member, the leaders issued a mandate at the Cologne Summit. Since Russia has become a member, the G8's attention to education has been focused and sustained. It reached a new height of attention and institutionalization as the Russian host in 2006 made education one of three priority topics, and institutionalized the G8 education ministers' forum by holding a second meeting.

The second component is controlled participation, by bringing to a particular summit those selected non-G8 member countries with the most to contribute to the particular issue at hand. This increases both the depth and breadth of the intelligence available to G8 leaders in their treatment of a subject, and the legitimacy, global understanding and effective diffusion of the directions and decisions they produce. This process of outreach again coincides with the great leap forward in twenty-first-century G8 global education governance. In 2000, Japanese Prime Minister

Obuchi attempted to secure the presence of four Asian leaders at his Okinawa Summit, but this endeavor ultimately failed due to a lack of agreement over which leaders should come. However, since 2001, the same four leaders of the leading democratic powers of Africa have come to almost every summit, accompanied by others from Africa, and in 2004, from the broader Middle East. Their participation directly reinforced the G8's direction-setting in education for development and education for democracy and social advance, and its expansion to the least-developed countries and peoples, and to Africa and the broader Middle East. The addition in 2003, 2005, 2006, 2007 and 2008 of the more systemically significant countries, with the Group of Five (G5) powers of India, China, Brazil, Mexico and South Africa at the core, have expanded these dynamics. The G5 and others have also been included in an expanding number of ministerial meetings. For example, at the 2006 G8 education ministers' meeting, the G5 along with Kazakhstan were all present. All of the many country additions except China have reinforced the core democratic character and commitment of the G8 itself.

The third component is the G8's occasional engagement since 1996 with relevant international institutions at the annual summit (such as the UN, the WTO, the IMF and the World Bank) to help formulate educational policy. MOs have played a role at the summit since their attendance at the 1996 Lyon post-summit breakfast, and a more vigorous role since 2001. The G8 also has a history of directing the actions of relevant educational institutions in order to work toward G8-established goals and commitments.

The fourth component is the growing premium on making the summit an occasion for informal, flexible encounters among leaders themselves. The first major move here was the 1998 Toronto Summit format of allocating specific time for leaders to be alone with other like-minded leaders in order to generate unstructured dialogue on education. From 1998 on, UK Prime Minister Blair eliminated foreign and finance ministers from the summit in order to allow more time for spontaneous leaders-only discussions and decision making. This new summit format corresponds with the great leap forward in G8 global education governance, starting in Bayne's view in 1998, but by all accounts in 1999. As only the G8 leaders, unlike their ministers, are popularly and directly elected, this leaders-only format encouraged leaders to connect more directly with their mobilized citizens at the summit, with the education-enhancing results that Bayne, Hart and others highlight.

Conclusion

The G8 has become an increasingly effective center of global education governance in the twenty-first century. It has sustained substantial performance across all of its tasks of domestic political management, direction-setting, decision making, delivery and development of global governance. Although the G8 has not performed equally strongly on all of these functions every year, the overall pattern is one of success.

This leap into effective global education governance has been driven by several forces. The first is the US's declining level of educational achievement and ability to attract foreign post-secondary students after the vulnerability-exposing shock of 9/11, despite its leading public expenditure on education and teachers' salaries and long years its students are formally enrolled in school. The US was increasingly ill-equipped nationally for the Internet-dependent knowledge economy of the twenty-first century, and found little multilateral help from a poorly performing UNESCO, a UNICEF with a partial mandate and an OECD with a partial membership. In contrast, the highly capable countries of the G8 gathered in an international institution devoted to the global promotion of open democracy, individual liberty and social advance. The G8 took up the task of educating Asia, where the free flow of information was still censored, with an aging G8 citizenry whose lifelong learning and multicultural openness had become critical for future economic and social success, and a rapidly democratizing Africa across a new North–South digital divide. A new generation of G8 leaders dedicated to education as a domestic priority, led by Prime Minister Tony Blair, President George Bush and President Vladimir Putin, brought education governance to the G8 summit. The G8's long history in governing global education meant that the 2006 St. Petersburg Summit was able to move to a new level of educational governance with relative ease and success. And in 2007 and 2008, education continued to remain and expand – not in attention, but in diversity – on the G8's agenda. The G8 could certainly work to improve its governing of education, particularly in complying with its education commitments; but compared to the UN and its other counterparts, it could serve to teach others how to successfully and effectively govern the issues of education in a global context.

Bibliography

Alden, Chris (2003), "Let Them Eat Cyberspace: Africa, the G8 and the Digital Divide," *Millennium – Journal of International Studies* 32(3): 457–76.

Bayne, Nicholas (2000), *Hanging in There: The G7 and G8 Summit in Maturity and Renewal* (Aldershot: Ashgate).

Bayne, Nicholas (2001), "Managing Globalisation and the New Economy: The Contribution of the G8 Summit," in John Kirton and George M. von Furstenburg, eds, *New Directions in Global Economic Governance: Managing Globalization in the Twenty-first Century*, (Aldershot: Ashgate).

Bayne, Nicholas (2005), *Staying Together: The G8 Summit Confronts the 21st Century* (Aldershot: Ashgate).

Dewitt, David and John Kirton (1983), *Canada as a Principal Power: A Study in Foreign Policy and Decisionmaking* (Toronto: John Wiley).

G8 Research Group (2002), "Issue Performance Assessment: Universal Primary Education," available at <http://www.g8.utoronto.ca/evaluations/2002kananaskis/assessment_upe.html>.

Hajnal, Peter (1999), *The G7/G8 System: Evolution, Role and Documentation* (Aldershot: Ashgate).

Hart, Jeffrey A. (2005), "The G8 and the Governance of Cyberspace," in Michele Fratianni et al., eds, *New Perspectives on Global Governance: Why American Needs the G8* (Aldershot: Ashgate).

Honderich, John (2006), "Getting Smart about Cities," *Literary Review of Canada* 14(4).

Kirton, John and Junichi Takashe, eds (2002), *New Directions in Global Political Governance* (Aldershot: Ashgate).

Kokotsis, Ella (1999), *Keeping International Commitments: Compliance, Credibility and the G7, 1988–1995* (New York: Garland).

Krasner, Stephen, ed. (1983), *International Regimes* (Ithaca, NY: Cornell University Press).

Labonte, Ronald, et al. (2004), *Fatal Indifference: The G8, Africa and Global Health* (Cape Town: University of Cape Town Press).

Lawton, Thomas C. (2001), "The New Global Electronic Economy: Consensus, Confusion, Contradictions," in John Kirton and George M. von Furstenberg, eds, *New Directions in Global Economic Governance: Managing Globalization in the Twenty-First Century* (Aldershot: Ashgate).

Mastroeni, Michele (2001), "Creating Rules for the New Global Information Economy: The United States and G8 Leadership," in John Kirton and George M. von Furstenberg, eds, *New Directions in Global Economic Governance: Managing Globalization in the Twenty-First Century* (Aldershot: Ashgate).

OECD (2004), *Knowledge Management: Innovation in the Knowledge Economy: Implications for Education and Learning* (Paris: OECD Publications Service).

Official Website of the G8 Presidency of the Russian Federation in 2006 (2006), "Education: The Problem," available at <http://en.g8russia.ru/agenda/education/>.

Okinawa G8 Summit (2000a), "Final Communiqué," available at <http://www.g8.utoronto.ca/summit/2000okinawa/finalcom.htm>.

Okinawa G8 Summit (2000b), "Okinawa Charter on Global Information Society," available at <http://www.g8.utoronto.ca/summit/2000okinawa/gis.htm>.

Putin, Vladimir (2006), "The Upcoming G8 Summit in St. Petersburg: Challenges, Opportunities, and Responsibility," March 1, available at <http://www.g8.utoronto.ca/whatsnew/putin060301.html>.

Putnam, Robert and Nicolas Bayne (1984), *Hanging Together: The Seven Power Summits* (Cambridge, MA: Harvard University Press).

Putnam, Robert and Nicholas Bayne (1987), *Hanging Together: Cooperation and Conflict in the Seven-Power Summits* (Cambridge, MA: Harvard University Press).

Stephens, Gina (2006), "G8 Institutionalization as a Cause of Compliance: The DOT Force Case," paper presented at the 47th Annual Convention of the International Studies Association, San Diego, CA, March 22–25, 2006, available at <http://www.g8.utoronto.ca/scholar/stephens_060326.pdf>.

UNDP (2005), *A Time for Bold Ambition: Together We Can Cut Poverty in Half* (New York: United Nations Development Programme).

UNESCO (2005), *Education Trends in Perspective: Analysis of the World Education Indicators* (Paris: OECD Publications).

UNESCO Education for All (2000), "Dakar Framework for Education," available at <http://www.unesco.org/education/efa/ed_for_all/dakfram_eng.shtml>.

UNICEF (2004), *UNICEF at a Glance* (New York: United Nations Children's Fund).

United Nations (2005), *The Millennium Development Goals Report* (New York: United Nations Department of Public Information).

UNICEF (2006), *The State of the World's Children 2006: Excluded and Invisible* (New York: United Nations Children's Fund).

United Nations (2000), *Millennium Declaration* (New York: United Nations Department of Public Information).

Von Furstenberg, George and Joseph Daniels (1992), *Economic Summit Declarations, 1975–1989: Examining the Written Record of International Co-operation*, Princeton Studies in International Finance 72 (Princeton, NJ: Princeton University Department of Economics.

World Summit on the Global Information Society (2005), "Tunis Commitment," available at <http://www.itu.int/wsis/docs2/tunis/off/7.html>.

Chapter 13

Information and Communication: G8 Institutionalization and Compliance in the DOT Force

Gina Stephens

The G8 is a rapidly evolving, increasingly influential institution that has a substantial impact on international cooperation and coordination. Especially following the end of the Cold War and the inclusion of Russia, this institution has expanded in depth and breadth to deal with a growing array of global economic, transnational and political issues. This growth has led some to view this institution as an evolving center for global governance in the post-Cold War era (Kirton 1997, Bayne 2000, Ikenberry 2001).

As the G8's focus has expanded beyond its original concern with economic policy coordination, so too have its instruments to assist in this expansion. In particular, the G8 practice of establishing issue-specific working groups has intensified. At the same time, G8 countries as a group have also demonstrated increasing levels of compliance with their summit commitments (Kokotsis 1999: 269). Thus, it seems that there is a connection between G8 institutional expansion (notably in the increasing number of expert working groups) and enhanced cooperation and compliance with G8 commitments. Using insights provided by constructivism and social identity theory, this chapter analyzes the case of the G8's Digital Opportunities Task Force (DOT Force). It argues that an increase in institutionalization and specialization in "top-down" created working groups changes their participant's interests and identities, thereby increasing cooperation and eventually compliance. These tightly focused groups, especially those tasked with policy areas that are relatively new (where there is little pre-existing or divisive national policy among G8 members – such as the issue area of information and communication technologies [ICT] and its role in development), provide a forum that favors the evolution of a group-centric identity that mitigates an overwhelming concentration on national conceptions of relative capability and competitive interests. Further, the creation of working groups that involve members from societal groups and countries beyond the G8, and whose work is embedded in a larger constellation of multilateral organizations (MOs) working in the same policy area, provides extra impetus for compliance. Indeed, it provides an innovative way of extending the G8's coherent global governance.

The DOT Force: Genesis and Achievements

The DOT Force was a G8 expert working group created as part of the Okinawa Charter on Global Information Society that was presented at the 2000 G8 Okinawa Summit (G8 2000). At this summit, the G8 leaders mandated the creation of the DOT Force in recognition of the need for a truly global strategy to address the concern of a developing "digital divide"[1] between the developed and developing world and the powerful potential of ICT to aid in development:

> [T]here is a need for greater international dialogue and collaboration to improve the effectiveness of IT [Information Technology]-related programmes and projects with developing countries, and to bring together the "best practices" and mobilize the resources available from all stakeholders to help close the digital divide. The G8 will seek to promote the creation of a stronger partnership among developed and developing countries, civil society including private firms and NGOs [non-governmental organizations], foundations and academic institutions, and international organizations. We will also work to see that developing countries can, in partnership with other stakeholders, be provided with financial, technical and policy input in order to create a better environment for, and use of, IT. (Shade 2003: 108)

The G8 presidency appointed a DOT Force secretariat that consisted of four individuals – two members from the World Bank and two members from the United Nations Development Programme (UNDP). This secretariat was responsible for the further construction of the rest of the 47-member task force. Each G8 country was asked to provide representatives from three societal sectors – government, the private sector and business – and from non-profit organizations (NPOs). Eight non-G8 developing countries were asked to provide governmental representatives.[2] This membership was further complemented by the addition of single members from several MOs, the European Commission, the Organisation for Economic Co-operation and Development (OECD), the UN Economic and Social Council (ECOSOC), the United Nations Educational, Scientific and Cultural Organization (UNESCO), the United Nations Conference on Trade and Development (UNCTAD), the International Telecommunications Union (ITU)

1 The term "digital divide" originated in the mid-1990s to describe the disparity between those who had access to the Internet and those who did not. Initially, the term was used simply to describe technical access, but later it began to encompass more complex measures of access such as social infrastructure (access to education, literacy rates) and content (the ability to produce and consume information on the Internet) (Shade 2003: 108).

2 The developing country members were Bolivia, Brazil, Egypt, India, Indonesia, Senegal, South Africa and Tanzania.

– and from the World Economic Forum, the Global Information Infrastructure Commission and the Global Business Dialogue on E-Commerce.

The objectives of the DOT Force were specified in the Okinawa Charter as follows: the facilitation of dialogue and discussion with a variety of stakeholders – developing countries, international organizations and NGOs; G8 coordination of ICT programs and projects; the promotion of policy dialogue and education and awareness programs; an examination of private sector inputs; and the reporting of findings and activities before the next annual meeting in Genoa. Four priority areas were established: fostering policy, regulatory and network readiness; improving connectivity, increasing access and lowering costs; building human capacity, and encouraging participation in global e-commerce networks.

The DOT Force was set up with a deliberate one-year timetable, mandate and reference to both the core MO (ITU) and other MOs to guide its actions. The first phase of its operation was to uncover and identify concrete methods and projects for bridging the digital divide and to ensure the full participation of developing countries in the global information society. To do this, the DOT Force was to hold three two-day plenary meetings for all the members (with meetings taking place in Tokyo, Cape Town and Siena). These plenaries were designed to create a final report that would then be presented to the G8 leaders at the 2001 G8 summit in Genoa, Italy. In between plenary meetings, member countries and organizations were to focus on consultations within their own countries, thereby building a broader network of stakeholders which would forward submissions for the Genoa report and provide key linkages within their own domestic contexts to assist the Task Force in its implementation phase.

The consultative process was taken very seriously by all members, although the representatives from developing countries pointed out that their ability to field an extensive domestic consultation was more constrained by both limited resources and the short time frame of less than a year (McSorley 2003). The most extensive, and arguably most effective, consultation process took place in Canada. The Canadian Civil Society Consultation was undertaken both physically (at various relevant events across the country) and virtually (via email lists and electronic message boards). It was organized by Maureen O'Neil, the Canadian NPO DOT Force representative from the International Development Research Centre (Delannoy 2001). A website (Dotciv) was set up as a hub for the overall consultation process, and invitations were sent out to civil society organizations to participate in developing the Canadian input to the DOT Force discussions.

The working documents that stemmed from the Dotciv initiative show that the consultative process was essential to the formation of a broader and richer Canadian position. A consistent thread in the early discussions between governmental representatives and civil society organizations was the need to move beyond a "narrow (emphasis on infrastructure, telecoms)" and "technicist (technical considerations driving the Canadian position rather than a development concern)" approach (Delannoy 2001). This suggestion was taken to heart by the Canadian DOT Force representatives. This theme appears in the Canadian contribution to the

Task Force's Genoa Plan of Action – particularly in emphasizing the importance of a gender focus in ICT development, which was an early Canadian contribution to the document.

The transformation and enrichment of the discussion surrounding the digital divide to one that went beyond merely technical considerations occurred within the DOT Force as a whole. It reflects the development of a group consensus on the norms that should underscore both the course of its own work and the projects and proposed solutions that the Task Force would put forward. The DOT Force explicitly sought, early on, to provide an overarching normative frame of reference in the area of ICT and development – a frame that would provide coherence and guidance both within the G8 and without. The summary documents that stemmed from the first plenary state that all participants agreed to several basic principles that should "undergird the work of the Task Force" (Dot Force Secretariat 2000). Of particular note is the stated need for G8 governments and other participants to "feel and actively demonstrate *ownership* of the DOT Force process" and that this should be an "iterative, participatory process" that is as "*inclusive* as possible given the time constraints" (original emphasis). Likewise, the first plenary document underscores the importance of embedding a solution to the digital divide within a broader development process, noting that "there is no dichotomy between the 'digital divide' and the broader social and economic divides at the heart of the development process."

The report that resulted from the consultative process, *Digital Opportunities for All: Meeting the Challenge*, was presented as expected to the G8 leaders in July 2001 in Genoa at the annual summit (Dot Force Secretariat 2001). The report explicitly highlighted the close linkage between the DOT Force's work and the UN's Millennium Declaration and Millennium Development Goals (MDGs), observing that advances in ICT could "contribute substantially to realizing *every* one of these goals" (Dot Force Secretariat 2001; original emphasis). The report also explored and supported the varying needs of different countries with regards to the implementation of ICT for development and suggested that developing countries must become producers, not simply consumers, of content. It encouraged the UN's ICT Task Force to continue to identify options for involving stakeholders from developing countries in the development of ICT policy internationally. It also identified the key role of community-based organizations and NGOs in providing the means to assist this process.

Perhaps the most important aspect of the report was how it situated the work of the DOT Force as a nexus and a focus for all relevant policy actors: MOs, national governments, the private sector, NPOs and individual citizens. It emphasized the importance of coordinated action between all actors, focusing on public–private partnerships and seeking to make considerations of ICT-related entrepreneurship an integral part of all development programs and funding projects undertaken by multilateral development banks, agencies and national governments. It also highlighted the role that ICT could play in the work of other MOs (such as the UNDP and the World Health Organization [WHO]) and their fight against HIV/AIDS. The detailed Plan of Action, designed to offer a "fresh vision of how to bridge the Digital Divide," sought to help establish and support developing countries and emerging economy national e-strategies; improve connectivity, increase access and lower costs; enhance human capacity development, knowledge, creation and sharing; foster enterprise and entrepreneurship for sustainable economic development; establish and support universal participation in addressing new international policy and technical issues raised by the Internet and ICT; establish and support dedicated initiatives for the ICT inclusion of less-developed countries; promote ICT to support health care and fight against HIV/AIDS and other infectious and communicable diseases; encourage national and international efforts to support local content and applications creation; prioritize ICT in the G8, as well as other development assistance policies and programs; and enhance the coordination of multilateral initiatives (Dot Force Secretariat 2001, Industry Canada 2002).

Following the acceptance of the Plan of Action at Genoa, the DOT Force moved into its implementation phase. Under the Canadian chair in 2002, seven implementation teams were created and assigned to the following areas: Access and Connectivity, National E-Strategies, Human Capacity and Knowledge, Enterprise and Entrepreneurship, ICT for Health, Global Policy Participation and Local Content and Applications. Members from the Task Force were assigned to each team, with the expectation that these seven teams would prepare reports on their individual initiatives as well as contribute to a general report card to be presented to the G8 leaders at the Kananaskis Summit. The teams operated "in an independent and decentralized fashion, stressing an informal and practical approach focused on results" (DOT Force Secretariat 2001). The implementation process was highly structured, featuring several progress reviews for each team throughout the year to assess whether the implementation of the Plan of Action was on target. These reviews resulted in concrete reports to the Canadian chair, who guided the process and oversaw the group's "stocktaking" meetings and the creation of their final report, which was released at Kananaskis. When this document was presented at the summit in 2002, the achievements that it chronicled were impressive.

Within one year, the DOT Force vision had moved much closer to realization. Participation had reached well beyond the original membership to include almost 100 stakeholder organizations, spanning more than 30 countries. Through the work of its implementation teams, the DOT Force generated more than 20 major bilateral and multilateral initiatives, operating across a broad range of areas crucial to balanced development – access, governance, entrepreneurship, health and education. In designing and implementing these initiatives, DOT Force members gave special attention to the needs of less-developed countries, and particularly to Africa, responding directly to the requirements articulated in the New Partnership for Africa's Development (NEPAD) (DOT Force Secretariat 2001).

Although the DOT Force was formally disbanded once its report was given, the work begun by the Task Force and the initiatives that it produced have continued through a variety of other bodies, both governmental and non-governmental. The United Nations Information and Communications Technologies Task Force (UN

ICT) took over as a focal point for continuing the process initiated by the DOT Force, assisted by the OECD's Development Assistance Committee (DAC).[3] In the private sector, former DOT Force partners such as the World Economic Forum, the Global Business Dialogue on Electronic Commerce and the International Chamber of Commerce also continued its work. Likewise, there was a regular summit system in the World Summit on the Information Society, which met twice – in Geneva in 2003 and Tunis in 2005 – to bring forward items stemming from work done through the DOT Force and through the UN ICT. A comprehensive system of implementation and follow-up continued following the Tunis Summit, with the UN's Commission on Science and Technology for Development assisting the UN's ECOSOC with the multitude of initiatives and "action lines" that were agreed to through this summit system. The legacy of the DOT Force's work can be seen as a continuous thread throughout this issue area, to the present time.

One of the key features of the DOT Force that proved to be the secret to its success was its ability to harness new and existing MOs that amplified its reach and implementation beyond those of just the G8 member governments. The UN ICT was created in November 2001, shortly after the formation of the DOT Force. Although the DOT Force did not specifically spawn the creation of the UN ICT (its creation was an output of an ECOSOC panel on ICT issues and, more broadly, from efforts to implement the MDGs), the DOT Force successfully harnessed the impetus of the UN ICT and leveraged its broader membership in order to establish strategic direction and maintain policy coherence in this area.

The UN ICT was replaced in 2006 by a new and more broadly inclusive organization, the UN's Global Alliance for ICT and Development (GAID). GAID's formation closely mirrors that of the DOT Force. It was created after "comprehensive worldwide consultations with governments, the private sector, civil society, the technical and Internet communities and academia" (United Nations Global Society for ICT and Development 2009).

While the UN ICT emphasized the role of ICT in achieving the MDGs, GAID was intended to achieve broader goals in that it would be "a truly global forum that would comprehensively address cross-cutting issues related to ICT in development" (United Nations Global Society for ICT and Development 2009).

GAID functions as a partnership and network supported by the UN, under the authority of the Secretary-General and the auspices of ECOSOC. GAID, like the DOT Force, was formed using a multi-stakeholder approach that includes representation from MOs, officials from developed and developing countries, members from the international ICT industry and civil society groups. It continues to expand on the seminal achievements of the DOT Force, leveraging many of the same structural and procedural characteristics that made the DOT Force so successful.

3 Throughout its tenure, the DOT Force harnessed extensive partnerships with a broad selection of multilateral organizations, including the OECD, the UN ICT Task Force, UNCTAD, the UNDP, ECOSOC, UNESCO and the World Bank.

Explaining G8 Compliance with DOT Force Initiatives

The issue area of ICT and development is a relatively new one for the G8, especially in terms of those aspects that pertain to Internet technologies. Yet there is evidence of G8 activity in the area as early as 1996, with communiqué commitments centering on the Global Information Society. Initially, performance in this issue area was poor – the summit's activities in this area were assigned a grade of C by the G8 Research Group (2006) in 1997. This record shows a marked improvement, however, with the creation of the DOT Force in 2000, garnering two successive A grades for 2001 and 2002 within that issue area.

Compliance with the DOT Force-related commitments was also extraordinarily high. It received 100 percent compliance across all eight countries for commitments made at the Okinawa Summit of 2000, followed by a nearly perfect score for the completion of commitments made in Genoa the following year. Here, all countries demonstrated full compliance, with the exception of Russia, which scored a -1 compliance rate, thereby bringing the total score down to 75 percent (G8 Research Group 2001).

What explains these extraordinarily high compliance scores? G8 compliance was positively affected in this case by five key factors: the creation of a working group; the structure and content of the working group and its particular policy task; the development of a group identity and norms; the existence of other MOs with a similar; and sometimes overlapping, membership and the chairing arrangements.

First, the creation of a working group by the G8 leaders represented a high measure of political will to seek results in this particular policy area – results that might not otherwise be achievable at other levels of the G8 system. The foreign ministers' process, for example, is quite vibrant, but is also broad in the number of different policy areas and initiatives that are brought forward during the summit cycle, making it difficult to achieve more detailed and focused policy results with attainable goals and commitments. A working group allows a tighter focus on a particular policy area and produces more substantial and detailed policy results. Likewise, it has been shown by previous studies that increased institutionalization has a positive effect on G8 compliance (Kokotsis 1999). Institutionalization creates an ongoing inter-summit focus on a particular area of policy. It also creates necessary linkages within G8 domestic political structures that favor follow-through on these commitments. The multi-stakeholder structure of the DOT Force multiplied this effect, as it mobilized not only members of the G8 countries' domestic bureaucracies, but also two other key societal sectors that had influence within the policy area: the business community and the non-profit civil society sector. DOT Force membership also leveraged the power of seven major MOs: ECOSOC, OECD, UNDP, UNCTAD, UNESCO, ITU and the World Bank. This unique structure, combined with the extensive consultation process that communicated the aims of the Task Force to a broader audience within the G8 countries and beyond, created the necessary "buy-in" at both the domestic and international levels, and mobilized consent for the financial expenditures required to fulfill the Task Force's work.

Second, the structure and work plan of the Task Force encouraged compliance. The goals of the organization were clearly stated at its creation, and a concrete work program with clear target dates and a tight one-year timetable for completion was established. These guided and focused the work, preventing any lags or confusion that might occur with a group of that size. Similarly, once in the implementation phase, the further split of the group into smaller units tasked with narrower goals and similarly tight timelines also provided focus. The institution of "stocktaking" exercises and the requirement for team progress reports during implementation further encouraged compliance by assigning transparent accountability. The effectiveness of the group's structure was apparent to the members of the group. This was noted explicitly in the plenary documents: "the tripartite, participatory, iterative, experimental nature of the process with developing countries at its center, permitted a degree of informality, speed, and creativity that might not always be possible in international fora" (DOT Force Secretariat 2000).

The increase in G8 compliance might also be caused by the particular task that the group worked on. In this case, the DOT Force's work involved an area that was relatively new in terms of policy. The Internet and its uses for development formed a subject that was fairly undeveloped within G8 governments and MOs. Therefore, there were few inherited, entrenched, well-defined conflictual policy stances between G8 members in this area. Likewise, the upper levels of the G8 structure were more likely to accept the recommendations of an expert group in an area that required technical knowledge – especially if those experts had been chosen by the G8 governments themselves. This potential for breaking new ground was also recognized by the Task Force early on in the plenary phase: "the multi-constituency, participatory nature of this Task Force could help to set the standard for international policy making bodies on the digital economy at a time when international policy frameworks and mechanisms are still fluid in this area" (DOT Force Secretariat 2000).

That working groups within the G8 structure should have such a significant effect has previously been observed in the academic community. Nicholas Bayne accurately noted that the increase in institutionalization is inevitable given the complexities of globalization, and further, that it is not surprising that these groups should have a wider effect beyond the G8:

> This expanding summit apparatus is not just the usual bureaucratic spread; … The most powerful influence on this proliferation is the iterative way in which the summits work. The summits grapple with difficult and unfamiliar issues. They often need several attempts before hitting the right solution. They handle subjects for which there are no satisfactory global institutions. In these conditions, it becomes natural to create G7 or G8 groups to work on the issues between summits, to prepare future decisions and to keep track of problems, even when they have been handed on to wider institutions. *These subsidiary*

> *groups, at ministerial or official level, gradually acquire a life of their own.* (Bayne 1999: 38; emphasis added)

Bayne implies the creation of a group-centric identity that may form in groups such as the DOT Force. This third factor of group identity and the formulation of group norms may then increase members' perception of the importance of the work and encourage compliance when those members return to their domestic bureaucracies.

The creation of a group identity within a group like the DOT Force has also been noted in the broader constructivist literature on MOs (Wendt 1999). As Martha Finnemore observes, actor and structure begin to act on each other in a feedback loop: "Actors create structures which take on a life of their own and in turn shape subsequent action" (Finnemore 1996: 30). The increase in the G8's institutional breadth and depth, especially in the post-Cold War period, has therefore created a dense system of groups in which the interaction of individuals creates policy outputs. The negotiation of these policy outputs is clearly shaped by the internal dynamic of the individuals comprising these groups. The social interactions which occur within these groups may shape not only what their members see as their individual interests, but ultimately how they view their own identities – especially when dealing with new problems where few pre-existing national policies exist. These individual estimations of interests and identities (and the social norms that engender them) may then be exported further to other G8 groups at different levels (for example, working groups to sherpas), to domestic bureaucracies, and/or other international fora. In this way, the interactions that shape interests and identities may play as powerful a role as material factors in shaping agenda-setting and policy outcomes. As Finnemore observes:

> The fact that we live in an international society means that what we want and, in some ways, who we are are shaped by social norms, rules, understandings, and relationships we have with others. These social realities are as influential as material realities in determining behavior. Indeed they are what endow material realities with meaning and purpose.

Alison Bailin (2001) also points to the importance of iterated group interaction and information-sharing in the summit on the formation of individual identity and its related impact on group cooperation:

> Summit discussions reinforce group identity. Summiteers develop personal relationships. The group designates roles for members through discussion. Each knows that fulfilling its role is critical for success. In such a small, exclusive group, it is easy to discern a single actor's contribution or effect on the situation.

Thus, the structure of the DOT Force – with its well-defined work program, replete with clear and close deadlines, frequent meetings, and smaller groups for implementation – allowed this effect to arise more fully.

Insights from the field of social psychology are also useful in explaining the importance of the group structures that have evolved within the Summit system in the post-Cold War era and their impact on the internal functioning of the G8, through their effect on the individual policymakers that comprise these groups. Social identity theory reveals the importance of group membership to the establishment of personal identity. In particular, Tom Tyler and Steven Blader (2001: 210) identify the role of group status (how influential/important a group is perceived to be) on the formation of individual identity. The more influential a group is, the more attractive group membership is to the individual since it reinforces positive perceptions of individual status, which in turn encourages the individual to increasingly act in ways that further the group's collective interest. In high-status groups, the individual's own identity becomes co-mingled with that of the group:

> Since the perceived quality of the group literally reflects on [the individual's] sense of self and their feelings of self-worth, the group's success can bring about benefits for their identity and vice versa. This leads to a link between the success of the group and the maintenance of a positive sense of self. Alternatively, they may be motivated to work on behalf of the group simply as a behavioral expression of their connection with the group. … We expect that when people are identified as such with their group, they will be more willing to act cooperatively toward the group – investing their time and energy in working to see the group succeed.

Most importantly, Tyler and Blader (2001), and other social psychologists, specify that this co-mingling of individual and group identity internally leads to changes in the individual's attitudes and values, and that this change in values is not motivated "by external contingencies such as resources" (Kohn 1999). This finding echoes the constructivist literature on norms, which posits that material factors may simply be a secondary motivator of compliant and cooperative behavior (Checkel 2004, Bernstein 2002, Finnemore 1996).

The fourth factor that influenced G8 members' compliance with the DOT Force commitments was the embeddedness of the group in other ongoing processes in the policy area that involved MOs with an overlapping membership. The DOT Force work was in line with other broader programs of development, adopting similar conclusions to that of the OECD's DAC on mainstreaming gender into bilateral and multilateral development programs. Similarly, the DOT Force also connected its own work to the larger G8 Africa Action Plan initiative presented at Kananaskis, allowing it to utilize the political momentum for the Africa plan to assist compliance with its own agenda. In addition, the DOT Force included representatives from relevant MOs that worked in the policy area of ICT and development (such as the UN, the OECD and the World Bank). It deliberately located its work within a constellation of like-minded organizations in order to ensure that work in the area (and the guiding norms that the DOT Force created) continued past its own end-date:

> As a process conducted under the G8, the DOT Force formally sunsets with this report. Its agenda, however, has now become the business of a number of other bodies that will carry on the leadership role of the DOT Force within the international community. The UN ICT Task Force, established by the Secretary-General in November 2001, shares the DOT Force vision and approach, and provides a focal point for establishing strategic direction, policy coherence and advocacy in relation to the global, ICT-based development agenda. Through its regional networks, the UN ICT Task Force provides an effective means for broader outreach and the effective involvement of developing countries in future implementation work. In the private sector, organizations such as the World Economic Forum, the Global Business Dialogue on Electronic Commerce, and the International Chamber of Commerce have also accepted the challenge of widening digital opportunities within the developing world. (DOT Force Secretariat 2001)

The DOT Force leveraged the political will and economic power in its constituting source (the G8). Further, instead of replicating the work of existing MOs or creating parallel work projects, the DOT Force sought to use existing resources and act instead as a focus and driver for the ICT development agenda.

Fifth, the fact that the Task Force was headed by a Canadian chair during the 2002 Canadian hosting of the G8 assisted in securing compliance during the implementation phase. The Canadians were motivated to ensure a smooth completion of the DOT Force's work and to provide a successful conclusion to an initiative that essentially showcased many successful Canadian projects in the area of ICT and development. These projects connected not only with the DOT Force initiative, but also with the larger Kananaskis priority of the Africa Action Plan.[4] Thus, Canada employed the hosting prerogative to place particular emphasis at the G8 leaders level on the Africa Action Plan, and within that, the DOT Force initiative.

Conclusion

The DOT Force represents a successful G8 experiment with the institutionalization of an expert working group that extends beyond the original G8 parameters.

4 There were three such Canadian initiatives: the Canadian e-Policy Resource Centre, the Centre for Connectivity in Africa, and Enablis (which was formerly the DOT Force Entrepreneurship Network.

Members of the DOT Force themselves recognized that their group represented a unique and almost magical formula for a successful task force:

> The DOT Force implementation teams have become the primary means of implementing the Genoa Plan of Action. Their initiatives illustrate the key elements in the DOT Force formula – they include innovative models of development that are scalable and replicable; they involve partners from developing countries in all phases, from design to delivery; they rely on public–private partnerships; and they carry minimal overhead, allowing for speedy implementation. Their autonomy and operational flexibility are key values to nurture in the deployment of projects, while seeking high-level support from global organizations. (DOT Force Secretariat 2001)

The unique structure and task of the DOT Force resulted in clear, detailed and achievable policy objectives. It also led to the expression of common values and the development of a group identity that encouraged compliance. The combination of separate societal sectors within the group and the unifying aspect of the working group in terms of identifying and prioritizing policy objectives also enhanced compliance. Likewise, the reporting structure and internally constructed measures of accountability throughout the consultative and implementation phases assisted greatly with maintaining the focus on the task at hand for all member countries, and transmitted this focus to G8 member bureaucracies, thereby ensuring compliance. G8 compliance scores relating to information technology rose considerably following the creation of the DOT Force. In 1997, the compliance score in this area had been 0.57 whereas in 2002, the score rose to 0.75, demonstrating the success of this group in its fulfillment of G8 commitments (G8 Research Group 2001). Its legacy, in terms of its catalytic effect on both MOs and on the creation of many private sector initiatives in this area, speak to an even broader success.

The case of the DOT Force represents a promising model for the construction of future working groups with the G8. The broad membership of a group like the DOT Force does much to debunk those who criticize the G8 for being unrepresentative of the developing world and the broader sectors of their own societies. The breadth and balance of its membership (drawn from well beyond a global electronically empowered techno-elite), employs a similar strategy to the WHO's Public Private Partnerships (WHO 2006). Such bodies extend the reach and the available resources of the G8 and long-established MOs to enact truly effective global governance.

Bibliography

Bailin, A. (2001), "From Traditional to Institutionalized Hegemony," *G8 Governance* 6, available at <http://www.g8.utoronto.ca/scholar/bailin/bailin2000.pdf>.

Bayne, N. (1999), "Continuity and Leadership in the Age of Globalisation," in Michael Hodges, John Kirton and Joseph Daniels, eds, *The G8's Role in the New Millennium*, (Aldershot: Ashgate), pp. 21–44.

Bayne, N. (2000), *Hanging in There: The G7 and G8 summit in Maturity and Renewal* (Aldershot: Ashgate).

Bernstein, S. (2002), "International Institutions and the Framing of Domestic Policies: The Kyoto Protocol and Canada's Response to Climate Change," *Policy Sciences* 35(2): 203–36.

Brown, R. (2000), "Social Identity Theory: Past Achievements, Current Problems and Future Challenges," *European Journal of Psychology* 30(6): 745–48.

Checkel, J. (2004), "Social Constructivism in Global and European Politics: A Review Essay," *Review of International Studies* 30(2): 229–44.

Delannoy, J-F. (2001), "Report on the dotciv discussion," available at <http://www.bellanet.org/dotforce/docs/dotciv_report.doc?ois=y;template=blank.htm> (last accessed March 2006).

DOT Force Secretariat (2000), "First Plenary Meeting of the Digital Opportunities Task Force (DOT Force)," Tokyo, Japan, November 27–28, available at <http://www.funredes.org/mistica/english/cyberlibrary/participants/docuparti/eng_doc_05.html>.

DOT Force Secretariat (2001), *Digital Opportunities for All: Meeting the Challenge*, available at <http://www.g8.utoronto.ca/summit/2002kananaskis/dotforce_reportcard.pdf>.

Ellemers, N., P. Koretakaas and J.W. Ouwerkerk (1999), "Self-Categorization, Commitment to the Group, and Group Self-esteem as Related But Distinct Aspects of Social Identity," *European Journal of Social Psychology* 29: 371–89.

Ellemers, N., R. Spears and B. Doosje (2002), "Self and Social Identity," *Annual Review of Psychology* 53: 161–96.

Finnemore, M. (1996), *National Interests in International Society* (Ithaca, NY: Cornell University Press).

G8 (2000), "Okinawa Charter on Global Information Society," Okinawa, July 22, available at <http://www.g8.utoronto.ca/g7/summit/2000okinawa/gis.htm>.

G8 (2001), "G8 Communique Genova 2001 Final," July 22, available at <http://www.g8.utoronto.ca/g7/summit/2001genoa/finalcommunique.html>.

G8 Research Group (2001), "G8 Compliance Report – Okinawa 2000," available at <http://www.g7.utoronto.ca/evaluations/2001compliance/2001reportDot.pdf>.

G8 Research Group (2006), "G8 Performance Assessment by Issue, 1996–2004," available at <http://www.g8.utoronto.ca/evaluations/assessments.htm>.

Hodges, M., J. Kirton and J. Daniels, eds (1999), *The G8's Role in the New Millennium* (Aldershot: Ashgate).

Hogg, M. and D. Abrams (1988), *Social Identifications: A Social Psychology of Intergroup Relations and Group Processes* (London: Routledge).

Ikenberry, J. (2001), *After Victory: Institutions, Strategic Restraint and the Rebuilding of Order after Major Wars* (Princeton, NJ: Princeton University Press).

Industry Canada (2002), "Report Released on Bridging Global Digital Divide," June 25, available at <http://www.ic.gc.ca/eic/site/ic1.nsf/eng/02756.html>.

Jervis, R. (1985), "From Balance to Concert: A Study of International Security Co-operation," *World Politics* 38: 58–79.

Kirton, J. (1989), "Contemporary Concert Diplomacy: The Seven-Power Summit and the Management of International Order," paper presented at the Annual Convention of the International Studies Association, March 29–April 1, London, available at <http://www.g8.utoronto.ca/scholar/kirton198901>.

Kirton, J. (1993), "The Seven Power Summits as a New Security Institution," in David Dewitt, David Haglund and John Kirton, eds, *Building a New Global Order: Emerging Trends in International* Security (Toronto: Oxford University Press), pp. 335–57.

Kirton, J. (1997), "Economic Co-operation: Summitry, Institutions and Structural Change," in John Dunning and Gavin Boyd, eds, *Structural Change and Co-operation in the Global Economy* (London: Edward Elgar).

Kirton, J. (1999), "Explaining G8 Effectiveness," in Michael Hodges, John Kirton and Joseph Daniels, eds, *The G8's Role in the New Millenium* (Aldershot: Ashgate), pp. 45–68.

Kohn, A. (1999), *Punished by Rewards: The Trouble with Gold Stars, Incentive Plans, A's, Praise, and Other Bribes* (Boston, MA: Houghton Mifflin).

Kokotsis, E. (1999), *Keeping International Commitments: Compliance, Credibility and the G7, 1988–1995* (New York: Garland Publishing).

Kokotsis, E. and John K. (2001), "Compliance with G8 Commitments: The Peace and Security and Conflict Prevention Agenda, From Okinawa 2000–Genoa 2001," paper prepared for the Department of Foreign Affairs and International Trade Policy Planning Division in preparation for the Canadian Presidency of the G8 Foreign Ministers' Process in 2002, available at <https://tspace.library.utoronto.ca/bitstream/1807/563/2/kirton-kokotis.pdf>.

Kupchan, C. and C. Kupchan (1991), "Concerts, Collective Security, and the Future of Europe," *International Security* 16: 114–61.

Kupchan, C. and C. Kupchan (1995), "The Promise of Collective Security," *International Security* 20: 52–61.

Martin, L.A. and B.A. Simmons (1998), "Theories and Empirical Studies of International Institutions," *International Organization* 52(4): 729–57.

McSorley, K. (2003), "The Secular Salvation Story of the Digital Divide," *Ethics and Information Technology* 5: 75–87.

Putnam, R.D. and N. Bayne (1987), *Hanging Together: Cooperation and Conflict in the Seven-Power Summits* (Cambridge, MA: Harvard University Press).

Shade, L.R. (2003), "Here Comes the DOT Force: The New Cavalry for Equity?" *Gazette: The International Journal for Communication Studies* 65(2): 107–20.

Simpson, R. (2003), "The G8 DOT Force," Presentation presented at the OECD Global Forum on Knowledge Economy, March 4–5.

Tyler, T. and S.L. Blader (2001), "Identity and Cooperative Behavior in Groups," *Group Processes & Intergroup Relations* 4(3): 207–26.

United Nations Global Society for ICT and Development (2009), "What Is GAID?," available at <http://www.un-gaid.org/About/WhatisGAID/tabid/892/language/en-US/Default.aspx>.

Wendt, A. (1999), *Social Theory of World Politics* (Cambridge: Cambridge University Press).

World Health Organization (2006), "Partnerships," available at <http://www.who.int/neglected_diseases/partnership/en>.

Chapter 14

Health Compliance in the G8 and APEC: The World Health Organization's Role

John Kirton, Nikolai Roudev, Laura Sunderland, Catherine Kunz and Jenilee Guebert

One of the most promising ways to bring health and foreign policy together in a comprehensive, coherent and consequential way comes when national leaders gather together in global summits, above all at the annual meetings of the informal, plurilateral Group of Eight (G8) and the Asia Pacific Economic Cooperation (APEC) forum.

Since its start in 1975, the G7/8 has dealt with a wide range of issues, including finance, trade, development, the environment and foreign policy. Since 1980, it has added health. Starting in 1989, it has involved other countries, with the most regular participants being the Group of Five (G5) leaders of China, India, Brazil, Mexico and South Africa, plus several African and other developing countries. Since 1996, it has added the heads of the major multilateral organizations (MOs), including the World Health Organization (WHO). The G8 summit has now made 234 specific, future-oriented, often ambitious health commitments, across the many issues at the forefront of global health governance today. More such commitments have come from G8 ministerial institutions for finance and foreign affairs, as well as the G20 forum of systemically significant countries created in 1999. Through the presence of the European Union (EU) and MOs in these forums and through other consultative processes, many of the world's other powers participate in shaping G8-centered global health governance.

APEC leaders have also been active in the health and foreign policy fields. Since they first started meeting in 1993, they have increasingly reached out beyond their classically conceived economic agenda to embrace health and foreign policy, to expand APEC membership and to move from deliberation and normative direction-setting to decision making expressed in collective commitments. Thirty health commitments were agreed to by these APEC leaders from a diverse group of countries across Asia and the Americas, North and South.

But do these G8 and APEC health commitments – created in the context of and in combination with foreign, climate, human rights and development policy – make any difference when the leaders and ministers return to their own countries to implement them? As the most powerful leaders of the world's most consequential governments, they should have the authority and capacity to ensure that the political will they express in their high-profile international meetings will be quickly translated into real action by their own governments, and the well-equipped civil and foreign services they contain. But at home they may also confront coalition and minority governments, competing priorities, breaking crises, fiscal and legislative constraints, and media and civil society demands to deal with other issues. Thus, the promises made on the sunny summit mountain-tops abroad may not become promises kept in the shadowy foothills and valleys back home.

Given the leadership shown by the G8 and APEC on global health governance, there is a need for its leaders and their stakeholders and citizens in the global community to know how well their commitments are being complied with and how this implementation could be improved. To address this subject, this chapter takes up four tasks. First, it maps and identifies trends in the health and foreign policy commitments made by the G8 summit, its finance, foreign and G20 ministerial forums, and by the APEC leaders' meeting. Second, it identifies patterns in the members' compliance with these commitments. Third, it considers the causes of this compliance, identifying factors coming from the international system, notably the role of multilateral organizations, members' domestic societies, their states and the leaders' own control. Fourth, it charts ways in which the member governments, with their different domestic constitutional systems and government structures, implement their commitments back home.

Commitments: Health and Foreign Policy in the G8 and APEC

The G8 Summit

The G8 summit has become an active forum for global health governance. In its annual two/three-day meetings, and in a set of public concluding declarations, statements and communiqués, it combines commitments that cover health and foreign policy, as well as climate, human rights and development, including the Millennium Development Goals (MDGs). Because leaders and their personal representatives (known as "sherpas") prepare, review and issue commitments in their leaders' name as a collective whole, these commitments are designed to offer a coherent package of priorities and connections among the component health and other issues.

The G8 summit first started making health commitments in 1980, as Appendix 14A shows. It has done so continuously since 1996, making several health commitments at every summit, in a ratchet-like upward rise. A new high of 61 health commitments was made at the 2006 St. Petersburg Summit, where infectious disease stood as one of the three priority themes, the 2007 Heiligendamm Summit made 43 health commitments, and the 2008 Toyako Hokkaido Summit produced 19. Together, these three summits produced 123 – or over half – of the 234 health commitments the G8 has made.

The G8 has concentrated on the issues of HIV/AIDS, making 41 commitments since 1996. It has also focused on multiple diseases, with 17 commitments since 1999, medicine/treatment with 14 since 1996, polio with 14 since 2002, malaria with 13 since 1998, and the Global Fund to fight AIDS, Tuberculosis and Malaria with 12 since 2001.

These health commitments have increasingly been issued along with foreign policy commitments, as Appendix 14B shows. Since 1978, almost every G8 summit has issued commitments on foreign policy, defined as the political-security subjects of East–West relations, terrorism, transnational crime and drugs, weapons non-proliferation, regional security, democratization, good governance, peace support and conflict prevention. It has done so in every year when it has issued a commitment on health. Its production of foreign policy commitments took off to sustained high levels in 1995, about the same time that its health performance did. Its foreign policy production peaked at 114 commitments in 2007, with a significant 105 in 2004, 74 in 2005, 82 in 2006 and 72 in 2008. Between 1975 and 2008, G8 summits produced 1,043 foreign policy commitments, almost five times as many as they made on health. But since 1996, the G8 summit has simultaneously been both a health and foreign policy global governor to a robust and rising degree.

The G8 has connected health not only with foreign policy, but also with climate change, human rights and development, including the MDGs. On human rights, the G8 summit started making commitments in 1981, has done so intermittently since 2002, and between 1975 and 2008 produced 59 in total, about a quarter of those on health. On climate, it started making commitments in 1987, has done so continuously since 1989, has moved to a sustained high volume since 2005, and has produced about three-quarters as many as on health. On development, it started making commitments in 1975, moved to a sustained high volume in 1995, and has now produced more than twice as many as on health. The G8 summit thus seems to more reliably create the health–development connection and the health–climate connection than it does the health–human rights one.

The G8 System

The broader G8 system has also combined health and foreign policy commitments in its ministerial forums, as Appendix 14C shows. Its foreign ministers' forum made five health commitments in 1999 and one in 2000, for a total of six. Its development ministers' forum, created in 2002, has made health commitments whenever it has met, producing five of its total of nine in 2007 alone. Even more active have been the G7 finance ministers, who have met for much longer and far more frequently each year. By 2008 they had produced 23 health commitments, all but one coming after 2000. And the G20 forum of finance ministers, produced a health commitment in 2000.

APEC

APEC leaders have also been increasingly involved in global health governance. They have made commitments on health continuously since 2000, as Appendix 14D shows. Their performance peaked with six health commitments in 2005. Their total of 26 health commitments from 2000 to 2008 compares with the 201 health commitments the G8 summit has made during the same period.

APEC leaders' 26 health commitments have dealt with nine issues. Tied for first, with six commitments each, are the "big three" of HIV/AIDS, diseases in general and avian influenza. Strategies for health and health services have two each, and severe acute respiratory syndrome (SARS), information exchange, pandemics, and health and safety each have one. Even more than the G8, APEC has focused on individual high-profile diseases, rather than health care systems or other cross-cutting issues. As in the G8, HIV/AIDS has come first.

APEC leaders' health commitments have increasingly been issued along with foreign policy ones. APEC leaders' 23 commitments on health issued between 2001 and 2007 were accompanied by 108, or more than four times as many, on foreign policy in the same period. They were also accompanied by 28 on climate change, 11 on development and 8 on human rights. But only health and foreign policy have each produced several commitments each year. APEC thus appears to be a particularly promising forum for authoritatively integrating health with foreign policy, primarily by getting more health commitments made there.

Compliance with Health and Foreign Policy Commitments

The G8 Summit

G8 leaders substantially comply with their health commitments within the year after they are made, as Appendix 14E shows. On the 46 health commitments measured for compliance from 1983 to 2008 (out of 225 made), the average score is +59 percent, on a 200-point scale ranging from -100 percent to +100 percent, where +100 percent is full compliance, 0 is partial or in-progress compliance, and -100 percent is no compliance at all or action opposite to what the commitment was. Translated to the more intuitively familiar scale of 0–100 percent, this represents a solid A- grade of 80 percent. Over the period 1983–2008, G8 compliance with health commitments was volatile, with a slight decline in 2005 and 2006, and an increase in 2007.

There is considerable variation in compliance across the different issues where the G8 leaders have made health commitments the most. The largest issue of HIV/AIDS has a compliance score of 69 percent (this and the other compliance scores below are reported on the 200-point scale). The Global Fund has compliance of 58 percent, malaria 100 percent and polio 41 percent. But medicine/treatment is at 25 percent and multiple diseases are at only 21 percent. While all issues have positive compliance scores, which indicates that G8 members generally make an effort to comply with the commitments, the G8 again performs better on individual high-profile diseases than on cross-cutting health systems and issues as a whole.

Compliance with health commitments varies considerably across G8 members, as Appendix 14F shows. The highest compliance comes from the US and Canada, tied at 78 percent, followed by the UK at 73 percent. The EU, France, Japan and Germany have 65 percent, 68 percent, 46 percent and 40 percent. Low but still positive scores come from Italy at 25 percent and Russia at 24 percent.

G8 summit compliance with foreign policy is approximately the same as for health, as Appendix 14G shows. While health has a slightly higher compliance score at 54 percent, foreign policy is close behind at 52 percent. Climate change and human rights come in at 51 percent each, while development comes at 47 percent. Trade is at 39 percent. It is only in finance, at 22 percent, that G8 compliance falls behind. The G8's summit's performance as a forum for inclusive, integrated global health diplomacy is reinforced by the fact that it both collectively decides on health, foreign policy, climate, human rights and development together, and substantially delivers its commitments in all these issue areas in the subsequent year.

The G8 System and the G20

The broader G8 system also seems to induce compliance, including from those countries which are not members of the summit-level G8 itself. The finance ministers' G20 meeting coaxes compliance from its non-G8 members, led by South Africa in the foreign policy field (see Appendix 14H). These non-G8 members also complied somewhat with the foreign policy, if not the health, commitments of the 2003 G8 Evian Summit, to which their leaders were invited for the first time. Such inclusion, which has become routine since 2005 for the G5, also appears to have induced compliance from them with the G8 summit's subsequent commitments on climate change (G8 Research Group Oxford 2007).

APEC

APEC members' compliance with their collective commitments is more difficult to trace, in part because of the larger number and more diverse nature of the members involved. The standard approach has been to focus on APEC's trade liberalization commitments and see how well members comply by assessing the individual action plans they construct to move toward their trade goals. The dominant view has been that compliance has been disappointing, with little chance that the goal of free trade among the developed country members by 2010 will be met (Bark, Moon and Paik 1998).

Causes of Compliance with Health and Foreign Policy Commitments

The causes of G8 members' compliance with their health, foreign policy and other commitments potentially come from a large number of sources, and from different levels of governance abroad and at home. In the international system, these include configurations of countries' relative capability and vulnerability, the international dynamics of emulation among countries, and the involvement of international institutions of a formal, broadly multilateral and informal, plurilateral G8-centered sort. In domestic societies, these include the pressure or support from public opinion for the issues that were committed to, or for the committing institutions or leaders themselves. In member governments, they include the direct control leaders have over their legislatures and relevant institutions such as central banks, and the way leaders themselves display their political will by crafting commitments at the summit that catalyze compliance with them beyond.

The evidence on causes of compliance with G8 commitments shows that changes in relative capability and vulnerability have an indirect effect at best (Kirton 2006a). The emulation effect as a defection dynamic among members does matter, suggesting individual G8 members can serve as compliance leaders to unleash an upward spiral of compliance across the group as a whole (Li 2001). Moreover, when G8 leaders have and use a powerful MO, a G8 institution and a coordinative center within their own government dedicated to the issue area, higher compliance results (see Kokotsis 1999, esp. pp. 3–36, 267–89). And when they craft their commitments in ways that embed particular compliance catalysts, so does higher compliance (Kirton 2006a, 2006b, Kirton et al. 2007, 2009). Thus, G8 governments and their leaders are not prisoners of systemic forces beyond their control, but are able to use international institutions, their own national governments and the design of their own summit commitments to deliver the compliance they presumably want. G8 leaders largely control their own compliance fate.

However, there are particular combinations, or specific cocktails, of compliance catalysts required in each issue area for compliance to rise. In the case of G8 health commitments, higher compliance comes when the commitment includes a one-year timetable for completion, invokes the WHO as the core MO to assist and does not ask any other MO for help. In the case of finance and development, considered as a combined issue area, higher compliance comes when G7 finance ministers deal with the issue before and after the leaders make the commitment, and when leaders set a one-year timetable for compliance and place the commitment in a priority position at the summit itself. On climate change, higher compliance comes when the leaders give the commitment priority placement, but do not invoke international law. Invoking the most relevant MO helps Canada but harms the United States in terms of compliance results.

Implementing Health and Foreign Policy Commitments

Leaders at the summit can thus carefully exercise their political will to improve compliance, and use international institutions abroad and their governments at home to help them in this task. But this push from the summit peak must still filter through the ongoing process of international institutions and national governments for the desired compliance to come about. Little is known about how these implementation processes operate, and how they can be improved.

International Institutions

Within international institutions, there are several ways in which G8 commitments are translated into commensurate action through the formidable resources these bodies control and through the often impressive influence they have on their member states.

In some MOs, such as the International Monetary Fund (IMF) and International Bank for Reconstruction and Development (IBRDs or the World Bank), the rules and decision-making procedures allow G7 and G8 members formally and informally to control the behavior of the organization. G7 members have certainly used this international organizational power, for example in responding to the Asian-turned-global financial crisis of 1997–99.

Other MOs of the 1940s generation, such as the WHO, are far less controlled and guided by the G8. They play a strong, autonomous role. The WHO's Director-General attended the G8 summit in 2001 and 2006. In 2000, the Director General played a catalytic role in Tokyo in creating the process that led the G8 to produce the Global Fund in 2001. But beyond this, little is known about how this firsthand connection inspired subsequent G8 or WHO action. The same can be said for the only G8 health ministers' meeting, in 2006, which was attended by the WHO, the UN Joint Programme on HIV/AIDS (UNAIDS), the Global Fund, the World Bank, the EU and the health ministers of the G5.

The G8 has often used the plurilateral Organisation for Economic Co-operation and Development (OECD), in part as a substitute for the secretariat that the G8 has deliberately and strongly renounced for itself since its foundation in 1975. Recently, it has used the OECD to help deliver its African development commitments. Here, the G8 is working in partnership with the African countries, some of whose leaders have attended the G8 summit regularly since 2000 and 2001. In 2007, the G8 also looked to the OECD to serve as the secretariat for the new Heiligendamm Process – a two-year structured dialogue on innovation/intellectual property, investment, development and energy efficiency that the G8 launched with the G5 (Cooper and Antkiewicz 2008).

Since its start, the G8 itself has largely relied on using its final meeting of the leaders' sherpas and their foreign affairs sous-sherpas (FASS) each year to review the results of the summit that year, including how its new commitments are being put into effect. Such meetings monitor implementation and identify where greater political engagement is necessary to push implementation ahead (Donnelly 2007: 49). But in practice this sherpa meeting largely focuses on the new, not the old, as attention tends to focus on what the incoming G8 host, about to take the chair on January 1, is planning for the following year's summit.

Over the years, G8 leaders have experimented with several processes to monitor, report on and thus improve compliance. These include remit mandates to report back to the leaders before or at the next summit, the creation of G8 official-level bodies to conduct and track implementation, and the issuing of public reports on a priority topic prepared by each member and released to the media at or after the subsequent summit. At the 2006 St. Petersburg summit, G8 leaders committed to conduct a regular review of the measures they would take against HIV/AIDS, tuberculosis and malaria. In the Autumn of 2007, following the subsequent summit at Heiligendamm, they issued their first report. Monitoring and implementing their health commitments was a major emphasis of G8 leaders at the Hokkaido Toyako summit in 2008. None of these measures, including the public reporting process, has thus far reliably helped to improve compliance or enhance the credibility of the G8 where compliance is concerned.

The G8 system has also developed its own G8-centered global governance in ways that have helped with implementation. Beyond the ministerial bodies noted above, since 1975 the G8 has created dozens of official-level bodies to help implement the G8 leaders' commitments, as well as to prepare recommendations for further action. Many of these bodies deal directly with health and foreign policy, as Appendix 14I shows. Some are also created from the start with, or expanded to embrace, non-G8 countries, especially in the foreign policy fields of nuclear proliferation, missile technology and financial crime. Very little is known about the operation or even existence of such groups, and how they advance the implementation task.

In the case of APEC, with its much larger membership, the leaders have created a small secretariat to help them with their preparatory and follow-up work. Because it is small and relies on a staff that rotates to some degree with APEC's annual host, it has the potential to stay closely attuned to what the APEC leaders want. APEC does track its members' progress toward their "goals," but not necessarily on an annual basis. APEC publishes reports, brochures and documents about what has been done and what needs to be done in order for the member economies to accomplish their goals. Member economies are also required to submit annual reports on their individual action plans and their collective action plans. They are in effect required to monitor their own compliance in this way. Members can also put forward "APEC Projects" that have to be seconded by one or two other members. The APEC Secretariat goes through these to approve them before allocating funds. If they are accepted, APEC assigns overseers to these projects, who are required to write a final report upon the project's completion.

National Governments

Within national governments, there are several ways to implement health and foreign policy commitments made at the summits of the G8 and APEC. For the G8, the lead responsibility usually resides with the leaders' sherpa, who upon returning from the summit assigns the various follow-up tasks to those individual parts of the bureaucracy whose subject responsibility is most closely involved. Here, the actual implementation process varies widely according to the institutional location of the sherpa. In countries such as Canada and Japan, where the sherpa has long been the deputy minister or associate deputy minister of the foreign ministry, the flows tend to run down to the G8 division in the foreign ministry, across to the functional divisions in the foreign ministry, and out from them to any and all of the relevant counterpart units in other departments. In countries such as the United States, where the sherpa often comes from one of the leader's own offices, the foreign ministry is less central but still substantially involved.

Whatever the cross-national variation, however, in no case is responsibility for implementation assigned to the chief civil servant in the government, or to the head of the leader's political staff. Nor are there comprehensive interdepartmental committees that meet regularly to undertake and review implementation. Therefore, implementation does not map a summit whose commitments are made by the leader across virtually the full range of what his or her government does. And the lead responsibility for implementing the results of the last summit remains with the sherpa, whose primary responsibility is to prepare for the next summit and ensure that his or her leader's priorities are reflected there.

The sherpa-centric implementation process does have some advantages. When the sherpa comes from the foreign ministry, the implementation process for G8 commitments can more readily be coordinated with that of APEC and other plurilateral summits in which all G8 members are engaged in (in a somewhat overlapping mix) and the relevant MOs in the international institutional world. This is especially the case if, as in Canada, the same foreign ministry units are responsible for both the G8 and APEC, as this allows for a coordinated cross-institution strategy to be produced. It also means that the center for G8 preparation and implementation is institutionally close to, if not embedded in, those responsible for the countries' involvement in MOs beyond the international financial institutions (IFIs).

Yet the reliance on the foreign ministry as the center for implementation can have costs as far as the integration of health is concerned. Few G8 sherpas have had previous experience in their national departments of health. Few G8 foreign ministers have previously served as health ministers, with the notable exceptions of France's Bernard Kouchner and Philippe Douste-Blazy and Canada's Pierre Pettigrew. The leaders themselves have occasionally had previous experience as foreign ministers, but rarely as health ministers. On only two occasions have they had both. Both of these health/foreign policy twins have come relatively recently and together, in the persons of Japan's Junichiro Koizumi and Italy's Silvio

Berlusconi, from 2001 to 2006 and from 2008, respectively. This again suggests that the G8 summit is a promising forum for practicing integrated global health diplomacy, but not necessarily on the implementation front, if emphasis is placed on the past experience and ongoing monitoring of the key individuals involved.

Non-governmental Organizations

Some non-governmental organizations, with their dedication to transparency and accountability in global governance, also monitor compliance with G8 commitments, in part on the assumption that "that which is measured is treasured," and thus is that which gets done. The G8 Research Group, as a global analytical network, has assessed annually G8 countries' compliance with selected priority commitments across all issue areas. It has issued a final compliance report every year since 1996, and an interim (six-month) compliance report every year since 2002. More recently, advocacy organizations have begun to monitor compliance, largely with the G8's African development commitments. The leading organization is ONE (formerly known as DATA), which is concerned with G8 compliance on debt, aid, trade and AIDS. Also active is the African Monitor, headed by the Anglican Archbishop of Capetown. While many of these efforts embrace health, only the G8 Research Group covers both foreign policy and health. And its focus is skewed to the priorities set by each presidency for its summit. Since 1996, these have seldom included foreign policy subjects. Only once, in 2006, have they included health.

Conclusion: Improving Implementation

The annual G8 summit and APEC leaders' meetings are thus promising forums for integrating health with foreign policy in ways that reflect the priorities of the WHO and the global community as a whole. Both are delivered directly by the most powerful leaders of many of the most influential countries in the world. These individuals are ultimately responsible, abroad and at home, for both health and foreign policy. They use their summits simultaneously to make many commitments in both fields and in the closely related ones of human rights, climate change and development, including the MDGs. Moreover, commitments made at G8 summits on these subjects are quickly complied with by the member governments to a substantial degree. Such compliance is caused, and can thus be improved, by leaders crafting their commitments in catalytic ways, and using their international institutions, including the MOs, and national governments in well-designed ways.

But the prevailing processes of implementing G8 and APEC leaders' commitments through international institutions, MOs, national governments or non-governmental networks are not currently conducive to enhancing compliance, monitoring and reporting, and thus integrating health and foreign policy in mutually supportive ways. There are many promising ways to improve compliance in support of this objective, including through a multi-stakeholder global health diplomacy network of civil society, national governments and multilateral organizations, including the WHO; however, it is not clear that any such improvements are being undertaken. And without these advancements, it is unlikely that health and foreign policy will move beyond the current status quo. They will not move to merge closer together in a more meaningful and cohesive way.

Bibliography

Bark, Taeho, Woo-Sik Moon and Jin-Hyun Paik (1998), "Strengthening Compliance with APEC Agreement: A Study on Member States' Compliance with APEC Agreement," *Policy Analyses II* 98-08, available at <http://www.kiep.go.kr/common/board_file_down.asp?131405|1> (in Korean).

Cooper, Andre W.F. and Agata Antkiewicz, eds (2008), *Emerging Powers in Global Governance: Lessons from the Heiligendamm Process* (Waterloo, Ontario: Wilfrid Laurier University Press).

Cooper, Andrew F., John Kirton and Ted Schrecker, eds (2007), *Governing Global Health: Challenge, Response, Innovation* (Aldershot: Ashgate).

Donnelly, Martin (2007), "Gleneagles G8 Summit Perspective," in Michele Fratianni, John Kirton and Paolo Savona, eds, *Financing Development: The G8 and UN Contribution* (Aldershot: Ashgate), pp. 43–51.

G8 Research Group Oxford (2007). "Governing Global Climate Change: St. Petersburg Compliance Report for the 'G8 Plus 5' Countries," available from: <http://www.g8.utoronto.ca/oxford/2006compliance-ox.pdf>.

Hajnal, Peter I. (2007), *The G8 System and the G20: Evolution, Role and Documentation* (Aldershot: Ashgate).

Kirton, John (2006a), "Explaining Compliance with G8 Finance Commitments: Agency, Institutionalization and Structure," *Open Economies Review* 17(4): 459–75.

Kirton, John (2006b), "Implementing G8 Economic Commitments: How International Institutions Help," paper prepared for a 2006 G8 pre-summit seminar, "On the Road to St. Petersburg: The Role of International Organizations in Implementing G8 Commitments," co-sponsored by the State University Higher School of Economics, and the G8 Research Group, University of Toronto, available at <http://www.g8.utoronto.ca/scholar/kirton2006/kirton_institutions_060622.pdf>.

Kirton, John, Nikolai Roudev and Laura Sunderland (2007), "Making Major Powers Deliver: Explaining Compliance with G8 Health Commitments, 1996–2006," *Bulletin of the World Health Organization* 85: 192–9.

Kirton, John, Nikolai Roudev and Laura Sunderland (2009), "Explaining Compliance with G8 Health Commitments, 1996–2006," in Andrew Cooper

and John Kirton, eds, *Innovation in Global Health Governance: Critical Cases* (Farnham: Ashgate).
Kokotsis, Ella (1999), *Keeping International Commitments: Compliance, Credibility and the G7, 1988–1995* (New York: Garland).
Li, Quan (2001), "Commitment Compliance in G7 Summit Macroeconomic Policy Coordination," *Political Research Quarterly* 54: 355–78.

PART V
The G8's St. Petersburg Summit and Beyond

Chapter 15
The G8 at St. Petersburg and Beyond

John Kirton

On July 15–17, 2006, the Group of Eight's (G8) 31st annual summit took place in St. Petersburg. It was the first regular summit Russia hosted since it joined the club as the eighth country member in 1998. As its priority themes for the summit, Russia chose energy security, infectious disease and education – the first time these subjects had been selected in advance as the substantive core of a summit's overall design. To the summit, Russia ultimately invited, for only the second time as a self-contained set, the leaders of the systemically significant countries of India, China, Brazil, Mexico and South Africa. Russia also invited from the very start, as a part of its summitry strategy, a large number of executive heads of several major multilateral organizations (MOs), including the United Nations (UN), the International Energy Agency (IEA), the World Health Organization (WHO) and the African Union (AU) and, for the first time ever, the International Atomic Energy Agency (IAEA) and the United Nations Educational, Scientific and Cultural Organization (UNESCO) (see Appendix 2A). And to help prepare the summit and deliver its results, Russia created an unprecedented Civil G8 mechanism that brought Russia and international civil society leaders into the summit process as never before.

After the summit, Russia's strategy and the summit's success inspired a great debate between critics and supporters of the St. Petersburg Summit and the G8 as a whole. The first school of major critics preferred global economic governance by the established MOs, rather than the informal, plurilateral G8. Former World Bank President James Wolfensohn, European Central Bank Governor Jean-Claude Trichet and Bank of England Governor Mervyn King explicitly and implicitly criticized the G8, its St. Petersburg Summit and its Group of Seven (G7) finance ministers' forum for their economic failings. These included not dealing with the mounting imbalances in the global economy, the simultaneous tightening of interest rates by national central banks and a looming financial crisis from asset inflation, general market euphoria and proliferating derivatives trading. The critics further saw the G8 as obsolete in a world where economic power was rapidly passing to India and China. They even suggested an end to the G7 finance ministers' forum, in favor of global economic governance through a reformed International Monetary Fund (IMF).

A second school of supporters, in sharp contrast, preferred the G8-centered soft law plurilateralism that St. Petersburg, under its Russian host, brought. Former German Chancellor Gerhard Schroeder and editorialists from around the world had a high opinion of the G8 and Russia as its 2006 host. Some saw the 2006 summit as a defensive event, with Russia using the unparalleled opportunity to showcase its economic revival and deflect criticism of its policies at home and abroad. Others more expansively concluded that Russia had hosted the G8 as well as any other country ever had, and had begun to serve as a representative of developing countries in the club. Schroeder himself went further, judging Russia's presidency to be efficient and successful, as President Vladimir Putin developed Russia in a democratic direction. And others even concluded that Russia would be a "hard act to follow," as Putin used his G8 presidency to reassert Russia's global role and brought it to a level not seen since 1989.

A close look at the available evidence suggests that the judgment of even the most optimistic supporters may be too modest in some important ways, for it misses the key to St. Petersburg's success on its multifaceted institutional innovations that included a new relationship between the soft law G8 and the hard law MOs. As a G8 host in 2006, Russia bore an extraordinary triple burden. It was asked to deliver a summit that would, as usual, address and help solve pressing global problems. It was further expected, for the first time in summit history, to produce one that would demonstrate, confirm and deepen the host's credentials and character as a democratic polity at home. And it was called upon to reform the G8 summit and system itself to include new rising powers, many MOs and a multifaceted globalized society in the G8 and around the world.

On the whole, Russia met this triple standard, and thus did much to shape G8 summitry in the years to come. It delivered a summit that made important advances and innovations on its three priority themes and on the burning political issue of the Middle East conflict that erupted that summer in Lebanon. Russia's responsibility of hosting, its acceptance of summit conclusions that affirmed democratic principles throughout, and its responsiveness to civil society at home and abroad helped empower democratic constituencies within Russia at a difficult and critical time. And for the future, Russia helped make the G8 a center of more genuinely global and domestic governance in several ways. It ultimately directly brought the capabilities, needs, diversity and legitimacy of the "Plus Five" powers of India, China, Brazil, Mexico and South Africa permanently into the summit club. It included many MOs from the start of the summit preparatory process through to the summit itself. And it involved civil society, legislators, youth, religious leaders and the media to help democratize the G8 itself.

Yet after St. Petersburg, there remained doubts about whether Russia as host had finally found the formula to ensure that the G8's often far-reaching and innovative democratic principles were actually implemented by its members and delivered to solve real problems in the global community as a whole. The Civil 8 process evaporated along with Russia's G8 presidency. Neither the old MOs nor the new G8 mechanisms were employed in the G8 compliance monitoring and implementation tasks. It is here that action is needed to make the G8 a genuinely accountable and effective center of global governance for today's twenty-first-century world.

St. Petersburg Summit Performance

The first accomplishments of Russia, as a regular host, were to set an agenda that combined innovation and iteration in the delicate blend that breeds summit success, and then deliver agreements on that agenda. While previous summits had dealt with energy security, infectious disease and education as important topics, never before had these subjects been identified so far in advance as the three central themes that constituted the core of the summit's overall design. The trilogy included two areas where there was a core UN MO – the WHO for disease and UNESCO for education – and one, energy, where there was not. As the energy and health priorities came directly from President Putin, Russia had no difficulty in getting its summit colleagues to accept and stick to this agenda. The trilogy built iteratively on the work of the G8 summits at Gleneagles in 2005 and before. Energy security flowed from Gleneagles's emphasis on climate change. Infectious disease and education were critical components of Gleneagles's concern with African development. And on all three priorities, Russia innovatively expanded and reframed the agenda. Energy security included, for the first time as an important component, physical energy security and energy poverty as links to African and global development. Infectious disease placed a new emphasis on the spread of HIV/AIDS into Eurasia. And education included the important dimension of the need for openness, multiculturalism and migration.

This agenda proved to be timely and well tailored in addressing the present and prospective needs of the G8 members and global community as a whole. Energy security was front and center in 2006, as world oil prices rose above $77 a barrel, a level in inflation-adjusted terms not seen since the last big oil shock in 1979. In a world where global terrorism and renewed nuclear proliferation had arrived, the concern with physical energy security was a new global priority that the G8 summit, unlike the fragmented and incomplete UN system with no bodies for terrorism or energy, could and did treat as an integrated, coherent whole. The concern with the Eurasian face of AIDS arose at a time when Russia was the G8 member suffering most at home from the disease, and when India was challenging South Africa as the country with the largest estimated absolute number of citizens living with HIV. And the education agenda well matched the needs of a world in an age where human capital and innovation and aging populations were central concerns. Rising shock-punctuated vulnerability in energy, chronic vulnerability in health and intensifying interdependence in education drove the G8 forward in these domains.

As a summit host, Russia proved able, willing and adept at accepting and adjusting to its partners' priorities and core interests, and getting them to adjust to Russia's in return. Faced at the start with a domestically driven German veto of any G8 mention of nuclear power as a legitimate part of a secure energy supply mix, Russia persisted with its supportive partners to get this changed. Hosting its first regular summit on the 20th anniversary of the 1986 Chernobyl nuclear explosion and the 10th anniversary of the Moscow Nuclear Safety Summit, Russia eventually got the Germans to relent. As a result, the G8 affirmed the value of safe and secure civilian nuclear power at home, and was thus able to speak with greater credibility to an Iran that was considering whether to accept a G8 offer to help create such nuclear power, if that country would give up its program leading to homegrown nuclear arms. Here, the G8 went well beyond the inadequate, established, hard law regime embedded in the International Atomic Energy Agency and Nuclear Non-Proliferation Treaty.

On infectious disease, Russia added and blended the concerns of those focused on the well-known dangers of HIV/AIDS, tuberculosis and malaria with those concerned about the new danger of a rapidly globalizing avian influenza (Cooper and Kirton 2009). It included the need to address such new diseases with immediate, intrusive measures within the sovereign jurisdiction of the originating state. And it dealt with older diseases such as measles, long defeated in G7 countries but a growing problem in Russia as its health care system declined. In doing so, the G8 largely reinforced the work of a WHO already active and effective in these domains.

On education, Russia accepted the arguments of the United States and Canada – both federal systems where classically defined education was the jealously guarded constitutional prerogative of sub-federal states and provinces – that the subject and summit action were better framed as human capital and innovation. This was a globally oriented, forward-looking approach that would avoid domestic political difficulties for the North American members at home. It was one that went well beyond the core competence of UNESCO and other UN bodies such as the UN Children's Fund (UNICEF) and the International Telecommunications Union (ITU).

As a result of such flexible adjustment and accommodation, the St. Petersburg Summit delivered some strong results (Appendix 15A). These came on most of the summit's six functions of domestic political management, deliberation, direction-setting, collective decision making, delivering its decisions and the development of global governance as a whole. Within Russia as the host country, the summit had a large imprint. The summit was selected by its citizens as the third most important and newsworthy international event of the year, and generally received favorable acclaim in public opinion polls and the major daily newspapers. It produced an extensive deliberative performance, as indicated by the number and length of the communiqués released. The summit set new normative directions, most notably in reframing energy security to put environmental protection and open markets in first place, and emphasizing the need for transparency, openness and the rule of law across all the three priority themes. The summit produced 317 clear, concrete, future-oriented collective decisions, the highest number in the 31-year history of the G7/8 summit to that time. It embedded those decisions to a considerable degree with the catalysts known to produce compliance on the part of the members during the following year. Compliance came at an overall level of +47 (on a scale from -100 to +100). And it did much to develop G8-centered global governance, most notably by hosting many subject-specific ministerial meetings to prepare and follow up on the summit, including the third G8 energy ministers' gathering in history and the first ever meeting of G8 ministers of health. This heavy reliance on G8 ministerials indicated that Russia, a charter member of the UN with a permanent veto on the Security Council (UNSC), was moving away from the UN in favor of a new identity as a member of a G8 whose institutionalized global governance system it sought to build. Russia thus proved it was a fully accomplished host of a regular G8 summit, producing one with a performance at or above average in most respects.

St. Petersburg also proved successful in the task of immediate crisis response in the field of political security. With a new conflict in the Middle East erupting on the eve of the summit, the Russians accepted a draft document, prepared on Canadian initiative with US support, that set forth an appropriate and novel response for coping with the immediate conflict and for laying a new foundation for breaking the recurrent cycle of violence and moving toward permanent peace in the years ahead. The G8 leaders ruled on the three contentious issues given to them in square brackets by their officials in a draft declaration, and did so in the way that President Putin as G8 host preferred. The final document was endorsed by the key summit participants, notably the UN Secretary-General, China – one of the UNSC Permanent Five veto powers – and the rest of the Plus Five countries at their meeting with the G8 the next day. This new G8 roadmap was then legally approved by the UN back in New York. It was subsequently adopted in its essence by other relevant plurilateral summit institutions such as la Francophonie. On this key political-security issue that had afflicted the world and the UN for sixty years, Canada led the G8, and the G8 led the UN. This was a clear case of G8-led governance through the MOs.

These St. Petersburg priorities and achievements served as the foundation for the German approach as G8 host in 2007. To be sure, the Germans exercised their prerogative as host to set their own priorities for the Heilgendamm Summit, giving pride of place as the start of their preparatory process to the many financial, economic, trade and investment issues that St. Petersburg, with its full agenda, did not adequately address. In doing so, the Germans and G8 showed their belief in the inadequacy of the UN system, with its pillar MOs of the IMF in finance, the WTO in trade and the World Bank and the United Nations Conference on Trade and Development (UNCTAD) in development. The Germans' first priority, economic growth, included resource use as one of its five components. This component focused on energy efficiency, climate change and the Kyoto Protocol, this last issue having been brought into force as ratified international law because of the critical role played by Russia, along with Canada and Japan. Germany's second priority of African development started with the health systems and HIV/AIDS, which Russia had highlighted through its priority on infectious disease. Germany's priority of African development ended with peace and security, where progress could help the peace process in the broader Middle East and North Africa, as a critical region for energy security, regional security, counterterrorism and the control of weapons of mass destruction.

Democratizing Russia and the G8

An even more impressive success of St. Petersburg came in the realm of process, above all in democratizing the G8 at home and on a global scale. This was an area in which the UN, devoid of any recognition of democracy in its charter or reliable democratic majority in the domestic character of its membership, was at best irrelevant or acted against this core mission of the G8.

Outreach

Russia's first advance in democratizing the G8 was to invite to the summit, under strong pressure from its G8 partners, the leaders of the systemically significant countries of India, China, Brazil, Mexico and South Africa. These Plus Five powers were critical to helping the G8 effectively address the priority of energy security, as the five were the great new energy demand powers straining a short-term, finite global supply. They were also key on the critical new front in the global war against infectious disease. Moreover, China's presence as a UNSC P5 member was important in the easy acceptance at St. Petersburg of the G8's new approach to peace in the Middle East and its subsequent legal endorsement at the UNSC. The presence of these five rapidly rising powers as important summit participants showed the world that the G8 Plus Five had the predominant power to govern the global community effectively, the open inclusiveness to incorporate rising powers in a way the UNSC P5 could not, and the diversity in geography, language, religion and level of development needed to enhance the G8's sensitivity, representativeness and legitimacy as a center of global governance as a whole. Furthermore, as all of the Plus Five but China were democratic polities, this particular set of participants deepened the democratic character of the G8. In addition, an ever-expanding, all-democratic European Union (EU) reinforced the power, democratic devotion, diversity and inclusiveness of the G8 itself.

St. Petersburg was only the second time that these Plus Five powers had been invited to participate in the summit as a set, having been invited to the Gleneagles Summit in 2005. Before, they had been part of a much larger group invited to the G8 Evian Summit in 2003. Russia's invitation, issued at the urging of its G8 partners, thus set a precedent that meant that the old G8 would become the new G8+5 on an ongoing, institutionalized increasing basis in future years (Cooper and Antkiewicz 2008). Thus, Germany invited from the start to its Heiligendamm Summit the same five powers, relabeled the "Outreach Five," or O5, and subsequently the Group of Five (G5). Germany further suggested to its G8 partners that these five would routinely participate in the G8 in all future years. As the partners looked with favor upon this suggestion, at St. Petersburg, as an iterative confirmation of the Gleneagles innovation, a new G8+5 had been born. By bringing all five new powers in together, with the force of the four democracies, it reinforced the democratic character of the G8 and gave it the best chance to socialize a rapidly opening China in this direction as well.

Downreach

St. Petersburg's second democratizing innovation was the unprecedented openness of the summit process. It came in part through a new Experts Council that Russia created at home to help prepare analytic papers to advance the priority agenda. In support of the regular sherpa preparatory process, the Experts Council allowed more knowledgeable individuals from inside and outside governments in Russia and the G8 to be involved in a meaningful and influential way.

To help prepare its summit and deliver its results, Russia also mounted an unprecedented Civil 8 mechanism that brought Russian and international civil society leaders into the summit process as never before (Pamfilova 2006). Through Civil 8, civil society was there from the start. For the first time, its members had direct face-to-face contact with all the sherpas (the leaders' personal representatives) together at several times throughout the year. Civil 8 successfully synthesized a large and diverse set of inputs and advice into an intelligent, coherent and helpful set of recommendations that were effectively communicated to G8 governors, including directly at the highest level, in the Civil 8-sponsored dialogue with President Putin two weeks before the summit's start. That hard-won direct dialogue, held for the first time, brought the G8 host leader together with 700 global civil society leaders in an open, freewheeling, two-hour public exchange. Through the free world media in attendance, that dialogue was available for all citizens of the global community to see, hear and read. President Putin not only listened politely and thanked civil society for its contribution, but also endorsed some of its recommendations, promised to raise them with his G8 colleagues, frankly noted sources of resistance and identified civil society as allies in his effort to convince his G8 colleagues to do the right thing. Through him as host, Civil 8 had become a *de facto* ninth member of the summit itself. The depth and durability of the civil society connection were driven to new levels, including through the post-summit Civil 8 meeting with the African Partnership Forum and through the Civil 8 meeting with the representatives of Russia's and Germany's sherpas as 2006 drew to a close.

This process of civil society participation made a difference at St. Petersburg. The leading independent publication at the summit, *G8 Summit 2006: Issues and Instruments*, started with a statement by the host leader, as it had in the 2005 edition, but then followed, for the first time, with a statement by and about Civil 8 (Fraser 2006). The chair of Civil 8, the exceptionally committed Ella Pamfilova, gave briefings and interviews at the summit in a way equal to senior figures of the Russian government itself. And perhaps encouraged by his earlier public Civil 8 encounter, President Putin ended every day at the summit by appearing before the world's media in a lengthy, open, unscripted session to discuss what had gone on behind closed doors during the day.

Moreover, some of Civil 8's many recommendations appeared in the summit communiqués. Civil society as a relevant and valuable actor was recognized in the chair's summary far more than ever before, and also throughout most of the individual communiqués. On the priority issue of energy security, when the Russian presidency had first circulated to its G8 partners its five-page concept paper in November 2005, environmental values had been virtually invisible. At the first Civil 8 workshop a few months later, the energy group was dominated by environmentalists. They kept up the pressure – on paper, in speeches and in guerrilla theatre T-shirts at the July civil society forum – right through to Civil 8's encounter with President Putin himself. Two weeks later at St. Petersburg, the G8 communiqué on energy security started with the importance of environmental security and spoke of this principle throughout. And on the road to St. Petersburg, President Putin made the expensive decision to re-route his new pipeline providing energy security to the east to protect Lake Baikal as the largest body of freshwater in the world.

In all, Civil 8 participants conducted a transparent, inclusive process that brought in a large and diverse group of civil society from many issue-focused communities, G8 countries and regions around the world. No one who wanted to contribute was turned away. Russia as G8 host was able, through the Civil 8, to show the world the growing strength of Russia's still fragile civil society, and the Russian government's respect for and responsiveness to it. Civil 8 demonstrated that a G8 that had long seemed to have a legitimacy deficit had now become more democratic, by proving that there was a meaningful place for civil society's voice inside the process, as well as from the rooms, the rock concerts and the thrown rocks and shouted slogans on streets outside.

Civil 8 and its G8 connection in 2006 thus set an unprecedentedly high standard that inspired the G8 as it looked ahead. Even before her year as host started in 2007, German Chancellor Angela Merkel indicated that she planned a dialogue with leaders of non-governmental organizations similar to that held by President Putin. The German sherpa team declared that the G8 dialogue with civil society pioneered by the Russians would continue on a permanent basis in their year and in those to come. Yet as the 2007 and 2008 summits unfolded, the role of civil society was far less robust than it had been in 2006.

Strengthening the Future G8

Despite these multidimensional accomplishments, there remained much to be done to build on St. Petersburg's success and thus strengthen the G8 Plus Five as an effective center of global governance in the years ahead.

The first step was to bring in Russia and the EU as full members of more parts of the G8 system. In the case of Russia, this included the G7 finance ministers' forum. Here, Russia's energetic hosting in the first half of 2006 of two G8 finance ministers' summit preparatory meetings proved Russia's reliability and the worth of a G8 finance ministerial. It did so most notably in affirming as early as February 2006 the need for the market-oriented approach to energy security that the G8 summit leaders ultimately endorsed. With Russia as the world's first-ranked, full-strength energy superpower and one of only two G8 members with a regular fiscal surplus, with its vast foreign exchange reserves, and as an emerging contributor to development assistance, there was now little on the G7 finance agenda that warranted Russia's exclusion. Russia still needed to be admitted to a revived trade ministers' quadrilateral, formed in 1981 by the United States, the European Union, Japan and Canada – especially as even the US had agreed that Russia should joint the WTO (Cohn 2002).

The second step was to develop a full set of regular G8 ministerial meetings that would cover most of the ministries that G8 governments have. Their agendas have now migrated outside their domestic polity in today's rapidly globalizing age. This included turning into annual events the intermittent G8 meetings for ministers of energy, development and health. Indeed, the case of health was especially important. Russia remained outside the Global Health Security Initiative, created in 2001 and including only the G7 members and Mexico. There was also an argument for creating a G8 defense ministers' forum to deal with issues such as peace and security in Africa and, above all, the perennial G8 issue of Afghanistan.

The third step was to strengthen the legislative, judicial and civil society institutions among the G8, so that this democratically devoted center of global governance went beyond governing only through and with its executive branch. Here, Russia took several useful steps forward in 2006 by creating G8 forums for religious leaders and the media. But a major leap could help with the G8 priorities of encouraging good governance and respect for the rule of law globally, including within Russia and other G8 members themselves. One concrete step, building on St. Petersburg's advance in education, would be to create a G8 scholarship exchange program so that promising postsecondary students from the G8 Plus Five powers could study in partner countries and thus learn at first hand about how things work there.

The fourth step was, on an *ad hoc* basis as dictated by the agenda, to add other countries, beyond the Plus Five, at the summit itself and to the ministerial and official-level groups that constitute the invisible, submerged body of the summit iceberg below. The Germans made a good start here, by promising once again to bring committed African leaders to their summit in 2007. But the entire system needed to be assessed to see how such expanded participation could both encourage more effective problem solving and also reinforce democratic principles and practices. This thrust could well include holding a meeting of the finance ministers' G20 at the leaders' level issues such as energy, health and trade where all the systemically significant countries are integrally involved. The advent of G20 summitry in November 2008, driven by an unprecedented global financial crisis, has responded to this need in part (Kirton and Koch, 2008, 2009a, 2009b). But there is much left off its crisis-focused agenda that deserves sustained G20 leaders' direct attention as well.

Delivering Effective Global Governance: The Accountability Gap

These steps were needed not only to help with global problem solving and democracy promotion in a rapidly globalizing world. They were also needed to help with the G8's greatest outstanding defect – effectively delivering its many, often pioneering promises to its many citizens, stakeholders and the many desperate people in the world as a whole. The G8 was deliberately created by it founders as a flexible, informal, soft law institution directed and delivered by democratically and popularly elected leaders, unconstrained by any rigidified, legally constrained, resource-short international bureaucracy that claimed to speak on its behalf. This core "constitutional" characteristic of the G8, recurrently reaffirmed by successive generations of G8 leaders, remains fundamental to the G8's success. There is thus no need for any permanent international G8 secretariat, either newly created by the G8 itself or volunteered by well-meaning existing bodies such as an Organisation for Economic Co-operation and Development (OECD), to which Russia does not belong.

The established MOs play an important role in implementing and otherwise contributing to G8 governance. In 2006, Russia made important advances in involving those organizations in the summit's preparations and production from the start. Based on this initiative and its solid results, it would be wise for the WTO, the OECD and the IEA to admit Russia as a full member, as a reciprocal step.

Others ways must also be found to solve the G8's great "commitment-compliance gap." While members' compliance with their priority G8 commitments has grown in recent years, it is still well short of what its citizens and their global colleagues expect and need. Moreover, the G8 Research Group's assessment of compliance with the St. Petersburg Summit's priority commitments six months after the summit showed that compliance was well below the level of summits in recent years. The final compliance score of +47 confirmed this result. Clearly, the strong commitment of Russia and the G8 in 2006 to do a better job of ensuring compliance with their commitments, and monitoring their compliance performance, was not sufficient to meet the objectives they as G8 governors themselves have set, nor was the strong presence of MO leaders at the summit itself.

There have arisen several exercises under way globally to assess by various methods compliance with and implementation of the G8's programs. But these accountability exercises, even as developed at Heligendamm in 2007 and Hokkaido Toyako in 2008, remain fragile and fragmented and, in the case of intra-governmental G8 efforts, opaque. The time has come to combine these efforts, in a multi-stakeholder, global "G8 compliance consortium," so that G8 governors can join with their own legislators, judiciaries, auditors general and civil society to know how well their promises at the summit are subsequently being transformed into practice on the ground. The democratically and popularly elected leaders of the G8 should be the ones who most want to know reliably whether their collective will is being converted by those below and beyond into the results they want.

And because "that which is measured is treasured," a more effective collective monitoring process should help convert G8 promises made into G8 promises kept.

Bibliography

Cohn, Theodore H. (2002), *Governing Global Trade: International Institutions in Conflict and Convergence* (Aldershot: Ashgate).

Cooper, Andrew and Agata Antkiewicz, eds (2008), *Emerging Powers in Global Governance: Lessons from the Heiligendamm Process* (Waterloo, Ontario: University of Waterloo Press).

Cooper, Andrew and John Kirton, eds (2009), *Innovation in Global Health Governance: Critical Cases* (Farnham: Ashgate).

Fraser, Maurice, ed. (2006), *G8 Summit 2006: Issues and Instruments* (London: Newsdesk).

Kirton, John and Madeline Koch, eds (2008), *G20: Growth, Innovation, Inclusion – The G20 at Ten* (London: Newsdesk).

Kirton, John and Madeline Koch, eds (2009a), *G20: The London Summit – Growth, Stability and Jobs* (London: Newsdesk).

Kirton, John and Madeline Koch, eds (2009b), *The 2009 G20 Pittsburgh Summit* (London: Newsdesk).

Pamfilova, Ella (2006), "The Civil G8 2006," in Maurice Fraser, ed., *G8 Summit 2006: Issues and Instruments* (London: Newsdesk).

Chapter 16
The 2006 St. Petersburg G8 Summit: Conclusions and Critiques

Andrew F. Cooper

The 2006 G8 summit was crucial in many ways for global governance. Its hosting marked a breakthrough in the expansion of the G7 beyond the traditional like-minded countries. The St. Petersburg Summit demonstrated the fundamental break with the bipolar architecture associated with the Cold War. In participation, however, the 2006 summit revealed more continuity than change. As in several previous summits, St. Petersburg put a heavy onus on opening up the process beyond the core membership. Although this was not always done robustly (with invitations to the big emerging countries coming late), it did not reverse the trends toward expanding the G8 in its outreach in state or non-state (via a forum of non-governmental organizations [NGOs]). The creation of the Civil 8 as well as the many other groupings stood out. So did the attention and participation Russia gave to the United Nations system, most notably a good number of specialized agencies. Such a focus reflected the priorities that Russia showcased.

Beyond the particular elements of the 2006 G8 animated by the central role of Russia, the St. Petersburg G8 stands out as an event that revealed the possibilities (but also the constraints) of connecting the informal nature of the G8 with hard law approaches via joint work on both a multilateral and a country-specific basis. Indeed, this is the theme that drives this book forward and provides it with its sustained importance. A second theme, as John Kirton demonstrates, is the need to do a better job of implementation within the G8 process to fill the "commitment–compliance gap."

Frameworks for Academic Analysis for G8 Governance

Kirton's chapter, "Multilateral Organizations and G8 Governance: A Framework for Analysis," asks some fundamental questions about the linkage between informal G8 and the hard law components of the international system:

> How do international institutions, led by the formal, hard law bodies of the Bretton Woods–United Nations (UN) system, and informal plurilateral bodies, led by the Group of Eight (G8), help each other change the world? More specifically, how have and can the world's other multilateral organizations (MOs) assist the G8 in

> enhancing its members' ability to consider, reach consensus on, commit to and comply with ambitious, appropriate agreements to address key global needs?

Kirton seeks to identify the relationship between MOs and compliance with G8 commitments. He reviews the current debate on the role that MOs play in improving G8 compliance, and then offers an analytical framework for considering the ways in which they can do this. He hypothesizes about why MOs help in improving G8 compliance, and then tests these ten hypotheses by applying them to the recent record on G8 compliance. He concludes by identifying the major policy questions about how MOs can better assist G8 compliance.

Kirton argues that dissatisfaction with the Bretton Woods-era institutions has reached a peak. Concurrently, the G8 has been making more commitments and pushing to ensure compliance, with growing reliance on assistance from other MOs. The recent case of Russia's heavy reliance on MOs in the lead-up to the St. Petersburg Summit and the multiple invitations it extended to MOs to attend shows that the G8 is turning to these institutions for help. What is needed therefore is a clear guideline about which MOs help the most, and when, where and why.

Kirton's analytical framework is meant to identify how MOs can help or harm G8 governance. He identifies three key dimensions: the level of connection between the MOs and the G8 (through key leaders or through their staff), the time of the connection (pre-summit, intra-summit or post-summit) and the intentionality of the MOs' contribution, on the part of each actor (what type of role each actor sees the other as playing). He then identifies 15 areas in which the MOs can contribute to G8 governance. These include information-gathering and analysis in the pre-summit phase, buying in to the ideas at the intra-summit phase and burden-sharing in the post-summit stage.

Finally, Kirton presents and tests ten hypotheses to explain MOs' assistance with G8 compliance: participation, communiqué incorporation, mission compatibility, membership overlap, managerial control, mutual experience, co-hosting responsibility, early involvement, government coordination and country-specificity. He uses data on compliance from the goals of the Okinawa, Sea Island and Gleneagles Summits.

Given Kirton's conclusions from these summits, it is not clear that increased references in G8 summits to MOs led to higher compliance with G8 goals. He suggests this might be because of contextual factors – compliance with the 2001 Okinawa Summit goals was hindered by the 9/11 attacks on the US, or related to the preferences regarding MOs inclusion on the part of the host country (multilateralist Japan versus skeptical United States). G8 reliance on MOs seemed to be more conclusive when the MO in question is smaller, more pluralistic and dominated by G7 members.

Kirton also identifies several key policy questions about how and why MOs can have a greater impact on G8 compliance. These include whether making Russia a greater participant in – and full member of – the World Trade Organization (WTO), the Organisation for Economic Co-operation and Development (OECD), the International Energy Agency (IEA) and similar institutions (as all other G8 members are) to help in G8 governance; whether the OECD should assume a stronger and more formal role of a particular sort as a "secretariat" for the G8, in some functions or overall, and whether MOs and their secretariats can assist more directly in the systematic monitoring of G8 compliance and implementation.

Kirton sees MOs as being either complementary or antithetical groups to the G8, but the G8 as dictating the agenda and the MOs just reacting. He sees many places in which MOs can assist the work of the G8, even to the point of having input in agenda setting, but the G8 still drives the agenda. Furthermore, he sees the G8 as dominating global governance, because the UN has shown an incapacity to reform its charter and Security Council. This has given informal bodies (namely the G8) that had previously been propping up and trying to help the UN reform, the opportunity to step in and take a greater role in solving global issues.

In Chapter 3, Marina Larionova asks what causes compliance with summit goals at the G8. Given the increased pressure on international institutions as a result of global governance, and the ensuing expansion of agendas, debates and commitments made, how has the relationship between the G8 and MOs evolved to ensure G8 compliance?

Larionova discusses the three most common models of G8 governance: G8 governance through MOs, governance against MOs and governance without MOs. She also presents a fourth framework through which to view G8 governance: governance in alliance with MOs. She uses a framework based on two assumptions. The first, a postdoctoral assumption, is that the G8 and MOs serve a common cause and thus should be natural allies. The second, a more constructivist assumption, is that the challenges of global governance, in conjunction with G8 members' preferences regarding the mode of interaction with the MOs, will tend toward G8 governance in alliance with the MOs, based on the democratic institutionalism and "network of networks" models of G8 governance. These assumptions form the core of Larionova's fourth model.

This model makes eight central claims. First, MOs are playing an increasing role in problem management and in reconciling domestic and international problems; however, their role in achieving the objectives of collective leadership remains negligible. Second, MOs are increasingly being involved at the pre-summit preparation stage, as many of them have expanded their mandates to fit them to G8 commitments. Third, G8–MO interaction modes and instruments can be classified as those common to all institutions and organization-specific. Fourth, the comprehensive nature of most of the 68 commitments determines the need for action by several MOs and the need for their coordination. Fifth, the tools and modes of the G8 and MOs constitute a global governance system. Sixth, the bureaucratization of the G8 sub-summit apparatus can enhance the relationship and coordination of a G8–MO relationship. Seventh, the capacity for peer-learning is dependent on the policy sphere between the actors, but is also restricted by the open method of coordination. However, MOs have accumulated sufficient capacity to search for the best solutions to G8-defined problems. Finally, the relationship and familiarity between the staff of G8 member counties and the MO dictates the capacity for implementation.

Larionova examines the documents from the sixth and seventh series (1998–2006), coinciding with the launch of the G8 cycle and its first sequence. She examines the following areas for references to MOs and organizations most commonly referred to and codifies what framework each reference would fall under: energy, development, education, security, information and communication, and innovation. The majority are UN bodies, with the next largest group coming from OECD-based organizations. The MOs she included in her analysis were those that had systemic ties to the G8.

Larionova's hypothesis of a trend toward G8 governance in alliance with MOs is confirmed. While G8 governance through MOs is the dominant mode (56 percent of the time), governance in alliance with MOs show a steady upward trend (32 percent). In contrast, governance against or without MOs was only referred to a combined total of 12 percent of the time. In some of the priorities examined there was a convergence of all four modes, but often only a combination of one or two. The chair's preferred mode usually only really mattered in the priority area of the summit. Governance in alliance with MOs as the preferred mode is pronounced in health, development and security. Governance through MOs is pronounced in energy and security, showing reluctance on the part of G8 leaders to limit national agenda-setting in those traditional spheres.

Overall, there is a steady increase in cooperation during 1998–2007. Conversely, while governance without or against MOs peaked in 2002–04, it has steadily declined since. Larionova makes key recommendations about how these findings can strengthen G8 global governance: increased early involvement for relevant MOs as the G8–MO relationship intensifies, increased support for building capacity both at the G8 and within the MOs to ensure their ability to meet commitments, and increased capacity-building and a deepening of organizational ties through investment in MOs on the part of Russia.

Larionova suggests that there is a global governance structure led by the G8 and assisted by MOs. Further, the MOs most commonly used to fulfill the goals of the G8, either as an instrument or as an ally, are UN-based. Therefore, Larionova implies that it is the informal structure of the G8 that is setting the agenda, while the formal bodies of the Bretton Woods system are the ones responsible for implementation. She advocates for increased cooperation and coordination between the two types of body, seeming to suggest that the divide between the informal and formal institutions (Bretton Woods-era versus G8) can be overcome to mutual benefit.

In his timely chapter, "Financial Crises, the International Monetary Fund and the G8," Ivan Savić argues that in a highly integrated global economy, financial crises are impossible to avoid and, given their complexity, difficult to correct. However, the world is in a much better position today than in past crises. Since the creation of the G8, a cooperative relationship between it and the International Monetary Fund (IMF) has emerged to address international financial crises. This relationship rests on a division of labor that allows the informal G8 system to work with the formal structures of the IMF. While room for improvement exists, Savić argues that under this system, problems are addressed better than ever before.

Savić discusses in turn the features of modern financial crises and the need for international response; the evolution of international response mechanisms, the current response structure, the G8–IMF record, the Asian financial crisis, current problems facing the international financial system and the success of the G8–IMF relationship as an international crisis response system.

Given the complexity of its modern international financial crises, the likelihood of spillover due to interconnectedness, and their relation to not only economic problems but ultimately political problems too, Savić posits that it is impossible to ignore the need for international cooperation in attempting to prevent and to correct financial crises. This has created a need for an international structure with the capability to both predict and attempt to avoid, as well as to offset the damage of international financial crises. Past attempts at fulfilling this need include the gold standard, the Bank for International Settlements and the Bretton Woods conference. Unfortunately, these attempts all failed.

In the aftermath of these failures, two key institutions have emerged: the IMF and the G8. Although they emerged at different times, the latter came about to fulfill some key functions that the former was accomplishing. Since the G8's emergence in the 1970s, the two institutions have operated under a division of labor, in which the IMF provides the benefits of a formal organization (bureaucracy, substantial independent resources, regular contact with member states) and the G8 provides the benefits of an informal institution (regular gathering of a few key state leaders in a forum that allows for a less formal discussion of problems). The G8 provides stability to the core of the international financial system by allowing for cooperation and consensus among the major financial powers, which come together annually to address major events as well as general, long-term desired objectives. The IMF then allows for a much broader conversation regarding these objectives, and provides institutional support, in areas such as monitoring capacity.

The institutional ties between these two institutions are likely why they can function effectively together. The G8 has a strong presence at the IMF (41 percent of voting rights) and therefore has a great deal of influence. However, the managing director of the IMF also plays a reciprocal role in influencing the G8 through regular attendance at the G8 summits. Furthermore, the vast amount of resources controlled by the G8 serves as backup when IMF resources are insufficient; this is what happened during the Asian financial crisis. Finally, the G8 lends credibility to IMF interventions in the eyes of investors, which restores confidence in the international financial system in times of crisis.

Criticisms such as the question of who benefits from this system emerge. Savić, however, uses the Asian financial crisis to show how the partnership has effectively functioned to overcome financial crises. Although the G7 was criticized for not responding rapidly enough, in the end it provided the necessary financial resources to back up loans from the IMF and other international financial institutions (IFIs), which also restored confidence to markets. Moreover, in the wake of the US sub-prime mortgage crisis, the IMF and G8 have been quick to respond together on possible corrective actions. The G8 has been looked to for leadership in this crisis and has presented a working guideline, which it has been implementing with the help of the IFIs.

As global interconnectedness has increased and past international financial systems have failed, the G8 and IMF have created a division of labor that has effectively dealt with crises since the 1970s. This division requires the IMF to use its formal institutional capabilities for operations such as monitoring and dealing with individual problems in emerging markets, while the G8 provides a stable core to the international financial system through the concert of key financial powers. While it is difficult to predict the outcome of the present crisis facing the system, the G8–IMF relationship provides reasons for optimism on the basis of past success. However, while Savić does mention that problems in the system exist, such as questions of legitimacy, conditionality and ideology, he does not provide a list of specific solutions or recommendations.

Savić suggests that the shortcomings of each institution are made up for by cooperation. The G8's informal nature allows for more effective decision making, and the IMF's formal nature provides capacity for activities such as monitoring and implementation. The relationship is symbiotic – each is valued for its separate contributions and approach, but ultimately it is a successful and desirable partnership.

In Chapter 5, John Kirton, Nikolai Roudev and Laura Sunderland ask whether the world's major powers keep the international commitments they make. Many G8 watchers and governors, they say, regard the group as a country club that does not follow through on decisions. They argue that the evidence suggests otherwise, and that since 1975 the G7/8 has moved beyond country club deliberations, extending to the "directional function of setting new principles and norms, the decisional function of collectively creating new rules or commitments, delivering on these commitments through the compliance of its members and creating new decision -making procedures by developing G8-centered global governance through G8 institutions of its own." Kirton et al. therefore raise a new question: what explains the rising compliance within the G8, since it has no legal charter or secretariat and its meetings occur only once a year? They offer a host of past analyses that sought to explain G8 compliance. However, all such attempts, including Kirton's own concert equality model, have failed to bring clear understanding. They argue that there has been an absence in research to date on the agency of individual leaders at G8 summits. They therefore argue that a new model must be constructed and tested, one that is comprehensive and multilevel, analyzing the causes of G8 compliance. Unlike past models, Kirton et al.'s new model begins with individual agency – examining how leaders deliberately craft their commitments in ways that help ensure compliance at home. This model then explores how the presence of a ministerial institution acts, for the most part, to reinforce the leaders' commitments and improve compliance. Finally, the model includes international system structure to determine whether agency and institutional forces act autonomously, or are controlled by system structure. These are the factors, according to the new model, that result in compliance within the G8.

The analysis concludes that agency matters most, but the institutional structure is also a factor. Leaders who embed timetables within their financial commitments and affirm the commitment's priority placement catalyze greater compliance, as do pre-summit commitments and post-summit affirmations by the 67 ministerial forums.

Kirton et al. use three previous works measuring G8 compliance to identify an increase in compliance over the course of the G7/8's existence: a study by George von Furstenberg and Joseph Daniels covering 1975–89, which placed G8 compliance at approximately 31 percent; the model developed by Ella Kokotsis covering 1988–95, which places overall G8 compliance at 39.3 percent, and Kirton's previous concert equity model, which covers 1996–2005 and scores overall compliance at an average of 46.3 percent. Once again, their primary issue is that none of the models in these studies satisfactorily answer the question of why compliance takes place. Why has compliance increased?

To answer this question, they first enquire about the degree and effectiveness of leaders' conscious collective agency within the summits as well as the creation and use of sub-summit-level institutions, to help secure collective compliance. They create a data set of 42 finance-related commitments from 1996 to 2005, including all commitments involving core G7 finance ministers' competences.

In analyzing the causes of increased compliance with G7/8 commitments, they ask to what extent greater compliance is caused "by conscious action of the agents who write them." This model shows that setting a timetable for compliance had a positive effect on overall compliance. Also, the placement of commitments as priorities had a strong effect in improving compliance. They also find that when sub-summit bodies are created, this distracts from G8 summit performance, and reduces compliance, insinuating that leaders then count on someone "other than themselves to ensure that their previous public summit promises are actually kept." They conclude by stating:

> To improve compliance with their summit financial commitments, leaders should give them priority placement and set a timetable for their completion, while finance ministers should act supportively during the six months before and six months after the summit year, but leave the leaders alone to do their own thing during the summit year itself.

Their final question concerns to what extent the decisions and actions undertaken by individual agents (leaders/finance ministers) are "merely responding unknowingly to more powerful forces from the structure of the international system." The proposed model responds by arguing that "changes in structural vulnerability and capability by themselves have no direct impact on compliance. … Structure matters only (albeit strongly) in spurring pre-commitment and recommitment … of these, only pre-commitment (along with post-affirmation operating autonomously) directly connects with compliance."

Their conclusion is that structural forces at the international level do not directly push G8 members to comply with leaders' commitments: "Only the individual leaders and finance ministers (in each case acting collectively and consciously) can do that." Structural forces can act as inspiration in creating greater knowledge of pre-commitment institutional factors such as vulnerability, internal equality and so on, but it is up to the individual agents to transform promises into promises kept. They suggest that these findings open a rich agenda for scholarly research, including adding agency and institutionalization to Kirton's previous concert equality model, the exploration of whether iteration increases compliance, and whether Kirton's findings relating to finance commitments and compliance translate into other areas of G8 compliance performance.

Practitioners' Perspectives

In Chapter 6, Robert Fauver looks at agenda stretch in the G8. G8 summits have expanded the agenda of the forum from its purely economic beginnings to its current focus on a host of non-economic issues. Fauver asks: do these summits matter? Do they accomplish anything? Is there follow-through on the commitments made by G8 leaders? The chapter concentrates on the effectiveness of MOs in implementing the commitments made by the G8. Primarily, the chapter focuses on the IMF and the World Bank, and asks whether or not institutions such as these should play a role in implementing G8 decisions, and should the G8 "play the role of a directoire for the MOs."

The original G7 meetings – those that were purely economic – converged effectively with the MOs, notably the IMF. The author argues that the decisions regarding the international monetary system, those in reaction to the instabilities brought about by the oil crisis of 1973/74 and the US abandonment of the dollar–gold link in 1971 set the stage for revising the Articles of Agreement of the IMF. This revision allowed the IMF to "perfectly" implement the commitments of the G7 summit. With the original G5 states having 38 percent of the voting power in the IMF and 37 percent in the World Bank, obtaining agreement for implementation of G8 decisions should have been "relatively straightforward" ever since.

Impeding implementation, however, is the feeling among finance ministers about decisions taken at G8 summits. At Naples in 1994, G8 leaders committed to adapting existing institutions and building new international institutions to ensure prosperity in the twenty-first century. But finance ministers had a consensus among themselves that IFIs were within their "individual purview" and were against government agencies involved in any review of their structure or framework. The author posits that if left to its own accord, the IFIs would be reluctant to undertake their own alteration due to their current management and staff being "heavily vested in the current institutional structures," and that an outside group would be required to perform a serious review of the adequacy of IFIs. He asks: "But what will be the impetus for the creation of such an outside group?"

Fauver argues that when not consulted prior to G7/8 summits, institutions can be overly uncooperative. This was also the case in the May 1986 leaders' meeting in Tokyo, where it was recognized that greater surveillance of macroeconomic policies was necessary. Leaders asked the IMF and the Group of Ten to create a system of economic indicators helpful for assigning responsibility for policy change to member countries. The IMF, however, has yet to fulfill such a request due to the lack of pre-summit communication. When not asked to participate in the summit process, MOs tend to resent being assigned tasks by the G8. If G7/8 states wish to effectively alter MOs such as the IMF or World Bank, reform must be pursued within the institutions themselves, through consensus-building.

In Chapter 7, Ade Adefuye begins by explaining why the annual G8 meetings have become "the defining moment in the annual global economic and political calendar." Africa's place within the agenda of these discussions has become increasingly important, Adefuye argues, due to an increasing awareness that allowing current conditions to persist would have unpleasant effects on the global economy. Since the G8's 2002 adoption of the Africa Action Plan at Kananaskis and, more important, the 2005 summit at Gleneagles where Africa topped the G8 agenda, the G8 has displayed a renewed commitment to combating poverty and disease. The chapter reviews the G8's commitments toward Africa from 2002 on. It explores the effectiveness and the amount of follow-through involved, and suggests what could be done to make the commitments more effective. It analyzes in particular the assistance of MOs such as the Commonwealth – an organization, the author argues, that has been at the forefront of the pursuit of political stability and sustainable development in the continent.

Through, notably, a series of measures Adefuye attributes to African leaders putting their house in order, the transformation of the Organization for African Unity into the African Union, the adoption of New Partnership for Africa's Development (NEPAD) and marked success in reducing inflation while increasing economic growth, the continent has garnered wide support in the international community, including the G8. Since 2001, the G8 has invited African leaders to each G8 summit, and has appointed Africa Personal Representatives (APRs) in charge of reviewing the Africa Action Plan.

The chapter then breaks down the commitments made by the G8 toward Africa into three categories, and details how the Commonwealth, along with other MOs, can help. First, in the case of peacekeeping and capacity building, the G8 has extended its support to the AU in establishing itself as the "prime interlocutor on peace and security on the continent," through the establishment of the AU's Peace and Security Council. The G8 has supported the council and its director, as well as its operations. The G8 has actively supported UN peacekeeping missions in Africa. The author argues, however, that more can be done, notably by placing attention on preventing state fragility and conflict resulting from structural weakness. This is where the Commonwealth can help the G8, thanks in part to the

Commonwealth's "soft, non-threatening approach," responsible for winning the confidence of member countries and allowing Commonwealth institutions such as Commonwealth Secretariat.

With regard to strengthening the second category of institutions and governance, the G8 has been overwhelmingly supportive of parliamentary institutions at both national and regional levels, including the NEPAD group of pan-African parliamentarians. The G8 has supported organizations such as the African Regional Commission, research and policy groups pertaining to money laundering countermeasures, good governance, and trade and gender issues. However, national difficulties instilling transparency and accountability have presented serious challenges. Primarily, the issue of illicit asset transfers outside of the continent requires action from states in Africa and the G8. Adefuye argues that here the Commonwealth can again aid the G8, as it had already established a commission to examine stolen assets in Africa in 2003. The 2005 report that followed argued that Commonwealth states needed to sign and implement the UN Convention Against Corruption. The report argues that Commonwealth heads of state and other ministers and public officials should not have immunity from prosecution, and that legislation needs to be passed regarding procedures for conviction in cases of illicit asset transfers. Adefuye argues that this is an area where both the Commonwealth and the G8 can work together through the G8's adoption of and assisted implementation of the Commonwealth group's recommendations.

In the third case of debt relief, Adefuye states that the G8 has been "instrumental in achieving progress on debt relief in Africa," citing the Heavily Indebted Poor Countries (HIPCs) Initiative and the $32 billion in debt relief it delivered. The 2005 G8 Gleneagles Summit is famous for the debt relief it granted some African states. However, Adefuye argues that the G8 must separate debt relief from development assistance. Adding debt relief to official assistance figures allowed the G8 to "take its foot off the accelerator in increasing the real volume of aid." The G8 must also do more to honor the recommendation of the Africa Action Plan which underlined the importance of encouraging investment in Africa, both from within and from outside the continent. The author notes the G8's support of investment measures such as the OECD/NEPAD Investment Initiative, the Investment for Development Project, the Common Market for Eastern and Southern Africa and the Southern African Development Community, and Canada's contribution through the Canada Investment Fund for Africa. The author notes, however, that certain G8 states failed to complete the Doha round of negotiations, due to resistance on agricultural subsidies. African states are thus currently unable to exploit their competitive advantage in agricultural production. The Commonwealth has been using its connections to "impress on the rich countries the need to effectively implement the program on trade liberalization and improved market access." The Commonwealth Heads of Governments' Valletta Statement of 2005, which reaffirmed the leaders' commitment to the WTO's Doha Development Agenda objectives, provides an opportunity to cement a rules-based international trading system. The Commenwealth called for the WTO ministerial conference in Hong Kong to agree on the elimination of all export subsidies by 2010.

Adefuye concludes that G8 governments need to be held to account for their impact on Africa, and that in general, greater political will within the G8 is needed to fulfill their commitments to the continent. Currently, there is no integrated evaluation effort regarding the G8's activities concerning Africa. The author argues that "it is of mutual advantage if the vested interests are removed," primarily agricultural subsidies. Finally, the author recommends: (1) the establishment of a new G8/Africa forum which would include both groups political leaders as well as the Secretary-General of the UN and the heads of IFIs and the African Development Bank; (2) the G8 giving central focus to the biennial report of UN Economic Council for Africa and the OECD's Development Assistance Committee, responding in detail; and (3) performing a comprehensive "development audit" on important areas of policy, including trade, investment and arms.

In Chapter 8, Roy MacLaren follows up the discussion on trade. He asks who the G8 is addressing when it argues for the quick conclusion of the Doha round of trade negotiations. He answers that its members actually address themselves, as it is they alone "who can make a success or failure of the Doha round" since it is they who are responsible for the trade issues at stake: "It is disingenuous to 'punt' the problem back to the WTO negotiations when in essence it remains a transatlantic issue." However, doing so, he argues, would mean profound changes in G8 members' domestic policies, particularly agriculture:

> If the United States and the European Union (EU) do not, for domestic reasons, choose to reduce sharply or to eliminate their various barriers to international trade in agriculture, despite their own exhortations at the annual G8 meetings, there is nothing that the WTO itself can do.

MacLaren argues that G8 states follow contradictory paths through their membership in the World Bank and IMF and their membership in the WTO. Policies to alleviate international poverty are for naught when trade policy emphasizes protectionism. For greater coherence, G8 states must coordinate their policies at home. The author argues that a binding, rules-based system, including a review procedure, would benefit world trade; however, as long as trade is governed by "narrow domestic priorities," such a system cannot exist.

MacLaren suggests that perhaps the G8 can salvage some sort of deal within the Doha round, by "papering over … the vast differences remaining among G8 states"; however, any impact of such a deal would be minimal. Ultimately, MacLaren argues, the WTO should be recognized as a location for negotiation of trade with proper review mechanisms. As bilateral and regional trade deals grow, the WTO can assess their impact on enhancing global trade. The G8 must also recognize that states such as India, Brazil and China are becoming major players in world trade – a failure that has contributed to the ineffectiveness of the WTO.

MacLaren concludes that the Doha round is a crucial test regarding the value of the G8, a forum which for the past thirty years has attempted to resolve international trade and investment. By failing the Doha round process, the G8 will be called into question over its ability to craft a healthy system for the future. The "cost of failure" is the systemic blow to the WTO and multilateralism in trade, the key governing structures, leading to greater bilateral deals which weaken the WTO's credibility.

St. Petersburg Priorities: Education, Education, Information and Health

In Chapter 9, Sylvia Ostry analyzes the trade and environment issues that have evolved into "sustainable development" in the global trading system. She provides a brief review of the Energy Charter Treaty and explores the options for policy cooperation between institutions regarding sustainable development.

Ostry charts out the history of environmental concepts within the global trading regime, beginning with the absence of environment references in the initial General Agreement on Tariffs and Trade (GATT) of 1948, to the creation of the GATT Group on Environmental Measures and International Trade formed after the 1972 Stockholm Conference on the Human Environment. The mainstream's initial view of environmental protectionism and sustainable development was built on a fear that it could lead to protectionist trading measures. The environmental movement, although more interested in the World Bank initially, began to focus on the GATT after it ruled in favor of Mexico during a dispute with US tuna embargos due to fishing practices endangering dolphins. This issue led environmentalist non-government organizations to lobby hard during the Uruguay round of negotiations. This lobbying led to the US government ensuring that sustainable development was referenced in the WTO agreement.

However, the ambiguity of the preamble complicated matters. Ostry labels it "a masterpiece of creative ambiguity." She also argues that "sustainable development" itself is ambiguous due to divides between the left and the right, as well as the global North and South (the latter favoring growth over the "post-materialism" of the rich countries of the North). Ostry argues, however, that although currently these divisions remain, the global atmosphere is much more receptive to concepts of sustainable development, as represented in the discussions surrounding WTO reform through the Doha round, and through the negotiations surrounding the Energy Charter Treaty.

In the case of the WTO and the Doha round, paragraph 51 called for the Committee for Trade and Environment and the Committee for Trade and Development to act as a forum where the environmental and developmental aspects of the negotiations could be debated in hopes of obtaining a consensus on sustainable development. Ostry argues, however, that tying sustainable development to the negotiations only hampered the ability to have a serious and informed debate due to the constraints it placed on participants. Instead, Ostry argues for a WTO policy forum, accompanied by research resources, to engage a wide range of actors including cities, provinces/states, and other concerned institutions.

With energy security a top priority for the majority within the OECD, Russia put energy at the top of its 2006 G8 summit agenda. This was a complex issue, especially since Russia has to refused to join the Energy Charter Treaty. Ostry traces the history of the charter from its beginnings in the early 1990s, when it was launched by the EU as a mechanism to help enhance cooperation between the East and West and to aid in the East's transition toward a market economy. Since coming into force in 1998, a number of states have entered, including several Asian states, However, the US, Canada, and Russia remain unattached. Ostry argues that the Treaty is the first broadly multilateral agreement covering investment, a first step in establishing clear and transparent rules reducing risk and encouraging financial support for energy supplies. Russia's refusal to join, however, remains an obstacle. Ostry argues that "Energy security without Russia is akin to *Hamlet* without the Prince."

Ostry concludes that the most significant measure the G8 could adopt for energy security would be for the US and Canada to sign the treaty as a measure to persuade Russia to do the same. However, Ostry recognizes that such a move is unlikely. The Energy Charter Treaty is too ambitious within the current geo-political context. The G8 should therefore initiate a step-by-step approach toward energy security and sustainability. The significant differences between states, especially with regard to their legal and regulatory systems, are important to the effectiveness of the Treaty. The G8 should launch a project analyzing the legal and regulatory systems with respect to foreign investment in energy. Such an analysis should include the WTO Secretariat to discuss trade-related investment and intellectual property measures. This study would provide information essential to understanding how to implement reasoned discussion surrounding energy security through an investment regime. Ostry once again calls for the establishment of a special forum which would discuss the urgency of delivering energy security. She concludes: "The world needs energy security to foster sustainable development. This is international coherence writ large."

In Chapter 10, Nodari A. Simonia explores concepts surrounding market risks in the energy sector and the reasons why exporting countries such as Russia justifiably insist that importing countries share the business risks connected to the commodities, as well as demanding guarantees in order to protect both producing countries and consumers from the volatility and unpredictability of the spot markets and speculation. This is why the St. Petersburg Summit's joint declaration and the plan of actions for the provision of global energy security established the idea of producers' and consumers' "mutual responsibility for sustainable and stable development of world energy."

Simonia opens with a detailed account of the Russian–Ukrainian gas price dispute of January 2006, in which Russia cut gas to the European country for three days. Simonia argues that Russia's claims against Ukraine were absolutely fair, but their implementation was "so clumsy, ill-conceived and immaturely unskillful that it simplified the task of developing a mass psychological attack on Russia and its leadership by anti-Russian politicians and by almost the entire Western mass media." This case displays the volatility of the energy market, and the risks involved for the exporter.

In the preparation for the St. Petersburg Summit, the most stubborn arguments concerned the definition of "energy security." For the West, energy security meant a secure guarantee of supply, or security for consumers. Russia, on the other hand, argued that a guarantee of supply must be supplemented with demand guarantees, and that consumer countries should share responsibility and risks with producing countries. Simonia argues that the pure market approach does not work in the energy sector. Oil and gas are not ordinary goods, for they are non-renewable raw materials unevenly distributed geographically with massive upfront capital costs. Finally, the main traditional oil and natural gas deposits are in a state of productivity decline, and new sources are difficult to access.

The general sentiment among many within the West is that the market must guide energy demand, and thus Russia–EU energy cooperation. The possibility of new technologies and new forms of more comfortable, cheaper energy may overtake oil and gas in the market, and consumers must have the right to use those sources if the prices are more agreeable. This negates the possibility of long-term demand contracts. However, current demand requires no stoppage of deliveries. This represents a conflict of interest for supplier nations like Russia, for they must invest large amounts of money in infrastructure, extraction and delivery, all of which remain beneficial only if demand remains high. Simonia argues that the same logic is behind the EU's stance on the Energy Charter Treaty and its ratification by Russia. The Charter provides for security of deliveries from Russia, the Caspian region and Central Asia. Simonia argues that the problems lie with "those rules worked out by the Brussels bureaucracy, which unilaterally protect only EU countries' interests. For Russia, a country that is at a different socio-economic development level … implementation objectively causes damage to its national interests. …"

Simonia argues that the guarantees Russia requires and the actions it has taken in ensuring its own energy security are well within reason. However, the nervous reactions of the EU generate a sense of impending dread: "But only toward Russia, which made up its mind to put its house in order, is the reaction exceedingly nervous." Simonia also argues that the call for greater diversification of sources (exporting states) to avoid monopolistic behavior is presented with a shade of aloofness, if not hostility, toward Russia. Simonia therefore suggests that the EU contradicts itself regarding its views toward Russian and energy: "It accuses Russia of an urge toward monopolization of European energy markets," but when Russia threatens to diversify exports, "the EU protests that these resources are not enough for everyone, and that Russia is blackmailing the EU."

Simonia contends, however, that there is a second level of interaction between Russia and the rest of Europe – cooperation between corporations from both parties, measured by diligent work at creating joint enterprises, exchanges of assets and rendering services. Simonia insists that Putin's calm reaction to ideological hostility in the West is due to the surefootedness of the corporate side of the relationship. Simonia details the cooperation that has taken place through the Nord Stream gas pipeline project, a pipeline from Russia to Germany, as one of many successful energy delivery relationships supported by Russia. Simonia contrasts this with the planned delivery system from Iran and Azerbaijan via Turkey, and its subsequent delays. Simonia argues that the failures of the latter are due to Brussels being more concerned with finding alternatives to Russia in energy delivery than ensuring secure and effective supply. Other accounts of effective Russian energy delivery within Europe are noted, too.

Simonia concludes by highlighting the divide between the heated rhetoric that comes from Brussels in the energy sector and the strong working relationship that exists between Russian and European businesses. He finishes by stating: "Efforts toward mutually dependant cooperation cannot and should not be depicted as Russia's insidious actions aimed at establishing its own energy monopoly and political dominance."

In Chapter 11, Victoria Panova provides a historical account of the G8 the IEA and global energy concerns as a focal point of the two groups existence and their relationship with each other. She begins by stating that indeed one of the main reasons that the G8 was created was due to the energy crisis of the early 1970s and the economic uncertainty that came in its wake. The same can be said for the IEA, which was established on November 15, 1974, in Paris within the OECD framework.

From the very beginning, differences of perception regarding the energy problem arose in the West. France called for the comprehensive international cooperation of all countries, hard law bodies such as the World Bank and established funds to make loans to those "too rich" to qualify for "soft" no-interest loans but too distressed to afford loans at the prevailing normal lending rates. In 1975, the global community witnessed the creation of the G6, later the G7 with Canada joining in 1976.

Panova argues that there have been four phases in how the G7/8 has dealt with energy activities: (1) during the energy crises of the 1970s and early 1980s; (2) the subsequent period, with excess supply; (3) the end of the 1980s–90s with the demise of the Soviet Union along with the G7's shift toward the problems of nuclear security (especially after the 1986 Chernobyl crisis); and (4) since 2000, when energy security has again recaptured the attention of the G8 members.

In her analysis of the first period, Panova introduces the Rambouillet Declaration of 1975, arguing that it serves as a charter for the G7/8 and outlining the reasons for the club's establishment. The declaration called for democracies to overcome high unemployment, continuing inflation and serious energy problems, and therefore to concentrate on the extraction of raw materials, including energy, since world economic growth was clearly linked to increasing the availability of energy sources. It also emphasized that members should "continue to cooperate in order to reduce their dependence on imported energy through conservation and the development of alternative sources." Following the declaration, leaders concluded that they would need to intensify technology exchanges and joint research while increasingly diversifying supply. The seriousness of the energy problem was also apparent in the establishment of the US Department of Energy in 1977, which consolidated the energy-related functions of the government into one cabinet-level organization.

The second oil crisis, however, shook the G7 once more. At the 1979 Tokyo Summit, the G7 thus committed to restricting oil consumption through setting maximum oil import targets. Each state created its own targets. The leaders also created a high-level group of representatives of G7 countries within the OECD. The key element of the ensuing discussion was the recognition of the role new technologies would play in creating any long-term freedom from energy vulnerability. This realization led to the establishment of the International Energy Technology Group linked to the OECD, IEA and other appropriate international institutions. It would review both plans and actions undertaken by G7 members. Out of this era, Panova argues that the key energy security criteria were maximum use of energy resources, energy efficiency, diversification and minimizing energy imports. The main lesson was that energy security could only be achieved within the framework of "effective market mechanisms functioning inside and outside the G7 countries."

The second era was marked by greater liberalization of the oil market, drops in prices, new technologies and increased energy efficiency, all of which created a reduction in fuel demand and increased supply. By the early 1990s, oil prices had dropped to pre-crisis levels and energy security lost its relevance. Economics became more political under Ronald Reagan in the US, Margaret Thatcher in the UK, as well as conservative governments under Helmut Kohl in Germany and Yasuhiro Nakasone in Japan. Within the summit, East–West relations took energy's place as the priority. The only passage on energy that came out of this period was the agreement that the oil price reduction should not lead to the cessation of energy-saving initiatives. Acknowledging that their coordinated policies were partly responsible for the reduction, leaders agreed to continue their policies to ensure long-term stability for the markets.

The post-Chernobyl era of the late 1980s and early 1990s was marked by an emphasis on environmental security. The G7 supported the creation of the European Energy Charter, which included an open non-discriminatory regime for commercial investments in energy. The 1989 Paris Summit agreed on greater cooperation with hard law organizations such as the International Maritime Organization to prevent oil spills. Consensus existed among G7 leaders regarding the dangers of greenhouse gas emissions. The G7 also shifted toward nuclear security, working with the IEA and World Bank to strengthen regulatory regimes and modernize standards. The 1990 Iraqi invasion of Kuwait did show that oil supplies and prices remained vulnerable to political crises. But the crisis was contained by effective market mechanisms, expanded supply by several exporting states and steps by the IEA to ensure the use of oil reserves.

The beginning of the twenty-first century was marked by the entrance of Russia within the G8. George W. Bush refused to ratify the Kyoto Protocol. Concern over energy prices returned, with the G8 arguing that "high and volatile oil prices" constituted a danger for the world economy, especially vulnerable developing states. Environmental energy was not forgotten. The 2003 Evian Summit argued for doubled hulls of oil tankers, despite resistance from Japan.

The stronger presence of security issues at G8 meetings came with Bush's America, which argued that terrorist activity creates volatility within the energy market. During the 2005 Gleneagles Summit, climate change and energy security were examined, although many – especially the Europeans – argued that the resulting document on climate change was weak. On oil specifically, G8 leaders acknowledged that there should be greater shared responsibility between producers and consumers with further investments in infrastructure, and emphasized the role of the International Energy Forum (not the IEA, of which Russia is not a member). It was also agreed that there must be greater transparency in reporting oil supply and demand.

Panova concludes by defending energy's place as a priority within the G8. Issue number one is now the rise of China, soon to be the biggest user of energy globally. But there has yet to be any global energy revolution (along the lines of the scientific revolution). Nuclear energy has failed to live up to its expectations, and the dangers of this form of energy remain fresh in the minds of those alive during Chernobyl. Complications arise due to the necessity of huge investments into further modernization of the industry. Russia's place, Panova argues, is only natural, as it is the second largest exporter of energy in the world. Finally, environmental concerns regarding greenhouse gases will keep energy at the forefront of G8 discussions.

Panova concludes that the G7/8 has, along with other agencies such as the IEA, contributed significantly to countering the energy shocks created by military, political and structural risks. The future of G8 discussions regarding energy will be geared toward furthering energy market stabilization, creating new infrastructure, assisting developing countries and reacting to international energy security threats. Panova calls for increased steps in energy security, including increased predictability in the market, greater transparency of flows, greater infrastructure and greater import–export coordination.

In Chapter 12, John Kirton, Laura Sunderland and Jenilee Guebert argue that although the G7 proclaimed in 1977 that it would promote the training of young people to build a skilled labor force "to take advantage of the upturn in economic activity as it develops," it was not until 1984 that education became its regular and rising concern. In the twenty-first century, education moved to center stage with Japan hosting the first meeting of G8 education ministers in 2000 and Russia choosing education as a priority for the 2006 summit. Kirton et al. argue that the G8 has been responsible for a "great leap forward in … global education governance" due to the rising vulnerability and declining capability of the US, now increasingly forced to look to G8 colleagues for help. The US has suffered declining educational achievement since 9/11, as it has been ill-equipped nationally for the "Internet-dependent knowledge economy." The highly capable states gathered in the G8 found it easy to take up the tasks of global education, especially regarding Asia, where the free flow of information was censored, and in an Africa that was rapidly democratizing but not developing, and suffering from a North–South digital divide.

The G8's deliberative performance on education has been rising. It received sporadic attention during the first summit cycle (1975–81), regular attention since 1983, and "particularly vigorous" attention from 2000 to 2006. The highest attention came in the summits focusing on Africa. Traditionally, education was thought of as a means to an end by the G8 (education for job training, education for health, education for development), rather than an end in itself. The great reversal came in 1999 at Cologne with "development for education." The Cologne Debt Initiative recommended that the IMF, World Bank and the Paris Club provide funding for the HIPCs, allowing them to divert resources to social programs such as education. Then came "information technology for education" at the Okinawa Summit, the Genoa Plan for Africa concluding action was required to build human capacity through education and training, the G8 Education Task Force report at Kananaskis, the Gleneagles Summit's focus on universal primary education in Africa and the 2006 St. Petersburg Summit, where education was one of the three priorities. Delivery on decisions made at the summit was relatively good in the twenty-first century. Okinawa achieved a perfect score in 2000, whereas the Education for All program at the 2004 Sea Island Summit achieved a much lower performance of 33 percent.

The authors argue that the explosion in the attention received by education in the twenty-first century was due to six factors: (1) the US's declining education achievement relative to its G8 and OECD peers; (2) the fact that this decline occurred while the US led in expenditures on education and teacher salaries, as well as the sustained enrolment of students; (3) a US poorly equipped for the Internet-dependent knowledge economy; (4) a G8 committed to promoting open democracy, individual liberty and social advance; (5) a new generation of G8 leaders led by Tony Blair and George W. Bush dedicated to education as a priority; and (6) the new post-1998 summit format, allowing leaders to deal more freely and flexibly with domestic issues. The decline in MO effectiveness also contributed, as the UN Educational, Scientific and Cultural Organization (UNESCO) and the UN's Children's Fund (UNICEF) were criticized as obsolescent and archaic.

Kirton and Sunderland conclude that the G8 has "become an increasingly effective center of global education governance in the twenty-first century." It has performed well in domestic political management, direction-setting, decision making, delivery and development of global governance, driven by the aforementioned forces. They conclude that "the G8's long history of achievement" in governing global education helped fuel the St. Petersburg Summit's success in this field.

In Chapter 13, Gina Stephens explores the extent to which G8 structural expansion and institutionalization have enhanced cooperation and compliance with G8 commitments. Specifically, she analyzes the impact of the G8's Digital Opportunities Task Force (DOT Force), observing that an increase in institutionalization and specialization in "top-down"-created working groups changes participants' interests and identities, thereby increasing compliance.

Stephens acknowledges that the breadth of topics discussed by the G7/8 since the end of the Cold War has expanded significantly. With this policy expansion has come an expansion in the instruments necessary for assisting the G8. The other trend in post-Cold War G8 summitry is that overall compliance to G8 commitments has steadily increased. Therefore, she argues: "it seems that there is a connection between G8 institutional expansion … and enhanced cooperation and compliance with G8 commitments." She further argues that when these working groups are created and involve members from societal groups and countries beyond the G8, embedded in a "larger constellation of multilateral organizations (MOs) working in the same policy area," they provide extra impetus for compliance.

To justify her claim, Stephens explores the workings of the DOT Force, a G8 expert working group created for the Okinawa Charter on Global Information Society at the 2000 Okinawa Summit. The G8 leaders mandated its creation as part of a global strategy to address the digital divide between developed and developing countries, as well as the potential of information and communication technologies (ICT) to aid in the advancement of development. The DOT Force Secretariat consisted of two members from the World Bank and two members from the United Nations Development Programme (UNDP), and was responsible for establishing the 47-member task force. Each G8 country contributed representatives from government, private sector business and non-profit organizations. Eight non-G8 developing countries participated as well. The task force also included members of the European Commission, the OECD, the UN's Economic and Social Council (ECOSOC), the United Nations Educational, Scientific and Cultural Organization (UNESCO), the United Nations Convention on Trade and Development (UNCTAD), the International Telecommunication Union (ITU), the World Economic Forum, the Global Information Infrastructure Commission and the Global Business Dialogue on E-Commerce. Four priorities were established: fostering policy, regulatory and network readiness; improving connectivity at lower costs; building human capacity; and encouraging participation in global e-commerce networks.

Through the DOT Force process, the discussion extended the "digital divide" beyond merely technical considerations, reflecting the development of group consensus on norms underscoring their work and their proposed solutions. *Digital Opportunities for All: Meeting the Challenge*, the report presented at the 2001 Genoa Summit, contained a nine-point action plan. Following its acceptance, the DOT Force moved to implementation, creating seven teams in areas such as "Access and Connectivity," "Human Capacity and Knowledge," "ICT for Health" and "Global Policy Participation." Final achievements of the project were chronicled in a report presented to the 2002 Kananaskis Summit. The impressive results included expansion of its membership, over 20 bilateral and multilateral initiatives and implementing initiatives and special attention to Africa, responding to requirements articulated by the NEPAD.

The performance of the G8 on the DOT Force was extraordinarily high, receiving successive A grades from the G8 Research Group. All states demonstrated full compliance, with the exception of Russia, with its -1 score bringing the average G8 score to 75 percent. Stephens suggests this high compliance depended on a few key factors: the creation of a working group, the structure and content of the working group in accordance with its specific task, the development of a group identity and norms, and the existence of other international organizations with a similar, sometimes overlapping, membership: institutionalization "creates a focus on a particular area of policy and also creates necessary linkages within G8 domestic political structures that favor follow-through on these commitments." Also, the DOT Force's multi-stakeholder structure multiplied this effect, mobilizing not only G8 member bureaucracies, but also other key societal sectors with influence within the policy area, including business, non-profit and civil society. Compliance may also have been caused by the particular task of this working group focused on an area novel in policy terms.

From a constructivist standpoint, the creation of a group identity within the DOT Force played a part in its effectiveness: "The social interactions which occur within these groups may shape not only what their members see as their individual interests, but ultimately how they view their own identities – especially when dealing with new problems where few pre-existing national policies exist." The interactions shaping interests and identities play as powerful a role as material factors in shaping the agenda. Stephens uses social identity theory to explain the effect of group membership on personal identity, arguing that the more successful the group, the more attractive the group is, reinforcing positive perceptions of individual status, and encouraging action to further the group's collective interests.

Stephens concludes that the DOT Force represented a successful experiment for G8 institutionalization beyond original G8 parameters. Its unique structure and task resulted in clear, detailed, achievable policy objectives, as well as an expression of common values and group identity, encouraging compliance. She concludes: "The breadth and balance of its membership … employs a similar strategy to the WHO's [World Health Organization's] Public Private Partnerships. Such bodies extend the reach and the available resources of the G8 and long-established MOs to enact truly effective global governance."

In Chapter 14, John Kirton, Nikolai Roudev, Laura Sunderland, Catherine Kunz and Jenilee Guebert note that the G8 and the Asia-Pacific Economic Cooperation (APEC) forum have both increasingly made commitments on global public health. They address whether G8 and APEC members have a strong record of compliance with these commitments, the reasons behind their compliance, and what can be done to enhance compliance. They specifically examine the role of the WHO and its relationship with these two informal organizations and their members.

The G8 began addressing health substantially at the 1996 summit; since then, the issue has steadily risen (especially in relation to the Millennium Development Goals [MDGs]). By 2008, commitments made by the G8 stood at 225, covering HIV/AIDS, infectious diseases and health generally as it relates to development, human rights and climate change. Health has also been included at the meetings of foreign ministers, development ministers and the G7 finance ministers. There was strong compliance within the first after commitments were made. However, compliance varies across member states. The G8 system also allows significant pressure to be placed on non-member states (such as G20 members) to extract compliance from them as well. Causes of compliance include the relative capacity of each member state, emulation by weak states of the stronger ones, and the direct political will and capability on the part of the committing leader. Furthermore, embedding compliance catalysts in the commitments brings greater compliance, as does the existence of domestic institutional structures that allow for inclusion of international objectives within health policy decision making. Including the WHO as the core MO to assist in this area is also a key factor in raising compliance. The G8 has partnered with several MOs in formulating health policy, namely the OECD, the IMF, the World Bank and the WHO. These partnerships are useful in assisting members to implement G8 health commitments. Finally, the sherpa-centric structure of the G8 system allows for some ease of agenda-setting because the sherpa can assist with coordination across groups.

Regarding APEC, commitments have been made on health issues since the forum was founded at the leaders' level in 1993, although they have been relatively few. They cover HIV/AIDS, infectious diseases, avian influenza, strategy and service delivery. Commitments have been fewer than those made by the G8, with only 24 related to health on the part of APEC since 2000. It is difficult to track the compliance of APEC members, but it is generally agreed that compliance levels are disappointingly low. A small secretariat to track and monitor compliance and implementation of member states has been created, but in effect states are still required to self-monitor. APEC's Secretariat has published pamphlets and reports on compliance, but has not actually generated it.

The G8 and APEC provide useful forums for discussing and creating foreign and health policy objectives that reflect objectives determined by the WHO. However, a formula for guaranteeing compliance and implementation has not been found. The role that MOs play in assisting compliance is relatively limited; the authors suggest that a multi-stakeholder global public health policy network is one of the ways in which implementation and compliance can be improved.

Informal bodies, namely the G8 and APEC, set the agenda in health policy; these bodies not only have the power and ability to set goals for their own members, but also for those with close affiliation (G20 members). However, while these bodies are useful agents in agenda-setting, the direction and priorities of health policy often originate with the WHO, because of its bureaucratic resources. With regard to monitoring and ensuring compliance and assisting with implementation, the authors suggest that partnering with more formal MOs has only had a limited impact on success. A more comprehensive global policy network that includes a number of actors (national governments, international institutions and non-governmental organizations) is needed to enhance compliance and implementation.

Moving the G8 Forward at St. Petersburg and Beyond

In Chapter 15, John Kirton argues that as president of the G8 in 2006, Russia did an exemplary job of hosting the annual summit. Successes included the timely selection of three key issue areas (energy security, infectious diseases and education), the participation of key emerging powers, and the inclusion of civil society leaders and actors. These successes opened up new opportunities for the G8 to increase its legitimacy and effectiveness. The central question, therefore, is whether this was just a glimpse of what the G8 could be, or whether there is now a likelihood that these reforms will continue. Moreover, Kirton looks at how these successes can be replicated and built upon.

Kirton provides significant praise of Russia's actions as G8 President. His analysis looks at the major successes of the summit, their implications for democratizing the G8, and the lessons that can be taken from this summit to strengthen the future of the G8. Finally, he addresses the record of the G8 since the 2006 summit, and comments on what further steps need to be taken.

According to Kirton, Russia had three tasks to fulfill: to host a successful summit for addressing global issues; to demonstrate its commitment to democracy at home and abroad, and to reform the G8 system to include rising powers and other key international actors. On the first, he concludes that Russia provided strong leadership in both its selection of agenda items and in its ability to adjust to other member states' priorities while having them adjust to their own. Second, the wide-reaching and unparalleled amount of access to the summit, including the creation of the Civil 8, as well as multiple forums for religious, civil, youth and media groups, proved the commitment of Russia's leadership to opening up the dialogue both internally and internationally. Finally, the inclusion of the Plus Five powers as well as leadership from a number of MOs (including, specifically, a number of UN agencies) exemplified Russia's commitment to including non-traditional G8 actors with an increasing stake in its decisions.

Building on the successes of the summit, Kirton lists four steps to further strengthen the G8. First, Russia and the EU need to be given full membership in the G8 system. Second, a set of regular G8 ministerial meetings covering the major ministries in G8 countries should be developed. Third, legislative, judicial and civil society institutions must be strengthened among G8 members to relieve some of the power of the G8 members' executive branches. Finally, on an *ad hoc* basis as determined by the agenda, more countries need to be invited to participate at the summit itself, even more than the Plus Five powers of Brazil, China, India, Mexico and South Africa alone.

These four steps are key to enhancing democracy at the G8 and to further ensuring compliance with summit goals and their implementation. While its informal nature remains the key to the G8's success, it must be partnered with more "hard law" approaches through joint work with MOs and other stakeholders. Russia successfully incorporated other actors into the summit and broadened the dialogue. These successes should be built upon. Finally, because the issue of implementation and the gap between commitment and compliance remains large, a "multi-stakeholder global 'G8 compliance consortium'" should be created to address implementation and further compliance monitoring.

Kirton's assessment of Russia's presidency indicates that he sees the need for G8 outreach in order to address questions of accountability and democracy. Although he does specify that the informal nature of the G8 is what makes it successful, he also advocates broader inclusion of both non-member states and non-state actors. Moreover, he acknowledges the problems of compliance and implementation. But his suggestion of a multi-stakeholder global "G8 compliance consortium" does little to address how this would take place. Kirton's suggestion, though, is that the desire of member state leaders to see their ideas implemented is what would likely drive this type of forum. This seems to suggest an expanded informal system rather than the development of a G8 bureaucracy. As Kirton fully appreciates, the G8 has a distinctive culture that emphasizes a reinforcement of its strengths by incremental means. That being said, the breakthrough in terms of Russia's hosting of the 2006 summit reveals that there is also an ability to make big leaps when they are necessary to keep the G8 at the center of the debates and structure of global governance.

Appendices

Appendix 2A: Multilateral Organizations at the Annual G7/8 Summit 1996–2008

1996 Lyon

United Nations: Boutros Boutros-Ghali, Secretary-General
International Monetary Fund: Michel Camdessus, Managing Director
World Bank: James Wolfensohn, President
World Trade Organization: Renato Ruggiero, Director-General

2001 Genoa

United Nations: Kofi Annan, Secretary-General
World Bank: James Wolfensohn, President
World Trade Organization: Renato Ruggiero, Director-General
World Health Organization: Gro Harlem Brundtland, Director-General
Food and Agriculture Organization: Jacques Diouf, Director-General

2002 Kananaskis

United Nations: Kofi Annan, Secretary-General

2003 Evian

United Nations: Kofi Annan, Secretary-General
World Bank: James Wolfensohn, President
International Monetary Fund: Horst Köhler, Managing Director
World Trade Organization: Supachai Panitchpakdi, Director-General

2005 Gleneagles

Commission of the African Union: Alpha Oumar Konare, Chair
International Energy Agency: Claude Mandil, Executive Director
International Monetary Fund: Rodrigo de Rato y Figaredo, Managing Director
United Nations: Kofi Annan, Secretary-General
World Bank: Paul Wolfowitz, President
World Trade Organization: Supachai Panitchpakdi, Director-General

2006 St. Petersburg

Commission of the African Union: Alpha Oumar Konare, Chair
Commonwealth of Independent States: Nursultan Nazarbayev, Chairman-in-office
International Energy Agency: Claude Mandil, Executive Director
International Atomic Energy Agency: Mohammed ElBaradei, Director-General
UNESCO: Koichiro Matsuura, Director-General
World Health Organization: Anders Nordström, Acting Director-General
World Trade Organization: Pascal Lamy, Director-General
United Nations: Kofi Annan, Secretary-General

2007 Heiligendamm

United Nations: Ban Ki-moon, Secretary-General
International Monetary Fund: Rodrigo de Rato y Figaredo, Managing Director
World Bank: Paul Wolfowitz, President
Organisation for Economic Co-operation and Development: Angel Gurria, Secretary-General
International Energy Agency: Claude Mandil, Executive Director
World Trade Organization: Pascal Lamy, Director-General
Commission of the African Union: Alpha Oumar Konare, Chair

2008 Hokkaido

United Nations: Ban Ki-moon, Secretary-General
World Bank: Robert Zoellick, President
International Monetary Fund: Dominique Strauss-Kahn, Director-General
International Energy Agency: Nobuo Tanaka, Executive Director
Organisation for Economic Co-operation and Development: Angel Gurria, Secretary-General
Commission of the African Union: Jean Ping, Chair

Appendix 2B: Analysis of multilateral organizations at the G8 Summit, 1989–2008

	Final compliance score	Interim compliance score	No. of MOs present	UN	IMF	World Bank	WTO	NAM	WHO	IEA	AU	CIS	IAEA	UNESCO	OECD
Overall average	47.4	34.8	4	80%	50%	60%	60%	20%	20%	40%	40%	10%	10%	10%	20%
Overall average with MOs	48.0	33.9													
Overall average without MOs	46.8	40.0													
1996–2008 average with MOs	50.0	33.9													
1996–2008 average without MOs	43.6	40.0													
1989	+07.8		1[a]					Yes							
1990	-14.0														
1991	00.0														
1992	+64.0														
1993	+75.0		1[b]					Yes							
1994	+100.0														
1995	+100.0														
1996	+36.2		4[a]	Yes	Yes	Yes	Yes								
1997	+12.8														
1998	+31.8														

Appendix 2B (continued)

	Final compliance score	Interim compliance score	No. of MOs present	UN	IMF	World Bank	WTO	NAM	WHO	IEA	AU	CIS	IAEA	UNESCO	OECD
1999	+38.2														
2000	+81.4														
2001	+49.5		4[c]	Yes		Yes	Yes		Yes						
2002	+35.0	+29.8	1[c]	Yes											
2003	+65.8	+47.1	4[c]	Yes	Yes	Yes	Yes								
2004	+54.0	+40.0													
2005	+65.0	+47.4	6[c]	Yes	Yes	Yes	Yes			Yes	Yes				
2006	+47.0	+33.0	8[c]	Yes			Yes		Yes	Yes	Yes	Yes	Yes	Yes	
2007	+51.0	+33.0	7[c]	Yes	Yes	Yes	Yes			Yes	Yes				Yes
2008	N/A	+13.0	6[c]	Yes	Yes	Yes				Yes	Yes				Yes

Notes:

[a] Met with all G7/8 leaders before or after summit (margins presence).

[b] Met with host only (proximity presence).

[c] Met with all G7/8 leaders during summit (integral presence).

The average scores in the table above for MOs are calculated out of the total number of summits where MOs have been present. The percentage of overall participation in summits from 1975-2008 is as follows: No. of MOs present = 1 (or 1.24); UN = 24% IMF = 15%; World Bank = 18%; WTO = 18%; NAM = 6%; WHO = 6%; IEA = 12%; AU = 12%; CIS = 3%; IAEA = 3%; UNESCO = 3%; OECD = 6%.

Compliance scores from 1990 to 1995 measure compliance with commitments selected by Ella Kokotsis. Compliance scores from 1996 to 2008 measure compliance with G8 Research Group's selected commitments.

The NAM members met with the G8 foreign ministers in Cologne on June 10, 1999, before the leaders' summit on June 18–20, 1999. They met again on July 13, 2000, before the July 20–23, 2000 leaders' summit.

Appendix 2C: A model of agency, institutionalization and structure

Agency: Compliance Catalysts

1. priority placement
2. target
3. timetable
4. remit mandate
5. money mobilized
6. agent
7. G8 body
8. international institution

Institutionalization

1. re-mentions by the G7/8 finance ministers
2. pre-mentions by the G7/8 finance ministers
3. post-mentions by G7-centered finance ministerial bodies
4. recommitment by G7/8 finance ministers
5. pre-commitment by G7/8 finance ministers
6. post-affirmation by G7/8 finance ministers

Structure

Vulnerabilities

1. percentage change in price of Brent Crude Oil barrel (London)
2. percentage change in price of gold (London)
3. percentage change in global stock markets index
4. average annual change in G7 economic confidence indicators

Capabilities

5. average G7 real GDP growth
6. US real GDP growth minus average G7 GDP growth
7. average appreciation of US$ versus other G7 currencies

Appendix 2D: Finance and development compliance and catalysts, 1996–2004

Issue area	Issue	Priority placement	Target	Timetable	Remit mandate	Money	Agent	G8-centered body	International institution	Total	Score
Macroeconomics	Macroeconomics	Yes	—	—	—	—	—	—	—	1	+1.00
Microeconomics	Microeconomics	Yes	—	—	—	—	—	—	—	1	+0.29
Development	ODA	—	—				—			0	0.00
IFI reform	UNCTAD	Yes	—	—	—	—	—	—	Yes	2	+0.29
UN reform I	$ obligations	Yes	—	—	—	—	—	—	Yes	2	+0.14
UN reform II	Development agenda	—	—	—	—	—	Yes	—	Yes	2	+0.14
Development	Africa	Yes	—	—	—	—	Yes	—	—	2	0.00
Microeconomics	Employment	—	—	—	—	—	—	—	—	0	+0.38
Debt	HIPC	—	—	—	—	—	Yes	—	Yes	2	0.00
Microeconomics	Employment	Yes	—	—	—	—	—	—	Yes	2	0.00
Debt	HIPC	—	Yes	—	—	—	Yes	—		2	+0.86
Macroeconomics	Macroeconomics	—	—	—	—	—	—	—	—	0	+1.00
Exchange rate	Exchange rate	—	—	—	—	—	—	—	—	0	0.00
Crime	FATF	—	—	—	—	—	—	Yes	—	1	0.00
Debt	HIPC	—	—				Yes	Yes	—	2	0.00
Debt	Decision points	—	Yes	Yes	—	—	Yes	Yes	—	4	-1.00
Debt	HIPC	—	—	—	—	—	—	—	—	0	0.00
IFI reform	IFI reform	—	—	—	—	—	Yes	Yes	—	2	-1.00
Debt	HIPC	—		—	—	—	—	—	—	1	+1.00
Health	Global Fund	—	—	Yes	—	Yes	—	Yes	Yes	4	+0.75
Terrorism	Terrorism	—	—	—	—	—	Yes	—	—	1	+1.00
Environment	GEF	Yes	—	—	—	—	—	Yes	—	2	-0.13

Issue area	Issue	Priority placement	Target	Timetable	Remit mandate	Money	Agent	G8-centered body	International institution	Total	Score
Africa	ODA	Yes	Yes	—	—	—	—	—	—	2	+0.50
Health	Polio	Yes	Yes	Yes	—	—	—	—	—	3	0.00
Economic growth	Agriculture & trade	Yes	—	—	—	—	—	—	—	1	+0.13
Debt	HIPC	Yes	—	—	—	Yes	—	Yes	—	3	+0.25
World economy	World economy	Yes	—	—	—	—	—	—	—	1	+0.25
Health	Global Fund	Yes	—	Yes	—	—	Yes	Yes	—	4	+0.88
Health	Polio	Yes	Yes	Yes	—	—	—	—	—	3	+1.00
Development	ODA	Yes	—	Yes	—	—	Yes	Yes	—	4	+0.88
Debt	HIPC	Yes	—	Yes	—	—	Yes	—	—	3	+0.38
Crime	Finance	Yes	—	—	—	—	—	—	Yes	2	-0.50
Terrorism	Finance	Yes	—	Yes	—	—	—	Yes	Yes	4	+1.00
Development	Doha	Yes	—	Yes	—	—	Yes	—	—	3	+1.00
Development	Private entrepreneur	—	—	—	—	—	Yes	Yes		2	-1.00
Africa	Darfur	Yes	—	—	—	—	—	—	—	1	+0.88
Health	Polio	Yes	—	Yes	—	—	Yes	—	—	3	+0.44
Crime	Finance	—	—	Yes	—	—	Yes	Yes	—	3	+0.11
Crime	Finance	Yes	—	—	—	—	Yes	—	Yes	3	+0.44
Debt	HIPC	Yes	Yes	Yes			Yes	Yes	—	5	+1.00
Africa	Famine	Yes	—	—	—	—	Yes	—	—	2	+0.67
World Economy	World economy	Yes	—	—	—	—	—	—	—	1	+0.22
		25/42	07/42	12/42	00/42	02/42	18/42	13/42	09/42	86	
		60%	17%	29%	00%	05%	43%	31%	21%	2	

Appendix 2E: Membership overlap in the OECD

	EU members represented at G7/8 (excluding G7/8 members)	Compliance score	No. of members in OECD	% of OECD held by G7/8 countries	% of OECD held by G7/8 countries + EU members
1975 (G6)	0	+57.1	24	25	25
1976 (G7)	0	+08.9	24	29	29
1977 (EU)	5[a]	+08.4	24	29	50
1978	5	+36.3	24	29	50
1979	5	+82.3	24	29	50
1980	5	+07.6	24	29	50
1981	6[b]	+26.6	24	29	54.2
1982	6	+84.0	24	29	54.2
1983	6	-10.9	24	29	54.2
1984	6	+48.8	24	29	54.2
1985	6	+01.0	24	29	54.2
1986	8[c]	+58.3	24	29	62.5
1987	8	+93.3	24	29	62.5
1988	8	-47.8	24	29	62.5
1989	8	+07.8	24	29	62.5
1990	8	-14.0	24	29	62.5
1991	8	00.0	24	29	62.5
1992	8	+64.0	24	29	62.5
1993	8	+75.0	24	29	62.5
1994	8	+100.0	25[d]	28	60
1995	11[e]	+100.0	26[f]	27	69.2
1996	11	+36.2	29[g]	24	62.1

	EU members represented at G7/8 (excluding G7/8 members)	Compliance score	No. of members in OECD	% of OECD held by G7/8 countries	% of OECD held by G7/8 countries + EU members
1997 (G8)[h]	11	+12.8	29	24	62.1
1998	11	+31.8	29	24	62.1
1999	11	+38.2	29	24	62.1
2000	11	+81.4	30[i]	23	60
2001	11	+49.5	30	23	60
2002	11	+35.0	30	23	60
2003	11	+65.8	30	23	60
2004	16[j]	+54.0	30	23	76.7
2005	16	+65.0	30	23	76.7
2006	16	+47.0	30	23	76.7
2007	18[k]	+51.0	30	23	76.7
2008	18	N/A	30	23	76.7

Notes:

[a] Belgium, Denmark, Ireland, Luxembourg, the Netherlands.

[b] Greece.

[c] Portugal, Spain.

[d] Mexico.

[e] Austria, Finland, Sweden.

[f] Czech Republic.

[g] Hungary, Korea, Poland.

[h] Russia is not a member of the OECD, therefore the addition of Russia does not affect the overall percentage the G8 holds within the OECD.

[i] Slovakia.

[j] Czech Republic, Hungary, Poland, Slovakia.

[k] Bulgaria, Romania.

Appendix 2F: Membership overlap in the United Nations, 1975–2005

	EU members represented at G7/8 (excluding G7/8 members)	Compliance score	No. of members in UN	% of UN held by G7/8 countries	% of UN held by G7/8 countries + EU members	% UNSC P5 held by G7/8 countries
1975 (G6)	5[a]	+57.1	144	4.2	7.6	60
1976 (G7)	5	+08.9	147	4.7	8.2	60
1977	5	+08.4	149	4.6	8.1	60
1978	5	+36.3	151	4.6	7.9	60
1979	5	+82.3	152	4.6	7.9	60
1980	5	+07.6	154	4.5	7.8	60
1981	6[b]	+26.6	157	4.5	8.3	60
1982	6	+84.0	157	4.5	8.3	60
1983	6	-10.9	158	4.4	8.2	60
1984	6	+48.8	159	4.4	8.2	60
1985	6	+01.0	159	4.4	8.2	60
1986	8[c]	+58.3	159	4.4	9.4	60
1987	8	+93.3	159	4.4	9.4	60
1988	8	-47.8	159	4.4	9.4	60
1989	8	+07.8	159	4.4	9.4	60
1990	8	-14.0	159	4.4	9.4	60
1991	8	00.0	166	4.2	9.0	60
1992	8	+64.0	179	3.9	8.4	60
1993	8	+75.0	184	3.8	8.2	60
1994	8	+100.0	185	3.8	8.1	60
1995	11[d]	+100.0	185	3.8	9.7	60
1996	11	+36.2	185	3.8	9.7	60

	EU members represented at G7/8 (excluding G7/8 members)	Compliance score	No. of members in UN	% of UN held by G7/8 countries	% of UN held by G7/8 countries + EU members	% UNSC P5 held by G7/8 countries
1997 (G8)	11	+12.8	185	4.3	10.3	80
1998	11	+31.8	185	4.3	10.3	80
1999	11	+38.2	188	4.3	10.1	80
2000	11	+81.4	189	4.2	10.1	80
2001	11	+49.5	189	4.2	10.1	80
2002	11	+35.0	191	4.2	9.9	80
2003	11	+65.8	191	4.2	9.9	80
2004	21[e]	+54.0	191	4.2	15.2	80
2005	21	+65.0	191	4.2	15.2	80

Notes:

[a] Belgium, Denmark, Ireland, Luxembourg, the Netherlands.

[b] Greece.

[c] Portugal, Spain.

[d] Austria, Finland, Sweden.

[e] Cyprus, Czech Republic, Estonia, Hungary, Latvia, Lithuania, Malta, Poland, Slovakia, Slovenia.

Appendix 2G: Multilateral organizational experience of the host Sherpa, 2005–06

	Compliance score	Sherpa	International institutional experience before hosting	International institutional experience after hosting
1975	+57.1	Raymond Barre		Prime Minister of France (1976–81)
1976	+08.9	George P. Shultz		
1977	+08.4	John Hunt		
1978	+36.3	Manfred Lahnstein		
1979	+82.3	Hiromichi Miyazaki		
1980	+07.6	Renato Ruggiero	Italian Mission to the European Community (1969–70s), spokesman for the President of the European Commission (1977–78)	WTO Director-General (1995–99)
1981	+26.6	Allan Gotlieb	Delegate to the United Nations General Assembly (1967–68)	
1982	+84.0	Jacques Attali		President of the European Bank for Reconstruction and Development (1991–93)
1983	-10.9	W. Allen Wallis		
1984	+48.8	Robert Armstrong		
1985	+01.0	Hans Tietmeyer		Chairman of the Bank for International Settlements (2003–05), Governor of the Fund for Germany at the IMF (1998)
1986	+58.3	Reishi Teshima		
1987	+93.3	Renato Ruggiero	Italian Mission to the European Community (1969–70s), spokesman for the President of the European Commission (1977–78)	WTO Director-General (1995–99)

	Compliance score	Sherpa	International institutional experience before hosting	International institutional experience after hosting
1988	-47.8	Sylvia Ostry	Head of the Economics and Statistics Department of the OECD (1979–83)	
1989	+07.8	Jacques Attali		President of European Bank for Reconstruction and Development (1991–93)
1990	-14.0	Richard T. McCormack		Chairman of the International Chamber of Commerce (2001–03)
1991	00.0	Nigel Wicks	Executive Director at the World Bank and the IMF (1983–85)	
1992	+64.0	Horst Köhler		Managing Director of the International Monetary Fund (2000–04)
1993	+75.0	Koichiro Matsuura		Chair of UNESCO's World Heritage Committee (1998–99); Director-General of UNESCO (1999–2005)
1994	+100.0	Pietro Calamia		
1995	+100.0	Gordon Smith	Delegation to NATO (1968); Permanent Representative and Ambassador to NATO (1985–90)	
1996	+36.2	Jean-David Levitte	Counsellor at the Permanent Mission of France to the United Nations (1982–85); Permanent Representative to the United Nations Office in Geneva (1988–90)	Permanent Representative to the United Nations (2000–02)
1997	+12.8	Daniel K. Tarullo		
1998	+31.8	John Holmes	Temporary duty at the British Mission to the UN (early 1970s)	
1999	+38.2	Klaus Gretschmann		Director-General, Economic Policy Directorate, Council of the European Union (2001–present)

Appendix 2G (continued)

	Compliance score	Sherpa	International institutional experience before hosting	International institutional experience after hosting
2000	+81.4	Yoshiji Nogami	Ambassador to the OECD (1997–99)	
2001	+49.5	Francesco Olivieri		Permanent Representative to the OECD (2001–05)
2002	+35.0	Robert Fowler	Ambassador to the UN (1995–2000)	
2003	+65.8	Maurice Gourdault-Montagne		
2004	+54.0	Gary Edson		
2005	+65.0	Michael Jay		
2006	+47.0	Igor Shuvalov		

Notes: Excludes all positions in the sherpa's national department of foreign or external affairs relating to international relations, trade, ambassadors to countries, etc. that are not explicitly involved with an international institution.
This list of experience is preliminary, and may not include all international institutional experience.

Appendix 3A: G8 commitments and compliance

	Sequences/series	Main series issues and summit achievements	No. of documents	No. of commitments[a]	Summit grade	Average compliance[b] score
	Sixth series	*Globalization and development*				
1998	Birmingham (first G8 summit)	New format, crime	7	73	B+	0.45
1999	Cologne	Debt, Kosovo, finance	5	46	B+	0.39
2000	Okinawa	Outreach, information technology	10	105	B	0.78
2001	Genoa	Infectious diseases, Africa	6	58	B	0.53
	Seventh series	*Fighting terrorism and its causes*				
2002	Kananaskis, Alberta	Africa, cleaning up WMD	8	187	B+	0.33
	Fifth sequence of the G7	Start of the G8: cycle and first sequence				
2003	Evian	Outreach, reconciliation	12	206	1+	0.51
2004	Sea Island, Georgia	Middle East	15	253	1+	0.54
2005	Gleneagles, Scotland (start of second G8 sequence)	Climate change dialogue, Africa[c]	15	212	A-[d]	0.65

Appendix 3A (continued)

	Sequences/series	Main series issues and summit achievements	No. of documents	No. of commitments[a]	Summit grade	Average compliance[b] score
2006	St. Petersburg	Energy security, health, education	15	317	B-[e]	0.45
2007	Heiligendamm	Shaping globalization, helping Africa to develop	12	329	A-[f]	0.51
2008	Hokkaido	Climate change and sustainable energy dialogue, Africa	6	280	B[g]	0.48

Notes:[a] According to the methodology, "commitment is a distinct, specific, identifiable, measurable, collectively agreed, future-oriented and publicly expressed statements of intent, promise or undertaking by leaders that they will take future action to meet or adjust to an identified target."

[b] Compliance is a conscious new or altered effort by national governments in the post-summit period aimed at implementing the provisions contained in aummit communiqués.

[c] Based on Bayne (2005).

[d] Reported by Kirton as Bayne's "preliminary grade." For details of the summits and their agenda, see Chapters 3 and 5 in Bayne (2005).

[e] Based on Bayne's methodology, reported by M. Larionova.

[f] Based on Bayne's methodology, assessment by J. Kirton.

[g] Based on Bayne's methodology, assessment by M. Larionova.

Source: Adapted from (Bayne 2005: 18, Table 2.1; 214, Table 14.1). Reproduced with Nicholas Bayne's permission.

Appendix 3B: 2006 St. Petersburg final compliance scores

Issue area	Canada	France	Germany	Italy	Japan	Russia	UK	US	EU	Issue average
1. Health (Global Fund)	1	1	0	0	*1*	*1*	0	*1*	0	0.56
2. Health (tuberculosis)	*1*	0	0	0	0	0	0	*1*	0	0.22
3. Health (polio)	1	0	1	-1	0	1	1	1	0	0.44
4. Energy (oil and energy reserve data collection)	1	1	1	1	1	1	1	1	1	1.00
5. Energy intensity	0	0	0	0	0	1	1	0	1	0.33
6. Surface transport	*1*	0	*1*	0	0	0	0	1	1	0.44
7. Renewable energy	1	0	1	*1*	1	1	1	*1*	1	0.89
8. Climate change	*0*	1	1	*1*	1	1	1	1	1	0.78
9. Education (academic mobility)	0	*1*	*1*	0	0	*1*	0	0	1	0.44
10. Education (qualification systems)	0	0	1	*0*	*0*	*0*	0	1	1	0.33
11. Education (gender disparities)	1	1	0	-1	0	0	1	0	0	0.22
12. Africa (security)	1	1	0	0	0	0	0	1	*1*	0.44
13. Africa (debt relief)	1	1	1	0	1	1	1	*1*	1	0.89
14. Transnational crime and corruption	0	0	0	0	0	0	0	0	0	0.00
15. Intellectual property rights	0	0	0	0	0	0	1	0	N/A	0.13
16. Trade (export subsidies, agriculture)	**0**	-1	1	-1	1	0	1	0	0	0.11
17. Counter-terrorism (energy)	*1*	*1*	0	0	0	0	*1*	*1*	1	0.56

Appendix 3B (continued)

Issue area	Canada	France	Germany	Italy	Japan	Russia	UK	US	EU	Issue average
18. Stabilization and reconstruction (UN)	0	0	0	0	0	0	0	0	0	0.00
19. Global partnership (non-proliferation)	1	0	1	0	1	1	1	0	0	0.56
20. Middle East (Lebanon)	1	1	1	1	1	1	1	1	1	1.00
Country average	0.60	0.40	0.55	0.05	0.40	0.45	0.60	0.60	0.58	
All-country average										0.47
All-issue average										0.47
2006 interim compliance average	0.45	0.25	0.45	-0.10	0.30	0.25	0.55	0.35	0.53	0.34
2005 final compliance	0.81	0.58	0.88	0.29	0.52	0.14	0.81	0.95	0.89	0.65
2005 interim compliance	0.52	0.48	0.33	0.43	0.52	-0.14	0.71	0.67	0.75	0.47

Note: Italics indicate increase since 2006 interim report; bold indicates decrease since 2006 interim report.

Appendix 3C: 2006 St. Petersburg final compliance scores by priority issues

No. Issue area	CAD	FRA	GER	ITA	JAP	RUS	UK	US	EU	Issue average
Health (infectious diseases)										
1. Health (global fund)	1	1	0	0	1	1	0	1	0	0.56
2. Health (tuberculosis)	1	0	0	0	0	0	0	1	0	0.22
3. Health (polio)	1	0	1	-1	0	1	1	1	0	0.44
2006 final health average										0.41
G8 health average since 1996										0.40
Energy security										0.50
4. Energy (oil and energy reserve data collection)	1	1	1	1	1	1	1	1	1	1.00
5. Energy intensity	0	0	0	0	0	1	1	0	1	0.33
6. Surface transport	1	0	1	0	0	0	0	1	1	0.44
7. Renewable energy	1	0	1	1	1	1	1	1	1	0.89
8. Climate change	0	1	1	1	1	1	1	1	1	0.78
2006 final energy security average										0.68
G8 energy + environment average since 1996										0.67
2006 environment average*										0.67
G8 environment average since 1996										0.61
Education										
9. Education (academic mobility)	0	1	1	0	0	1	0	0	1	0.44
10. Education (qualification systems)	0	0	1	0	0	0	0	1	1	0.33
11. Education (gender disparities)	1	1	0	-1	0	0	1	0	0	0.22
2006 final education average										0.33
G8 education average since 1996										0.48

Appendix 3D: Markers (G8–multi institutions interaction models markers)

G8 governance against multilateral organizations	G8 governance in alliance with the multilateral organizations	G8 governance through the multilateral organizations	G8 governance without multilateral organizations
We set up We convene (a conference) We decided to forge a new partnership We launched	We must (will) engage We remain engaged We commit ourselves With our partners Together with Partnership We will work with In (close) consultations with We will (jointly) cooperate We must ensure (implementation) We will implement (an MO's initiative) Incorporation in … We welcome endorsement We support (on a regular basis) We reaffirm our support Maintain solid support We pledge our support Provide assistance In close collaboration with We will endeavor with all our partners Signing and ratifying We met with We make engagements Provide (technical and financial) assistance Strengthening and assisting Adhere to Coordination with We reaffirm our commitment Provide funding Implementation In conjunction with We have secured the entry into force Working under auspices We are working to (deliver) Financial contributions Working in support of	We welcome We urge We call on/for We support (as an acknowledgment) We encourage We attach strong importance We note with approval We note Drawing on (experience) We invite We commend (An MO) should/must … We look to We endorse We will pursue … through We forge Through We take note of We back	We will ask our ministers Among ourselves In our individual and collective capacities

Appendix 3E: The distribution of references on priority issues

Sphere/mode	Against		In alliance		Through		Without		Total
	No.	% of total	No.	% of total	No.	% of total	No.	% of total	No.
Development	27	4	232	38	332	54	23	4	614
Security	40	6	196	29	375	55	68	10	679
Energy	17	8	51	24	128	61	15	7	211
Health	5	3	94	47	91	46	10	5	200
Education	2	2	19	21	64	72	4	4	89
ICT	11	33	4	12	18	55	0	0	33
Innovations	3	13	10	42	10	42	1	4	24
Other	10	4	56	24	152	66	13	6	231

Appendix 3F: The distribution of references across issues

	Total no. of MOs mentions	No. of MOs mentions				% of MOs mentions			
		Against	In alliance	Through	Without	Against	In alliance	Through	Without
1998	93	6	17	50	20	6	18	54	22
1999	93	5	32	45	11	5	34	48	12
2000	153	9	34	98	12	6	22	64	8
2001	119	10	36	70	3	8	30	59	3
2002	128	13	52	58	5	10	41	45	4
2003	142	14	43	78	7	10	30	55	5
2004	247	25	77	131	14	10	31	53	6
2005	321	11	128	168	14	3	40	52	4
2006	279	3	70	194	12	1	25	70	4
2007	506	19	173	278	36	4	34	55	7
Total	2,081	115	662	1170	134	6	32	56	6

Appendix 5A: G7/8 summit performance, 1975–2008

	Bayne grade	No. of commitments	Compliance score
1975	A-	14	+57.1
1976	D	07	+08.9
1977	B-	29	+08.4
1978	A	35	+36.3
1979	B+	34	+82.3
1980	1+	55	+07.6
1981	1	40	+26.6
1982	1	23	+84.0
1983	B	38	-10.9
1984	1-	31	+48.8
1985	E	24	+01.0
1986	B+	39	+58.3
1987	D	53	+93.3
1988	1-	27	-47.8
1989	B+	61	+07.8
1990	D	78	-14.0
1991	B-	53	00.0
1992	D	41	+64.0
1993	1+	29	+75.0
1994	1	53	100.0
1995	B+	78	100.0
1996	B	128	+36.0
1997	1-	145	+27.0
1998	B+	73	+45.0
1999	B+	46	+39.0
2000	B	105	+80.0
2001	B+	58	+53.0
2002	B+	187	+33.0
2003	1	206	+51.0
2004	1+	253	+55.0
2005	A-	212	+54.0
2006	N/A	317	+47.0
2007	N/A	329	+51.0
2008	N/A	296	+13.0

Note: Compliance scores are from von Furstenberg and Daniels for 1975–89 (on all economic and energy commitments), Kokotsis for 1990–5 (on four-issue sustainable development and Russian assistance areas), and the G8 Research Group for 1996–2008 (on priority commitments across all issue areas).

Appendix 5B: The G7/8 summit compliance record, 1975–2008

Summit year	Von Furstenberg and Daniels compliance scores (%)	Kokotsis compliance scores (%)	G8RG compliance scores (%)	Amalgamated compliance scores (%)
1975	57.1			57.1
1976	8.9			8.9
1977	8.4			8.4
1978	36.3			36.3
1979	82.3			82.3
1980	7.6			7.6
1981	26.6			26.6
1982	84.0			84.0
1983	-10.9			-10.9
1984	48.8			48.8
1985	1.0			1.0
1986	58.3			58.3
1987	93.3			93.3
1988	-47.8			-47.8
1989	7.8	-50.0		-50.0
1990		-14.0		-14.0
1991		0.0		0.0
1992		64.0		64.0
1993		75.0		75.0
1994		100.0		100.0
1995		100.0		100.0
1996			36.0	36.0
1997			13.0	13.0
1998			45.0	45.0
1999			39.0	39.0
2000			80.0	80.0
2001			53.0	53.0
2002			33.0	33.0
2003			51.0	51.0
2004			55.0	55.0
2005			65.0	65.0
2006			47.0	47.0
2007			51.0	51.0
2008			48.0[a]	48.0
Average	30.8	39.3	47.4	39.6

Notes: The above table contains compliance scores from three separate data sets:

1. First and Second Summit Cycles (1975–81, 1982–88): G. von Furstenberg and J. Daniels (1991), "Policy Undertakings by the Seven 'Summit' Countries: Ascertaining the Degree of Compliance," *Carnegie-Rochester Conference Series of Public Policy* 35: 267–308.
2. Third Summit Cycle (1989–95): E. Kokotsis (1999), *Keeping International Commitments: Compliance Credibility and the G7, 1988–1995* (New York: Garland), Appendix.
3. Fourth and Fifth Summit Cycles (1996–2002, 2003–): G8 Research Group. All information is available online at <http://www.g8.utoronto.ca/compliance>.

Appendix 5C: Compliance with G7/8 commitments by country, 1996–2008

	1996	1997	1998	1999	2000	2001	2002 (interim) final	2003 (interim) final	2004 (interim) final	2005 (interim) final	2006 (interim) final	2007 (interim) final	2008 (interim) final
France	+0.26	0.00	+0.25	+0.34	+0.92	+0.69	(+0.38) +0.64	(+0.50) +0.75	(+0.39) +0.50	(+0.48) +0.57	(+0.25) +0.40	(+0.17) +0.52	(-0.05) +0.20
US	+0.42	+0.33	+0.60	+0.50	+0.67	+0.35	(+0.25) +0.36	(+0.50) +0.50	(+0.44) +0.72	(+0.71) +0.81	(+0.35) +0.60	(+0.78) +0.91	(+0.45) +0.80
UK	+0.42	+0.50	+0.75	+0.50	+1.00	+0.69	(+0.42) +0.55	(+0.58) +0.50	(+0.50) +0.67	(+0.67) +0.95	(+0.55) +0.60	(+0.61) +0.70	(+0.45) +0.80
Germany	+0.58	+0.17	+0.25	+0.17	+1.00	+0.59	(+0.08) +0.18	(+0.42) +0.50	(+0.50) +0.67	(+0.33) +0.88	(+0.45) +0.55	(+0.48) +0.57	(+0.40) +0.60
Japan	+0.21	+0.33	+0.20	+0.67	+0.82	+0.44	(+0.10) +0.18	(+0.42) +0.42	(+0.33) +0.39	(+0.52) +0.52	(+0.25) +0.40	(+0.04) +0.30	(-0.10) +0.35
Italy	+0.16	-0.50	+0.67	+0.34	+0.89	+0.57	(0.00) -0.11	(+0.38) +0.25	(+0.39) +0.44	(+0.43) +0.29	(-0.05) +0.05	(+0.13) +0.17	(-0.20) +0.10
Canada	+0.47	+0.17	+0.50	+0.67	+0.83	+0.82	(+0.77) +0.82	(+0.58) +0.83	(+0.50) +0.72	(+0.52) +0.81	(+0.40) +0.60	(+0.22) +0.65	(+0.25) +0.75
Russia	N/A	0.00	+0.34	+0.17	+0.14	+0.11	(+0.14) 0.00	(+0.42) +0.33	(0.00) +0.06	(-0.14) +0.14	(+0.25) +0.45	(+0.17) +0.30	(+0.05) +0.25
EU	N/A	N/A	N/A	+0.17	N/A	N/A	N/A	N/A	(+0.44) +0.72	(+0.75) +0.89	(+0.53) +0.58	(+0.39) +0.48	(+0.20) +0.55
Average	+0.36	+0.13	+0.45	+0.39	+0.80	+0.53	(+0.27) +0.33	(+0.47) +0.51	(+0.39) +0.55	(+0.47) +0.65	(+0.33) +0.47	(+0.33) +0.51	(+0.16) 0.58

Source: G8 Research Group, Annual Compliance Studies, available at <http://www.g8.utoronto.ca/compliance/>.

Appendix 5D: G7 compliance, 1975–89

By issue	**Score**
International trade	0.734
Energy	0.660
Real GNP growth	0.397
Inflation multi-country	0.266
Aid and schedules	0.265
Fiscal adjustment	0.259
Demand composition	0.233
Interest rate	0.221
Inflation rate	0.221
Foreign exchange rate	-0.700
By country	
United Kingdom	0.413
Canada	0.409
Germany	0.346
Italy	0.274
Japan	0.262
United States	0.246
France	0.240

Source: Von Furstenberg, G. and Daniels, J. (1992), *Economic Summit Declarations, 1975-1989: Examining the Written Record of International Co-operation*, Princeton Studies in International Finance 72, Princeton, N.J., Department of Economics.

Appendix 5E: Compliance with G7/8 commitments overall and by issue area, 1996–2008

Issue area	1996	1997	1998	1999	2000	2001	2002 (interim) final	2003 (interim) final	2004 (interim) final	2005 (interim) final	2006 (interim) final	2007 (interim) final	2008 (interim) final
Total (average *n*)	+36.1 (19)	+12.8 (6)	+31.8 (6)	+43.5 (6)	+80.8 (12)	+45.9 (9)	(+29.8) +35.8 (13)	(+47.1) +51.0 (12)	(+40.0) +55.0 (18)	(+47.3) +65.0 (21)	(+33.0) +47.0 (20)	(+0.33) +0.51 (23)	(+0.13) +0.48 (20)
Economic issues													
World economy	—	—	—	—	+0.86	—	—	(+0.13) 0.25	(+0.33) +0.22	—			(+0.67) +1.00
IFI reform	+0.29	—	—	—	—	-1.00	—	—	—	—			
Exchange rates	—	—	—	0.00	—	—	—	—	—	—			
Macroeconomics	+1.00	—	—	+1.00	—	—	—	—	—	—			
Microeconomics	+0.29	—	—	—	—	—	—	—	—	—			
Employment	—	+0.38	0.00	—	—	—	—	—	—	—			
Raw materials												(+0.22) +0.11	
Corruption												(+0.22) (+0.33)	(+0.67) +0.67
Aging	—	—	+0.33	—	+0.86	—	—	—	—	—			
ICT/IPR	+0.57	—	—	—	+1.00	+0.75	—	(+1.00) +0.75	—	—	(+0.13) +0.13	(+0.22) +0.33	(+0.56) +0.78
Trade	+0.29	—	+0.33	-0.25	+1.00	+0.88	(+0.14) -0.13	(-0.25) -0.38	(+0.22) +0.56	(+0.11) 0.00	(+0.22) +0.11	(+0.33) +0.67	
Africa: trade										(+0.67) +0.33			(+0.11) +0.33
LDC: trade										(+0.33) +0.44			

Issue area	1996	1997	1998	1999	2000	2001	2002 (interim) final	2003 (interim) final	2004 (interim) final	2005 (interim) final	2006 (interim) final	2007 (interim) final	2008 (interim) final
Agricultural trade	—	—	—	—	—	—	(0.00) +0.13	—	—	—			
Trade Doha	—	—	—	—	—	—	—	—	(+1.00) +0.88	—			
Development (general/ODA)	0.00	0.00	—	—	—	0.00	(+0.50) +0.50	(+0.88) +0.88	(-1.00) -1.00	(+0.22) +0.22		(+0.44) +0.44	(-0.67) +0.44
Debt/HIPC	—	—	0.00	+0.86	—	+1.00	(-0.50) +0.25	(0.00) +0.38	(+1.00) +1.00	(0.00) +1.00	(+0.33) +0.89	(+0.22) +0.33	
Africa: growth										(+0.22) +0.56		(0.00) +0.33	
Education	—	—	—	—	—	+0.58	(N/A) +0.63	—	—	(+0.56) +0.33	(+0.15) +0.33	(+0.11) +0.44	(-0.22) +0.11
Global transnational issues													
Energy	—	—	—	—	—	—	—	(0.00) +0.75	(+0.89) +0.78	(+1.00) +1.00	(+0.67) +0.74	(+0.56) +0.70	(+0.48) +0.94
Environment	+0.14	+0.50	+1.00	—	—	+0.17	(0.00) +0.57	(+0.38) +0.50	(0.00) +1.00	(+1.00) +0.89	(+0.56) +0.78	(+1.00) +1.00	(+0.45) +0.64
Water	—	—	—	—	—	—	(+0.50) +0.57	—	—	—			
Tsunami										+0.67 (+1.00)			
Biotech	—	—	—	—	+0.75	—	—	—	—	—			
Human genome	—	—	—	—	+0.80	—	—	—	—	—			
Health (general)	—	—	—	—	+1.00	+0.75	(+0.25) N/A	—	—	—		(+0.56) +0.67	(0.00) +0.78
Global Fund	—	—	—	—	—	—	—	—	—	—	(+0.11) +0.56	(+0.44) +0.67	
TB	—	—	—	—	—	—	—	—	—	—	(0.00) +0.22		

Appendix 5E (continued)

Issue area	1996	1997	1998	1999	2000	2001	2002 (interim) final	2003 (interim) final	2004 (interim) final	2005 (interim) final	2006 (interim) final	2007 (interim) final	2008 (interim) final
HIV/AIDS	—	—	—	—	—	—	—	(+0.88) +0.88	(+0.33) +0.56	(+0.22) +0.33		(+0.22) +0.33	
Tropical diseases	—	—	—	—	—	—	—	—	—	—	—	—	(-0.89) -0.33
Polio	—	—	—	—	—	—	—	—	(0.00) +0.44	(+0.44) +0.11	(+0.44) +0.44		
Cultural diversity	—	—	—	—	+0.63	—	—	—	—	—			
Nuclear safety	+0.29	—	—	—	—	—	—	—	—	—			
Crime and drugs	+0.43	0.00	+0.25	0.00	+0.88	—	(+0.25) +0.25	—	(0.00) +0.11	(+0.11) +1.00	(0.00) 0.00		
Terrorist financing	—	—	—	—	—	—	—	(+0.25) -0.50	(-0.11) +0.44	—		(+0.67) +0.78	
Political/security issues													
East/West relations	+0.86	—	—	—	—	—	—	—	—	—			
Terrorism	+0.71	—	—	+1.00	+0.40	+1.00	(+1.00) +1.00	(+1.00) +1.00	—	(+0.89) +1.00	(+0.11) +0.56		(-0.78) -0.22
Arms control	+0.29	—	—	—	+0.88	—	(+0.63) +0.25	—	—	—			
Landmines	+0.71	+0.75	—	—	—	—	—	—	—	—			
Human rights	+0.71	—	—	—	—	—	—	—	—	—			
Transport security	—	—	—	—	—	—	—	(+0.38) +0.63	(+0.11) 0.00	(+0.56) +0.67	(+0.22) +0.44	(+0.22) +0.22	
WMD	—	—	—	—	—	—	—	(+1.00) +1.00	(+0.78) +0.78	(+0.44) +1.00	(+0.78) +0.56	(0.00) +0.30	(0.00) +0.33
Regional security													
Asia	-0.43	—	—	—	—	—	—	—	—	—			
Europe	+0.86	—	—	—	—	—	—	—	—	—			

Issue area	1996	1997	1998	1999	2000	2001	2002 (interim) final	2003 (interim) final	2004 (interim) final	2005 (interim) final	2006 (interim) final	2007 (interim) final	2008 (interim) final
Middle East	-0.43	—	—	—	—	—	—	—	(+1.00) +1.00	(+1.00) +1.00	(+1.00) +1.00		(-0.22) 0.00
Iraq	—	—	—	—	—	—	—	—	(0.78) +0.89	(+0.25) +0.88			
Russia	—	-0.86	—	—	—	—	—	—	—	—			
Conflict prevention	—	—	—	—	+0.63	—	(+0.60) +0.38	—	(+0.78) +0.89	(+0.89) +0.89			
Food security	—	—	—	—	—	—	—	—	(+0.67) +0.67	—			(0.00) +0.44
Peace-building/ keeping	—	—	—	—	—	—	—	—	(+0.44) +0.67	(+0.44) +0.67		(+0.11) +0.44	(+0.22) +0.67
UN reform I ($)	+0.14	—	—	—	—	—	—	—	—	—			
UN reform II (development agenda)	+0.14	—	—	—	—	—	—	—	—	—	(0.00) 0.00		
Good government (Africa)	—	—	—	—	—	—	(+0.50) +0.25	—	—	(—0.11) +0.25	(+0.22) +0.44	(+0.78) +0.78	
Peer review (Africa)	—	—	—	—	—	—	(0.00) 0.00	—	—	—			
Other													
Heiligendamm process	—	—	—	—	—	—	—	—	—	—	—	(+0.22) +1.00	

Source: G8 Research Group, Annual Compliance Studies, available at <http://www.g8.utotonto.ca/compliance/>.

Appendix 5F: Finance scores, 1996–2004: Compliance-generating precursors and commitments coding, $n = 42$

Commitment	Issue area	Issue	Priority placement	Target	Timetable	Remit mandate	Money	Agent	G8-centered body	International institution	Total	Score
1996	Macroeconomics	Macroeconomics	I								1	+1.00
1996	Microeconomics	Microeconomics	1								1	+0.29
1996	Development	ODA									0	0.00
1996	IFI reform	UNCTAD	I							1	2	+0.29
1996	UN reform I	$ obligations	I							1	2	+0.14
1996	UN reform II	Development agenda						1		1	2	+0.14
1997	Development	Africa	1					1			2	0.00
1997	Microeconomics	Employment									0	+0.38
1998	Debt	HIPC						1		1	2	0.00
1998	Microeconomics	Employment	1							1	2	0.00
1999	Debt	HIPC		1				1			2	+0.86
1999	Macroeconomics	Macroeconomics									0	+1.00
1999	Exchange rate	Exchange rate									0	0.00
1999	Crime & drugs	FATF							1		1	0.00
2000	Debt	HIPC						1	1		2	0.00
2000	Debt	Decision points		1	1			1	1		4	-1.00
2000	Debt	HIPC									0	0.00
2001	IFI reform	IFI reform						1	1		2	-1.00

Commitment	Issue area	Issue	Priority placement	Target	Timetable	Remit mandate	Money	Agent	G8-centered body	International institution	Total	Score
2001	Debt	HIPC		1							1	+1.00
2001	Health	Global Fund			1		1		1	1	4	+0.75
2001	Terrorism	Terrorism						1			1	+1.00
2001	Environment	GEF							1		2	-0.13
2002	Africa	ODA	1	1							2	+0.50
2002	Health	Polio	1	1	1						3	0.00
2002	Economic growth	Agricultural trade	1								1	+0.13
2002	Debt	HIPC	1				1		1		3	+0.25
2003	World economy	World Economy	1								1	+0.25
2003	Health	Global Fund	1		1			1	1		4	+0.88
2003	Health	Polio	1	1	1						3	+1.00
2003	Development	ODA	1		1			1	1		4	+0.88
2003	Debt	HIPC	1		1			1			3	+0.38
2003	Crime & drugs	Finance	1							1	2	-0.50
2003	Terrorism	Finance	1		1				1	1	4	+1.00
2004	Development	Doha	1		1			1			3	+1.00
2004	Development	Private entrepreneur						1	1		2	-1.00
2004	Africa	Darfur	1								1	+0.88

Appendix 5F (continued)

Commitment	Issue area	Issue	Priority placement	Target	Timetable	Remit mandate	Money	Agent	G8-centered body	International institution	Total	Score
2004	Health	Polio	1		1			1			3	+0.44
2004	Crime & drugs	Finance			1			1	1		3	+0.11
2004	Crime & drugs	Finance	1					1		1	3	+0.44
2004	Debt	HIPC	1	1	1			1	1		5	+1.00
2004	Africa	Famine and food security	1					1			2	+0.67
2004	World economy	World economy	1								1	+0.22
Total			25/42	07/42	12/42	00/42	02/42	18/42	13/42	09/42	86	
Average			60%	17%	29%	00%	05%	43%	31%	21%	02	

Notes: Definition: Finance as an issue area within the G8 includes all commitments with references to international financial institutions, development, economic growth, official development aid, debt relief and heavily indebted poor countries, any time money is committed, and any time finance, or finance ministers are mentioned. Finance does not include trade, but does include the above aspects of trade, such as trade for development or trade for economic growth.

Appendix 5G: The Integrated Model of Agency, Institutionalization and Structure

Agency: Compliance Catalysts

1. priority placement
2. target
3. timetable
4. remit mandate
5. money mobilized
6. agent
7. G8 body
8. international institution

Institutionalization

1. presence of G7-centered ministerial bodies, e.g., (G5?) G7/8 finance ministers, G20, number by year finance ministers
2. meetings of the G7/8 finance ministers, annual total of meetings, frequency.
3. outside participation in G7-centered finance ministerial bodies
4. presence of G7/8-centered official-level bodies, e.g., FATF
5. recommitment by G7/8 finance ministers in the calendar year summit took place
6. pre-commitment by G7/8 finance ministers in the 12 months prior to the summit
7. reaffirmation by G7/8 finance ministers in the 12 months after the summit

Structure

Vulnerabilities

1. percentage change in price of Brent Crude Oil barrel (London)
2. percentage change in price of gold (London)
3. percentage change in global stock markets index
4. average annual change in G7 economic confidence indicators

Capabilities

5. average G7 real GDP growth
6. US real GDP growth minus average G7 GDP growth
7. average appreciation of US$ versus other G7 currencies

Appendix 12A: Pattern of G8 education performance (includes core and related agenda)

	G8RG score	Bayne score	Deliberative	Directional	Decisional: total commitment	Decisional: money	Delivery	Developmental global governance
1975	—	A-	—	—	—	—	—	—
1976	—	D	—	—	—	—	—	—
1977	—	B-	1	—	1	—	—	—
1978	—	A	1	—	1	—	—	—
1979	—	B+	—	—	—	—	—	—
1980	—	1+	—	—	—	—	—	—
1981	—	1	—	—	—	—	—	—
1982	—	1	—	—	—	—	—	1
1983	—	B	1	—	3	—	—	—
1984	—	1-	2	—	1	—	—	—
1985	—	E	2	—	2	—	—	—
1986	—	B+	1	—	—	—	—	—
1987	—	D	2	—	—	—	—	—
1988	—	1-	4	—	1	—	—	—
1989	—	B+	1	—	2	—	—	—
1990	—	D	3	—	3	—	—	—
1991	—	B-	3	—	2	—	—	—
1992	—	D	1	—	—	—	—	—
1993	—	1+	2	—	1	—	—	—
1994	—	1	2	—	1	—	—	—
1995	—	B+	1	—	1	—	—	—
1996	—	B	3	—	1	—	+1.00	—
1997	B	1-	6	—	1	—	+0.38	—

1998	1	B+	1	—	2	—	—	—
1999	B-	B+	35	—	—	—	—	—
2000	A/A-	B	28	1	5	—	+1.00	1
2001	A/A-/D+	B	9	—	10	—	+0.67	1
2002	—	B+	97	2	21	—	+0.57	—
2003	—	1	15	1	7	—	—	—
2004	B+	1+	52	2	28	—	—	1
2005	—	A-	28	1	11	—	+0.33	—
2006	B	—	63	8	50	—	+0.33	1
2007	B-	—	9	1	9	—	+0.39	—
2008	A+	—	11	2	14	$1bn	-0.11	—

Notes: Deliberative = number of paragraphs in G8 summit documents related to education (core and related).
Directional = number of paragraphs in communiqué chapeau or chair's summary related to education.

Appendix 12B: G8 research group education performance assessments, 1997–2008

	Issue	Grade
1997	Reaffirm 1994 OECD job strategy	B
1997	Global information society	1
1998	Employability	A-
1999	Education and human capital	B-
2000	Information technology	A-
2000	Education	A
2001	DOT Force	A
2001	Africa Action Plan	A-
2001	Universal primary education	D+
2004	Broader Middle East Initiative	B+
2006	Education	B
2007	Development	B-
2008	Africa and education	A+

Source: G8 Research Group <http://www.g8.utoronto.ca/compliance/>.

Appendix 12C: The G7/8 core education agenda

	Total paragraphs	Total education paragraphs	% education	EFS	HLE	DOK	IIP	CC	DF	TX	DRE	AFE	PFE	HE
1975	15	0	0											
1976	25	0	0											
1977	49	0	0											
1978	51	0	0											
1979	38	0	0											
1980	54	0	0											
1981	52	0	0											
1982	20	0	0											
1983	22	0	0											
1984	59	0	0											
1985	46	0	0											
1986	45	1	2	1										
1987	103	1	1		1									
1988	69	0	0											
1989	122	0	0											
1990	124	1	1			1								
1991	172	0	0											
1992	143	0	0											
1993	77	0	0											
1994	92	1	1				1							

Appendix 12C (continued)

	Total paragraphs	Total education paragraphs	% education	EFS	HLE	DOK	IIP	CC	DF	TX	DRE	AFE	PFE	HE
1995	222	0	0											
1996	296	1	<1				1							
1997	147	0	0											
1998	129	0	0											
1999	169	32	19	1				29		1				
2000	213	2	1						2					
2001	108	3	3						2		1			
2002	211	87	41	1					78[a]	2	1	1	2	2
2003	427	8	2						2			6		
2004	672	21	3	4					9	7			1	
2005	236	16	7	2			1		6			7		
2006	224	44	20	21	1	4		1	8	1		1	1	6
2007	307	6	2	2					3			1	0	
2008	137	4	3	2					2					

Notes: [a] Introduction of the G8 Education Task Force to operationalize education for all in the G8 Africa Action Plan and A New Focus on Education For All.

EFS: education for itself, for the future, society, etc.; HLE: conference of high-level experts on education; DOK: diffusion of knowledge; IIP: investment in people; CC: Cologne Charter; DF: Dakar Framework (universal primary education), Education For All, includes education for girls and women; TX: teacher exchanges, teacher training (includes providing teachers with better resources, textbooks, etc.); DRE: debt relief for education; AFE: aid for education; PFE: programs for increased enrolment, meet broad community needs for education; HE: higher education.

The year 1999 marks the introduction of the Cologne Charter on lifelong learning, which has its own 28-paragraph document.

Appendix 12D: The G7/8 education-related agenda

	Total paragraphs	Total education paragraphs	% education	TYP	EAIDS	TIP	TFM	EFD	EFE	EFD	TFS	GIS	TFP
1975	15	0	0										
1976	25	0	0										
1977	49	1	2	1									
1978	51	1	2	1									
1979	38	0	0										
1980	54	0	0										
1981	52	0	0										
1982	20	0	0										
1983	22	1	5	1									
1984	59	2	3	2									
1985	46	2	4	2									
1986	45	0	0										
1987	103	1	1		1								
1988	69	4	6	1		3							
1989	122	1	1	1									
1990	124	2	2	1			1						
1991	172	3	2			1		2					
1992	143	1	1			1							
1993	77	2	3			2							
1994	92	1	1					1					

Appendix 12D (continued)

	Total paragraphs	Total education paragraphs	% education	TYP	EAIDS	TIP	TFM	EFD	EFE	EFD	TFS	GIS	TFP
1995	222	1	<1	1									
1996	296	2	1					2					
1997	147	6	4	1		1	1		1	1	1		
1998	129	1	1	1									
1999	169	2	1	2									
2000	213	26	12	1				4				21[b]	
2001	108	6	6			1	1			3		1	
2002	211	10	5							1		8	1
2003	427	7	16			1	1				5		
2004	672	31	5	8		2	3			7	8	2	1
2005	236	12	5	2		1				4	2	2	1
2006	224	19	8	4	3	1		1			8	1	1
2007	307	3	1	1	2								
2008	137	7	5		2		2		2				1

Notes: [a] If the section says "education for increased employment and growth," it will be categorized as TIP.

[b] The year 2000 marks the release of a 19-paragraph document on GIS.

TYP: training for employment/flexibility of labor (includes life-long learning, active aging); EAIDS: education to prevent AIDS; health education; TIP: training for increased productivity, economic growth/reform; TFM: training for management (including management of biotechnology, agriculture, etc.); EFD: education for development; EFE: education for the environment; EFD: education for drug-use prevention; TFS: training for skills (law enforcement, seafarers, judges, journalists, doctors, etc.); GIS: Global Information Society (includes DOT Force); TFP: training for peacekeeping.

Appendix 12E: G7/8 education commitments

	Overall	Education (core)	Education (related)	Ratio (education/overall)	Follow/support MO	Lead MO	Independent of MO
					For core commitments only		
1975	14	0	0	—	—	—	—
1976	7	0	0	—	—	—	—
1977	29	0	1	3%	—	—	—
1978	35	0	1	—	—	—	—
1979	34	0	0	—	—	—	—
1980	55	0	0	—	—	—	—
1981	40	0	0	—	—	—	—
1982	65	0	0	—	—	—	—
1983	38	0	3	8%	—	—	—
1984	31	0	1	3%	—	—	—
1985	24	0	2	8%	—	—	—
1986	39	0	0	—	—	—	—
1987	54	0	0	—	—	—	—
1988	27	0	1	4%	—	—	—
1989	61	0	2	3%	—	—	—
1990	78	1	2	4%	—	—	1
1991	53	0	2	4%	—	—	—
1992	40	0	0	—	—	—	—
1993	29	0	1	3%	—	—	—
1994	53	0	1	2%	—	—	—
1995	76	0	1	1%	—	—	—
1996	128	0	1	1%	—	—	—
1997	111	0	1	1%	—	—	—

Appendix 12E (continued)

	Overall	Education (core)	Education (related)	Ratio (education/overall)	Follow/support MO	Lead MO	Independent of MO
1998	73	0	2	3%	—	—	—
1999	46	0	0	—	—	—	—
2000	163	1	4	3%	1	—	—
2001	58	6	4	17%	3	1	2
2002	188	12	9	11%	3	2	7
2003	206	0	7	3%	—	—	—
2004	265	8	20	11%	—	2	6
2005	212	5	6	5%	—	1	4
2006	317	39	11	16%	—	—	—
2007	329	6	3	3%	—	—	—
2008	296	9	5	5%	3	0	0
Totals	2,120	33	70	5% (average)	10	6	20

Notes: Follow/support multilateral orgaization (MO): The initiative is in collaboration with another MO which has acted as the instigator; lead MO: The initiative is in collaboration with another MO and instigated by the G8, or the initiative is in the form of instructions to another MO. Independent of MO: There is no mention in the initiative of involvement of another MO.

Appendix 12F: G8 education compliance by country and issue area

Issue	Average	US	Japan	Germany	UK	France	Italy	Canada	Russia	EU
	+100	+100	N/A	+100	+100	+100	N/A	+100	N/A	N/A
Global information society	+1.00	+1	N/A	+1	+1	+1	N/A	+1	N/A	N/A
	+38	+100	+100	00	+100	00	00	+100	-100	N/A
Employment	+0.38	+1	+1	0	+1	0	0	+1	-1	N/A
	+100	+100	+100	+100	+100	+100	+100	+100	+100	N/A
Digital divide/DOT Force	+1.00	+1	+1	+1	+1	+1	+1	+1	+1	N/A
	+67	+50	+100	+50	+100	+100	+50	+100	-100	N/A
Universal primary education/ Education for All	+0.58	0	+1	0	+1	+1	0	+1	N/A	N/A
Digital divide/DOT Force	+0.75	+1	+1	+1	+1	+1	+1	+1	-1	N/A
	+57	+100	+100	00	+100	+100	N/A	+100	-100	N/A
Universal primary education/ Education for All	+0.57	+1	+1	0	+1	+1	N/A	+1	-1	N/A
	+33	0	0	+100	+100	+100	0	0	0	0
Universal primary education/ Education for All	+0.33	0	0	+1	+1	+1	0	0	0	0
	+33	+33	00	+67	+33	+67	-33	+33	+33	+67
Academic mobility	+0.44	0	0	+1	0	+1	0	0	+1	+1
Qualification systems	+0.33	0	0	+1	0	0	0	0	0	+1
Gender disparities	+0.22	+1	0	0	+1	+1	-1	+1	0	0
	+39	+100	0	0	+100	+100	-50	+50	-50	+100
Education for All	+0.44	+1	0	0	+1	+1	0	0	0	+1
S&R education	+0.33	+1	0	0	+1	+1	-1	+1	-1	+1

Appendix 12F (continued)

Issue	Average	US	Japan	Germany	UK	France	Italy	Canada	Russia	EU
	-22	-100	0	0	+100	0	-100	-100	0	0
Education	-0.22	-1	0	0	+1	0	-1	-1	0	0
	+53% (97)	+67% (12)	+45% (11)	+50% (12)	+83% (12)	+83% (12)	00% (10)	+67% (12)	-20% (10)	+67% (6)

Notes: The 1996 and 2002 scores are different from those in the G8 Research Group's online report, due to mathematical errors. Education encompasses all levels of public and private instruction, from primary through university into lifelong learning. It includes technical, vocational and professional training and mobility, the employment and labor market, productivity, innovation and competitiveness in the new knowledge economy, and the governance of cyberspace. It further embraces social and political subjects, such as gender equality in education, education to prevent the spread of disease, education as an MDG, access to education in developing countries, literacy and free information flows.

Appendix 12G: G7/8- centered education institutions

Working Group on Technology, Growth and Employment (1982–86)

The Working Group on Technology, Growth and Employment was launched at the 1982 summit to work with international institutions, particularly the OECD, to develop programs to create the appropriate economic, social and cultural conditions where technology will develop and flourish. The working group's final report was commented on at the 1986 summit.

Digital Opportunities Task Force (DOT Force) (2000–01)

The DOT Force was established in 2000 to recommend global action to bridge the international information and knowledge divide. It released its report in 2001.

G8 Task Force on Education (2001–02)

The 2001 Genoa Communiqué noted: "We will establish a task force of senior G8 officials to advise us on how best to pursue the Dakar goals in co-operation with developing countries, relevant international organisations and other stakeholders. The task force will provide us with recommendations in time for our next meeting" (Genoa, 22 July, 2001, Communiqué). In 2002, the task force released its document *A New Focus on Education For All*, which also incorporated opinions from individuals and organizations.

G8 Expert Group to Develop Criteria and Procedures for Evaluating Educational Outcomes and Qualifications (2006)

The 2006 Chair's Summary noted: "We underlined the need to increase exchanges in science and technology and other areas of education at all levels and promote better understanding, recognition and transparency of foreign qualifications and educational outcomes. In this connection, Russia proposed the establishment of an expert group to develop criteria and procedures for evaluating educational outcomes and qualifications. The group could include representatives of state organizations, business and civil society."

Appendix 14A: G8 Summit health commitments by issue, 1975–2008

	Total	Health and safety	Research	Development	HIV/AIDS	Medicine	Narcotics	Children	Diseases	WHO	Aging	Malaria	Multiple disease	Tuberculosis	General health	Awareness	Partnership	Strategy	Biotech
1980	1	1																	
1981	1	1																	
1983	1		1																
1991	1			1															
1996	6		1	1	1	1	2												
1997	7			1	2			1	1	1	1								
1998	4				2					1		1							
1999	3				1								2						
2000	15		1		2	2					1	1	2	1	1	1	1	1	1
2001	5			1									1						
2002	19		1		5	1		1					1				1		
2003	16		2		1	4			1	1	1		1						
2004	10				4														
2005	13				2							1	1	1	1				1
2006	61		2		8	2			7	1		5	6	1					1
2007	43		2		10	4		1	1	1		4	1				1		
2008	19				1			2	2			1	1		3			2	
Total	225	2	10	4	39	14		5	12	5	3	13	16	3	5	1	3	3	3

	Global Fund	Intellectual property	Polio	Technology	Workers	Mother–infant	Services	SARS	Education	Health systems	Avian influenza	Natural disasters	Information exchange	Financial institutions	Anti-retrovirals	Measles	Funds	Public health	Management	Reproductive	Tropical diseases
1980																					
1981																					
1983																					
1991																					
1996																					
1997																					
1998																					
1999																					
2000																					
2001	2	1																			
2002	2		2	2	1	1	1														
2003	3		1					1													
2004			5						1												
2005	1		1		2				1	1											
2006	2	1	3		1				2	1	8	3	2	1	1	3					
2007	2		1	1	2	2			2	2							4	1	1		
2008			1		2					2										1	1
Total	12	2	14	3	6	3	1	1	6	6	8	3	2	1	1	3	4	1	1	1	1

Note: No health commitments were made at the G8 leaders' level in the years that do not appear here.

Appendix 14B: G8 Summit commitments by issue area, 1975–2008

	Total	Subtotal	Finance	Trade	Development (includes MDGs)	Climate change	Human rights	Foreign policy/ political security	Health
1975	14	7	4	2	1				
1976	7	5		1	3			1	
1977	29	21	4	8	9				
1978	35	10		4	3			3	
1979	34	12		3	6			3	
1980	55	29	5	6	6			11	1
1981	40	30		6	10		1	12	1
1982	23	19	6	7	3			3	
1983	38	29	8	6	9			5	1
1984	31	24	1		17			6	
1985	24	4	1		3				
1986	39	40	4	4	8			24	
1987	53	40	8	8	4	1		19	
1988	27	23	1	6	5			11	
1989	61	52	1	6	4	4	3	34	
1990	78	61		10	15	7		29	
1991	53	38		9	3	5		20	1
1992	41	35	1		4	7		23	
1993	29	27		3	6	4		14	
1994	53	35		5	5	4		21	
1995	78	63	7	10	16	7	2	21	
1996	128	103	9	12	23	3	5	45	6
1997	145	117	10		18	9	6	67	7
1998	73	53	1	6	11	7	1	23	4
1999	46	42		5	19	4		11	3
2000	105	84	6	6	23	2		32	15
2001	58	42	3	2	20	4		8	5
2002	187	158		1	43	1	12	82	19
2003	206	113	2	9	14	4		68	16
2004	253	224		6	91	3	9	105	10
2005	212	142		3	25	27		74	13
2006	317	189		7	6	20	13	82	61
2007	329	256		3	48	44	4	114	43
2008	296	194	7	12	27	54	3	72	19
Total	3,197	2,321	89	176	508	221	59	1,043	225

Notes: The foreign policy/political security issue area comprises of commitments relating to terrorism, East–West relations, crime and drugs, non-proliferation, regional security, conflict prevention, peace support, and democratization/good governance.
The development issue area includes Millennium Development Goals.

Appendix 14C: G8 system ministerial health commitments, 1975–2008

	G8 summit	Finance	Foreign affairs	Trade	Environment	Development	G20	Total
1975	0	0	0	0	0	0	0	0
1976	0	0	0	0	0	0	0	0
1977	0	0	0	0	0	0	0	0
1978	0	0	0	0	0	0	0	0
1979	0	0	0	0	0	0	0	0
1980	1	0	0	0	0	0	0	1
1981	1	0	0	0	0	0	0	1
1982	0	0	0	0	0	0	0	0
1983	1	0	0	0	0	0	0	1
1984	0	0	0	0	0	0	0	0
1985	0	0	0	0	0	0	0	0
1986	0	0	0	0	0	0	0	0
1987	0	0	0	0	0	0	0	0
1988	0	0	0	0	0	0	0	0
1989	0	0	0	0	0	0	0	0
1990	0	0	0	0	0	0	0	0
1991	1	0	0	0	0	0	0	1
1992	0	0	0	0	0	0	0	0
1993	0	1	0	0	0	0	0	1
1994	0	0	0	0	1	0	0	1
1995	0	0	0	0	0	0	0	0
1996	6	0	0	0	1	0	0	7
1997	7	0	0	0	24	0	0	31
1998	4	0	0	0	1	0	0	5
1999	3	0	5	0	2	0	0	11
2000	15	4	1	0	3	0	1	24
2001	5	4	0	0	9	0	0	18
2002	19	0	0	0	4	1	0	24
2003	16	2	0	0	3	3	0	24
2004	10	1	0	0	0	0	0	11
2005	13	7	0	0	0	0	0	20
2006	61	4	0	0	0	0	0	65
2007	43	0	0	0	0	5	0	48
2008	19	0	0	0	1	2	0	22
Total	**225**	**23**	**6**	**0**	**49**	**11**	**1**	**293**

Notes: Numbers indicate the health commitments that were made in G7/8 statements. G8 Summit: based on commitments determined by the G8 Research Group, University of Toronto. Finance: based on commitments made in documents issued at G7/8 Finance Ministers' meetings. Foreign Affairs: based on commitments made in documents issued at G7/8 foreign affairs ministers' meetings. Trade: based on commitments made in documents issued at trade ministers' quadrilateral meetings. Environment: based on commitments made in documents issued at G7/8 environment ministers' meetings. Development: based on commitments made in documents issued at G7/8 development ministers' meetings. G20: based on commitments determined by the G8 Research Group, University of Toronto.

Source: G8 Research Group, G7/8 Ministerial Meetings and Documents, available at <http://www.g8.utoronto.ca/meetings.html>.

Appendix 14D: APEC leaders' health commitments by issue

	Total	HIV/ AIDS	Diseases	Strategy	Services	SARS	Avian influenza	Information exchange	Pandemics	Health & safety
2000	1	1								
2001	1				1					
2002	4		3		1					
2003	4		3			1				
2004	2	2								
2005	6			2			3	1		
2006	4	2					2			
2007	2	1					1			
2008	2								1	1
Total	26	6	6	2	2	1	6	1	1	1

Appendix 14E: G8 summit health compliance by issue, 1975–2008

	Total	Research	Development	HIV/AIDS	Multiple disease	Aging	Malaria	Tuberculosis	Global Fund	Intellectual Property	Medicine	Children	General diseases	Polio	Mother–infant	Workers	SARS	Education	Tropical disease
1983	100(1)	100(1)																	
1997	50(2)		00(1)	100(1)															
1998	22(2)			22(2)															
1999	32(2)			63(1)	00(1)														
2000	82(5)			100(1)	43(1)	67(1)	100(1)	100(1)											
2001	88(2)								75(1)	100(1)									
2002	43(8)			75(2)					25(1)		38(1)	33(1)		00(1)	100(1)	00(1)			
2003	80(6)					100(1)			89(1)		13(1)		100(1)	100(1)			78(1)		
2004	50(2)			56(1)										44(1)					
2005	44(6)			100(1)	25(1)			67(1)	33(1)					11(1)		29(1)			
2006	37(5)			50(1)				22(1)	56(1)	13(1)				44(1)					
2007	73(5)			100 (2)					67(1)							67(1)		33(1)	
2008	-45(2)												00(1)						-89(1)
Total	59(46)	100(1)	00(1)	69(12)	21(3)	83(2)	100(1)	62(3)	58(6)	59(2)	25(2)	33(1)	100(1)	41(5)	100(1)	36(3)	78(1)	33(1)	—

Notes: The 2008 scores are interim results. They are not included in the overall averages or totals. Averages do not necessarily equal the totals listed in the columns or rows, as information for certain countries is unavailable for some commitments. See Appendix 14F for further information.

Appendix 14F: Compliance with Health Commitments by Issue Area, 1983–2008

Average (n = 46)	**54%**	**78%**	**46%**	**40%**	**73%**	**58%**	**25%**	**78%**	**24%**	**65%**
Commitment	**Average**	**US**	**Japan**	**Germany**	**UK**	**France**	**Italy**	**Canada**	**Russia**	**EU**
Research	100%	100%	N/A	N/A	N/A	N/A	100%	100%	N/A	N/A
1983	1.00	1	N/A	N/A	N/A	N/A	1	1	N/A	N/A
Development	0%	100%	0%	100%	100%	-100%	-100%	-100%	N/A	N/A
1997	0.00	1	0	1	1	-1	-1	-1	N/A	N/A
HIV/AIDS	69%	100%	22%	22%	80%	100%	56%	100%	-13%	100%
1997	1.00	1	N/A	N/A	1	1	N/A	1	N/A	N/A
1998	0.33	1	0	0	1	1	-1	1	-1	1
1998	0.11	1	-1	-1	1	1	-1	1	-1	1
1999	0.63	1	1	-1	1	1	1	1	0	N/A
2000	1.00	1	1	1	1	1	1	1	N/A	1
2002	1.00	1	N/A	N/A	N/A	1	N/A	1	N/A	N/A
2002	0.50	1	1	1	-1	1	1	1	-1	N/A
2004	0.56	1	-1	1	1	1	1	1	-1	1
2005	1.00	1	1	1	1	1	1	1	1	1
2006	0.50	1	-1	-1	1	1	1	1	1	N/A
2007	1.00	1	1	1	1	1	1	1	1	1
2007	1.00	1	1	1	1	1	1	1	1	1
Multiple diseases	21%	0%	67%	0%	0%	0%	0%	0%	33%	100%
1999	0.00	0	0	0	0	0	0	0	0	N/A

Appendix 14F (continued)

Average (n = 46)	**54%**	**78%**	**46%**	**40%**	**73%**	**58%**	**25%**	**78%**	**24%**	**65%**
Commitment	**Average**	**US**	**Japan**	**Germany**	**UK**	**France**	**Italy**	**Canada**	**Russia**	**EU**
2000	0.43	0	1	0	N/A	N/A	0	1	0	1
2005	0.25	0	1	N/A	N/A	N/A	N/A	-1	1	N/A
Aging	83%	100%	100%	100%	100%	100%	50%	100%	0%	100%
2000	0.67	1	1	1	1	1	0	1	-1	1
2003	1.00	1	1	1	1	1	1	1	1	1
Malaria	100%	100%	100%	100%	100%	100%	100%	100%	N/A	100%
2000	1.00	1	1	1	1	1	1	1	N/A	1
Tuberculosis	62%	100%	67%	33%	67%	33%	33%	100%	50%	67%
2000	1.00	1	1	1	1	1	1	1	N/A	1
2005	0.67	1	1	0	1	0	0	1	1	1
2006	0.22	1	0	0	0	0	0	1	0	0
Global Fund	58%	67%	67%	33%	50%	67%	33%	83%	67%	50%
2001	0.75	0	0	1	1	1	1	1	1	N/A
2002	0.25	0	0	0	0	0	1	1	0	N/A
2003	0.89	1	1	0	1	1	1	1	1	1
2005	0.33	1	1	0	0	0	-1	0	1	1
2006	0.56	1	1	0	0	1	0	1	1	0
2007	0.67	1	1	1	1	1	0	1	0	0
Intellectual property	59%	50%	50%	50%	100%	50%	50%	50%	50%	100%

Average ($n = 46$)	54%	78%	46%	40%	73%	58%	25%	78%	24%	65%
Commitment	**Average**	**US**	**Japan**	**Germany**	**UK**	**France**	**Italy**	**Canada**	**Russia**	**EU**
2001	1.00	1	1	1	1	1	1	1	1	1
2006	0.13	0	0	0	1	0	0	0	0	N/A
Medicine	25%	0%	50%	0%	50%	0%	0%	100%	0%	0%
2002	0.38	0	1	0	1	0	0	1	0	N/A
2003	0.13	0	0	0	0	0	0	1		0
Children	33%	100%	0%	0%	100%	0%	-100%	100%	0%	100%
2002	0.33	1	0	0	1	0	-1	1	0	1
General disease	100%	100%	100%	100%	100%	100%	100%	100%	N/A	N/A
2003	1.00	1	1	1	1	1	1	1	N/A	N/A
Polio	41%	80%	0%	80%	80%	-20%	-40%	80%	40%	75%
2002	0.00	0	0	0	0	0	0	0	0	N/A
2003	1.00	1	1	1	1	1	1	1	1	1
2004	0.44	1	0	1	1	-1	-1	1	1	1
2005	0.11	1	-1	1	1	-1	-1	1	-1	1
2006	0.44	1	0	1	1	0	-1	1	1	0
Mother–infant	100%	100%	100%	100%	100%	100%	100%	100%	100%	100%
2002	1.00	1	1	1	1	1	1	1	1	1
Workers	36%	33%	33%	33%	0%	100%	0%	33%	100%	33%
2002	0.00	0	0	0	0	N/A	N/A	0	N/A	0
2005	0.29	0	1	0	-1	1	N/A	0	N/A	1

Appendix 14F (continued)

Average (*n* = 46)	**54%**	**78%**	**46%**	**40%**	**73%**	**58%**	**25%**	**78%**	**24%**	**65%**
Commitment	**Average**	**US**	**Japan**	**Germany**	**UK**	**France**	**Italy**	**Canada**	**Russia**	**EU**
2007	0.67	1	0	1	1	1	0	1	1	0
SARS	78%	100%	100%	0%	100%	100%	100%	100%	0%	100%
2003	0.78	1	1	0	1	1	1	1	0	1
Education	33%	100%	0%	0%	100%	100%	-100%	100%	-100%	100%
2007	0.33	1	0	0	1	1	-1	1	-1	1
Health systems and infectious disease	56%	100%	-100%	100%	100%	100%	0%	100%	-100%	-100%
2008	0.56	1	-1	1	1	1	1	1	0	-1
Tropical diseases	33%	0%	-100%	-100%	0%	-100%	-100%	0%	-100%	-100%
2008	-0.33	-1	-1	-1	0	-1	-1	0	-1	-1

Appendix 14G: G8 Summit Compliance

	Average	Sub-average	Finance	Trade	Development (includes MDGs)	Climate change	Human rights	Foreign policy/ political security	Health
1975									
1976									
1977									
1978									
1979									
1980									
1981									
C1									
1982									
1983	100(1)	100(1)							100(1)
1984									
1985									
1986									
1987	50(1)	50(1)				50(1)			
1988									
C2 average	60(3)	60(3)				40(2)			100(1)

Appendix 14G (continued)

	Average	Sub-average	Finance	Trade	Development (includes MDGs)	Climate change	Human rights	Foreign policy/ political security	Health
1989	-10(2)	-10(2)				-10(2)			
1990	43(1)	43(1)				43(1)			
1991	38(2)	38(2)				38(2)			
1992	71(3)	71(3)				71(3)			
1993	57(2)	57(2)				71(2))			
1994	71(2)	71(2)				72(2)			
1995	29(1)	29(1)				29(1)			
C3 average	46(13)	46(13)				46(13)			
1996	48(24)	42(13)	40(1)	33(1)	00(1)	57(1)	83(1)	42(8)	
1997	16(10)	13(9)			00(1)	29(2)		-03(4)	36(2)
1998	44(11)	49(9)		33(1)	00(1)	100(3)		33(2)	22(2)
1999	44(11)	39(10)	00(1)	-25(1)	86(3)	22(1)		56(2)	31(2)
2000	75(29)	73(23)		100(2)	00(4)			90(12)	82(5)
2001	43(18)	41(13)	-14(2)	88(1)	50(2)	-4(3)	57(2)	100(1)	88(2)
2002	35(28)	36(28)		00(2)	15(5)	89(1)	79(2)	34(10)	43(8)
C4 average	47(131)	45(104)	3(4)	41(8)	25(17)	43(11)	71(5)	52(38)	52(21)
2003	61(18)	64(15)		-38(1)	61(2)	88(2)		54(4)	80(6)

	Average	Sub-average	Finance	Trade	Development (includes MDGs)	Climate change	Human rights	Foreign policy/ political security	Health
2004	55(30)	62(28)		77(3)	100(3)	89(2)		51(18)	50(2)
2005	62(26)	62(26)		26(3)	73(5)	80(5)	33(1)	81(6)	44(6)
2006	39(25)	37(23)		11(1)	89(1)	33(9)	33(2)	40(5)	37(5)
2007	56(26)	57(22)		56(1)	37(3)	72(2)	44(1)	53(9)	72(6)
2008	47(20)	43(14)	100(1)	33(1)	78(1)	56(3)	11(1)	39(5)	11(2)
C5 average	53(145)	55(128)	100(1)	37(10)	71(15)	59(23)	31(5)	53(47)	54(27)
Averages	50	50(248)	22(5)	47(72)	51(49)	57(43)	51(10)	52(85)	54(49)

Notes: All numbers have been rounded to the nearest percentage point.C1 C2 etc. refer to summit cycles, beginning with france and ending with Canada.
Numbers in parentheses indicate numbers of commitments measured.
Overall averages and issue area averages may not tally with averages in other tables, as averages are calculated from yearly averages and do not take unavailable data into account. For more specific breakdowns of the commitments, see <http://www.g8.utoronto.ca>.
All commitments are mutually exclusive.
The following categories are included in the overall yearly averages but do not appear in their own separate columns above: macroeconomics +73(6), microeconomics +7(5), social policy +61(7), environment +48(8), information and communication +60(10), nuclear safety +29 (1), UN reform + 14(2), migration +44(1), energy: +81(4) and Heiligendamm Dialogue Process +100(1).

Appendix 14H: G20 compliance

2003 G20 Morelia Commitments

Issue area	Australia	India	South Africa	Total
Foreign policy	00(1)	00(1)	+100(1)	+33%(1)
Finance	-33(3)	00(2)	00(3)	-13%(8)
Trade	+100(1)	+100(1)	+100(1)	+100(1)
Micro	+100(1)	+100(1)	+100(1)	+100(1)
Subtotal	00%(5)	+25%(4)	+40%(5)	+21%(14)
Total	+17(6)	+40(5)	+50%(6)	+35(17)

Note: Subtotal includes the areas of foreign policy, finance and trade. Numbers in parentheses indicate the total number of commitments measured.

G20 Compliance with 2003 G8 Evian Priority Commitments

Issue area	Australia	India	South Africa	Total
Health	00(1)	-100(1)	+100(1)	00%(1)
Foreign policy	+75(4)	+50(4)	+50(4)	58%(4)
Trade	00(1)	00(1)	+100(1)	+33%(1)
Development	00(2)	-50(2)	00(2)	-17(2)
Environment	+100(1)	+100(1)	+100(1)	+100(1)
Energy	+100(1)	+100(1)	+100(1)	+100 (1)
Macro	00(1)	00(1)	+100(1)	+33(1)
Information and communication	00(1)	00(1)	+100(1)	+33(1)
Subtotal	+38%(8)	00%(8)	+50%(8)	+29(24)
Total	+42%(12)	+17%(12)	+67%(12)	+42%(36)

Notes: Subtotal includes the areas of health, foreign policy, development and trade. Numbers in parentheses indicate the total number of commitments measured. Priority commitments have been identified by Ella Kokotsis.

Appendix 14I: G8 official bodies 1975–2008

First Cycle (8)

1975	London Nuclear Suppliers Group
1977	International Nuclear Fuel Cycle Evaluation Group
1979	High Level Group on Energy Conservation and Alternative Energy
1979	International Energy Technology Group
1979	High Level Group to Review Oil Import Reduction Progress
1980	International Team to Promote Collaboration on Specific Projects on Energy Technology
1980	High Level Group to Review Result on Energy
1981	Missile Technology Control Regime

Second Cycle (9)

1982	Working Group on Technology, Growth and Employment
1982	Consultations and Coordination on East–West Relations
1982	Representatives to control exports of strategic goods
1982	Procedures for multilateral surveillance of economic performance
1985	Expert Group for Foreign Ministers
1985	Expert Group on Desertification and Dry Zone Grains
1985	Expert Group on Environmental Measurement
1986	Group of Experts on Terrorism
1987	International Ethics Committee on AIDS

Third Cycle (14)

1989	Financial Action Task Force (FATF) (with others, secretariat from OECD)
1989	International Ethics Committee on AIDS
1990	Chemical Action Task Force, 1990–92 (with others)
1990	Task Force to Study the State of the Soviet Economy
1990	Permanent Working Group on Assistance to Russia
1990	Gulf Crisis Financial Coordination Group
1992	Nuclear Safety Working Group
1992	Group of Experts on the Prevention and Treatment of AIDS
1993	Support Implementation Group (SIG)
1993	G8 Non-Proliferation Experts Group
1995	Counter-Terrorism Experts Group
1995	G7/P8 Senior Experts Group on Transnational Organized Crime (Lyon Group)
1995	Global Information Project National Coordinators
1995	Development Committee Task Force on Multilateral Development Banks

Fourth Cycle (16)

1996	Nuclear Safety Working Group
1996	Lyon Group
1997	Expert Group on Financial Crime
1997	Subgroup on High Tech Crime (of the Lyon Group)
1997	Officials Group on Forests
2000	Conflict Prevention Officials Meeting
2000	Renewable Energy Task Force
2000	Digital Opportunities Task Force (DOT Force)
2000	Global Fund to Fight AIDS, Malaria and Tuberculosis
2001	G8 Task Force on Education
2001	Personal Representatives for Africa (APR)
2002	Energy Officials Follow-up Process
2002	G8 Global Partnership Review Mechanism
2002	G8 Nuclear Safety and Security Group
2002	G8 Experts on Transport Security
2002	Global Health Security Laboratory Network

Fifth Cycle (41)

2003	High Level Working Group on Biometrics
2003	Counter-Terrorism Action Group
2003	Radioactive Sources Working Group
2003	Senior Officials for Science and Technology for Sustainable Development
2003	G8 Enlarged Dialogue Meeting
2003	Forum for the Partnership with Africa
2003	Global Health Security Action Group Laboratory Network
2003	Technical Working Group on Pandemic Influenza Preparedness
2004	Global Partnership Senior Officials Group
2004	Global Partnership Working Group
2004	Global HIV Vaccine Enterprise
2004	Microfinance Consultative Group
2004	Best Practises Microfinance Training Centre
2004	Democracy Assistance Dialogue
2004	Task Force on Investment
2004	G8 Expert-Level Meetings on Peace Support in Africa
2004	Friends of the Convention on Corruption
2004	G8 Accelerated Response Teams on Corruption
2004	International Partnership for a Hydrogen Economy
2004	International Partnership for a Hydrogen Economy Implementation-Liaison Committee
2004	Carbon Sequestration Leadership Forum
2004	Renewable Energy and Energy Efficiency Partnership

2004	Generation IV International Forum
2004	Global Earth Observation System of Systems (GEOSS)
2005	Dialogue on Sustainable Energy
2005	Working Group on Innovative Financing Mechanisms
2005	Experts on Intellectual Property Rights Piracy and Counterfeiting
2005	Global Bioenergy Partnership
2005	African Dialogue Follow-up Mechanism (Africa, paragraph 33)
2006	G8 expert group to develop criteria and procedures for evaluating educational outcomes and qualifications
2006	G8 expert group on the possibilities of strengthening the international legal framework pertaining to IPR enforcement
2006	G8 expert, UN and other international organization group on the feasibility of implementing stabilization and reconstruction measures
2006	G8 expert group on securing energy infrastructure
2007	Structured high-level dialogue with major emerging economies (Heiligendamm Process)
2007	Sustainable Buildings Network with G8 and major emerging economies
2007	Regional Micro Small and Medium Enterprises Investment Fund
2007	International Working Group on Land Transport Security composed of G8 and non-G8 countries
2008	G8 Experts Group to monitor implementation on food security
2008	Climate Investment Funds
2008	Energy forum
2008	Global Remittances Working Group

*Note*s: This does not include one-off meetings or conferences.
Italics indicate bodies that are related to foreign policy as per political security; bold indicates bodies that are related to health.
Numbers in parentheses represent the total number of bodies created during that cycle.
First Cycle = 1975–81; Second Cycle = 1982–88; Third Cycle = 1989–95;
Fourth Cycle = 1996–2002; Fifth Cycle = 2003–10.

Appendix 15A: Summit performance

St. Petersburg 2006 Compliance Scores

Issue Area	Canada	France	Germany	Italy	Japan	Russia	UK	US	EU	Issue Average
Health (Global Fund)	1	1	0	0	1	1	0	1	0	0.56
Health (Tuberculosis)	1	0	0	0	0	0	0	1	0	0.22
Health (Polio)	1	0	1	-1	0	1	1	1	0	0.44
Energy (Oil and Energy Reserve Data Collection)	1	1	1	1	1	1	1	1	1	1.00
Energy Intensity	0	0	0	0	0	1	1	0	1	0.33
Surface Transport	1	0	1	0	0	0	0	1	1	0.44
Renewable Energy	1	0	1	1	1	0	1	1	1	0.89
Climate Change	0	1	1	1	1	0	1	1	1	0.78
Education (Academic Mobility	0	1	1	0	0	1	0	0	1	0.44
Education (Qualification Systems)	0	0	1	0	0	0	0	1	1	0.33
Education (Gender Disparities)	1	1	0	-1	0	0	1	0	0	0.22
Africa (Security)	1	1	0	0	0	0	0	1	1	0.44
Africa (Debt Relief)	1	1	1	0	1	1	1	1	1	0.89
Transnational Crime and Corruption	0	0	0	0	0	0	0	0	.0	0.00
Intellectual Property Rights	0	0	0	0	0	0	1	0	n/a	0.13
Trade (Export Subsidies, Agriculture)	0†	-1	1	-1	1	0	1	0	0	0.11
Counter-terrorism (Energy)	1	1	0	0	0	0	1	1	1	0.56

Issue Area	Canada	France	Germany	Italy	Japan	Russia	UK	US	EU	Issue Average
Stabilization and Reconstruction (UN)	0	0	0	0	0	0	0	0	0	0.00
Global Partnership (Non-Proliferation)	1	0	1	0	1	1	1	0	0	0.56
Middle East (Lebanon	1	1	1	1	1	1	1	1	1	1.00
Country Average	0.60	0.40	0.55	0.05	0.40	0.45	0.60	0.60	0.58	0.47
All Issue Average										0.47
2006 Interim Compliance Average	0.45	0.25	0.45	-0.10	0.30	0.25	0.55	0.35	0.53	0.34
2005 Final Compliance	0.81	0.57	0.88	0.29	0.52	0.14	0.81	0.95	0.89	0.65
2005 Interim Compliance	0.52	0.48	0.33	0.43	0.52	-0.14	0.71	0.67	0.75	0.47

Appendix 15A (continued)

Overall Summit Performance, 1975–2008

	Domestic political management			Deliberative			Directional	Decisional	Delivery	Development of global governance	Attendees	
	Bayne grade	% Mem	Average no. of references	No. days	No. statements	No. words	No. references to core values	No. comments	Compliance	No. bodies min./off.	No. members	No. participants 1/MO
1975	A-	33	0.33	3	1	1,129	5	14	57.1	0/1	4/6	0/0
1976	D	33	1.00	2	1	1,624	0	7	08.9	0/0	7	0/0
1977	B-	50	1.50	2	6	2,669	0	29	08.4	0/1	8	0/0
1978	A	75	3.25	2	2	2,999	0	35	36.3	0/0	8	0/0
1979	B+	67	3.33	2	2	2,102	0	34	82.3	1/2	8	0/0
1980	1+	20	0.40	2	5	3,996	3	55	07.6	0/1	8	0/0
1981	1	50	3.75	2	3	3,165	0	40	26.6	1/0	8	0/0
1982	1	75	1.75	3	2	1,796	0	23	84.0	0/3	9	0/0
1983	B	60	3.00	3	2	2,156	7	38	-10.9	0/0	8	0/0
1984	1-	25	0.50	3	5	3,261	0	31	48.8	1/0	8	0/0
1985	E	33	1.00	3	2	3,127	1	24	01.0	0/2	8	0/0
1986	B+	80	4.40	3	4	3,582	1	39	58.3	1/1	9	0/0
1987	D	25	6.00	3	7	5,064	0	53	93.3	0/2	9	0/0
1988	1-	25	0.50	3	3	4,872	0	27	-47.8	0/0	8	0/0
1989	B+	50	1.00	3	11	7,125	1	61	07.8	0/1	8	0/0

	Domestic political management			Deliberative			Directional	Decisional	Delivery	Development of global governance	Attendees	
	Bayne grade	% Mem	Average no. of references	No. days	No. statements	No. words	No. references to core values	No. comments	Compliance	No. bodies min./off.	No. members	No. participants 1/MO
1990	D	33	0.67	3	3	7,601	10	78	-14.0	0/3	8	0/0
1991	B-	20	2.80	3	3	8,099	8	53	00.0	0/0	9	1/0
1992	D	33	1.33	3	4	7,528	5	41	64.0	1/1	8	0/0
1993	1+	33	1.00	3	2	3,398	2	29	75.0	0/2	8	1/0
1994	1	40	1.80	3	2	4,123	5	53	100.0	1/0	8	1/0
1995	B+	25	0.25	3	3	7,250	0	78	100.0	2/2	8	1/0
1996	B	40	0.40	3	5	15,289	6	128	41.0	0/3	8	1/4
1997	1-	40	0.40	3	4	12,994	6	145	12.8	1/3	9	1/0
1998	B+	60	1.00	3	4	6,092	5	73	31.8	0/0	9	0/0
1999	B+	80	1.60	3	4	10,019	4	46	38.2	1/5	9	0/0
2000	B	25	9.50	3	5	13,596	6	105	81.4	0/4	9	4/3
2001	B	40	1.20	3	7	6,214	3	58	55.0	1/2	9	0
2002	B+	17	0.17	2	18	11,959	10	187	35.0	1/8	10	0
2003	1	75	1.25	3	14	16,889	17	206	65.8	0/5	10	12/5
2004	1+	33	0.67	3	16	38,517	11	245	54.0	0/15	10	12/0
2005	A-	50	0.50	3	16	22,286	29	212	65.0	0/5	9	11/6
2006	N/A	25	0.25	3	15	30,695	256	317	47.0	0/4	10	5/9
2007	N/A	75	1.25	3	8	25,857	651	329	51.0	0/4	9	9/9

Appendix 15A (continued)

	Domestic political management			Deliberative			Directional	Decisional	Delivery	Development of global governance	Attendees	
	Bayne grade	% Mem	Average no. of references	No. days	No. statements	No. words	No. references to core values	No. comments	Compliance	No. bodies min./off.	No. members	No. participants 1/MO
2008	N/A	33	1.33	3	6	16,842	TBC	296		1/4	9	15/6
Total				95	195	313,915	1052	3,118		13/92	289	74/43
Average all	B-	43	1.74	2.8	5.7	9,233	31.9	91.7	41.35	0.38/2.71	8.5	2.17/1.26
Average Cycle 1	B-	47	1.94	2.1	2.9	2,526	1.1	29	32.46	0.14/0.71	7.43	0/0
Average Cycle 2	1-	46	2.45	3	3.3	3,408	1.3	34	32.39	0.29/1.14	8.43	0/0
Average Cycle 3	1+	33	1.26	3	4	6,446	4.4	56	47.54	0.58/1.29	8.14	0.57/0
Average Cycle 4	B	43	2.04	2.9	6.7	10,880	5.7	106	42.17	0.58/3.57	9.00	0.86/1.00
Average Cycle 5	B-	49	0.88	3	12.5	25,181	177	255.67	56.56	0.17/6.16	9.50	10.67/6.0

Notes: NA = not available; TBC = to be calculated.
domestic political management (national policy addresses): % Mem is the percentage of measured G8 countries that referred to the G7/8 at least once that year in their national policy address(es).
Directional: number of references in the communiqué's chapeau or Chair's Summary to the G8's core values of democracy, social advance and individual liberty. Compliance scores from 1990 to 1995 measure compliance with commitments selected by Ella Kokotsis. Compliance scores from 1996 to 2007 measure compliance with the G8 Research Group's selected commitments. Bodies min/off is the number of new G7/8 countries' institutions created at the ministerial (min.) and official (off.) level at or by the summit, or during the hosting year, at least in the form of having one meeting take place. The first number represents ministerials created; the second number represents official-level bodies created. Attendees refers to the number of leaders of full members, including those representing the European Community from the start, and the number of invited participants of countries and/or of multilateral organizations at the G8 leaders' session. Russia started as a participant in 1991 and became a full member in 1998. In 1975, the G4 met without Japan and Italy; later that year, the G6 met. 1 = countries; MO = multilateral organizations. The first number represents non-G8 countries that participated, the second number represents multilateral organizations that participated.

Appendix 15A (continued)

St. Petersburg Summit Performance

Domestic Political Management:

- percentage of measured G8 countries that referred to the G7/8 at least once that year in their national policy address(es): 25%
- average number of references for the measured countries: 0.25

Deliberative:

- says the summit was held: 3
- number of statements released by the leaders at the summit: 15
- number of words in the leaders' documents issued at the summit: 30,695

Directional:

- number of core values referenced in the summit documents: 256
- number of commitments issued at the summit: 317
- Compliance score for 2006 commitments measures: +47.0%

Development of global governance:

- number of ministerial meetings and/or official-level meetings held in 2006: 4

Index

Global Finance Series

Full series list

G8 against Transnational Organized Crime
Amandine Scherrer
ISBN 978 0 7546 7544 0

Governing Global Derivatives Challenges and Risks
Chiara Oldani
ISBN 978 0 7546 7464 1

Financing Development The G8 and UN Contribution
Edited by Michele Fratianni, John J. Kirton and Paolo Savona
ISBN 978 0 7546 4676 1

The New Economic Diplomacy Decision-Making and Negotiation in International Economic Relations (Second Edition)
Edited by Nicholas Bayne and Stephen Woolcock
ISBN 978 0 7546 7047 6 (hbk)
ISBN 978 0 7546 7048 3 (pbk)

The G8 System and the G20 Evolution, Role and Documentation
Peter I. Hajnal
ISBN 978 0 7546 4550 4

Corporate, Public and Global Governance The G8 Contribution
Edited by Michele Fratianni, Paolo Savona and John J. Kirton
ISBN 978 0 7546 4046 2

Elements of the Euro Area Integrating Financial Markets
Edited by Jesper Berg, Mauro Grande and Francesco Paolo Mongelli
ISBN 978 0 7546 4320 3

New Perspectives on Global Governance Why America Needs the G8
Edited by Michele Fratianni, John J. Kirton, Alan M. Rugman and Paolo Savona
ISBN 978 0 7546 4477 4

Governing Global Banking The Basel Committee and the Politics of Financial Globalisation
Duncan Wood
ISBN 978 0 7546 1906 2

Global Financial Crime Terrorism, Money Laundering and Offshore Centres
Edited by Donato Masciandaro
ISBN 978 0 7546 3707 3

Sustaining Global Growth and Development G7 and IMF Governance
Edited by Michele Fratianni, Paolo Savona and John J. Kirton
ISBN 978 0 7546 3529 1

Governing Global Finance New Challenges, G7 and IMF Contributions
Edited by Michele Fratianni, Paolo Savona and John J. Kirton
ISBN 978 0 7546 0880 6